Java Message Service (JMS) for J2EE

Edition

1   Java and Enterprise Applications   **3**

2   Enterprise JavaBeans (EJB)   **35**

3   Enterprise JavaBeans Examples   **65**

II   Introduction to a Message Service

4   Middleware and Message-Oriented Middleware   **93**

5   Concepts and Fundamentals of JMS Programming   **109**

6   JMS Programming Techniques with Examples   **143**

III   Java Message Service

7   JMS Reliability   **175**

8   JMS and XML   **197**

9   Message-Driven Beans   **221**

10   JMS and the Web   **243**

IV   Java Message Service Applications

11   Developing Applications Using the JMS API   **257**

V   Appendixes

A   J2SE and J2EE Settings   **281**

B   Application Deployment Tool   **307**

C   Java Message Service (JMS) API Vendors   **331**

D   Overview of JMS Package Classes   **343**

Index   381

Java Message
Service (JMS)
for J2EE

Levent Erdogan

New Riders

www.newriders.com

201 West 103rd Street, Indianapolis, Indiana 46290
An Imprint of Pearson Education
Boston • Indianapolis • London • Munich • New York • San Francisco

Java Message Service (JMS) for J2EE

Trademarks

Warning and Disclaimer

Publisher
David Dwyer

Associate Publisher
Stephanie Wall

Production Manager
Gina Kanouse

Managing Editor
Kristy Knoop

Acquisitions Editors
Deb Hittel-Shoaf
Elise Walter

Development Editor
Anne Marie Walker

Senior Marketing Manager
Tammy Detrich

Publicity Manager
Susan Nixon

Project Editor
Beth Trudell

Indexer
Ginny Bess

Manufacturing Coordinator
Jim Conway

Book Designer
Louisa Klucznik

Cover Designer
Brainstorm Design, Inc.

Cover Production
Aren Howell

Composition
Jeff Bredensteiner

To my grandfather, Ilyas, and grandmother, Kaya, who dedicated their life to me.
To my real and longtime friends who are with me whenever I need them.

❖

The answer is wherever the difficulty is.
Mevlana

Table of Contents

I   **Introduction to Java Enterprise Edition**

1   **Java and Enterprise Applications   3**

Java 2 Standard and Enterprise Edition   7

J2EE Architecture   8

J2EE APIs   11

Classification of J2EE Technologies   14

JNDI   15

Summary   32

Questions and Answers   32

2   **JavaBeans and EJBs   35**

History of EJB   36

JavaBeans and EJB   38

EJB Architecture   39

EJB Container   41

Using EJB   43

Session Bean   45

Entity Beans   51

EJB and the Web   60

EJB and JMS   61

Summary   62

Questions and Answers   62

3   **Enterprise JavaBeans Examples   65**

Creating a Session Bean   65

Creating an Entity Bean   72

Presentation Tier on EJB   80

EJB and the Web   85

Summary   88

Questions and Answers   89

II   Introduction to a Message Service

4 Middleware and Message-Oriented Middleware   93

History of MOM   93

Types of Messaging Models   102

Summary   106

Questions and Answers   107

5 Concepts and Fundamentals of JMS Programming   109

What Is a Messaging System or Service?   109

What Is the JMS API?   112

Concepts of JMS Programming   115

Summary   140

Questions and Answers   140

6 JMS Programming Techniques with Examples   143

Basic Steps for Writing a JMS Application   143

A p2p Messaging Example   146

A pub/sub Messaging Example   155

A pub/sub Messaging Example with a Message Selector   164

Summary   169

Questions and Answers   170

III   Java Message Service

7 JMS Reliability   175

What Is Reliability?   175

Basic Reliability Mechanisms   176

Advanced Reliability Mechanisms   181

Clustering for Reliability   192

Summary   195

Questions and Answers   195

8   **JMS and XML   197**

What Is XML?   198

Processing an XML Document   203

Validation of XML   203

Processing Technologies   207

A Sample Application Using the JAXP API
in JMS   210

Summary   218

Questions and Answers   218

9   **Message-Driven Beans   221**

What Is a Message-Driven Bean?   221

Architecture of a Message-Driven Bean   223

Combining a Message-Driven Bean with Session
and Entity Beans   225

A Message-Driven Bean Example   226

Summary   240

Questions and Answers   240

10 **JMS and the Web   243**

Architectures of a JMS Provider and a
Web Client   243

A Sample Application Using JMS through a Web
Client   246

Summary   254

Questions and Answers   254

IV   **Java Message Service Applications**

11 **Developing Applications Using the
JMS API   257**

The Design Layout of the "Ask Advance
Payment" Application   258

Design Samples of JMS Applications   275

Summary   278

V   Appendixes

A   J2SE and J2EE Settings   281
J2SE   282
J2EE   293
Forte for Java Community Edition   299
Web Server for J2EE Applications   303

B   Application Deployment Tool   307
Starting the Deployment Tool   307
Adding a New Application   310
Adding an Enterprise Bean to the
Application   312
Deploying the Application   318
Adding a Web Component to the
Application   321

**C   Java Message Service (JMS) API
Vendors   331**
Criteria to Choose an Appropriate
JMS Vendor   332
BEA Systems Inc. (WebLogic Server)   333
IBM (MQSeries)   335
iPlanet (JMQ or iMQ)   335
Sun Microsystems (J2EE 1.3 Reference
Server)   336
TIBCO/Talarian (SmartSockets for JMS)   337
Progress (SonicMQ)   337
Fiorano (FioranoMQ)   338
Softwired (iBus)   339
ExoLab (OpenJMS)   340
Macromedia (JRun)   340

**D   Overview of JMS Package
Classes   343**
Class Hierarchy for the javax.jms Package   343
Interface Hierarchy for the javax.jms
Package   346

Index   381

About the Author

Levent Erdogan holds a master's degree in Electronics and Communications Engineering from Istanbul Technical University (ITU). He began his career as a computer technology lecturer and then worked as a system analyst, network supporter, and software application developer in several companies in Turkey and in the United States. Levent has been developing database and Internet applications since 1997. After developing Internet and enterprise applications, he realized the power of Java and decided to write a book on Java technologies.

His hobbies include writing short stories, being an activist on social issues (particularly consumer rights), and writing computer technology books. He also likes to relax in the warm seas of the lovely Mediterranean and watch *The Simpsons*, *Friends*, and *Will & Grace*.

Levent published three computer books prior to writing this book. He currently works as a software application developer in the United States, Canada, and Turkey while writing books. He expects to obtain his doctoral degree within a year from ITU. Because he loves mathematics and teaching, Levent wants to become a mathematics teacher whenever he decides to leave the software engineering field.

You can reach Levent at `info@JMSbook.com`.

About the Technical Reviewers

These reviewers contributed their considerable hands-on expertise to the entire development process for *Java Message Service (JMS) for J2EE*. As the book was being written, these dedicated professionals reviewed all the material for technical content, organization, and flow. Their feedback was critical to ensuring that *Java Message Service (JMS) for J2EE* fits our reader's need for the highest quality technical information.

Mandar Chitnis is a senior associate (Level II – Technical Architect) in the reputed consulting firm of Cap Gemini Ernst and Young (CGEY). Over the past eight years, he has worked extensively with Java/CORBA, Oracle, OOAD, C/C++, and Java. His major area of expertise is designing and developing different middle-ware technical architecture solutions for web-enabling enterprise applications.

Steve Heckler is a freelance web developer, editor, writer, and trainer based in Atlanta, Georgia. Prior to being self-employed, Steve served more than six years as a trainer and manager at a leading IT training firm. An avid developer, trainer, and writer on Java, .NET, and XML-related topics, Steve holds bachelor's and master's degrees from Stanford University.

Acknowledgments

I'd like to thank my friends because they encouraged me to write this book and supported me with their constructive criticism. I'd also like to thank the Tourism Ministry of Turkey for providing lots of pictures of Turkey for the book's cover.

Deborah Hittel-Shoaf, my Acquisitions Editor, deserves a great deal of credit because she helped me carry out this project since the beginning of our talks about the book. She gave me the idea at the beginning. We solved many technical and procedural problems together to bring this book to the readers. Elise Walter, my other Acquisitions Editor, was also very helpful when I needed her as I authored this book.

And I can't forget my Development Editor's, role on the book; Anne Marie Walker did a great job reading, correcting, and completing other editing tasks.

Lots of thanks to the many other folks at New Riders for their incredible effort in completing this book. To Mandar Chitnis and Steve Heckler for technical editing, to Mike LaBonne for the drawing of graphs and charts, to Kristy Knoop for project editing, to Ginny Bess for indexing, and to Jeff Bredensteiner for layout.

Tell Us What You Think

As the reader of this book, you are the most important critic and commentator. We value your opinion and want to know what we're doing right, what we could do better, what areas you'd like to see us publish in, and any other words of wisdom you're willing to pass our way.

As the Associate Publisher for New Riders Publishing, I welcome your comments. You can fax, email, or write me directly to let me know what you did or didn't like about this book—as well as what we can do to make our books stronger.

Please note that I cannot help you with technical problems related to the topic of this book, and that due to the high volume of mail I receive, I might not be able to reply to every message.

When you write, please be sure to include this book's title and author as well as your name and phone or fax number. I will carefully review your comments and share them with the author and editors who worked on the book.

Fax:	317-581-4663
Email:	stephanie.wall@newriders.com
Mail:	Stephanie Wall
	Associate Publisher
	New Riders Publishing
	201 West 103rd Street
	Indianapolis, IN 46290 USA

Introduction

As a Java developer, you definitely have the right to say "Java is the king of the computer language world." You have probably developed many great applications with other object-oriented or structured languages. They are great languages in their own right, but Java is not only a computer language, it is also a set of technologies. You are sure to see how useful the language is when you develop an enterprise application using Java. It makes a developer's life easier and more productive. It also lowers development costs by decreasing development time and effort.

The Java 2 Enterprise Edition (J2EE) platform has greatly improved software development for thousands of developers. Java Naming and Directory Interface (JNDI), Enterprise JavaBeans (EJB), JavaServer Pages (JSP), and servlets are a few examples of the technologies included in J2EE. Java Message Service (JMS) is a Java API, which is similar to JNDI or Java Database Connectivity (JDBC), and adds additional functionality to the Java language. It allows Java applications to easily send and receive messages through message service providers. Java and non-Java applications can also communicate with and understand each other through messaging services. The JMS API bridges the compatibility gap between different messaging providers with its widely accepted specifications. JMS provides a universal message format and API that make JMS providers interoperable with each other

JMS is integrated as part of J2EE and is included as a default in J2EE version 1.3. In version 1.3, J2EE also introduces a new bean, the message-driven bean. The message-driven been is used for asynchronous messaging-based applications in addition to session and entity beans, which are used for synchronous messaging. Message-driven beans are part of the EJB 2.0 specification.

Enterprise applications written by developers are independent of vendor-specific issues because of the JMS API. It is similar to the JDBC API for database tasks and the JNDI API for naming and directory service tasks. You only need to know what the message format is and how you can create, send, receive, and read a message. The JMS API provides a consistent interface for developers to communicate with messaging systems provided by different service providers, and the JMS API handles message provider-specific issues. Particularly, a messaging-based application provides a significant advantage by solving network-based problems, which are nightmares for enterprise application developers. The message you want to send is transferred even if there is a networking fault.

JMS, whose latest version is 1.0.2 at the time of this writing, was created by Sun Microsystems in collaboration with leading enterprise messaging vendors. Sun is not a JMS vendor. Sun defines JMS specifications, and in turn, JMS vendors (including Sun) adopt and implement these specifications in their products as much as is required. Message-oriented middleware (MOM)-based products have existed for quite a while in the market. These products allow enterprise applications to communicate with each other using a loosely coupled message service. JMS is designed for applications that are written in the Java language in order to make MOM vendors' products communicate with each other and get the most benefit from these products. JMS supports common features of traditional MOM-based products for Java-based enterprise applications. JMS facilitates reliable asynchronous communication between components in a distributed environment. Communication between components of a JMS application is secure and reliable.

What You Need For the Book

In this book, you will not only find concepts and their definitions, but also examples and sample applications. Therefore, you first need to install and configure some software on your computer to get the most from this book. Software such as the Java 2 Standard Edition (J2SE) and J2EE definitely must be installed and configured on your computer if you want to run Java applications (standard or enterprise). Other software programs, such as Forte for Java, are optional. You can choose any other similar software depending on your project requirements. For example, you can write your Java source code in any text editor such as Notepad or in any free software program such as Forte for Java Community Edition. Other tools are available to write Java code and create Java applications. They include full-featured Integrated Development Environments (IDEs) such as Visual Café, JBuilder, JDeveloper, and CodeWarrior—all of which you must purchase for use after a free evaluation period.

In this book, freeware or shareware software is used as much as possible. The book focuses on concepts and their applications, not on a specific vendor's product. You can find some brief information about the JMS vendors and their products in Appendix C, "Java Message Service (JMS) API Vendors." All the software packages used in the book are Windows versions. Particularly, applications are written and tested on Windows XP. As you know, Java is a platform-independent technology; therefore, the source code of all applications listed in this book will work on any platform regardless of the platform where you write or run the code.

If you develop commercial or more professional projects, consult each particular vendor for development tools or enterprise applications and messaging servers. Appendix C lists vendors' web site addresses, so you can access their latest product information.

Who Should Read This Book

Intended audiences for this book include

- Java enterprise application developers with mid-level experience.
- Java application developers who do not have enterprise application experience and are willing to learn enterprise applications and JMS.
- Students in master's programs in computer software departments at universities.
- Students with mid-level Java experience in certification programs or high-level computer courses.

Who This Book Is Not For

For this book, it is assumed that you know the Java language and have mid-level Java project/work experience.

If you do not have Java enterprise application experience, you can still benefit from this book because three chapters provide information about the J2EE platform and enterprise edition technologies.

Overview

This book is logically designed to take you from low-level Java enterprise application development to mid-level JMS application development. (I assume that you have standard edition experience, but you might not have enterprise edition experience.) Therefore, the book is divided into four parts as follows:

Part I, "Introduction to Java Enterprise Edition". It is highly recommended that you read through the first three chapters if you are new to this topic. If you are experienced in enterprise applications, you can move on to Part II.

- Chapter 1, "Java and Enterprise Applications"—In this chapter, you will learn about the J2EE architecture, its technologies, and JNDI in detail, which are very important in JMS applications.
- Chapter 2, "Enterprise JavaBeans (EJB)"—In this chapter, you will learn about EJBs, the most important part of the J2EE platform. You will find detailed information about session beans and entity beans. EJBs have a very important role in JMS applications: They were the only beans before message-driven beans were introduced.
- Chapter 3, "Enterprise JavaBeans Examples"—This chapter provides simple but very useful examples for understanding EJB technologies. If you apply the techniques provided and practice them in sample projects, you will rapidly learn how to develop enterprise applications.

Part II, "Introduction to a Messaging Service". This part describes the history and fundamentals of JMS. I highly recommended that you read this section of the book. In particular, if you are new to messaging service concepts, you need to know why developers need JMS.

- Chapter 4, "Middleware and Message-Oriented Middleware"—This chapter provides detailed information about middleware technology and message-oriented middleware technology. They are the technologies on which JMS is based.

- Chapter 5, "Concepts and Fundamentals of JMS Programming"—In this chapter, you will learn the basic concepts and components of JMS programming.

- Chapter 6, "JMS Programming Techniques with Examples"—This chapter provides simple JMS applications so you can easily understand the concepts.

Part III, "Java Message Service". This part provides detailed information about JMS. If you have little JMS experience, you should definitely read the following chapters.

- Chapter 7, "JMS Reliability"—In this chapter, you will learn the basic and advanced reliability of JMS.

- Chapter 8, "JMS and XML"—This chapter provides some brief information about eXtended Markup Language (XML) and how to use XML in JMS applications.

- Chapter 9, "Message-Driven Beans"—This chapter explains message-driven beans, which are the most important components of J2EE version 1.3 for developing asynchronous JMS applications. Message-driven beans are a part of the EJB 2.0 specification (part of J2EE 1.3).

- Chapter 10, "JMS and the Web"—In this chapter, you will learn how to use the web component of the J2EE platform in JMS applications.

Part IV, "Java Message Service Applications". This part presents a summary of the book. If you are a student, this part provides you with a final laboratory project. You will apply all the information you learned throughout the book.

- Chapter 11, "Developing Applications Using the JMS API"—The sample applications are provided to enhance your ability to develop JMS applications. You will not only learn how to develop JMS applications, but also learn the difference between each type of bean.

In addition, there are four appendixes in **Part V, "Appendixes"**.

- Appendix A, "J2SE and J2EE Settings"—This appendix provides information on where you can download and how to install and configure J2SE, J2EE, and Forte for Java Community Edition, which you might need when you develop sample applications provided in the book.

- Appendix B, "Application Deployment Tool"—This appendix provides information on how to deploy an enterprise application in the J2EE platform version 1.3 Reference Implementation Server.

- Appendix C, "Java Message Service (JMS) API Vendors"—This appendix provides some brief information about JMS vendors and their JMS products.
- Appendix D, "Overview of JMS Package Classes"—This appendix provides some brief information about interfaces of JMS packages and how to use them. It is recommended that you read this appendix before developing a JMS application.

Conventions

This book follows a few typographical conventions:

- A new term is set in *italics* the first time it is introduced. For example: RPC is a technology used by middleware technologies such as *Java Remote Method Invocation* (RMI), *Common Object Request Broker Architecture* (CORBA), and *Microsoft's Distributed Component Object Model* (DCOM).
- Program text, methods, and URLs are set in a fixed-pitch font—for example: A message-driven bean is designed as an enterprise bean, and it contains methods such as `onMessage()`, `setMessageDrivenContext()`, `ejbCreate()`, and `ejbRemove()`.
- Sidebars are used to indicate important points. They look like this:

Tools to Write an XML File
XML can be written using any text editor or word processor, even Notepad. You have to save the file as a text file with a .xml extension.

- When you need to run a program or an application at a command prompt, the command you type is indicated in the main text like this:
  j2ee −verbose
- Source code for the sample applications uses the following font:

```
queueReceiver = queueSession.createReceiver(queue);
 queueConnection.start();
```

I

Introduction to Java Enterprise Edition

1 Java and Enterprise Applications

2 Enterprise JavaBeans (EJB)

3 Enterprise JavaBeans Examples

Java and Enterprise Applications

THIS CHAPTER PROVIDES BASIC INFORMATION about the Java language and how common it is used in the computer world by software developers. This book is aimed at providing developers with detailed information about the Java Message Service (JMS). I'll review the Java language and some important technologies of the Java language, which play key roles in the Java 2 Enterprise Edition (J2EE) and includes the JMS.

In 1995, Java was launched as a programming tool to develop simpler and more reliable software. Not only is Java a language, but it also includes a number of related programming technologies. Java is very different from other comparable programming languages. It is a secure, portable, cross-platform language. It has different editions and can be quite small compared to other languages in terms of its interpreter size when it is used in small appliance computer chips. Java and its technologies are used in many different fields in the computer world. If you need to program a chip on a washing machine, you can use Java. If you need to develop a stand-alone application for a desktop computer, you can use Java. If you want to develop web-enabled applications, Java applets, Java servlets, and JavaServer Pages (JSP), you can use Java. If you need a database connection, you can use Java Database Connectivity

(JDBC). If you need an enterprise application for your business-to-business (B2B) project, you can use Java (with enterprise edition). It is easy to extend examples of using areas of the Java language family. The following list describes the Java language's aspects:

- Java is easy to learn. Java is simpler than comparable languages as long as you understand the Object-Oriented Programming (OOP) language model. At first it might seem as though it is a difficult language. If you understand its underlying philosophy, you will see it is really very easy. Particularly, C++ programmers will find it easier. The creator of the Java language intended to make it easy to write, compile, debug, and learn the language. Its syntax and object-oriented structure comes from C++. Despite Java's similarities to C++, the complex aspects of the C++ language have been excluded from Java. The C++ syntaxes are also different from the Java language. The difficulties of learning the Java language is very close to other programming languages, such as Visual Basic and Delphi. Unfortunately, it is more complicated than learning HTML and JavaScript. Some developers believe that it is best to have some programming background if you want to develop Java applications. Of course, any programming experience is very helpful. Other developers disagree. Because the Java object-oriented model is different from structural programming, they believe that it is better to learn and develop Java applications if you do not have structural programming background.

- Java is a great language for Internet applications. Java is a programming language in which you can create web-enabled applications quickly and easily. Applets once were the most popular technology in the Java language, although their popularity has been surpassed by other technologies, such as Java servlets and JSP, because of some technological restrictions. Many people substitute the word Java with applets. Programs called applets appear in a web page like images, but applets can be interactive. An applet can take user input, respond to it, and change the content of the applet. Applets are downloaded over the World Wide Web just like HTML pages, graphics, or any other web site elements.

- Many users only think of Java for Internet applications, but Java is an excellent language for writing stand-alone applications. Many developers prefer Java because of its reliability and portability. Java can access resources on your computer for desktop applications, just as it can access resources on a network for a distributed application.

- Java is an OOP language. The main features of the OOP model are encapsulation, modularization, and reusability. The modularization feature of OOP provides a way of making programs modular and interactive with each other. Java includes many OOP structures and concepts from the C++ language, but it excludes some complicated aspects such as multi-inheritance.

- Java is a cross-platform language, which is one of its most significant characteristics. It is cross-platform, that is, platform independent. This means that you can run Java applications on different platforms and operating systems regardless of where they are developed. For example, you can write and compile your Java program on Windows operating systems, and you can run it on UNIX with no modifications.

If you write your programs using platform-specific languages such as C++, Visual Basic, or Delphi, your code will be compiled depending on the platform and operating system. The compiler creates binary files for the platform. This binary file is a machine code file that can be executed only by that computer platform. If you want to run the same program on a different platform or operating system, you have to recompile the source code for the new platform. You might also need to modify your source code if it contains lines that depend on the operating system. Figure 1.1 shows how a platform-specific language compiles the source code and runs it.

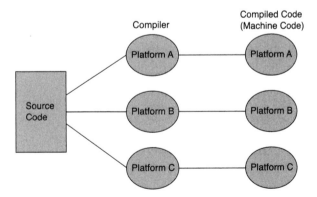

Figure 1.1   How a platform-specific compilation works.

Java programs owe their platform independence to a Java Virtual Machine (JVM), which is like a computer within a computer. A virtual machine is also known as Java interpreter or Java runtime. If you write your programs in Java, which is a platform-independent language, the source code is compiled into Java bytecode. Java bytecode is the JVM's version of machine code. A Java application compiled to bytecode is not platform specific. You can move the bytecode onto any platform that has a Java interpreter (JVM or a Java runtime). The Java interpreter then executes the bytecode of the Java program. Figure 1.2 shows how Java, a platform-independent language, compiles the source code and runs it.

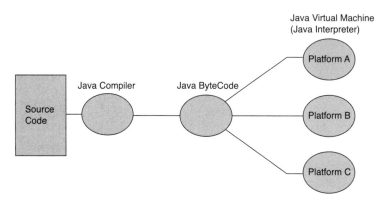

Figure 1.2 How a platform-independent compilation works.

Unfortunately, you lose some performance in Java applications because of its platform-independence. If you need speed in your Java program, you can use the Just-in-time compiler as your development tool. In this case, your Java source code will be compiled for a specific platform to gain speed. You will lose the most important aspect of the Java language, but you will still be writing your program in a great language. Java is more secure and more reliable than many other languages.

- Java goes beyond a desktop programming language tool: It has three different editions for different size applications and projects:
  - The Java 2 Standard Edition (J2SE) is used for developing desktop applications or applets.
  - J2EE is used for developing enterprise applications such as e-commerce projects. J2EE is an extension of J2SE and JMS comes with Enterprise Edition. If you install, J2EE 1.3 or later, it will install JMS 1.0.2 as well (refer to Appendix A, "J2SE and J2EE Settings," for detailed information on how to install J2EE).
  - The Micro Edition is used for developing applications for smart appliances such as cellular phones, interactive television, and so on.

- Java does not require a development tool. Java files are saved as plain text files with the .java extension. After you compile these files, the extension becomes .class. You do not need any special development tools, although there are some great tools available such as Forte for Java, Visual Café, JBuilder, CodeWarrior, and so on. You can see your syntax errors visually, and you can save some time coding certain components by using these development tools. These development tools have many advantages, such as code check in/check out, line-by-line debugging, integrated package references, automatic syntax checking, templates, clear explanations, locating syntax errors during compiling, and so on.

- Java is free of charge: Java programming language and other related technologies can be obtained from Sun Microsystems free of charge. As a developer or learner, you do not have to pay any license fees. Refer to Appendix A to learn how to obtain Java products.

Java 2 Standard and Enterprise Edition

As mentioned earlier, the Java 2 programming language comes in three editions: Standard, Enterprise, and Micro. The Micro Edition is beyond the scope of this book. Actually, the J2SE is also beyond the scope of this book. This book assumes that you have some experience with the Java language, particularly with J2SE. This book is intended to provide detailed information and examples for JMS, which is part of J2EE. We'll skip the fundamentals of the Java language and related examples and focus on J2EE and JMS.

Applications written using J2SE mostly consist of individual programs such as applets or stand-alone programs. Although you can develop enterprise applications with J2SE, it is not as easy, reliable, and scalable as J2EE. In J2SE, developers must handle many administrative issues, which are already done in J2EE.

The most important part of the J2EE application model is to minimize application programming. J2EE is a platform that provides solutions to develop, deploy, and manage multitier applications. J2EE significantly reduces the cost and complexity of multitier programming.

Enterprise JavaBeans (EJB) technology is at the heart of J2EE. You can develop enterprise applications easier by combining the EJB component architecture with other enterprise technologies.

If you need more information about J2EE, visit `http://java.sun.com/j2ee`. You can find the latest news, changes, updates, and specifications on this site.

J2EE Architecture

To explain how J2EE works, let's talk about application models. Before enterprise application servers, client-server applications were based on the two-tier model (see Figure 1.3).

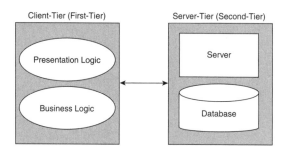

Figure 1.3   The two-tier client-server model.

In a two-tier model, the first tier (that is, client side) contains the presentation logic and the business logic on the same layer. On the client side, you can capture data from the user, process the business rule of the application, and present the result of the process on the client. On the server side, which is known as enterprise information systems (EIS), you can store and organize the data and related services.

If your application size is not very big and the number of clients or accesses by clients to the server side are reasonably low, this model works very well. The two-tier application model provides scalability to some degree, but it is not enough for complex applications. Installing and maintaining business logic are the major problems.

The main weak point is putting the business and presentation logic on the same layer. If you need to change something—even to make a small change—in business logic, you have to change the entire first tier. You have to update every client installation. If you cannot update the user side properly, your application can have more than one version in use, which is not desired.

In a two-tier model, when a user requests a statement from a database (that is, a request from the first tier to the second tier), it causes performance and network traffic problems in addition to security problems. This model has many disadvantages. The desktop computer, which contains the presentation and business layers, might not be powerful enough to process the request. The application might be forced to make too many requests, which increases network traffic. A three-tier model can handle the same request with a single access to the database. A two-tier model also allows clients to access the database directly, which can cause security problems.

A multitier client-server application can solve the weak points of a two-tier model. The best known and most commonly used multitier model is the three-tier model as shown in Figure 1.4.

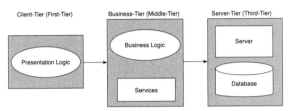

Figure 1.4   The three-tier client-server model.

In a three-tier model, you isolate the business logic from the presentation logic. Scalability of a three-tier model, in which you can expand and redesign the layer with new requirements and considerations without affecting the application, is better than a two-tier model. For complex enterprise applications, you can first design them using the three-tier model, and then increase the tiers, if you need to, after testing application and reviewing its performance, compatibility, and scalability issues. The main skeleton is the same for three or more tiers.

The first tier of an enterprise application consists mostly of the user interface for all systems such as a stand-alone Java application or a web browser. Presentation logic lies on the first tier and defines what the user interface displays and how a user's action will be handled. In some applications, presentation logic can have a server-side presentation layer with a connection to the client-side presentation layer.

The second tier is the business logic layer, which defines the business rules of the application. It is located on the server side, which is called the business logic server, not on the client side. This has two major advantages. First, if you change the business logic, you do not have to update the client side, which avoids having more than one version of the application. Second, the processing of user input as per the business rules is accomplished on the business logic server, which probably has more power to handle processes than a PC or any kind of client-side access point. On this layer, there can also be other services that make a developer's life easier and minimize programming costs.

On the server-side, data and related services can be found.

J2EE is based on a three-tier application model to enhance scalability and modularization. The first tier (client tier) contains the client-side presentation layer; the second tier (middle tier) contains the server side presentation layer and business logic layer; and the third tier (data tier) contains the data layer. All of the tiers rely on the Java programming language and the JVM. Figure 1.5 shows the architecture of J2EE.

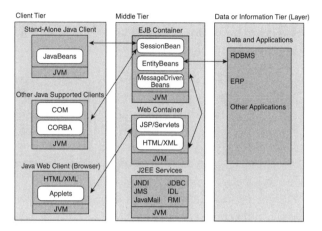

Figure 1.5   The three-tier architecture of the J2EE model.

In the first tier of J2EE architecture, information is displayed and input is collected from the user. The user interface can be developed as an HTML client, applets, XML documents, stand-alone Java clients, and non-Java client applications supported by J2EE, such as Common Object Broker Architecture (CORBA) and Component Object Model (COM).

The middle tier of the architecture has two main containers: an EJB container and a web container. Actually, if you need to make your application more than three tiers, you can divide these two containers into two separate tiers. A web container accepts user input and responds to the user. This tier can be implemented by Java servlets or JSP. A Java web client cannot access the EJB container directly. A web user sends a request to the web container, and the web container handles this request by communicating with the EJB container.

An EJB container organizes and implements application business logic. Java stand-alone clients and other non-Java clients supported by J2EE can access the EJB container directly. EJB technology is at the heart of J2EE, which provides the scalable architecture to execute business logic in a distributed computing environment. There are three types of EJBs:

- *Session beans* provide client processing on the server side.
- *Entity beans* support data persistence.
- *Message-driven beans* are specific beans for JMS.

Clients cannot access the application tier directly, which means that requests to the database or applications must be handled by the EJB container. This is the biggest advantage of an enterprise application—it reduces unnecessary network traffic and provides scalability, load balancing, and location independence.

J2EE APIs

J2EE includes other technologies as well. Technically, they are called Application Programming Interfaces (APIs). As a developer, you use these APIs to write programs that are more efficient, shorter, and reliable. For example, in your project, if you need to connect and use a SQL compatible database such Microsoft Access, Microsoft SQL Server, MySQL, Oracle, Sybase, and so on, you do not have to know every database. Java provides you with the JDBC API. You only need to know how to use JDBC. It handles and implements database specific tasks on your behalf as long as you define your statements, stored procedures, and functions properly in the application.

JMS is one of the J2EE APIs. You'll work with it a lot, but it is good to know a little bit about other available APIs in J2EE. The following list briefly describes some additional APIs:

- JMS—JMS provides message queuing and publish and subscribe types of message-oriented middleware (MOM) services.

- Java Naming Directory Interface (JNDI)—Internet applications must use naming and directory services to access network resources. You can share information related to users, machines, remote applications, and other network services with these services. JNDI is an API that is a standard Java library that is used for accessing naming and directory services such as Lightweight Directory Access Protocol (LDAP), Domain Naming Service (DNS), and Remote Method Invocation (RMI). You can even access the local file system (directory structure) on your computer.

- EJB—Beans are similar to a component model of the Java language. J2EE provides EJBs to distributed component model developers.

  A Java application user or web user can call an EJB from an EJB container in the server to complete certain tasks. EJB is pretty complicated, but extremely useful in your enterprise applications. It can be combined with other Java technologies—particularly JSP or Java servlets—to make a complete application.

  The roles of the three types of EJBs—session beans, entity beans, and message-driven beans—are very different, although they have a similar structure. A session bean must be used when the server needs to provide a particular service to a client, such as a calculation or database query. Entity beans are data objects. They represent a part of a database or application. Entity beans are persistent. They can be accessed by multiple users at the same time. Message-driven beans are dedicated to JMS applications.

- JDBC—Today's many applications use large amounts of data, which cannot be easily delivered with the applications. Many years ago, data was bundled with the application, but recent technology and software applications are based on database programs such as Oracle, Sybase, SQL Server, MySQL, and so on. If you work with databases, you know how difficult they are to master. Today's developers must be familiar with many different technologies, but it is extremely difficult and unnecessary to learn every type of database. The solution is JDBC.

  JDBC is a Java interface that resides between applications and databases, and can access any database. Each database that supports JDBC must have its own JDBC driver. As a developer, you do not have to know database-specific issues. After a connection is made, all commands and implementations are the same for all databases. You only need to know basic information (database, table and field structures, and so on). The main idea is simplicity. It is a developer's responsibility to implement simple and common tasks with a simple JDBC driver. The complex part is done by the driver.

- RMI—RMI is a Java API for distributed object application. In an enterprise application, one application might need to invoke a method on another application, which is part of the same enterprise application. RMI provides this mechanism. In other words, RMI manages communication between two programs, objects, or applications. RMI is like a communication or protocol API for enterprise applications.

  Distributed computing means that an application's code, data, or actual computation can be located on any computer or across multiple computers. In a distributed object model, an object in the application needs to send a message to another object running in another memory space (on any computer across the network). As a developer, you are used to handling issues such as heterogeneous platforms, locations, memory management, network communication, and different languages in addition to your application business logic issues. With RMI, you can focus on the business logic of your application without worrying about communication issues between objects. RMI is a mechanism that allows one Java object on one JVM to invoke methods on any other object running on another JVM.

- Java servlets—Many people think that a servlet is a server-side applet written in Java. This idea is not totally wrong, but Java servlets were launched as an alternative to the Common Gateway Interface (CGI), which is a type of web application that runs on the server side. A Java servlet is platform-independent and scalable, and it provides better performance. It has a very important role in J2EE. Servlets are the controllers of the application, although some developers accept them as the presentation layer. Although it is platform independent, to run a servlet, a web server, which holds servlets, must support servlets and must have a servlet engine. If your web server does not support servlets, you can still benefit from servlet technology through third-party software. For example, if you install JRun 3.1, you can run servlets in Microsoft Internet Information Server (IIS) 5.0.

- JSP—Is it a servlet or a server page? It is hard to classify this parent-child technology. JSPs are servlets. So, what is JSP?

  A servlet's structure and syntax are very strict. A servlet can be called in any HTML document, JSP, and other servlets, but it is a pure Java application. This technology can easily be used by advanced developers. JSP technology makes other web-related people's lives easier. A web server, which holds JSP applications, must have a JSP engine, which converts them into Java servlets. Instead of spending time on syntax or language problems, you can focus on your own business problem, which is directly related to your application. In other words, JSP is an alternate source code language for writing servlets. JSP is not a different technology. It is just an engine that makes servlet coding simpler. This is why people are confused by the difference between JSPs and servlets. Some developers think JSPs and servlets are the same, but they are incorrect. Briefly, if you need to separate presentation and business logic in a JSP application, you can encapsulate business logic into EJBs, and then embed them into presentation logic, JSP.

- Java Transaction API (JTA)—JTA is used for implementing distributed transactional applications. The idea of JTA is the same as a JDBC driver. It links transactions with other sources such as EJBs, JMS messages, and other JDBC connections. Under JTA, there is another API, Java Transaction Service (JTS). As a developer, you do not have to get involved with either JTA or JTS because they are hidden from programmers if you use higher-level interfaces such as JMS, JDBC, and EJB.

- JavaMail—The JavaMail API allows developers to build Java-based mail applications that are platform-independent and protocol-independent. JavaMail provides a layer on top of a mail provider.

- Java Interface Definition Language (IDL)—CORBA objects use IDL to specify a contract. Developers can define contracts between the Java world and the CORBA world with Java IDL.

- LDAP—LDAP is a protocol that defines how an application should access data on a server regardless of how data is stored on the server. In the future, LDAP will replace many "flat file" or "hashed file" systems to store user information. It provides a single data store of information about a user instead of lots of different files. You can access any entity (information) about a user while searching from any application. You do not have to keep similar information on many different servers.

Classification of J2EE Technologies

As mentioned previously, J2EE consists of many technologies called APIs. You can easily develop multitier applications by using these technologies. These technologies can be classified into three main categories: component, service, and communications. In this section, I discuss these technologies and their classifications.

Components

Developers use components to create user interfaces and business logic for enterprise applications. The component technologies allow you to reuse components in multiple enterprise applications. A component is the basic part of an application. You already know two components in J2SE: JavaBeans (not EJB, but the standard version) and applets. Because J2EE is an extension of J2SE and these components can be used in J2EE client-side applications, JavaBeans and applets are classified in the component category in J2EE technologies.

Other parts of component technologies are EJBs, client applications, and web components. JavaBeans, client applications, and applets run on the client side; EJBs and web components run on the server side.

Applets, which are very popular examples of component technologies in J2SE, and client applications, run on their own JVM. They serve as gateways to objects and the J2EE service, which you will read about in the next section.

A web component is a program that provides a response to a user request. It is a user interface for a web application. Web components can either be Java servlets or JSPs. Both can be integrated with HTML or XML documents. Many developers prefer JSP rather than Java servlets because of its simplicity.

EJBs are used to develop and deploy business logic in an enterprise application.

Services

J2EE service technologies provide certain advantages to developers. They allow developers to create their enterprise applications in a uniform manner. They also reduce programming costs and increase integrity and reliability.

The most popular service is the JDBC API, which provides database-independent connectivity between enterprise applications and databases. You can connect and authenticate to a database server, manage transactions, and execute SQL statements and stored procedures. Actually, JDBC is part of J2SE. Some developers categorize it as part of J2EE, which is an extension of J2SE, because JDBC is very common in J2EE applications.

Other services are JTA and JTS, which are usually invisible to developers. JTA allows applications to access transactions. JTS supports JTA.

The JNDI API provides naming and directory service to developers. Its main intent is that of Java: platform independence. In your application, you can use JNDI to access multiple naming and directory services such as LDAP, Novell Directory Service (NDS), DNS, and Network Information Service (NIS).

Communication Services

Communication technologies in the Java language provide a mechanism that enables you to contact the objects on the client side using the objects on the server side. A J2EE communication mechanism is based on the TCP/IP protocol, HTTP protocol, and Secure Sockets Layer (SSL). RMI, Java IDL, JavaMail, and JMS fall into the communication service classification.

The RMI service allows developers to develop distributed enterprise applications. Java IDL is a link between Java clients and CORBA objects.

JavaMail is a set of abstract classes and interfaces for an electronic mail system. These abstract classes and interfaces support many different message stores, formats, and transports.

JMS is a service for enterprise messaging systems. JMS supports point-to-point and publish-subscribe messaging types. This book will provide you with a great deal of information and sample applications for JMS.

JNDI

Actually, JNDI is not within the scope of this book, but it has a very important role in J2EE applications and JMS. Therefore, I provide some information about JNDI and its characteristics in this section. JNDI is a J2EE API that provides access to many different directory and naming services.

What Are Naming and Directory Services?

Obviously, naming and directory services has two parts: directory services and naming services.

Directory services are used to access hierarchical tree objects such as directories on the file system of your computer. If you need to access an object by name, naming services will help you. LDAP is an example of a directory service. You can find an entity such as an employee ID, phone number, department, location, and so on by entering its *key entities* such as a person's first and last name. Key entities allow you to uniquely access an object and its other entities.

DNS is an example of a naming service. A naming service provides computer users with a natural way to access objects on a computer system. You can reach a web site by entering its name instead of a group of numbers (called an IP address) using DNS. As a concept, you should be familiar with naming services in computer applications. It is usually integrated with other services. For example, a spreadsheet has a naming service for cells and macros.

What Is JNDI?

JNDI is an API that describes a standard Java library for accessing naming and directory services. Today, Internet and intranet applications are based on naming and directory services to access network resources. JNDI is very similar to the JDBC API. When you develop an application involved with a database, you do not need to know database-specific issues as long as you use JDBC in your Java application and have enough background in SQL. JNDI also provides developers with similar independence. You can access DNS, LDAP, RMI, and even file systems on the computer by using JNDI. You do not have to know every naming and directory service implementation as long as you know the basic concepts.

JNDI is not only independent of a specific directory or naming service implementation, but also enables invisible access to directory objects through multiple naming facilities.

A printer access example is a very good example of JNDI. If a Java application needs to access a printer, you'll usually lines of source code that look like this:

```
prt = (Printer)secondfloor.lookup("salesLaser3");
prt.print(document);
```

where secondfloor is the naming context that represents a physical building. In this example, the code looks for the object salesLaser3.

JNDI Architecture

The JNDI architecture shown in Figure 1.6 has four main layers to connect Java applications to directory and naming services: JNDI API, JNDI Naming Manager, JNDI Service Provider Interface, and vendor-specific service providers.

On top of the JNDI architecture is your Java application, which needs to use directory and naming services. These services are at the bottom of the architecture.

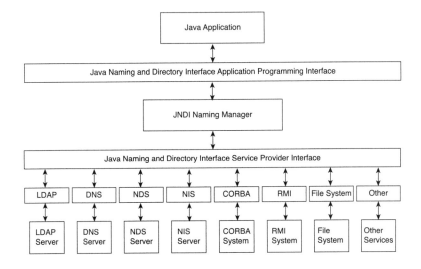

Figure 1.6   JNDI architecture.

JNDI resides between the application and the naming service. It isolates your Java application from a specific naming service implementation. A Java application uses JNDI to locate object names advertised by the directory and naming service. When an application requests an object by name and it uses JNDI, JNDI returns a reference to the remote object. What does this isolation provide? It provides an object advertised by its name through JNDI. Your application cares about its advertised name. At the bottom of the architecture, changes can occur in terms of configuration, provider vendor, and so on. As long as the advertised name stays the same for that object, your application is not affected by any change.

The JNDI API consists of four packages for naming and directory services: javax.naming, javax.naming.directory, javax.naming.event, and javax.naming.ldap. The JNDI Service Provider Interface (SPI) is contained in one package: javax.naming.spi.

JNDI Naming and Naming Packages

Before I explain naming packages, let's look at some naming services terms and concepts:

- Name and naming convention—In naming services, every name must obey a naming convention, which depends on the service.

- Atomic name—An atomic name is the smallest part of the component name, which means that it cannot be divided into smaller parts—it is indivisible.

- Compound name—Zero or more atomic names form a compound name based on the naming convention. For example, in the Internet DNS, atomic names are separated by a period (.) and are ordered from right to left. If you see a DNS name such as Boston.Massachusetts.USA, its sequence of atomic names are USA, Massachusetts, Boston.

- Binding—When you associate a name to an object, it is called binding. It is like a mapping between a name and a unique object. A file system is a good example of binding. When you create a directory or a file, you give them a name. You can reach these objects by using those names. When you change the name of file or directory, you rebind the file to a new name.

- Context—A context is an object whose state is a set of bindings with distinct atomic names. Every context has an associated naming convention. A context provides a lookup operation, which is known as *resolution*. It returns an object when you look up the object with the binding name.

- Subcontext—If an atomic name in one context object is bound to another context object of the same type, it is called a subcontext. Subcontexts form compound names.

- Naming system—A naming system is a connected set of same type contexts. It must have the same naming convention, and it provides the same set of operations.

- Namespace—A namespace is the set of all names, which are unique, in a naming system. For example, on the file system of your computer, each file in a directory must have a unique name. You cannot have two files with the same name, but you can have two files with same name if the files are in different directories (such as namespace).

- Composite name—A composite name spans multiple naming systems (such as namespaces), which can have zero or more components. Each component must come from a namespace of a single naming system. For example, the URL `http://www.mywebsite.com/sales/finalreport.htm` is a composite name. The http (protocol) comes from the URL scheme-id namespace, www.mywebsite.com (the name of the server) comes from the DNS name, and sales/finalreport.htm (name of the resource) comes from a file namespace.
- Initial context—A client can obtain an initial context object, which provides a starting point for the resolution of names.

The fundamental role of a naming service is to associate objects with names and to find objects with their given name. In real life, you might have a tax number, a citizen number, or a social security number. At tax filing time, governmental organizations will process all information about you by using one of these unique numbers. Fortunately, your parents and friends will never call you by these numbers. You have a name. Society binds a name to every person, although in the background (banks, credit card companies, tax administration), transactions are completed using your unique number.

Naming Package

javax.naming is part of the JNDI API package and contains classes and an interface to access naming services. With a naming package, you can access a context (including listing and searching), rename, move, add, replace, or remove a binding for an object, and store references to Java objects.

JNDI Directory Objects and Directory Package

Concepts and terms that you learned in the previous section "JNDI Naming and Naming Packages," are valid in directory services as well. Although a directory service cannot work without a naming service and a naming service cannot work without a directory service, it is hard to distinguish a directory service from a naming service. Some developers think these two services are the same. They cannot be separated from each other easily. Directory service is similar to a naming service, which organizes objects and data. The Yellow Pages is a very good example of a directory service in that it collects and organizes names, addresses, and phone numbers. A file system on your computer as well as networking are other examples of directory services. You can access the location of network printers and software on the network by, for example, using a service like Novell Directory Service (NDS).

As you might expect, directory services are hierarchical. Each node and directory forms a tree starting from the root. In a file system on your computer, you can organize your directories under a root directory, which is \ in Windows for example. Clients mostly focus on accessing a specific subdirectory and a file in that subdirectory. For example, if you need to access the file FinalReport.xls in the directory CurrentSales, which is under the SalesDept directory in the root (\), you have to change your current directory to \SalesDept\CurrentSales and access the file by referring to it by its given (binding) name FinalReport.xls.

A directory object is a special object in a naming system, and it represents a variety of information on the computer system. A directory object can have attributes. Each node of a directory hierarchy is called a *context*. Directory services allow you to create attributes, and read, remove, and modify attributes attached to contexts, which are directory objects. Directory services also have the capability to search a context using those attributes as a filter. The LDAP service is a good example of a directory service. For example, you can organize your company by physical locations (or departments or any other organizational style). Later, you can search a certain department in these locations. In this situation, a department name is the value of the name attribute of the department you are searching. If you search in all the locations or specific locations for people that have worked more than 10 years, the people's working duration is the value of the name attribute of the working duration you are searching.

Each directory service requires a service provider, which is linked to JNDI. When an application requests something from JNDI, JNDI sends that request to a directory service through a service provider. Directory services are very different in the way they organize information, search directories, and modify attributes. JNDI masks these differences for developers, so developers only need to know how the JNDI API works.

Directory Package

The javax.naming.directory is part of the JNDI API package. It extends the javax.naming package and contains classes and interfaces to access directory services in addition to naming services. With the directory package, you can search a directory using filters (for specific attributes or values), control and optimize search results, and modify attributes of an object.

JNDI URL and Composite Names

Uniform Resource Locators (URLs) are special composite name representations for directory and naming services. There are different URLs for different services. For example, your application might use the following URL for an LDAP server to search the sales department within a company in a different physical location:

```
ldap://ldap.chicago.com/ou=sales
```

In this URL, ldap:// is the directory service; ldap.chicago.com is the host server name; and ou=sales is the attribute of the directory object you are searching. Also, ou represents an organization unit in the LDAP architecture.

Another example might be a download page on an FTP server, which looks something like this:

```
ftp://technology.centurybooks.com/download/jms_newriders.zip
```

In this URL, ftp:// is the Internet protocol; technology.centurybooks.com is the name of the host server; and download/jms_newriders.zip is the file name in a specific directory on the computer system.

JNDI defines a composite name syntax to implement composite names. It allows Java applications to refer to the objects using multiple namespaces.

Where Can You Use JNDI?

JNDI has a very important role in Java enterprise applications. It works with many directory and naming services including LDAP, CORBA, File Systems, DNS, and RMI. Your enterprise applications can reach the directory and naming services from different providers through JNDI. Some examples for using JNDI follow:

- User authentication—In secure systems, you must be authenticated before logging on to a system such as a computer or network. For example, an LDAP server is used for user authentication before a user can access any resources. The Unix operating system prompts for a password before logging in.

- Electronic mail—An electronic mailing system is similar to a directory service. It provides a mapping between users and their email addresses. You can find an email address for a specific user or user group by using this service.

- Network printing—If you need to add a network printer to your system, you would search or select it by using a unique network card number or IP number. As a user or as a developer, it is always good to access a network printer by a meaningful name. The problem with using a network printer in an application is that the printer configuration or physical address or location might change. To avoid this problem, you can use a JNDI directory service for printing services in an application.

- Databases—By using the JDBC API, you can find attributes and their values on a database. By using JNDI directory service, you can locate database servers. In your applications, you can use the binding name of a database server instead of a physical name. If the database server needs reconfiguration, it will not affect your application as long as the binding name stays the same.

Using JNDI

LDAP is a very good example of showing how to use JNDI in an application. In the example shown Listing 1.1, the Java application tries to authenticate the user ID and its password on an LDAP server. If it is successful, it will verify the message; if not, it will display a failed message. To use directory and naming services in a Java application, you should import the proper packages like this:

```
import java.util.*;
import javax.naming.*;
import javax.naming.directory.*;
```

You can then decide on a name for your class. In Listing 1.1, the class file name is LDAPAuthenExample. Don't forget to save this file name with a .java extension as a plain text file. Your class skeleton will look like this:

```
public class LDAPAuthenExample {

} //end of LDAPAuthenExample
```

You need to assign values to the JNDI related constants. The first constant is CTXINIT. In Listing 1.1, it looks like this:

```
private static final String CTXINIT = "com.sun.jndi.ldap.LdapCtxFactory";
```

The CTXINIT constant's value depends on the directory and naming service. The second constant, CTXURL, is the directory and naming server location's URL. In the example, the server is an LDAP server and looks like this:

```
private static final String CTXURL ="ldap://montreal.javaapp.com:389
```

The server must be installed and running somewhere on the network. You should substitute this URL with your LDAP server name. The third constant, CTXBASE, is assigned to Base DN. For the example shown in Listing 1.1, it looks like this:

```
private static final String CTXBASE = "ou=people, dc=javaapp, dc=com";
```

You should check your LDAP server to find its Base DN. In your application source code, you might need to create some variables to use in the class, such as ldapEnv, userLogin, and userPassword.

After creating variables and assigning values to constants, you should create a constructor method of the class to initialize the values like this:

```
public LDAPAuthenExample {

    ldapEnv = new Hashtable();
    ldapEnv.put(Context.INITIAL_CONTEXT_FACTORY, CTXINIT);
    ldapEnv.put(Context.PROVIDER_URL, CTXURL);

}  //end of constructor class
```

You can also create some setter methods, such as `setUserLogin()` and `setUserPass()`, to assign values to variables in the class.

The heart of this application is the `isAuth()` method, which performs authentication. It returns a boolean value. If authentication is done through an LDAP server, it returns a true value; if it fails, it returns a false value and an exception message.

In the `main()` method, create an instance of the class like this:

```
LDAPAuthenExample ld= new LDAPAuthenExample();
```

Then, assign a User ID and its password by calling the `setUserLogin()` and `setUserPass()` methods. The next step is to call the `isAuth()` method of the instance. If you get a true boolean value, authentication is complete; otherwise it fails. This example aims to familiarize the user with the JNDI API.

In the example, authentication and assigning a user ID and password are in the same application, which you usually don't see in a real application. In a real application, you can create an authentication class separately without a `main()` method (maybe in a JavaBean), and you can call it from another application, or you can embed it into a JSP application. Just make sure that security is maintained in your applications.

Listing 1.1 contains the full source code of the Java application.

Listing 1.1   **A JNDI Authentication Example**

```
 1:  package jndiSamples;
 2:
 3:  import java.util.*;
 4:  import javax.naming.*;
 5:  import javax.naming.directory.*;
 6:
 7:  public class LDAPAuthenExample {
 8:
 9:  // Using JNDI to access LDAP
10:     private static final String CTXINIT = "com.sun.jndi.ldap.LdapCtxFactory";
11:  // LDAP URL, substitute with your LDAP server name
12:     private static final String CTXURL = "ldap://montreal.javaapp.com:389
13:  // Base DN is needed, find it from your LDAP server
14:     private static final String CTXBASE = "ou=People, dc=javaapp, dc=com";
15:
16:     private Hashtable ldapEnv;
17:     private transient String userLogin;
18:     private transient String userPassword;
19:
20:  //  building constructor class
21:     public LDAPAuthenExample {
22:
23:         ldapEnv = new Hashtable();
24:         ldapEnv.put(Context.INITIAL_CONTEXT_FACTORY, CTXINIT);
25:         ldapEnv.put(Context.PROVIDER_URL, CTXURL);
26:
27:     } //end of constructor class
28:
29:     public void setUserLogin(String uid) {
30:         this.userLogin = uid;
31:     }
32:
33:     public void setUserPass(String password) {
34:         this.userPassword = password;
35:     }
36:
37:  // The Authentication takes place here
38:     public boolean isAuth() {
39:
40:     //Building string for userDN with userid
41:         String userDN = "uid=" + userLogin + ", ou=People,  dc=javaapp, dc=com";
42:         boolean auth = false;
43:
44:         try {
45:                 ldapEnv.put(Context.SECURITY_PRINCIPAL, userDN);
46:                 ldapEnv.put(Context.SECURITY_CREDENTIALS, this.userPassword);
47:                 DirContext ctx = new InitialDirContext(ldapEnv);
```

```
48:                    System.out.println("Directory Context created Authentication");
49:                    ctx.close();
50:                    auth=true;
51:              } catch (AuthenticationException e1) {
52:          System.out.println("Directory Context couldn't be created…"+e1.toString());
53:                    auth = false;
54:              } catch (Exception e1) {
55:          System.out.println("Errorrrrr…"+e1.toString());
56:              } catch (NamingException e2) {
57:          System.out.println("Naming Exception Errorrrrr…"+e2.toString());
58:              }  /end of try and exceptions
59:
60:          return (auth);
61:     } //end of isAuth()
62:
63:     public static void main(String args[]) {
64:
65:          LDAPAuthenExample ld = new LDAPAuthenExample();
66:          ld.setUserLogin("levent");
67:          ld.setUserPass("pass123");
68:          if (ld.isAuth()) {
69:              System.out.println("Password verified");
70:          } else {
71:              System.out.println("Incorrect Password");
72:          }
73:
74:     }  // end of main
75:
76: } //end of LDAPAuthenExample class
```

Developing a Simple Java Application

In the next chapter, I provide you with more information about EJBs and enterprise applications, but now I'd like to show you how you can create a simple Java application by using the Forte for Java development tool. The Community Edition of Forte for Java is free of charge to developers and is an adequate tool for beginners and students. If you need more features in a development tool, you can purchase an upgrade to Forte for Java Professional Edition, or you can buy another development tool, depending on your project's requirements. This book is based on free and shareware programs, which anyone can easily acquire. Although there are other free programs on the market, I prefer the ones from Sun Microsystems or those that are suggested by Sun.

The source code for the examples of this simple application can be found in Listings 1.2 and 1.3. The output of these listings will display a kind of Hello World message. This application has two methods: main() and sayHello(), which are called in the main() method. By typing and running this example, you will see how to use a development tool and execute a simple Java application.

Let's start developing a very simple Java application (not an enterprise application). Click the Forte for Java icon on your desktop, or choose it from the program list. You might only see the top part of the Integrated Development Environment (IDE) on your screen, as shown in Figure 1.7. You need to display the Explorer window of the Forte for Java IDE on your screen; otherwise, you cannot work with the files.

Figure 1.7   The top part of the IDE in Forte for Java.

From the menu bar, select Window, Windows, and then GUI Editing. Click Explorer (see Figure 1.8).

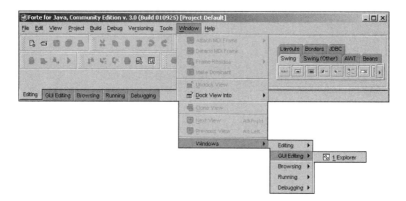

Figure 1.8   The top part of the IDE in Forte for Java with pull-down menus open.

You will then have an open Explorer window in the top part of the Forte for Java IDE (see Figure 1.9).

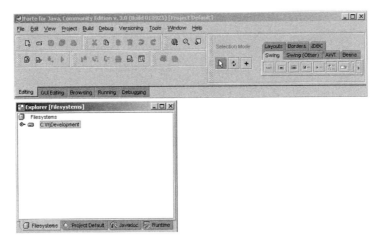

Figure 1.9   The top part of the IDE in Forte for Java and the Explorer window.

Now you are ready to create a simple Java application. In the Forte for Java development tool, be sure to create a working directory for your applications, which is technically called a package for your application. When the mouse is on the Forte for Java Development directory name, which is ffjDevelopment in this example, right-click the mouse button. The menu shown in Figure 1.10 is displayed.

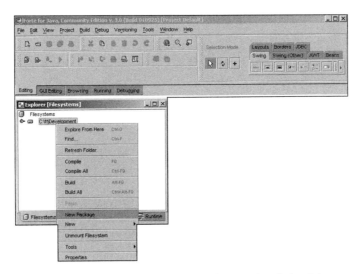

Figure 1.10   Forte for Java Explorer menu after a right-click of the mouse.

Choose New Package from this menu, and in the input box, enter the name SimpleJavaTest for this example (see Figure 1.11).

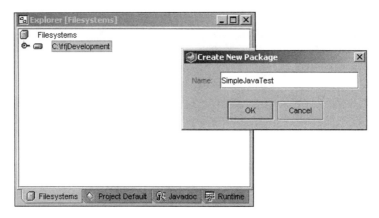

Figure 1.11   Input box to enter the new package name.

You can then create your Java applications in a new package (which is a kind of file organization). Highlight the new package name that you created in the previous step, and right-click. Select New to display menus containing different templates and wizards, which assist you in creating applications easily (see Figure 1.12). You can still create all of these by using any text editor, but development tools will increase your productivity dramatically.

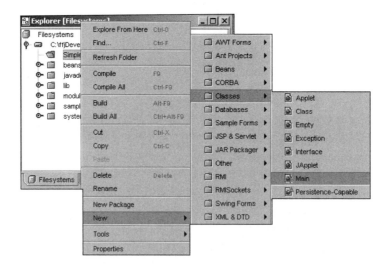

Figure 1.12   Template and Wizards menus after right-click on
the new package created.

The simplest one to use is the Empty template under the Classes choice. You can write your source code on a blank page like you do in any text editor. For this example, let's choose `main()`, which is displayed as Main under Classes. It will create the `main()` method of the class in addition to the other standard parts of the class. Click Main under Classes. The New Form Template Wizard will take you through the process to complete creating the object (instance). Five more steps are left to finish the process after choosing `main()` under Classes. (Choosing `main()` is assumed as the first step.) The other five steps are briefly explained as follows:

1. The wizard will then ask the name of the object. In the sample source codes in Listings 1.2 and 1.3, the name given to the object is HelloFromJMS.

2. Define the basic class definitions, such as superclass, interfaces to implement, and the class type.

3. Create fields (variables) and define their type and initial values.

4. Select inherited methods to override. If you did not choose a superclass in the second step, HelloFromJMS will only inherit the Object class, which is inherited by all Java classes by default. You can also override the public methods of the Object class such as `clone()`, `equals()`, `finalize()`, `hashCode()`, and `toString()`.

5. Create methods for your class. To make this simple example a little more difficult, let's add one more method, `sayHello()`. Instead of putting everything in `main()` method, let's put the business logic of the application in the `sayHello()` method. This method will be called from the `main()` method after creating an instance of the class.

At the end of process, Forte for Java will create template source code for your application as you can see in Figure 1.13. It is up to you to complete the rest of the application.

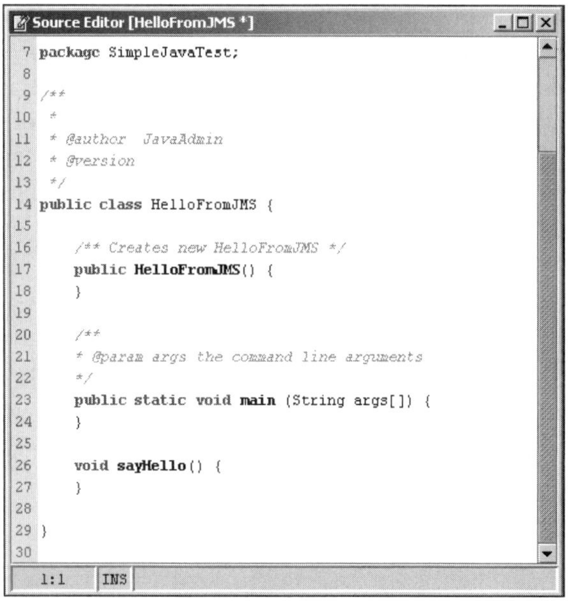

Figure 1.13 Template source code for the sample application.

To complete the application, you have to fill in two methods, `sayHello()` and `main()`. The `sayHello()` method is designed to provide some on screen messages to the user. For this example, write the code for the `sayHello()` method in Listing 1.2.

Listing 1.2 *sayHello( )* **Method of Example Application**

```
1:     void sayHello() {
2:
3:         System.out.println("Entering HelloFromJMS.sayHello()");
4:         System.out.println(" ==== Hello from JMS example! ====");
5:         System.out.println("Leaving HelloFromJMS.sayHello()");
6:
7:     }
```

The `main()` method code must also be written. You should first create an instance of the class, and then call this instance method, which in this case is `sayHello()`, to execute the application. Modify the `main()` method with the code in Listing 1.3.

Listing 1.3 *main( )* **Method of the Sample Application**

```
1:    public static void main (String args[]) {
2:
3:        System.out.println("Entering HelloFromJMS.main()");
4:        HelloFromJMS helloObj = new HelloFromJMS();
5:        helloObj.sayHello();
6:        System.out.println("Leaving HelloFromJMS.main()");
7:
8:    }
```

After you complete the source code, right-click on the application name, which is HelloFromJMS. When you select Execute from the menu, it will compile your source code and run it. If some errors occur during the compilation, there will be warnings in the IDE. If everything goes well, the results of executing the application will be displayed in the Output Window (see Figure 1.14).

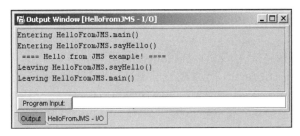

Figure 1.14   Output of the execution of the application.

After compiling the source code of the application, the Forte for Java development tool creates a class file of java source code with a .class extension and locates it in the same location. With some development tools, you can separate the .java extension source code file and the .class extension compiled files into different locations. The development tool sends the compiled files to the defined location in the file system after compilation.

You can see how easy it is to develop a Java application using a development tool. You can also develop an enterprise application by using these tools, but you also need a deployment tool to deploy them, which is explained in Appendix B, "Application Deployment Tool."

Summary

In this chapter, you learned about Java platforms, J2SE, J2EE, and how they are related.

I also discussed enterprise application architecture. Two types of architectures are common: the two-tier and the three-tier models. Prior to J2EE, the two-tier model was used for enterprise applications too. In this model, the business logic and presentation logic are on the same layer. Database and enterprise information systems make up the second layer.

Because of the two-tier model's weak points in large-scale projects—in terms of security, scalability, performance, and reliability—the three-tier model is more appropriate for use in the enterprise world. In the three-tier model, business logic is separated from the presentation logic. Database and enterprise information systems make up the third tier and can be reached only from the business logic tier of the model. With new editions of J2EE, even business logic is divided into sublayers when necessary. The client-side presentation layer makes up the first tier, the server-side presentation layer makes up the second tier, the business logic layer makes up the third tier, and the database and enterprise system make up the fourth tier.

You saw other features of J2EE such as the APIs and other technologies. You learned about JNDI in more detail because it has a very important role in JMS. An LDAP authentication example was also provided to show you how JNDI is used in Java applications.

You created a simple Java application by using the Forte for Java development tool. You will use this tool when you develop standard or enterprise applications, which will increase your developing speed and productivity, and substantially reduce your development time.

Questions and Answers

1. I develop enterprise applications using JSP technology. All JSPs are on the server-side. Users can call a JSP page from their browser. Database connections and queries are also implemented in JSP. If the presentation logic is on server-side, is the application using a two-tier or three-tier model?

It is using a two-tier model because the presentation logic and business logic are on the same layer, even though your presentation layer is on the server-side.

2. The two-tier model developed by JSP works well for my application. The number of clients using the application is almost 100, and only two or three clients at most need to access the application at the same time. Should I convert it to a three-tier or four-tier model?

It depends on your application. When the number of clients and requests from clients increase, you might face some performance problems. Additionally, it is always good to isolate database and enterprise information services from the presentation layer for security and reliability reasons.

3. Java applets are client-side elements used to create web applications. Is an applet part of J2EE?

Definitely, yes. J2EE is an extension of J2SE. All technologies, classes, and interfaces of J2SE are also part of J2EE. Java applets can be used on the client-side presentation layer to connect to the web container on the server-side.

4. Does J2EE come with a directory and naming server such as LDAP?

No. Java provides JNDI to developers to access a naming and directory service, but it does not provide a naming and directory server. You have to find and install these kinds of servers on your system as you do on database servers. JNDI, like JDBC, is just an interface between your application and the servers.

5. What is the role of JMS in J2EE applications?

JMS is one of the services included with J2EE. With J2EE 1.3, you can develop your application, which contains JMS, with message-driven beans as you do with session beans and entity beans. You will study JMS in detail throughout the rest of the book.

2

Enterprise JavaBeans (EJB)

IT WOULD BE CORRECT TO SAY THAT Enterprise JavaBeans (EJB) is the foundation of Java 2 Enterprise Edition (J2EE). What is an EJB? What does it do? What is its role in Java Message Service (JMS)? All the details of EJB technology cannot be explained in one chapter, but it is vital to include a discussion of EJB at the beginning of a book about JMS.

Briefly, EJB is a server-side component model of J2EE. If you develop a Java distributed application, you might need EJB in your project. In the past, there were mainly two types of programming models: programs written for personal computers or programs written for hosts. Personal computers (PCs) and hosts (mainframes) existed in two totally different worlds. PC programmers did not need to spend any effort learning the mainframe part of the computer world and vice versa.

Actually, today's server-side programming model goes back to mainframe programming models. In the basic client-server model, one computer contained all resources, and its dumb clients accessed this main resource to run applications. In this kind of model, you could still isolate your applications from EJB or other server-side models. Today, programs run on different computers and access data or other applications on different computers. Programs and data can be located on a local area network (LAN) or anywhere on the Internet.

When you develop distributed applications, you will have different options in addition to Java and its enterprise technology, EJB. Why do you need EJB? Java is a platform-independent language. Its slogan is "write once, run everywhere." Additionally, EJB is implementation-independent. It is very similar to a Java Database Connectivity (JDBC) API. The database that you need to access can be on a UNIX or Windows operating system, or any other operating system. You do not have to know the details of the database implementation as long as it has a JDBC driver and you know Structured Query Language (SQL). Similarly, an EJB can be developed and deployed to any application server as long as it is J2EE compliant.

History of EJB

Before examining some basic parts of EJB technology, let's discuss the evaluation of server-side technologies.

Distributed Programming and Applications

In a distributed application, the various parts of the application can be placed in separate locations. You can put the business layer, data layer, and access layer on different environments. Different users such as customers, vendors, and others can use the system at anytime from anywhere. Distributed programming is based on distributed objects. Common Object Request Broker Architecture (CORBA), Microsoft Distributed Component Object Model (DCOM), and Java Remote Method Invocation (RMI) are distributed technologies. These technologies allow objects to run on one machine while being used from another machine.

If you have developed an application on any kind of mainframe in the past, you are familiar with the distributed programming model. Mainframes actually represented the first three-tier model—a program resembling a database resided on one machine as the third tier, programs written in COBOL or similar languages resided on another machine as the second tier (the business layer), and dumb terminals represented the first tier (the presentation layer). In modern three-tier models, you develop a more user-friendly graphical user interface (GUI) or more sophisticated business layer or relational database, but the main idea of structure is the same. All parts of this model are similar to a distributed object model (DOM).

Server-Side Programming

The most important part of the older three-tier model was the business layer. To make the business layer more flexible and reusable, it is currently written in object-oriented languages (OOLs), such as C++ or Java. OOLs helped develop better GUIs, access data, and encapsulate the business logic. The encapsulation of the business layer into business objects has come to be considered the most important step. Developers designed business layers as business objects with the server-side component model. It resides in the middle tier of three-tier model and allows developers to make distributed objects easily.

Server-side components can be developed separately and can run on many environments without modification of the source code as long as the server supports the component model. The advantage of this model is that you can update changes on business logic very easily. If you need to change something on the business layer, you can modify your source code and redeploy. The basic step when you design a distributed software application is to design business layers as business blocks and glue them together properly.

Application Servers

As a developer today, if you need to develop an application, you have to consider many different technologies such as databases, web servers, message-oriented middleware (MOM), and so on. As a result, application servers came to the market to manage different technologies and make developers' lives easier. Application servers provide connectivity between client applications and the distributed objects. The first application servers were Object Request Brokers (ORBs), which allowed client applications to use distributed objects.

ORBs sometimes failed for large-scale applications or high volume users. System-level considerations were still developers' responsibilities; therefore, component transaction monitor (CTM) appeared in the distributed application world for more complicated and large-scale distributed applications. CTMs manage transactions, object distribution, concurrency, security, persistence, and resource management automatically. They provide solutions for high-volume users and mission critical applications. Application servers also provide a consistent and stable platform on which to develop and deploy enterprise applications.

Enterprise JavaBeans (EJBs)

So what is an EJB? It's a server-side component model used on component transaction monitors. This technology was introduced to software application developers by Sun Microsystems.

EJB technology is based on and is the heart of distributed object technologies. It resides in the middle tier of the three-tier model. See Figure 2.1.

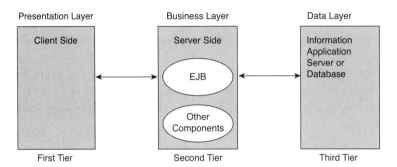

Figure 2.1   The three-tier model.

In the three-tier model, client applications (the presentation layer) are located on the first tier; business logic (the business layer) is located on the middle or second tier; and the database or application information server (the data layer) is located on the third tier. In the rest of this chapter, you will find more information about EJB technology. You will also explore examples in more depth in Chapter 3, "Enterprise JavaBeans Examples." This technology has a very important role in JMS.

JavaBeans and EJBs

EJBs are components that meet the server-side component model specification. They use the Java language as well as a set of classes and interfaces from the javax.ejb package. Some developers are confused by JavaBeans being called standard JavaBeans and EJBs. An EJB is a JavaBean for enterprise applications, but JavaBeans use different packages called java.beans. They are not designed for distributed applications, although they are a component model. You can use them on the client side (in the middle tier in some applications via web components) of the three-tier (or n-tier) model but not on the server side. EJBs are components, but they are designed for the server side. You can use EJBs on the client side through another web component such as a JavaServer Page (JSP) element or a Java servlet. EJBs are not designed as a client-side component. Therefore, JavaBeans and EJBs are different concepts.

Standard JavaBeans are components that are mostly used in a GUI for an item such as button, text field, or any other component. Nowadays, JSP makes heavy use of JavaBeans in the middle tier as a component. A standard JavaBean is

- Reusable—It can be used in almost every application without modifying the source code.
- Flexible— It can be modified based on your application requirements without having to modify the source code for the underlying bean. Doing this is as easy as calling the appropriate methods of the bean.
- Portable—It can be used on many different platforms that support the JavaBeans specification without modifying the source code.

As mentioned earlier, an EJB is a component that is located on the server side. It is designed as a business object deployed in an EJB server and is used in any business application. An EJB is

- Reusable—It can be used in almost every application without modifying the source code.
- Portable—It can be used on many different platforms that support the EJB specification without modifying the source code.

An EJB, unlike a standard JavaBean, is an object that is deployed in an application; it is not a GUI. There are three types of EJBs: *session bean*, *entity bean*, and *message-driven bean*.

Standard JavaBeans and EJBs have one commonality: They can both be called from a web component such as a JSP or a Java servlet. Particularly, standard JavaBeans are used more widely in the middle tier with JSP elements.

EJB Architecture

EJBs work in the J2EE environment, which is based on a distributed architecture. As you can see in Figure 2.2, there is a client component on the client side and a remote component on the EJB side. They are connected to each other through the network. The client component sends a request to the remote component across the network. The J2EE platform provides naming and directory service via a Java Naming Directory Interface (JNDI) API. It advertises a service component and resolves client references to the service component.

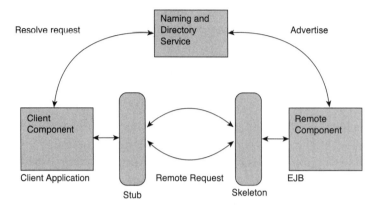

Figure 2.2   EJB architecture.

If the remote object exists, it advertises through a naming service using a logical name. A client uses the same logical name through the naming service when it makes a request. The naming service translates this logical name to the physical location. After a connection is established between the client component and the remote component, the client can send requests to the remote component. This process is not terribly complicated. Just remember, the naming service connects the client and remote objects by assigning a name to the EJB. Consider this analogy: Your parents (your naming service) named you (EJB) with a name (logical naming), registered you at the town hall (physical naming), told their family and friends your name (advertising from the naming service), and your friends (client) can call you (advertising) and ask you to do something (client request).

As you can see in Figure 2.2, there are three main parts of the architecture: the EJB, the skeleton, and the stub. The EJB is the business object, which is sometimes called an "object server." The stub and the skeleton identify where the EJB runs regardless of where it resides.

EJBs are located on the middle-tier, but it seems as though they are running on the client side by the stub and the skeleton. This is done through a distributed object protocol. An RMI protocol such as Java RMI, CORBA, or Microsoft DCOM falls in the object protocol classification.

The skeleton is also located in the middle tier. Every instance on the object server has a matched instance on the skeleton. The skeleton is set up on a port and listens to requests from the client (stub).

The stub is located on the client side and is connected to the server through a network. It provides communication between the client and the server. Actually, communication between the client and the server is implemented between the stub and the skeleton by using the RMI protocol.

Let me explain it in another way: Your EJB stays somewhere (middle tier), and it has a walkie-talkie (skeleton). Your client is at another location (first tier) and has a walkie-talkie (stub) too. They have a communication line via the air (network), and they speak the same language (RMI protocol). They set their channel to a specific channel (port), and the EJB walkie-talkie listens to requests coming from the client walkie-talkie. Although this explanation might sound silly, it is a very good way to create links between concepts and the real world when you are learning something new.

EJB Container

As a developer, you can develop and deploy enterprise applications using many technologies. But, you definitely need EJB. EJB technology offers some extra services to developers, such as transaction and security management and scalability management—among others. You can benefit from using EJBs even if you have lots of experience.

Some developers confuse the difference between an EJB server and an EJB container. Although it appears that they are the same, the EJB container runs on top of the EJB server. It handles system-level programming (see Figure 2.3). Interactions between a bean and its server are managed by a container. The container creates new instances and also ensures that the server stores the beans on the server properly.

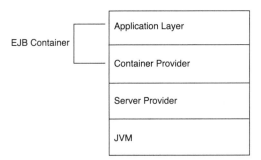

Figure 2.3   EJB server layers.

An EJB container resides within the server, and all bean instances only interact with the container. All communication with the bean instances first pass through the container.

Today, most of you have a direct line or direct access to the phone line at your desk. Not very long ago, there were one or more receptionists at every company who would forward or direct incoming calls from outside the company to you. The container has a similar role in EJB technology. It does not affect the communication, it only manages it. The only difference is that an EJB container never criticizes what you wear to its friends!

An EJB server runs on top of the Java Virtual Machine (JVM). The server provides system services such as management of distributed transactions and handles lower-level system services.

When a client application requests something from an EJB, the request first goes to the container and is then forwarded to the EJB. The container handles security, memory management, and other necessary transactions. After the process finishes, the response goes to the container and is forwarded to the client.

When a client needs to access an EJB, it contacts the EJB Home object. The EJB Home object carries out transactions, security, and memory management and creates an EJB instance or finds the proper EJB instance if it exists.

After creating or finding the appropriate EJB instance, the EJB Home object associates the EJB instance with the EJB object, and then returns to the client a distributed reference to the EJB object. When the client needs to run business methods, it is directed to the EJB object (also called the *remote object*). Every business method on the EJB object has a corresponding business method in the bean class. After accomplishing this process with security and other transaction issues, the EJB object forwards business method execution requests to the bean instance, and then returns the results to the client. See Figure 2.4.

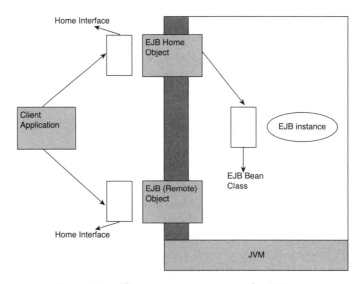

Figure 2.4   Client request process to the EJB.

An EJB container can be divided into two parts based on the functionality support provided for: the *bean provider* (called the application layer) and the *container provider*.

The bean provider includes three items: a bean class of EJB, its home interface, and its remote interface. In the bean class, the provider (you, the developer) implements business and creator methods. The bean provider supplies and implements home and remote interfaces. The client uses those interfaces to contact the EJB. The container uses the interfaces to generate the EJB Home and EJB object. The home interface is a subinterface of the javax.ejb.EJBHome interface. The remote interface is a subinterface of the javax.ejb.EJBObject interface.

The container provider generates EJBHome and EJBObject classes, which implement the EJB Home interface and the EJB Remote Object interface defined by the bean provider. EJBHome and EJBObject classes handle transactions, memory management, and security issues, and then send client requests to the EJB instance.

Home and remote parts are written as interfaces rather than classes because they represent the remote objects of the EJB on the client side. These interfaces are used by both client and container, and they provide interaction between the client and the container.

The client application uses the home and remote interfaces to communicate with the EJB instance. It uses JNDI to locate the object that implements the EJB Home interface. Then, the client application invokes the creator or finder method to acquire an EJB object. The client contacts the EJB to execute business processing.

Using EJB

Before J2EE version 1.3, there were only two types of EJBs: session beans and entity beans. Version 1.3 has launched a new type of EJB that is related to the subject of this book: *message-driven beans*. Some brief information about session beans and entity beans is in this chapter. Message-driven beans are examined in Chapter 9, "Message-Driven Beans" in more detail. In this section, you will learn how and when to use session and entity beans, and their differences. As you can see in Figure 2.5, in the three-tier model, EJBs reside in the middle tier.

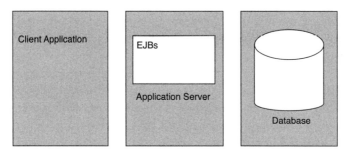

Figure 2.5   The location of EJBs in the three-tier model.

Session Bean

A session bean handles processes or tasks. It implements some actions on the server side on behalf of the client application. It might connect to a database to inquire or update, but it cannot represent data from a database. It represents the transactional part of an application. Its main responsibility is not database activities. A session bean is not data persistent.

Developers use a session bean when the application server should provide a specific service to the client. For example, you can implement mathematical formulas, such as adding or multiplying two numbers, just as you can query a simple SQL statement from a database.

Entity Bean

An entity bean is an object in the real world, which is usually a persistent record in a database. It represents the database part of an application. A session bean does not represent something in a database. Entity beans are used for activities related to a database, and they are persistent.

Classes and Interfaces

When you develop session and entity beans, you have to define two interfaces and one class. They are as follows:

- Home interface—Its methods are designed to create new beans, remove beans, and find beans. It extends `javax.ejb.EJBHome`. These methods define a bean's life cycle. When you use a home interface in a project, it is called an EJB Home or an EJB Home object.

- Remote interface—It defines the bean's business logic methods. It extends javax.ejb.EJBObject. It is like a representation of the bean to the world. When you use a remote interface in a project, it is called an EJB object or an EJB Remote object.

- Bean class—It is the main part of the bean. It contains the bean's business methods. An entity bean implements a javax.ejb.EntityBean; a session bean implements a javax.ejb.SessionBean. EntityBean and SessionBean extend a javax.ejb.EnterpriseBean. A bean class has methods that match the signature of the methods in the remote interface. It also matches some life-cycle methods in the home interface.

In addition to the two interfaces and one class, there is one more class of EJB: *primary key*. It provides a pointer into the database. It is only needed by an entity bean because only an entity bean is data persistent. The primary key implements java.io.Serializable.

It might seem a little confusing with all of these interfaces and classes. Don't worry—you will understand them much better after you see the examples in Chapter 3. I'll provide you with some brief information about the enterprise bean concepts before diving into the source code of the sample applications.

Session Bean

As discussed previously, a session bean handles processes or tasks. It interacts with a database, but it is not data persistent. In this part of the chapter, I will discuss session beans in detail. The most important feature of a session bean is its state. There are two types of session beans: *stateful* or *stateless*. The bean developer decides on the session bean type when it is designed.

A stateful session bean belongs to one and only one client for the client session. The session bean exists and serves the same client until either the client removes itself or the session is over (times out). If you need the conversational state, sometimes called the conversational history, between a client and a bean, you have to use a stateful session bean. It stores the conversational state it had with its client.

A stateless session bean does not remember the conversation between the client and the bean. It remembers the duration of a single method call. The client might not get the same bean. The bean can be called by different client requests, and this assignment is handled by the container.

From the view of a client programmer, stateless and stateful session beans are the same when writing the client application.

Stateful Session Bean

A stateful session bean belongs to one client and serves it during the session. The container has separate EJB objects and assigns every EJB instance to each client. On subsequent method calls, the client returns to the same EJB instance (see Figure 2.6).

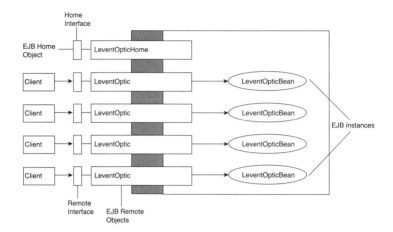

Figure 2.6 Stateful session bean.

If you use a stateful session bean, you do not store the history between the bean and the client on the client side. It is the container's responsibility. This increases the container's workload. The container must maintain a larger set of stateful session beans—one for each client.

If the bean stays inactive for a while, it is passivated by the container by saving its state information to secondary storage. It might be sent to garbage collection or be reused by another client. Passivation decreases memory consumption.

You might be wondering what happens if the client invokes a method on a passivated bean instance. The container manages this problem very well by activating the bean instance. It restores the state data to a new bean instance before executing the method call. Inactivity time can be defined during deployment.

Stateless Session Bean

Stateless session beans do not belong to only one specific client—they can be used by different clients. There is a pool of EJB instances in the container. All clients have the same reference to the same object. When a client calls a method (that is, makes a request), the container forwards this request to the first available EJB instance in the pool. If the client makes another request, it might go to another instance in the pool (see Figure 2.7).

Unlike the stateful type, the container does not need to grow or shrink the pool of stateless session beans when the clients call the `create()` and `remove()` methods.

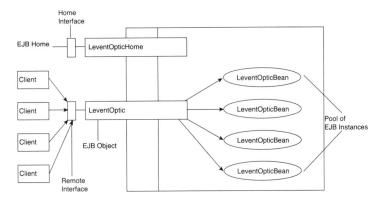

Figure 2.7   Stateless session bean.

The only problem is providing enough EJB instances by container for simultaneous requests from clients. The pool must be large enough for the simultaneous requests. The container does not have to maintain the number of simultaneous clients. The pool size might be smaller than the number of session bean clients.

Client Access to a Session Bean

Stateless or stateful session beans are the same from the view of the client. The client developer writes the program in the usual way. A client looks for the home object, asks to create a session bean, invokes the business logic methods, and then asks to remove the session bean.

As a developer, you must identify and understand the client usage type. If the client needs the session bean to remember data sent in a previous request, you should use a stateful session bean. Otherwise, you should choose a stateless session bean.

Although implementations such as accessing the bean or calling a method in the bean seem the same from the clients view, it is very different from the container's perspective. The container treats stateless and stateful session beans differently. If the bean is stateful, the container has the responsibility of providing the same EJB instance to the client. If the session bean is stateless, the container has flexibility and can use different EJB instances for each request. If your EJB has two or more methods (it is very rare that an EJB has only one method), every method uses the same EJB instance when the bean is stateful. Methods might call different EJB instances when the bean is stateless. This case is illustrated in Figure 2.8.

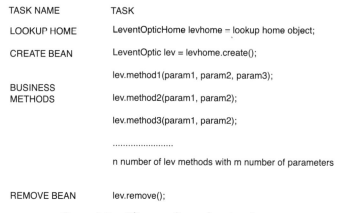

TASK NAME	TASK
LOOKUP HOME	LeventOpticHome levhome = lookup home object;
CREATE BEAN	LeventOptic lev = levhome.create();
BUSINESS METHODS	lev.method1(param1, param2, param3);
	lev.method2(param1, param2);
	lev.method3(param1, param2);
	....
	n number of lev methods with m number of parameters
REMOVE BEAN	lev.remove();

Figure 2.8   Client coding of session beans.

In Figure 2.8, if a session bean named LeventOptic is stateful, the client gets the same instance from creation to removal. It might be passivated if the bean is inactive, but the information about the bean state is stored and transferred to the new bean.

Alternatively, if LeventOptic is stateless, methods such as method1, method2, and method3 in the figure might be handled by different bean instances in the pool. Although the client uses `create()` and `remove()`, the container brings the bean instances from the pool and sends them back to the pool.

Session Bean Methods

As explained previously, an enterprise bean has three items: the home interface, the remote interface, and the bean class. The bean class contains business logic (such as business methods). Those methods are called by the container. A client cannot access those methods directly; it can access the home interface and the remote interface. These interfaces are implemented by the classes generated by the container.

The home interface of a session bean implements the javax.ejb.EJBHome interface; the remote interface implements the javax.ejb.EJBObject interface; and the bean class implements the javax.ejb.SessionBean interface.

The home interface provides methods to create and remove the session bean. The client creates the session bean and then invokes any business method of the bean. After completing the use of a business method, the client removes the bean. The remote interface provides a remove method and application-specific methods.

Which methods should be used in which interface or class? Because these methods might seem a little confusing, I'll provide you with some concepts and brief descriptions about them throughout this section. The more you develop EJB applications, the better you'll understand their structure. Examples are provided in Chapter 3 to help you.

Each session bean must have at least one creator method pair. One is the `create()` method, which is located in the home interface, and the other is the `ejbCreate()` method, which is located in the bean class. These methods' parameters must be matched, but their return types can be different. When there is a client request to the EJB home object's `create()` method, the container transfers its parameters to the bean instance's `ejbCreate()` method. The `create()` method return type is the EJB remote object that implements the remote interface. The `ejbCreate()` method returns void.

The `create()` method in the home interface throws all of the application exceptions thrown by `ejbCreate()`, javax.ejbCreateException, and java.rmi.RemoteException.

If the session bean is stateless, you cannot put parameters into the creator pair because it cannot store the client information. If the session bean is stateful, you can put parameters into the creator methods. These parameters are client-specific information, which the bean stores for the duration of the session. The creator methods can be overloaded because different clients might need different ways to initialize the stateful session bean.

The bean class implements the javax.ejb.SessionBean interface. The container can communicate with the bean by means of this interface. The SessionBean interface requires the `ejbPassivate()`, `ejbActivate()`, `ejbRemove()`, and `setSessionContext()` methods. The bean class contains the business logic's methods in addition to those methods.

Table 2.1 summarizes the methods in a session bean.

Table 2.1 **Session Bean Methods**

Home Interface	Remote Interface	Bean Class
create		`ejbCreate`
	Business Methods	Business Methods
remove	remove	`ejbRemove`

The following list summarizes the life-cycle methods in a session bean:

- `setSessionContext`
- `ejbPassivate`
- `ejbActivate`

Each business method in the bean class must have a corresponding signature in the remote interface. The client calls the business method through the remote object. It is forwarded to the bean instance's business method, and the result is returned. Briefly, the home interface and the remote methods are called by the client; the bean class methods are called by the container.

The remote interface's methods throw all of the application exceptions thrown by the bean class's business methods and java.rmi.RemoteException.

The bean provider must supply an `ejbRemove()` method in the bean class, but the `remove()` method in the home and remote interfaces are already provided by the home and remote superinterfaces, javax.ejbHome and javax.ejbEJBObject. The `remove()` method does not need to be provided explicitly like the `create()` method.

What Do Session Bean Methods Do?

The following is a brief description of the methods that are used in a session bean:

- `ejbCreate()`—Every session bean must have a creator method pair. One is the `create()` method in the home interface; the other is the `ejbCreate()` method with the same signature in the bean class as an infrastructure. The client starts the bean instance's life cycle by calling the `create()` method on the home interface.

  For a stateless session bean, there is no parameter in the method. In a stateful session bean, you can put in necessary parameters to save the conversation between the bean and the container.

  When the client calls the `create()` method in the home interface, it invokes the `ejbCreate()` method in the bean class. Developers should write the proper code in the `ejbCreate()` method to allocate resources, which the bean instance needs, and to initialize the values of the bean.

- `ejbRemove()`—Calling the `remove()` method from the client invokes the `ejbRemove()` method on the session bean instance, and then the bean instance is removed. For a stateless session bean, you do not have to add `remove()` explicitly—the container handles the removing task.

- `setEntityContext()`—This method is the first method used after a bean instance is created. It is called just before the `ejbCreate()` method. It passes the bean instance a reference to a javax.ejb.SessionContext, which is the bean instance's interface to the bean container. It creates a kind of communication between the bean instance and the bean container. setEntityContext has the same role in the entity bean. If you need to use the SessionContext object later, you have to code it in the `setEntityContext()` method.

- `ejbActivate()`—The container calls the `ejbActivate()` method if a passivated bean instance is requested by the client. It reads the bean instance from the storage area, which is saved before passivation. Activation of a bean is for a stateful session bean. The container does not activate a stateless session bean because it does not passivate it.

- `ejbPassivate()`—The container calls the `ejbPassivate()` method if a bean instance is not recently used. Before passivating, the container saves its state to the secondary storage associated with the EJB object to get it back whenever the bean instance is needed to reactivate. Passivation of a bean is for a stateful session bean. The container does not passivate a stateless session bean because it does not activate it.

In Chapter 3, you will learn more about session beans and be provided with an example.

Entity Beans

An entity bean is different from a session bean. It is designed for database mapping, and it is data persistent. In the session bean, you are advised to accomplish some tasks. Session beans can access a database but cannot represent persistent data. Because its structure is simple and it allows database tasks in addition to other tasks, technically you can use session beans for database activities. But this is not smart choice if you have a huge database and many clients who want to access the database. Session beans will connect to the whole database, whereas you can access a small part of a huge database and work with that part by using an entity bean. Its benefits are performance, of course.

In Figure 2.9, you see an entity bean mapping to a table in a database. You fetch one or more rows, depending on the query, using the primary key field, and then link them to an entity bean object.

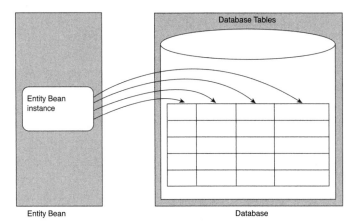

Figure 2.9   Entity beans mapping to a table in a database.

In Figure 2.10, you see an entity bean mapping to two or more tables in a database. You fetch rows from different tables, depending on the query, using the primary key field, and then link them to an entity bean object.

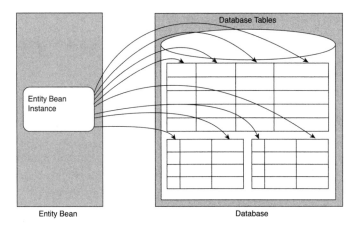

Figure 2.10   Entity beans mapping to two or more tables in a database.

By mapping a database with an entity bean, you do not create a new database: You still use the same database, but you create a link to that database. You extract a small part of the original database by making a query with a primary key. You can select, insert, delete, update, and perform other SQL commands on a representative data object, which allows you to affect the original database. Thus, you can prevent your application from interacting with the database continuously. In other words, an entity bean is like a view of data in the database. You can use objects with this view instead of the underlying database tables. You access and work with what you need. Consider which is better and cheaper—to rent the whole Empire State Building or one floor if you need just one floor?

Many developers working on a complicated project prefer using session beans and entity beans together for database activities. Entity beans connect to the database and create representative data. Session beans connect to this representative data instead of to the database directly (see Figure 2.11). In a session beans and entity beans combined design architecture, you have to design the beans' roles very well. You have to think about what the session beans need from the database. Then, you have to design entity beans, which are the objects that represent the data in the database. Objects in the entity beans will serve the session beans.

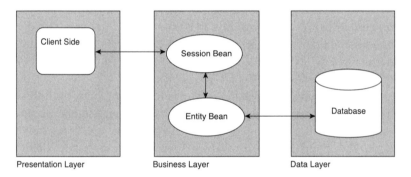

Figure 2.11   Session and entity beans together to connect a database.

Characteristics of an Entity Bean

An entity bean lives in a data store. This data store might be a relational database, a flat file, or any kind of data storage. An entity bean links the business object with the representation in the database. As a developer, you design and develop the business objects, such as business logic or business methods, and then map them to the underlying tables.

For an entity bean, you can design it as a *bean-managed transaction* or a *container-managed transaction*. If you choose the bean-managed transaction type, you have to code transactions explicitly by using the Java Transaction API (JTA). The container controls the entity bean's transaction if you choose container-managed as long as you set the transaction attribute.

Another important characteristic of an entity bean is the primary key, which uniquely describes each EJB object created for the entity. You can use the primary key class file or any other Java data type as the primary key.

Types of Data Persistence

A session bean has two types: stateless and stateful. An entity bean has two types as well: *bean-managed persistence (BMP)* and *container-managed persistence (CMP)*.

With the BMP type, as a developer you have to write the database access code, which are all the SQL statements including selecting, inserting, updating, and deleting in addition to JDBC coding that controls the interaction with the database. The container's responsibility is to invoke the entity bean methods whenever they are needed. This type of bean is the most difficult to use. As a developer, you have to take care of almost every database implementation and control, but it offers a very important advantage—it is container-independent. You can run a BMP type bean in any EJB container. It has very few disadvantages besides coding all database actions. It is not database-independent. If you use database-specific extensions to SQL, you might need to port the bean code to different types of databases.

With the CMP type, as a developer you only have to focus on business logic. The container has the responsibility of carrying on database accessing issues such as inserting, deleting, updating, and handling JDBC controls for interaction with the database. You map the entity bean's persistent fields to database columns. The container generates the required SQL statements on behalf of the developer. As you can guess, the CMP type bean is database-independent.

In Chapter 3, you will work on an example that shows how an entity bean works. In the example, you will use the BMP type of entity bean to explain the methods, even though it is more difficult than the CMP type.

Client Access to Entity Beans

CMP and BMP are the same from the view of the client. They are both server-side design issues that concern performance, database independence, and EJB container independence. The client developer writes the program in the usual way. The client looks for the home object, asks to create an entity bean, invokes the business logic methods, and then asks to remove the entity bean.

Actually, as a developer, a session bean and entity bean can be the same for you as well. You know there is a bean that does something or maps a database. It is not your concern how these issues are handled on the server side. You just need to access the bean and call the methods you need.

Although implementation of the entity bean regardless of its persistence type seems the same from the client's view, it is very different from the container's perspective. The container treats CMP and BMP entity beans differently. If the bean is CMP, the container has the responsibility of mapping the persistent fields. If the entity bean is BMP, the developer must write the proper SQL codes of infrastructure methods in the bean class.

Parts of an Entity Bean

An entity bean consists of four items; three of which are similar to session bean items: home interface, remote interface, and bean class. These items' purposes are the same as session beans items' purposes. An entity bean can also have an additional class: the primary key class.

The home interface of an entity bean implements the javax.ejb.EJBHome interface; the remote interface implements the javax.ejb.EJBObject interface; the bean class implements the javax.ejb.EntityBean interface; and the primary key class implements the java.io.Serializable interface.

The bean class contains business logic (such as business methods). Those methods are called by the container. A client cannot access those methods directly. A client (an application on the client side or a session bean) can, however, access the home interface and the remote interface. These interfaces are implemented by the classes generated by the container.

As you know, in the session beans, the home interface provides methods to create and remove the session bean. In the entity beans, the `create()` method is optional. There can be zero or more `create()` methods. If there is one or more `create()` methods, there must be the same number of `ejbCreate()` methods with the same signature in the bean class. If you need to do something after invoking the `ejbCreate()` method, you can use the `ejbPostCreate()` method as well. For both methods, you have to code them if you choose the BMP type persistence.

The `create()` method in the home interface throws javax.ejbCreateException and java.rmi.RemoteException in addition to all of the application exceptions thrown by the `ejbCreate() method`.

The find primary key method (`findByPrimaryKey()` method) must be in the home interface of an entity bean. In the bean class, you should use the `ejbFindByPrimaryKey()` method and write proper SQL codes to find the data row in the database if you use the BMP type of entity bean.

The `findByPrimaryKey()` method in the home interface throws all of the
application exceptions thrown by the ejbfindByPrimaryKey() method in addition to javax.ejbFinderException and java.rmi.RemoteException.

There can be additional finder methods. Their syntaxes must be
`findByXXX()`, where XXX represents a persistent data field in the database. In the
bean class, you should use the `ejbFindByXXX()` method and write proper SQL
codes to find the data row in the database if you use the BMP type of entity
bean.

The `findByXXX()` method in the home interface throws all of the
application exceptions thrown by the `ejbfindByXXX()` in addition to
javax.ejbFinderException and java.rmi.RemoteException.

The remote interface provides signatures of application-specific methods,
which are located in the bean class. If you need to, you can use the `remove()`
method in the remote interface of an entity bean. All methods in the remote
interface must throw `java.rmi.RemoteException`.

Entity beans must have a primary key object. It can be either a class file,
which you can define, or a valid Java data type. The primary key class must be
a serializable object. The fields in the primary key class must be a subset of the
entity beans' persistent fields. It must identify the EJB object uniquely. The primary key can be either a single primary key or a compound of primary keys.
An entity bean's primary key class requires a default constructor and must
implement two methods: `hashCode()` and `equals()`. At deployment time, the
primary key class is mapped to a persistent field used as the primary key in the
entity data store.

Table 2.2 contains the entity bean methods. Methods in the home interface
and the remote interface are called by the client; the methods in the bean class
are called by the container.

Table 2.2 **Entity Bean Methods**

Home Interface	Remote Interface	Bean Class
create		ejbCreate
		ejbPostCreate
	Business Methods	Business Methods
findByPrimaryKey		ejbFindByPrimaryKey
findByXXX		ejbFindByXXX
remove	Remove	ejbRemove

The following list contains the instance life-cycle methods of an entity bean:

- `ejbStore`
- `ejbLoad`
- `setEntityContext`
- `unsetEntityContext`
- `ejbActivate`
- `ejbPassivate`

The entity bean primary key class methods include

- `hashCode()`
- `equals()`

Recall that for a session bean there are three infrastructure methods of the bean class:

- `setSessionContext()`
- `ejbActivate()`
- `ejbPassivate()`

They do not have signatures in either the home interface or the remote interface. For the entity bean, there are six infrastructure methods of the bean class:

- `ejbStore()`
- `ejbLoad()`
- `setEntityContext()`
- `unsetEntityContext()`
- `ejbActivate()`
- `ejbPassivate()`

They do not have signatures in either the home interface or the remote interface. The container uses these methods to manage the entity bean instance's life cycle.

What Do Entity Bean Methods Do?

The following list provides a brief description of some methods that are used in an entity bean:

- `ejbLoad()`—Synchronizes the entity bean instance and the database. The container calls this method whenever the instance needs to be refreshed with the state in the database. Mostly, the container calls the `ejbLoad()` method before the first business method transaction.

With CMP type persistence, as a developer, you do not need to code this method. Insert an empty method like this:

```
public void ejbLoad() {  }
```

With BMP type persistence, you should code the SQL statements inside the method to select the appropriate columns from the database and load them into the instance's persistent fields. In the example in Chapter 3, you will learn how to code this method.

- ejbStore()—Also synchronizes the entity bean instance state and the database. The container calls this method whenever the instance needs to store its data in the database. This synchronization always happens at the end of a successful transaction. In the middle of a transaction, the container calls the ejbStore() method when it passivates the instance.

  With CMP type persistence, as a developer, you do not need to code this method. Insert an empty method like this:

  ```
  public void ejbStore() {  }
  ```

  With BMP type persistence, you should code the SQL statements inside the method to update the appropriate columns in the database. In the example in Chapter 3, you will learn how to code this method.

- ejbCreate()—If you use the create() method in the home interface, you must use the ejbCreate() method with the same signature in the bean class as an infrastructure. It is used to insert a new record into the database through the entity bean instance. The client invokes the create() method, and then the home object fetches an instance from the container's entity bean pool. This method invokes the corresponding ejbCreate() method on the instance.

  With CMP type persistence, as a developer, you do not need to code this method. With BMP type persistence, you should code the SQL statements inside the method to insert the values into the database. I will explain how you can use the create() method in Chapter 3.

- ejbPostCreate()—If you use the ejbCreate() method, you can add this method to perform some tasks after the completion of the ejbCreate() with matching arguments. Regardless of your need, put an empty ejbPostCreate() method into the bean class to satisfy the requirement of the interface if you use an ejbCreate() method. Its return type must be void, and the parameter list must be the same ejbCreate() method.

- `ejbRemove()`—Deletes a record from the database. As a client, you can delete a record by calling the `remove()` method from either the home object or the remote object. Calling the `remove()` method invokes the `ejbRemove()` method on the entity bean instance.

  With CMP type persistence, you do not code ejbRemove(); it can be used like this in the bean class:

  ```
  public void ejbRemove() throws RemoteException {    }
  ```

  With BMP type persistence, it's the developer's responsibility to code methods to delete records from the database.

- `setEntityContext()`—Is the first method called by the bean container after a bean instance is created. It passes the bean instance a reference to a javax.ejb.EntityContext, which is the bean instance's interface to the bean container. It creates a communication between the bean instance and the bean container. setSessionContext has the same role in the session bean: It allocates resources held for the instance's lifetime.

- `unsetEntityContext()`—At the end of the instance's life (after the bean is removed permanently), this method is called. It stops the context connection (communication) between the bean instance and the bean container. Deallocate resources before the instance is destroyed. In the session beans, the `setSessionContext() method` is similar to the `setEntityContext()` method, which is found in the entity bean class. But there is no `unsetSessionContext()` method in the session beans like the `unsetEntityContext()` method in the entity bean class. Let me explain why there is no `unsetSessionContext()` method in the session bean class. The entity bean instance begins its life as a collection of files, At this stage, no instance of the bean exists. By using the setEntityContext() method, the entity bean instance is brought to the instance pool to be used. At the end of the bean's life, an entity bean is sent to garbage collection from the pool by using the `unsetEntityContext()` method. The `ejbRemove()` or `ejbPassivate()` methods of the entity bean class sends the bean to the pool, not to garbage collection. In the session bean class (either stateless or stateful), you can remove the session bean instance and send it to the garbage by using the `ejbRemove()` method of the session bean class. There is no pool in the session bean life cycle. Therefore, there is no `unsetSessionContext()` method in the session bean class.

- `ejbActivate()`—Bean instances are created by the container. These instances are called *pooled state*. The container assigns them to a specific client, which is called the *ready state*. The container calls the `ejbActivate()` method after it assigns a pooled instance to an EJB object and moves it to a ready state.

- `ejbPassivate()`—The container calls the `ejbPassivate()` method before it moves a bean instance from a ready state to a pooled state.

- `ejbfindByPrimaryKey()`—Is the most important method of the bean class. It locates the records from the database by using the primary key. It is called *the primary key finder method*. It must be paired with the `findByPrimaryKey()` method in the home interface. In a Relational Database Management System (RDBMS), the primary key attribute usually maps to a primary key in a table. In an object-oriented database, the primary key attribute might point to a unique identifier. Session beans do not have finder methods.

  With CMP type persistence, implementation of this method is done automatically at deployment. With the BMP type, the developer must write proper code in the method of the bean class.

  In the entity bean design, there can be an entity bean without creator methods, but there cannot be any without finder methods.

- `ejbFindByXXX()`—Entity beans allow the developer to use additional finder methods in the primary key finder method. In this method, XXX represents a persistent field name in the bean instance. For example, if one of the persistent field names is FirstName, you can add an `ejbFindByFirstName()` finder method. Its corresponding signature will be `findByFirstName()` in the home interface. If you use CMP type persistence, you have to define how the finder method should work to the container at the time of deployment. If you use BMP type persistence, you must write the proper code for `ejbFindByXXX()` in the home interface.

  All finder methods, including the primary key finder, must throw FinderException and CreateException.

EJB and the Web

The Web plays a very important role in enterprise applications. A client can access an EJB, which is located on the server side, by using a web browser such as Internet Explorer or Netscape. Client web applications cannot only contain

HTML documents, which cannot use EJB. JSP and Java servlets allow the client to access EJB. Actually, JSP and Java servlet files reside on the web server, which is technically in the business tier. But they are accepted as part of the client tier, not the business tier, because they are used for presentation purposes.

Some developers write applications and put the presentation logic and the business logic in a JSP file. For small applications, this choice works well. (If a web application is accessed by a few hundred users and only a few of them access the site at the same time, the web application is classified as a small application for some developers). The JSP file does reside on the server side (web server), but this model cannot be used in a three-tier model. You can put the presentation tier and the business tier on the same layer by combining them in a JSP file. However, this is contrary to the design of the three-tier model. It is actually a two-tier model and is not a distributed application.

In the section "EJB and the Web" in Chapter 3, you will find some examples pertaining to a web client for an enterprise application.

EJB and JMS

This book focuses on the JMS API. You might wonder, then, why I'm discussing EJB (session and entity) and providing examples in the next chapter. If I only covered information about JMS without explaining the EJB technology, I believe that this book would not provide enough foundational information about JMS.

EJB is the heart of the Java enterprise technology. JMS is, by default, part of the Java enterprise technology in version 1.3. If you need to develop JMS applications, you need to understand this technology as a whole, even though you might not use it everyday.

Before message-driven beans were introduced, JMS applications were done via session and entity beans. I provide some JMS applications implemented by session and entity beans in Chapter 3.

To understand the message-driven bean, you have to understand historically its similar technologies.

You will be provided with more and more detail about JMS in the rest of the book. I recommend that you have a good deal of experience in other J2EE technologies such as session beans, entity beans, JSP, Java servlets, JNDI, and so on to develop an enterprise application project. Although you might not need to know these technologies in depth to develop JMS projects, it would be good to know other J2EE technologies in addition to JMS API so you can combine them in your projects.

Summary

In this chapter, I discussed session and entity beans, which are the foundation of J2EE. I explained JavaBeans and EJBs and talked about their differences. EJB architecture and containers were discussed as well as the concepts and structure of session beans and entity beans. You worked with a session and entity bean's home interface, remote interface, bean class, and their methods while designing an enterprise application. I also provided information about EJB's role in JMS and the Web.

Questions and Answers

1. I have almost 200 users, and no more than three users are allowed to connect to my enterprise application at a time. Can I perform database tasks with only a session bean?

Technically, yes. Honestly, no. I do not advise this. For this number of users, you will not have a lot of trouble, but it is always good idea to use an entity bean for database activities. Map the database to an entity bean and connect to the entity bean from the session bean.

2. Can I do other tasks such as adding numbers with an entity bean instead of a session bean?

Again, technically, yes. Honestly, no. The design of a session bean is simpler than that of an entity bean. You will spend a great deal of effort mapping a database, and you won't even use it. After a while, you will see that coding and maintenance of an entity bean is more difficult when you need to improve or modify your project.

3. If I put business logic methods into a Java servlet instead an EJB, is it still an enterprise application?

No. Even though a Java servlet resides on the server side like an EJB, it still is part of the presentation layer. In this case, it is called a two-tier model, and it is not a distributed object model. But if you do not need a distributed object model, this model is very good way to design server-side web applications.

4. In a stateful session bean, is it possible not to put parameters into the `create()` method?

In a stateful session bean, you can put parameters into the `create()` method, or you can leave it empty. If you do, you will decrease memory performance because the container will assign a specific bean instance. Between creation and remove, the container will force itself to remember its state.

5. What does the container do if a stateless session bean is inactive?

Nothing. A container does not passivate a stateless session bean because the container sends it back to the pool after the client request is done. The container assigns another bean instance for each client request.

6. In an entity bean, should I use the `create()` method?

No. In a session bean, you start the bean instance life cycle by using the `create()` method, but in an entity bean, the `create()` method has different role. It is used to insert a new record into the database. In an entity bean, the life cycle starts with invoking the `findByPrimaryKey()` method.

7. What should I do to delete a record from the database when I use an entity bean?

Use the `ejbRemove()` method and code it properly if it is a BMP type or define it at deployment if it is a CMP type.

8. What is the best EJB design architecture?

It depends on your project and its considerations. If there are transactional tasks (except database tasks) such as calculating formulas, you can use one or more session beans. But I do not think you can have an enterprise application without a database. You must use an entity bean, although you can handle database tasks with a session bean. For the most part, developers combine session and entity beans. The session bean handles database tasks with other tasks, but it is not recommended to connect to the database directly. Entity beans are used as database representations and serve session beans as an artificial database. This way, you will not increase database activity during heavy network traffic.

3

Enterprise JavaBeans Examples

IN CHAPTER 2, "ENTERPRISE JAVA BEANS," you studied the concepts and theories about session and entity beans in detail. Now it is time to put this information into practice. Analyzing an example after a long discussion is the best way to learn something new.

In this chapter, I will only provide sample applications and their source code. Refer to Appendix B, "Application Deployment Tool," to learn how to deploy these sample applications if you are using the Java 2 Enterprise Edition (J2EE) Reference Implementation.

Creating a Session Bean

I'll create an imaginary scenario to develop a session bean application. Let's first summarize what you need to do if you are going to develop a session bean:

1. Create the home and remote interfaces.

2. Create the session bean class.

3. Add the `create()` method to the home interface and the `ejbCreate()` method to the bean class.

4. Add the `ejbRemove()` method to the bean class.

5. Add the `remove()` method to the home or the remote interfaces if needed.

6. Add business logic methods to the session bean class.

7. Add business logic methods' signatures to the remote interface.

8. Set infrastructure methods in the bean class such as `setSessionContext()`, `ejbPassivate()`, and `ejbActivate()`.

Let's apply these steps to an example. In the example, I'll show how to use a session bean. Therefore, we will work on a very simple project. It is just a little more difficult than an Hello World example.

I will use an Access database (see Figure 3.1). It will be the laboratory database for these simple examples (both session bean and entity bean examples). I will use a UserLogin table in the database for this example. In the UserLogin table, there are three text type fields: LoginName, LoginPassword, and PersonID. The example will only have five rows.

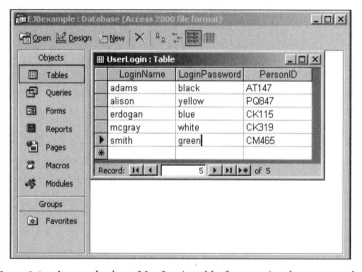

Figure 3.1   Access database UserLogin table for a session bean example.

In the example, I will try to access the database and make some queries through a session bean in an enterprise application. I assume that you know how to handle database tasks, such as connections and queries, using the Java language. I will use a JDBC-ODBC bridge for the database connection because there is currently no Java Database Connectivity (JDBC) driver for MS Access; therefore, I first need to create an Open Database Connectivity (ODBC) connection to the database. To create this connection, go to the ODBC Data Source Administrator in your administrative tool.

In the System DSN, create a new data source, which makes a connection to a database. In the example, the ODBC name for the database is EJBExampleODBC (see Figure 3.2).

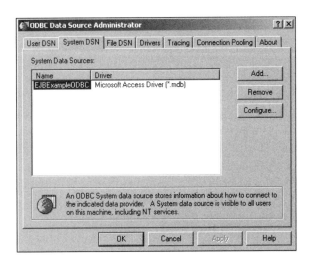

Figure 3.2   DSN name Access database.

As you know, ODBC works like JDBC, but it only works in a Microsoft environment. I used an ODBC driver because the examples are written and tested on Windows XP. The database is in MS Access, which is part of the Microsoft environment. If you want to work with another database such as Oracle, SQL Server, or mySQL, you need to change two lines in your source code in the database: `Class.forName()` and `DriverManager.getConnection()`. If you have to, you can use your database vendor's JDBC driver, or you can still use the JDBC-ODBC bridge (if possible). It is recommended by professional developers that you use a JDBC driver because the JDBC-ODBC bridge is slower.

To make the example simple, I will provide the LoginName and LoginPassword in the query, and I will get the PersonID back through a session bean. This is a way to check the user name and password against a database. You can enhance this idea in your projects and make it more complicated. Instead of a database, you can use Lightweight Directory Access Protocol (LDAP), a flat file, or any other technology.

As mentioned previously, you need three items in the session bean: a home interface, a remote interface, and a bean class. Let me start with the home interface. The simplest home interface, whose name in this example is LeventOpticHome, can be written like this:

```
1. import javax.ejb.*;
2. public interface LeventOpticHome extends EJBHome {
3. } //end of home interface
```

Its superinterface is javax.ejb.EJBHome. It must have a `create()` method, as you might remember from Table 2.1 in Chapter 2 "Enterprise JavaBeans." This `create()` method's return type must be a remote interface of the same session bean. (In this example, I can use the name LeventOptic to complete the home interface source code.) It cannot take any parameters because this session bean will be a stateless session bean in the example. If you need to design a stateful session bean, you can put parameters in this `create()` method in addition to the `ejbCreate()` method in the bean class of this session bean. The `create()` method must throw a RemoteException and a CreateException. After adding the `create()` method, the home interface source code will look like Listing 3.1.

Listing 3.1 **Home Interface of the Sample Session Bean**

```
1. package SessionExample;
2. import java.rmi.RemoteException;
3. import javax.ejb.*;
4. public interface LeventOpticHome extends EJBHome {
5.   public LeventOptic create() throws RemoteException,
6.         CreateException;
7. } //end of home interface
```

The next step is to code the remote interface. The simplest remote interface will look like this:

```
1. import javax.ejb.*;
2. public interface LeventOptic extends EJBObject {
3. } //end of remote interface
```

The remote interface, whose name is LeventOptic, is a subinterface of javax.ejb.EJBObject. It does not have a `create()` method. If needed, it might have a `remove()` method. It must have signatures of business logic methods in the bean class with the same return type and same parameter list. Those methods must throw a RemoteException. Let's assume that in the bean class the getPersonID business method signature will look like this:

```
String getPersonID(String pUserID, String pUserPass)
```

After adding this signature to the remote interface, its final source code will look like Listing 3.2.

Listing 3.2   **Remote Interface of the Sample Session Bean**

```
1. package SessionExample;
2. import java.rmi.RemoteException;
3. import javax.ejb.*;
4. public interface LeventOptic extends EJBObject {
5.    public String getPersonID(String pUserID,
6.            String pUserPass) throws RemoteException;
7.} //end of remote interface
```

The third step is to design a bean class for the stateless session example. I'll show a bean class without a business logic method to demonstrate the main structure of a bean class. A bean class that includes business methods will be too long for this example. This simple bean class, whose name is LeventOpticEJB, will look like Listing 3.3.

Listing 3.3   **Simple Bean Class of the Sample Session Bean**

```
1. import javax.ejb.*;
2. public class LeventOpticEJB implements SessionBean {
3.    public LeventOpticEJB() {  }
4.    public void ejbCreate() throws CreateException { }
5.    public void setSessionContext(SessionContext sc) { }
6.    public void ejbRemove()  { }
7.    public void ejbActivate() { }
8.    public void ejbPassivate() { }
9.  }  //end of bean class
```

A bean class is a subclass of javax.ejb.SessionBean. It must have the `ejbCreate()`, `setSessionContext()`, `ejbPassivate()`, `ejbActivate()`, and `ejbRemove()` methods, as you recall from Table 2.1 in Chapter 2. The `ejbCreate()` method must throw a CreateException. You can now have any number of business methods in the bean class as long as you put their signatures into the remote interface with the same return type and parameter list.

In this example, there will only be one business method whose name is getPersonID. It will take the user ID and user password as its parameter, and then it will query them against the database. It will return the PersonID according to the parameters. If there is no field for these parameters, the user will get a null value. I will not explain every line of this method. My goal is to show how a session bean works with a business method. You can replace this method with a simpler or more complicated one. As long as it is compiled and it returns something, it is okay to use. The source code for this method is shown in Listing 3.4.

Listing 3.4 **The Source Code for the Business Method of the Sample Session Bean**

```
1.    public String getPersonID(String pUserID,
2.           String pUserPass) {
4.      String myResult = null;
5.      Connection con ;
6.      ResultSet rs ;
7.      Statement stmt ;
8.    try {
9.    /*
10.   Loading the JDBC-ODBC bridge
11.   */
12.       Class.forName("sun.jdbc.odbc.JdbcOdbcDriver");
13.    } catch (Exception e)
14.    {
15.      System.out.println("JDBC-ODBC driver failed to load");
16.    }
17.    try   {
18.   /*
19.   connection to an ODBC data source called
20.   "EJBExampleODBC" second and third parameters are userid and
21.   password for this database, which is empty for this example*/
22.      con =        DriverManager.getConnection(
23.             "jdbc:odbc:EJBExampleODBC","","");
24.   // Creating a statement and
25.   //using it to execute a query into the database.
26.      stmt = con.createStatement();
27.   /*
28.   This returns a result set.
29.   */
30.      rs = stmt.executeQuery("SELECT * from UserLogin
31.      where LoginName = '" + pUserID + "' and
32.      LoginPassword = '"+ pUserPass + "'");
33.   /*
34.     We will find a value from the query
35.   */
36.      rs.next();
37.      myResult = rs.getString("PersonID");
38.   /*
39.     We are done with the statement and connection,
40.     so we close them.
41.   */
42.      stmt.close();
43.      con.close();
44.    } catch (Exception e)
```

```
45.     {
46.      System.out.println("database tasks failed"+e);
47.     }
48.     return myResult;
49.    } // end of getPersonID method
```

Because the business method is lengthy, I will not show the final source code of the bean class source code. You should insert business methods into the simplest bean class code. Do not forget to put the following line at the beginning of the code as you do in the home and remote interfaces if you organize the codes in a package.

```
package SessionExample;
```

Because this method is a kind of database activity method, you should import the java.sql classes. Therefore, use the following line while importing other classes into your class.

```
import java.sql.*;
```

Once you have finished writing the source code for the home interface, remote interface, and bean class, compile them in your development tool, which for this book is Forte for Java. If you have some syntax errors, correct them. After you compile without any syntax errors, you can deploy your enterprise application. You might have a deployment tool provided by your vendor. In this book, I'll use a deployment tool provided by Sun Microsystems, which comes with J2EE free of charge. Refer to Appendix B if you need to know how to deploy an enterprise bean.

Session Bean or Entity Bean: Which Do You Use for Database Actions?

In this session bean example, you connected to a database and made a query. But session beans are used for the transactional part of an enterprise application. Although you can make a query, insert, delete, or update tasks against a database, for the most part, developers do not prefer session beans for database activities. Entity beans are better for database activities because of their design specifications and architecture, as you will see in the next section of this chapter.

Let's look at a very simple business method for a bean class of a session bean. This method calculates the maximum number of two numbers given by the user. You can code the source like this:

```
1.    public int findMaxOne (int a, int b)
2.    {
3.      int maxnumber ;
4.      if (a>b) maxnumber = a; else maxnumber = b;
5.      return maxnumber;
6.    } // end of findMaxOne()
```

After adding this business method to the bean class, you must add its signature to the remote interface. You also must add the "throws RemoteException" clause to the same method signature in the remote interface. Its signature can look like this:

```
public int findMaxOne (int x1, int x2) throws
          RemoteException;
```

> **Redeploying the Enterprise Bean**
>
> After any changes are made in the remote interface, home interface, or bean class, including adding a new method, you should redeploy the enterprise bean. Otherwise, the changes will not be reflected.

Most likely, your next question is what about the client side? You might be wondering how you can access and use the enterprise bean. This is explained in detail in the section "Client Access to a Session Bean," which follows the discussion of entity beans because the client side of a session bean and entity bean are identical.

Creating an Entity Bean

Let's use an entity bean in an example to see how it works and what it does. I'll create an imaginary scenario to develop an entity bean application. Let's first summarize what you need to do in order to develop an entity bean:

1. Create the home and remote interfaces.

2. Create the entity bean class.

3. If you need a primary key class, create it. In the example, you will use a String type of key as the primary key. Thus, you do not need a primary key class.

4. Add the findByPrimaryKey() method to the home interface and its matching ejbFindByPrimaryKey() method to the bean class.

5. Add findByXXX() finder methods to the home interface and its matching ejbFindByXXX() methods to the bean class if necessary.

6. If necessary, add one or more create() methods to the home interface and add their matching ejbCreate() methods to the bean class. Creator methods are optional in the entity bean and are used to insert a new record into the database.

7. If you put an ejbCreate() method in the bean class, you can use ejbPostCreate() to implement some actions after ejbCreate() is invoked.

8. Add an `ejbRemove()` method to the bean class.
9. You can add the `remove()` method to the home or the remote interfaces if you need to delete records from the database.
10. Add business logic methods to the entity bean class.
11. Add business logic methods' signatures to the remote interface.
12. Set infrastructure methods in the bean class such as `setEntityContext()`, `unsetEntityContext()`, `ejbPassivate()`, `ejbActivate()`, `ejbStore()`, or `ejbLoad()`.
13. If you're using BMP type persistence, write the proper SQL code in the `ejbFindByXXX()` method. If you are using the CMP type persistence, show the container how it works at deployment.
14. If you design BMP type persistence, you need to write the proper SQL code for `setEntityContext()`, `unsetEntityContext()`, `ejbPassivate()`, `ejbActivate()`, `ejbStore()`, `ejbLoad()`, and `ejbRemove()`. For CMP type persistence, the container implements these methods.

Let's apply these steps to the example to show how to use an entity bean. As in the session bean example, a very simple project is used.

I will use the same Access database that I used in the session bean example, but the table is different (see Figure 3.3). In the entity bean example, I'll use the PersonInfo table in the database. In the PersonInfo table, there are four text type fields: PersonID, FirstName, LastName, and City. This example will only have five rows.

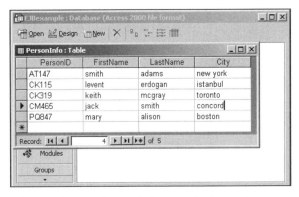

Figure 3.3   Access database PersonInfo table for the entity bean example.

In this example, I will link a database to an entity bean object by mapping it. Again, I assume that you know how to handle database tasks such as connection, query, and so on using the Java language. As in the session bean example, I will use a JDBC-ODBC bridge for database connection. Refer to the session bean example in Listing 3.4 for how to create an ODBC data source and how to use a JDBC-ODBC bridge in a Java application.

In the example, I will map the PersonInfo table and get a City Name for a given PersonID from the table. Because you will use BMP type persistence, you have to code many methods in the bean class. In CMP type persistence, you will not have to type these methods. They are the container's responsibility. Although developing a BMP type bean application is a little more difficult than a CMP type bean application, I wanted to demonstrate how entity beans work.

As mentioned earlier, you need three items in an entity bean: a home interface, a remote interface, and a bean class. In this example, you will use the String type of key as the primary key. Thus, you do not need a primary key class. The simplest home interface, whose name is BMPPeopleHome, can be written like this:

```
1. import javax.ejb.*;
2. public interface BMPPeopleHome extends EJBHome {
3. } //end of home interface
```

The home interface must contain at least one method, which is the primary key finder method. You can also add creator and other types of finder methods. For this example, you will use just the primary key finder method, which throws a RemoteException and a FinderException. After adding this method, the home interface can be written as shown in Listing 3.5.

Listing 3.5 **Home Interface of the Sample Entity Bean**

```
1. package BMPEntityExample;
2. import javax.ejb.*;
3. import java.rmi.RemoteException;
4. public interface BMPPeopleHome extends EJBHome {
5.   public  BMPPeople findByPrimaryKey(String key)
6.           throws RemoteException, FinderException;
7. } //end of home interface
```

The primary key is a String type. If you need to, you could create a primary key class and provide the data type of the key in a parameter list of the finder method. The primary key finder return type is the remote interface. You can also use additional finder methods. Their return types can be different, and their key must be one of the persistent fields.

You should locate a `create()` method inside the body of the interface using something like `findByPrimaryKey()`. If you need to add a `create()` method, it can look like this:

```
public BMPPeople create(String PerID)
        throws RemoteException, CreateException;
```

You can add to your application as many creator methods as you need. Their name and return types must be the same as the matched signatures in the remote interface, but their parameter lists must be different.

Don't forget—if you just put creator and finder signatures in the home interface, you should put their matching methods inside the body of the bean class.

The next step is to write the remote interface. The simplest remote interface will look like this:

```
1. import javax.ejb.*;
2. public interface BMPPeople extends EJBObject {
3. } //end of remote interface
```

This remote interface, whose name is BMPPeople, is a subinterface of javax.ejb.EJBObject. It must have signatures of business logic methods in the bean class with the same return type and same parameter list. Those methods must throw a RemoteException. Let's assume that in the bean class there will be a `getCity()` business method signature like this:

```
String getCity() throws RemoteException
```

After adding this signature to the remote interface, its final source code will look like Listing 3.6.

Listing 3.6 **Remote Interface of the Sample Entity Bean**

```
1. package BMPEntityExample;
2. import javax.ejb.*;
3. import java.rmi.RemoteException;
4. public interface BMPPeople extends EJBObject {
5.     public String getCity() throws RemoteException;
6. } //end of remote interface
```

The last step is to design a bean class for the entity bean example, omitting a business logic method. This simple bean class, whose name is BMPPeopleEJB, will look like Listing 3.7.

Listing 3.7   **Simple Bean Class of the Sample Entity Bean**

```
1. import javax.ejb.*;
2. public class BMPPeopleEJB implements EntityBean {
3.    public BMPPeopleEJB() {  }
4.    public void setEntityContext(EntityContext sc) {}
5.    public void unsetEntityContext( ) {}
6.    public void ejbCreate() throws CreateException {}
7.    public void ejbPostCreate() throws CreateException {}
8.    public void ejbActivate() { }
9.    public void ejbPassivate() { }
10.   public void ejbLoad() { }
11.   public void ejbStore() { }
12.   public void ejbRemove()  throws RemoveException { }
13. } //end of bean class
```

A bean class is a subclass of javax.ejb.EntityBean, and it must have
setEntityContext(), unsetEntityContext(), ejbPassivate(), ejbActivate(),
ejbLoad(), ejbStore(), and ejbRemove() methods. The container is responsible
for managing the life cycle of entity beans. In the BMP type persistence bean,
you have to write their proper SQL codes. If you have a create() method in
the home interface, you should add an ejbCreate() method and write its code
in BMP type persistence, or show the container how it works at the time of
deployment in CMP type persistence.

You will use an additional method if you are using BMP type persistence:
ejbFindByPrimaryKey(). This method matches the findByPrimaryKey() method
in the home interface. With CMP type persistence, this method is not written
by a developer. The container is responsible for implementing the method's
functionality. This is achieved at deployment time, using the tools provided by
the vendor.

You will have at least one business method and helper or utility methods,
which help business methods in the bean class. You should put business methods' signatures into the remote interface with the same return type and parameter list. In this example, the business method is getCity(). It provides the
City field value for a given PersonID, which is the primary key.

There are some helper methods used to connect the database and to load or
store data. The helper (utility) methods' names are selectByPrimaryKey(),
opendbConnection(), loadDBRow(), and storeDBRow() for this example.

If there is no primary key field value in the database, the client application
will get a null value. Every line of the business method and helper methods
will not be explained. The goal is to show how an entity bean works with a
business method. You can replace this method with another one or add additional methods. As long as it is compiled and returns something, it is okay
to use.

In the source code of the example, a business method and utility methods are provided separately in Listing 3.9 to make the code more readable. Do not forget to add them to the bean class body. The source code for the bean class is shown in Listing 3.8.

Listing 3.8   **The Source Code for the Entity Bean**

```
1.   package BMPEntityExample;
2.   import javax.ejb.*;
3.   import java.rmi.*;
4.   import java.sql.*;
5.   import javax.sql.*;
6.   import javax.naming.*;
8.   public class BMPPeopleEJB implements EntityBean {
9.     public static  String beanPerID;
10.    public static  String beanFName;
11.    public static  String beanLName;
12.    public static  String beanCity;
13.    public static  EntityContext context;
14.    public static  Connection dbConnect;
15.    public BMPPeopleEJB() { }
16.
17.  //setting and unsetting Entity context
18.  public void setEntityContext(EntityContext ctx) {
19.        context = ctx;
20.  }
21.  public void unsetEntityContext() throws
22.        EJBException, RemoteException {
23.        context = null;
24.  }
25.  //activating and passivating the bean instance
26.  public void ejbActivate() throws
27.        EJBException, RemoteException {
28.        beanPerID = (String)context.getPrimaryKey();
29.  }
30.  public void ejbPassivate() {
31.        beanPerID = null;
32.  }
33.  // remove method
34.  public void ejbRemove() throws RemoveException {  }
35.  // load and store methods
36.  public void ejbLoad() {
37.        beanPerID = (String)context.getPrimaryKey();
38.        try {
39.        loadDBRow(); // a utility method
40.        } catch (Exception e) {
41.            throw new EJBException("ejbLoad: "
42.                    +e.getMessage());
43.        }
44.  } // end of ejbLoad()
```

continues

Listing 3.8 **Continued**

```
45.  public void ejbStore() {
46.       beanPerID = (String)context.getPrimaryKey();
47.       try {
48.       storeDBRow(); // a utility method
49.       } catch (Exception e) {
50.           throw new EJBException("ejbStore: "
51.                   +e.getMessage());
52.       }
53.  } // end of ejbStore()
54.  // primary key finder method
55.  public static String ejbFindByPrimaryKey (String key)
56.           throws FinderException {
57.       beanPerID = key;
58.       try {
59.       if (!selectByPrimaryKey(beanPerID))
60.           throw new ObjectNotFoundException("Row for
61.             PersonID = " + key + " not found.");
62.       } catch (Exception e) {
63.           throw new EJBException("ejbFindByPrimaryKey:
64.                   " +e.getMessage());
65.       } //end of try
66.       return beanPerID;
67.  } //end of ejbFindByPrimaryKey
68.
69.  // put getCity() business method here
70.  // put selectByPrimaryKey() utility method here
71.  // put opendbConnection()utility method here
72.  // put loadDBRow()utility method here
73.  // put storeDBRow()utility method here
74.  } //end of bean class
```

For a very simple BMP type entity bean, this code is pretty long, even though a business method and utility methods were not added. You will find these methods to complete the bean class source code in Listing 3.9.

Note that the database connection is opened and closed in each of the business and utility methods. This is just an example to demonstrate how an entity bean works. This example is not optimized. Because database connections are expensive to open, ideally, these should be opened once, and then reused throughout the entity bean methods in your applications.

Listing 3.9   **Business and Utility Methods of the Entity Bean**

```
1.   public static String getCity() {
2.    return beanCity;
3.   } //end of getCity business method
4.    private static boolean selectByPrimaryKey(String key)
5.             throws SQLException {
6.      Statement stmt;
7.      ResultSet result;
8.      String stQuery;
9.      boolean resultexist = false;
10.     opendbConnection();
11.     try {
12.         stmt = dbConnect.createStatement();
13.         stQuery = "SELECT PersonID from PersonInfo
14.           where PersonID = '" + key + "'" ;
15.         result = stmt.executeQuery(stQuery);
16.         resultexist = result.next();
17.         stmt.close();
18.         dbConnect.close();
19.         } catch (Exception e)
20.         { System.out.println("selectByPrimaryKey
21.             finding failed"+e);
22.         } //end of try
23.         return  resultexist;
24.   } //end of selectByPrimaryKey()
25.   public static void opendbConnection() {
26.         try  {
27.     // Loading the JDBC-ODBC bridge
28.          Class.forName("sun.jdbc.odbc.JdbcOdbcDriver");
29.         } catch (Exception e)
30.         { System.out.println("JDBC-ODBC driver
31.             failed to load");
32.         }
33.         try           {
34.    /* connection to an ODBC data
35.      source called "EJBExampleODBC"   */
36.      dbConnect = DriverManager.getConnection(
37.         "jdbc:odbc:EJBExampleODBC","","");
38.      } catch (Exception e)
39.      { System.out.println("database tasks failed"+e);
40.      }
41.   } // end of opendbConnection()
42.   public static void loadDBRow() {
43.   Statement stmt;
44.   ResultSet result;
45.   String stQuery;
46.   opendbConnection();
47.   try {
48.   stmt = dbConnect.createStatement();
49.     stQuery = "SELECT * from PersonInfo
```

continues

Listing 3.9   **Continued**

```
50.        where PersonID = '" + beanPerID + "'" ;
51.   result = stmt.executeQuery(stQuery);
52.   if (result.next()) {
53.   beanFName = (result.getString("FirstName")).trim();
54.   beanLName = (result.getString("LastName")).trim();
55.   beanCity = (result.getString("City")).trim();
56.   } else {
57.     throw new NoSuchEntityException("Row for personID 58.        " +
        ➥beanPerID + " not found in the database. ");
59.   } // end of if
60. stmt.close();
61. dbConnect.close();
62. } catch (Exception e)
63. { System.out.println("database tasks failed"+e);
64. } //end of try
65. } // end of loadDBRow()
66. public static void storeDBRow() {
67. Statement stmt;
68. ResultSet result;
69. String stQuery;
70. opendbConnection();
71. try {
72. stmt = dbConnect.createStatement();
73. stQuery = "UPDATE PersonInfo SET"
74.     + " FirstName = '" + beanFName.trim() + "'"
75.     + ", LastName = '" + beanLName.trim() + "'"
76.     + ", City = '" + beanCity.trim() + "'"
77.     + " WHERE PersonID = '" + beanPerID + "'";
78. int countResult = stmt.executeUpdate(stQuery);
79. if (countResult == 0)
80.     throw new EJBException("Storing row for personID "
81.         + beanPerID + " failed. ");
82. stmt.close();
83. dbConnect.close();
84. } catch (Exception e)
85. System.out.println("database tasks failed"+e);
86. } //end of try
87. } // end of storeDBRow()
```

A couple of simple methods produce 87 lines. Good luck with your entity bean, particularly you BMP type entity bean developers.

Presentation Tier on EJB

In previous sections, session and entity beans were explained. Beans reside on the server side and are part of the business tier of the three-tier model. In your application, clients need to access the business tier. In this section, I will discuss how a client can access a session bean and an entity bean.

Client Access to a Session Bean

For a client to access a session bean, follow these steps:

1. Create a new context by using InitialContext like this:

   ```
   Context varNameOfContext = new InitialContext().
   ```

2. Look up the Java Naming Directory Interface (JNDI) name of the EJB by using the name you provided at the time of deployment like this:

   ```
   Object varNameOfResult = c.lookup("jndiName");
   ```

3. Narrow the result at the second step to obtain the home object of the EJB from the advertised objects via JNDI and assign it a variable whose type is the home interface, like this:

   ```
   theHomeInt myTheHomeVar =
   (theHomeInt)javax.rmi.PortableRemoteObject.narrow(varNameOfResu
   lt, theHomeInt.result);
   ```

4. Call the `create()` method by using the variable name, which is created in the third step and assign it a variable whose type is the remote interface type.

5. Call any business methods by using the variable name, which is created in the fourth step.

6. Call the `remove()` method.

Listing 3.10 contains the complete source code of a client application for the sample session bean shown in Listings 3.1 through 3.4. This application finds the EJB whose JNDI name is JNDISessionOptic, and then finds the PersonID for a person whose first name is "adams" and last name is "black".

Listing 3.10   **Client Access Source Code of the Sample Session Bean**

```
1.   package ClientSession;
2.   import javax.naming.*;
3.   import javax.rmi.*;
4.   import SessionExample.*;
5.   import java.util.*;
6.   public class ClientSessionTest
7.          {
8.   public ClientSessionTest() {  }
9.   public static void main(String args[]) {
10.    System.out.println("Person ID query from
11.       the database");
12.    try {
13.     Context myContext = new InitialContext();
14.     System.out.println("Context done: ");
```

continues

Listing 3.10   **Continued**

```
15.     Object myResult =
16.          myContext.lookup("JNDISessionOptic");
17.     System.out.println("lookup done ");
18.     LeventOpticHome myHome =
19.       (LeventOpticHome)javax.rmi.PortableRemoteObject.
20.       narrow(myResult, LeventOpticHome.class);
21.     System.out.println("narrow done ");
22.     LeventOptic myRemote = myHome.create();
23.     System.out.println("myRemote done ");
24.     System.out.println("Person ID for adams & black
25.         is " + myRemote.getPersonID("adams", "black"));
26.     myRemote.remove();
27.     } //end of try
28.     catch (Exception e) { System.out.
29.          println("Error Session Bean Access : " +e); }
30.   } //end of main
31. } //end of class
```

When writing the client source code to access this session bean, it is assumed that the EJB's JNDI name is provided as JNDISessionOptic at the time of deployment. If you provide a different JNDI name for the EJB at deployment, substitute that name in line 16 of Listing 3.10.

You have two options to develop a client application. First, you can bundle the client application with the EJB at the time of deployment. This way, it gets the information about the EJB and the enterprise application such as the bean class, the remote interface, and the home interface. You can run it like any other program. Second, you can develop a stand-alone client application, which is independent of your enterprise application. In this case, you have to add the client JAR file, which is created at deployment of the enterprise application, to the CLASSPATH of your system. This JAR file contains stub classes for your application components such as a bean class, a remote interface, and a home interface deployed to the J2EE runtime environment. In this way, clients can connect with J2EE components remotely.

After you run your client application (Listing 3.10), the results are displayed on your command line or in your application output window. Listing 3.11 shows the results of the client application for a session bean.

Listing 3.11   **The Screen Output After Running the Client Application of the Sample Session Bean**

```
Person ID query from the database
Context done:
lookup done
narrow done
myRemote done
Person ID for adams & black is AT147
```

The output shows a PersonID value of AT147 where the first name is "adams" and the last name is "black."

Client Access to an Entity Bean

For a client to access an entity bean, follow these steps:

1. Create a new context by using InitialContext like this:

```
Context varNameOfContext = new InitialContext().
```

2. Look up the JNDI name of the EJB by using the name that you provided at the time of deployment, like this:

```
Object varNameOfResult = c.lookup("jndiName");
```

3. Narrow the result at the second step and assign it a variable whose return type is the home interface, like this:

```
theHomeInt myTheHomeVar =
(theHomeInt)javax.rmi.PortableRemoteObject.narrow(varNameOfResu
lt, theHomeInt.result);
```

4. Call the `findByPrimaryKey()` method by using the variable name, which is created in the third step, and assign it to a variable whose return type is the remote interface. You might have other finder methods for other fields. You can call these finder methods after calling the primary key finder method. For example, you can add the `findByCity()` finder method after the `findByPrimaryKey()` method. Finder methods must have corresponding `create()` and `ejbCreate()` methods with proper parameter lists for that finder method.

5. Call any business method by using the variable name, which is created in the fourth step.

6. Call the `remove()` method.

In Listing 3.12, you'll find the complete source code of a client application for the sample entity bean shown in Listings 3.5 through 3.8. This application finds the EJB whose JNDI name is JNDIEntityPeople, and then finds the city name for the primary key value, which is PersonID, or AT147 for this example.

Listing 3.12   **Client Access Source Code of the Sample Entity Bean**

```
1.  package ClientEntity;
2.  import javax.naming.*;
3.  import javax.rmi.*;
4.  import BMPEntityExample.*;
5.  import java.util.*;
6.   public class ClientEntityTest
7.       {
8.   public ClientEntityTest() {  }
9.   public static void main(String args[]) {
10.    System.out.println("Obtaining a city name
11.        for a person ID");
12.    try {
13.     Context myContext = new InitialContext();
14.     System.out.println("Context done: ");
15.     Object myResult =
16.           myContext.lookup("JNDIEntityPeople");
17.     System.out.println("lookup done ");
18.     BMPPEopleHome myHome =
19.      (BMPPEopleHome)javax.rmi.PortableRemoteObject.
20.      narrow(myResult, BMPPEopleHome.class);
21.     System.out.println("narrow done ");
22.     BMPPEople myRemote = myHome.
23.        findByPrimaryKey("AT147");
24.     System.out.println("findByPrimaryKey done ");
25.     System.out.println("City name for  AT147 is " +
26.        myRemote.getCity("AT147"));
27.     myRemote.remove();
28.    }  //end of try
29.    catch (Exception e) { System.out.
30.        println("Error Entity Bean Access : " +e); }
31.   }  //end of main
32. } //end of class
```

When writing the client source code to access this entity bean, it is assumed that the EJB's JNDI name is provided as JNDIEntityPeople at the time of deployment. If you provide a different JNDI name for the EJB at deployment, substitute that name in line 16 of Listing 3.12.

As mentioned earlier when I discussed client application design for access to a session bean, you have two options to develop a client application. To review those options, refer to the "Client Access to a Session Bean" section. After you run the client application (Listing 3.12), the results are displayed on your command line or in your application output window. The results of running the client application for an entity bean are shown in Listing 3.13.

Listing 3.13 **The Screen Output After Running the Client Application of the Sample Entity Bean**

```
Obtaining a city name for a person ID
Context done:
lookup done
narrow done
findByPrimaryKey done
City for AT147 is new york
```

The output shows a City value, which is new york, for PersonID "AT147."

EJB and the Web

In this section, more details on how you can use Java Servlet technology (by the way, a JavaServer Pages (JSP) file becomes a servlet when it is compiled) on your presentation layer will not be provided. Instead, I will modify the client application source code in Listings 3.10 and 3.12 as a JSP file for access to a session bean and an entity bean.

JSP technology was chosen instead of Java Servlet technology because it is simpler to use and does the same thing. It is an alternative source code format for writing servlets. You do not have to spend half a day on syntax problems. I'll assume that you know JSP technology and have developed at least a few simple web sites using JSP.

When you deploy an enterprise bean, you can add JSP files as web components to your application and test them on a web browser after deployment. You can use a Tomcat web server, which is free of charge and supports JSP technology if you want to develop and test your applications on the free software suggested in this book. Tomcat is available for download at `http://jakarta.apache.org/tomcat/index.html`. Currently, it has two versions: version 3.x and version 4.x.

Web Client Access to a Session Bean and an Entity Bean

Listing 3.14 shows the complete source code of a web client application for
the sample session bean. It was adopted from the stand-alone client source
code in Listing 3.10. The main idea is the same as in a stand-alone application.
The only differences are the syntax and some minor modifications for the
JSP file.

Listing 3.14   **Web Client Access to the Sample Session Bean**

```
1.  <%@page contentType="text/html"%>
2.  <%@ page import="javax.naming.*, javax.rmi.*,
3.      SessionExample.*, java.util.*"%>
4.  <html>
5.  <head><title>JSP Page</title></head>
6.  <body>
7.  <%
8.  out.println("Person ID query from the database");
9.  out.println("<BR>");
10. Context myContext = new InitialContext();
11. out.println("Context done: ");
12. out.println("<BR>");
13. Object myResult =
14. myContext.lookup("JNDISessionOptic");
15. out.println("lookup done ");
16. out.println("<BR>");
17. LeventOpticHome myHome =
18. (LeventOpticHome)javax.rmi.PortableRemoteObject.
19. narrow(myResult, LeventOpticHome.class);
20. out.println("narrow done ");
21. out.println("<BR>");
22. LeventOptic myRemote = myHome.create();
23. out.println("myRemote done ");
24. out.println("<BR>");
25. out.println("Person ID for adams & black is  " +
26.    myRemote.getPersonID("adams", "black"));
27. out.println("<BR>");
28. myRemote.remove();
29. %>
30. </body>
31. </html>
```

When you call this JSP file, which is located on the web server, from you web
browser, you'll see a screen similar to Figure 3.4.

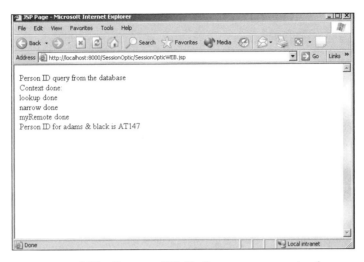

Figure 3.4   Web client as a JSP file for access to a session bean.

Web Client Access to an Entity Bean

Listing 3.15 shows the complete source code of a web client application for the sample entity bean. It is adopted from the stand-alone client source code in Listing 3.12. The main idea is the same as in a stand-alone application. The only differences are the syntax and some minor modifications for the JSP file.

Listing 3.15   **Web Client Access to the Sample Entity Bean**

```
1.  <%@page contentType="text/html"%>
2.  <%@ page import="javax.naming.*, javax.rmi.*,
3.    BMPEntityExample.*, java.util.*"%>
4.  <html>
5.  <head><title>JSP Page</title></head>
6.  <body>
7.  <%
8.  out.println("Obtaining a city name for a person ID");
9.  out.println("<BR>");
10. Context myContext = new InitialContext();
11. out.println("Context done: ");
12. out.println("<BR>");
13. Object myResult = myContext.lookup("JNDIEntityPeople");
14. out.println("lookup done ");
15. out.println("<BR>");
16. BMPPeopleHome myHome =
17. (BMPPeopleHome)javax.rmi.PortableRemoteObject.
18.    narrow(myResult, BMPPeopleHome.class);
19.  out.println("narrow done ");
```

continues

Listing 3.15 **Continued**

```
20.  out.println("<BR>");
21.  BMPPeople myRemote = null;
22.  try  {
23.    myRemote = myHome.findByPrimaryKey("AT147");
24.    out.println("myHome.findByPrimaryKey(AT147) done");
25.    out.println("<BR>");
26.  } catch (Exception e)
27.  { out.println("myHome.
28.      findByPrimaryKey(AT147) failed " +e);
29.    out.println("<BR>");
30.  } //end of try
31.  try  {
32.    out.println("City for AT147 is  " +
33.        myRemote.getCity());
34.    out.println("<BR>");
35.    out.println("myRemote.getCity() done");
36.    out.println("<BR>");
37.  } catch (Exception e)
38.  { out.println("myRemote.getCity()  failed " +e);
39.    out.println("<BR>");
40.  } //end of try
41.  try  {
42.    myRemote.remove();
43.    out.println("myRemote.remove() done");
44.    out.println("<BR>");
45.  } catch (Exception e)
46.  { out.println("getCity() and remove() failed " +e);
47.    out.println("<BR>");
48.  } //end of try
49.  %>
50.  </body>
51.  </html>
```

Summary

In this chapter, I provided examples for the concepts discussed in Chapter 2. I designed a session bean with a home interface, a remote interface, and a bean class. I provided client access for both session beans and entity beans. At the end of the chapter, I provided information on how to reach a session bean and an entity bean as a web client. Only source codes and how they work were provided in this chapter. Deployment issues are discussed in Appendix B.

Questions and Answers

1. In what order do you suggest writing parts of an EJB?

In the examples, I first wrote the home interface, then the remote interface, and then the bean class. Actually, writing them in the reverse order is better. If you design and write a bean class, you can put business methods into the remote interface. It is better to write the home interface after the remote interface because the `create()` and `findByPrimaryKey()` methods' return types will be in the remote interface. If you use a primary key class for an entity bean, you can write this class code before the bean class because you will need it in the `ejbFindByPrimaryKey()` method.

2. Which type of client access is better, a Java client or a web client?

It depends on your client type. The main idea and codes are identical. If your client is in the same physical network such as an intranet, Java client access might be the better solution. If you have clients all around the Internet, web client access is a must.

3. Is there any difference between a stateless and a stateful session bean for the client?

No. Clients access the session bean in the same way. If it is a stateless bean, the client must be able to handle saving some necessary information. If it is stateful, the container handles saving the conversation between the client and the bean instance.

4. Is there any difference between the BMP and CMP type persistence entity beans for the client?

No. Clients access the entity bean in the same way. A bean provider (developer) takes care of writing proper SQL codes in the bean class if the entity bean is the BMP type. Otherwise, the container handles it. It does not affect client access.

II

Introduction to a Messaging Service

4 Middleware and Message-Oriented Middleware

5 Concepts and Fundamentals of JMS Programming

6 JMS Programming Techniques with Examples

4

Middleware and Message-Oriented Middleware

I N THIS CHAPTER, YOU WILL LEARN about the history of middleware and different types of middleware technologies. Middleware is the foundation of message-oriented middleware (MOM) on which Java Message Service (JMS) is based. The information provided in this chapter revolves around general concepts of messaging technologies—it is not specific to JMS.

History of MOM

Computer technology has changed from the dumb terminals-host server model to an enterprise (sometimes called distributed) computing model. One of the needs for computer applications has stayed the same: Exchanging data between different parts of the computer world. In the 1980s, users via a kind of client application requested some actions from the mainframe (host), that is, the user invoked some methods on another location. The mainframe processed and returned the result to a dumb terminal screen or a printer (see Figure 4.1). During this process, mainframe type servers probably connected to a database for tasks such as inquiry, inserting, updating, and deleting. This process can actually be considered the first type of exchanging data or sharing information between two different applications, which was the first example of middleware.

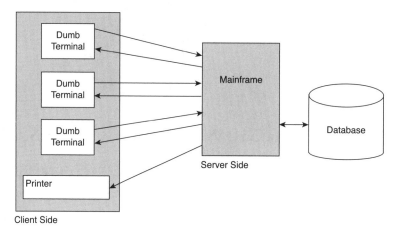

Figure 4.1   Terminal–host architecture.

Middleware is defined as transportation software that transfers information from one application to one or more other software applications. It is not just software that resides between different applications. MOM handles dependencies such as operating systems, hardware, and communication protocols and enables developers to focus on developing their applications. It allows developers to write applications to exchange data between all types of environments.

The enterprise computing model, in terms of the distributed component model, has found a place today's computing world. The middleware concept in the sense of exchanging data is extended to be message-oriented. In this model, information called data is sent between applications (or objects in broader definition) using messages. It is similar to data packets on a network. Messages have headers and actual data. This model is called MOM. Figure 4.2 shows the simplest architecture of the MOM model.

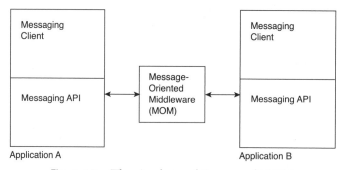

Figure 4.2   The simplest architecture of MOM.

Within the architecture, you see two new concepts: messaging client and messaging API. Messaging clients and MOM are the two basic parts of the messaging systems. Clients can be any application or component of the system. They send messages to MOM by using messaging APIs. MOM then distributes the message to other messaging clients.

In the following sections, you will learn about the other branches of middleware in addition to MOM.

Transaction-Processing Monitors (TPMs)

TPMs are not good for general-purpose application-to-application communication. TPMs are primarily used for transaction applications that access relational databases. This means that they provide communication between an application and a relational database.

In this model, the client invokes methods (procedures) on a server, which has a SQL database engine. These procedures contain a group of SQL statements (transactions). The server executes them, but there is no way that some can succeed and the rest fail—either all succeed or all fail as one unit.

Some applications based on transaction servers called on-line transaction processing are mission-critical applications. The key features for these applications are rapid response, tight controls over security, and integrity of the database.

Services and standards for TPMs are defined by the X/Open group whose work is supported by many vendors. TPMs work well when transactions are coordinated and synchronized over multiple databases.

Remote Procedure Call (RPC)

RPC is a technology used by middleware technologies such as Java Remote Method Invocation (RMI), Common Object Request Broker Architecture (CORBA), and Microsoft's Distributed Component Object Model (DCOM). It describes a distributed computing model. The Enterprise JavaBeans (EJBs) that were examined in Chapter 2, "Enterprise JavaBeans (EJB)," are built on this model. RPC-based technologies are some of the earliest forms of exchanging data or communication between systems. They will continue to be a solution for many applications.

In the RPC structure (see Figure 4.3), a method in one application invokes a method (procedure) in another (remote) application, and results from the remote application are returned to the sender. In this model, the application components communicate with each other synchronously; that is, one of them (the sender) sends the request and waits for a reply from the receiver.

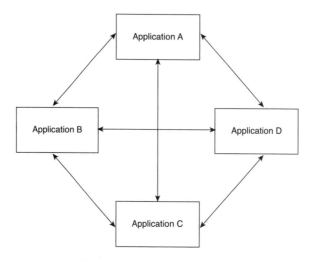

Figure 4.3 RPC architecture.

RPC-based technologies are used in point-to-point type messaging rather than publish-subscribe messaging and work well for small applications. They are not recommended for large applications because they do not scale well. They are not good for mission-critical applications either because many important details are left to the developer's responsibility šuch as portability (running on different environments), synchronization between applications, handling multiple connections, handling network or system failures, buffering, and flow control.

Object Request Brokers (ORBs)

An ORB is a type of object-oriented RPC. There are three ORB architectures on the market today:

- CORBA
- Microsoft DCOM
- Java RMI

Java RMI has a definite disadvantage when compared to CORBA and DCOM. It is designed for communication between two applications written in Java and does not address other programming languages, unlike CORBA and DCOM.

The most important aspect of ORB is its object orientation. If you need a definite object-oriented approach, you should consider ORB. It is similar to RPC in terms of its messaging type. ORB-based technologies are mostly synchronous and work for point-to-point type messaging as well.

Their disadvantage is that they count on the communication (transport) layer, which can fail at anytime.

The Object Management Group (OMG), which supports CORBA, has approved the Asynchronous Messaging Service, but it is not very common on CORBA deployments yet.

In-House Developed Middleware

So what do you do in your company (particularly if it's a small company) when you need a type of middleware layer for some applications? Often, IT managers or higher level directors might not be willing to purchase middleware software packages. If they have their own developers who are able to write middleware-like solutions, this layer will definitely be developed within the firm.

The first time you develop in-house middleware, this approach works very well, but later on, you will potentially encounter some problems such as lack of scalability and flexibility. Be aware—this in-house solution will turn out to be more expensive after fixing these prospective problems. Additionally, inexperienced developers who have not previously written such applications will increase the hidden cost of this approach.

MOM

The most important problem with RPC and ORB is application availability, that is, synchronization. If one application requests something from another application, both must be up and running. The sender sends and waits until it receives a reply. In MOM-based products, the information is transported from one application to another in a message asynchronously. The sender does not have to wait for a reply.

Another advantage of MOM is that it does not rely on the transport layer. It tries to address the communication layer problems instead of hiding them. Most MOM products have additional services that do not exist in RPC or ORB products, such as translating data, security, broadcasting data to multiple applications, locating resources on the network, error recovery, better debugging, and so on.

There are two types of messaging:

- Message queuing (also called application-to-application or point-to-point)
- Message passing (also called publish-subscribe)

I will provide more information about MOM and other messaging concepts in the remainder of this chapter.

Networking Features of MOM

Today, the distributed (enterprise) computing model has found popularity in the computer world. The key feature of a distributed application is to share or exchange data between applications. There wouldn't be any problems if there was only one environment and a no-fault communication layer. Applications run on different environments, from UNIX workstations to Windows-based PCs. Network structure and protocols can be different too. Particularly, networking is a very important factor for a mission-critical application.

Prior to MOM, developers were responsible for programming networking issues. When they wrote enterprise applications, they used low-level interprocess communication primitives such as sockets, shared memory, pipes, and RPCs. These applications work well if they are small applications, particularly those running on a LAN. Dealing with these networking issues becomes more complicated and difficult to handle as the enterprise application grows and runs on a variety of networking structures and protocols.

It is not only difficult to develop networking as part of an enterprise computing application, but it is also very risky and expensive. The latest MOM products implement and handle many difficult and troublesome networking aspects on behalf of developers. These networking aspects include

- Data translation—Information travels between applications regardless of the platform. It can be on an Intel-based PC, an HP-UNIX machine, or a Sun Solaris computer. Unfortunately, different platforms have different data types (integer, floating point, strings), which are incompatible with each other. The data sent by the sender is translated to a proper data type at the destination by MOM in order to make sure the receiver can understand the data.

- Flow control—In an enterprise application, components (applications) can be busy with other tasks when they receive information, which is called flow. Flow control must be handled by a MOM product. Otherwise, the enterprise application needs very complicated programming, which consumes large amounts of system resources.

- Encoding the information—Information (data, message) that is transferred from one application to another (or maybe more than one) must be formatted to make sure all recipients can understand whatever they receive. Some MOM products define the encoding/decoding rules in an interface definition language by using RPC or ORB. Some use self-describing messages. When the message is received, the message itself can be queried to understand how to encode the message contents. This is also called encapsulating message metadata along with the message.

- Multiprotocol support—Distributed applications run on different platforms with different network protocols, for example, Transmission Control Protocol/Internet Protocol (TCP/IP) or IBM's Systems Network Architecture (SNA). MOM products transfer information from one application running one network protocol to another application running another protocol. This feature is called *context bridging*.

- Finding resources—In distributed computing, resources are located at different locations. They must know where they are in order to communicate with each other. The location of resources changes frequently when a new application or server joins the system. *Naming services* are used by resources to identify their locations.

- Portability—There are different standards for transferring information across a network, for example, sockets, streams, named pipes, RPC, and ORB. Unfortunately, a standard that is designed for one network environment might conflict with others. MOM products handle different incompatibility problems between standards of different environments.

- Asynchronization—The most important feature of the MOM model is asynchronization. In a messaging system, an application sends the information without waiting for a response or reply. The application can continue processing while it waits for the remote application to return a reply message. Reply messages can come in the future at anytime. This feature cannot be easily achieved by a developer. However, one way a developer can achieve asynchronization is to use callbacks; the other is to use threads.

- Configuring resources/applications on the network—In a distributed computing system, computers, applications, and other related peripherals are located in different places and are identified uniquely by a naming scheme such as an IP address form for TCP/IP networks. MOM products can reconfigure a system easily when a part, either a machine or an application, is added to or removed from the network.

- Hardware/software failures—A programmer's and user's nightmare is when components, such as the network, a computer, a peripheral, or an application, on the enterprise system fail. In most cases, complete recovery is not possible. Many problems are caused by network failures, which mostly depend on protocols. TCP/IP often hides the problems and tries to fix them. It does not inform the client or system administrator unless the problem is unrecoverable. If you do not know about the problem in time, it might be impossible to recover. This is very important for mission-critical applications. MOM products help the client take action whenever problems occur.

- Handling the network bandwidth—In a distributed computing system, applications can exchange information over many connections. For example, a sender might want to transmit a message to multiple recipients using a single operation. In another example, a sender might be willing to choose the destination taking into consideration whether the recipient state is busy or not. A MOM product can easily handle coordinating multiple applications running across a heterogeneous network.

- Changing hardware—Today, the latest computer technology is usually obsolete within six months. New computers and equipment ranging from printers to routers are added or replaced very frequently. In particular, if interface definition languages such ORB or RPC are used, it is very difficult to manage this dynamic environment because these languages rely on static definitions, and they are not able to update these kinds of frequent changes in the system. MOM products are designed to handle this management nightmare.

Types of MOM Architecture

There are three types of MOM architecture: *centralized*, *decentralized*, and *hybrid*. They are examined briefly in the following sections.

Centralized Architecture

In a centralized architecture, the enterprise system is based on a message server, which is also called the message router. It is located in the center, and clients connect to that server. It has a kind of "hub and spoke" structure.

The message server delivers messages from one messaging client to another. Clients are separated (decoupled) and do not see each other. The system is very flexible in adding or removing clients without affecting the entire enterprise computing environment. Figure 4.4 shows a centralized architecture for *m* number of messaging clients. The advantage of this system is that the failing of one client does not affect the others' work. All other clients except the failed one can still use the system as usual.

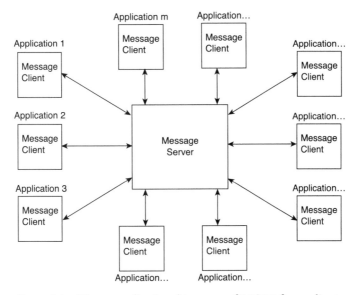

Figure 4.4 The centralized architecture of MOM for *m* clients.

Decentralized Architecture

In a decentralized architecture (see Figure 4.5), there is no central server. Functions such as security, transactions, and data persistence of the server in the centralized model are distributed to different servers called local servers, which are actually on the messaging client machines. Messaging clients and the local servers communicate with each other through a router on the network. A decentralized architecture uses IP multicast at the network level.

A message is delivered to the recipients via the network layer, which is based on the Internet Protocol (IP) multicast protocol.

Hybrid Architecture

The centralized model is mostly based on TCP/IP for message delivery. The decentralized model is based on IP multicast. Some MOM vendors' architectures might combine both architectures. Some clients communicate using IP multicast and some using TCP/IP.

All three architectures have advantages and disadvantages when compared to each other. Which architecture you choose depends on your project. As a developer, you can choose a single architecture depending on your project considerations. Many developers prefer a centralized architecture because it is a more convenient architecture in which to develop.

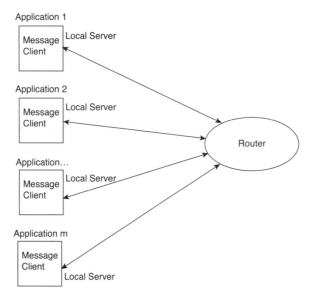

Figure 4.5   The decentralized architecture of MOM for *m* clients.

Types of Messaging Models

The messaging model can be divided into two different classifications: *synchronization type* and *message-sending type*.

Synchronization Type Models

The synchronization type of messaging model can be classified into two types: *synchronous* and *asynchronous* messaging.

Synchronous Type Messaging

In synchronous type messaging, both parts of the system must be up and running at the same time during any process. Component-based architectures such as EJBs (session or entity) are examples of this type of messaging. If one of the applications is down or fails to receive the message for any reason—networking problems, busy with another process, and so on—the process including messaging cannot be completed and fails.

Figure 4.6 shows the basic architecture of synchronous type messaging. Application A might be the first tier of the three-tier model, Application B the second tier, and Application C, the third tier. Application D might be another application, which can have a connection with the first tier and the second tier but is independent from the three-tier model.

   Applications can be connected to each other by any type of networking model such as a LAN, a WAN, an intranet, or the Internet. There is virtually a one-to-one connection between applications through the network.

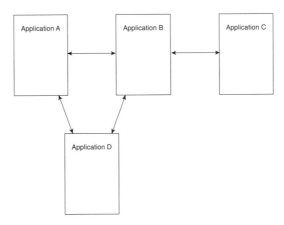

Figure 4.6   Synchronous type messaging.

The three-tier model, which you learned about in Chapter 1, "Java and Enterprise Applications," is synchronous. Business logic resides on the middle layer, presentation logic on the first layer, and data on the third layer. When a remote process is invoked on the business layer from the presentation layer, both parts (presentation layer and business layer) must be up and running. After a remote process starts processing, it might request something from the data layer. In this case, both parts again (business layer and data layer) must be up and running. The request is performed sequentially. The client who sends the request or message is blocked until the server has completed the process and responds to the client. This is one of the disadvantages of synchronous type messaging.

Asynchronous Type Messaging

In asynchronous type messaging, the two applications that are communicating do not need to be up and running at the same time during any process. Message-driven type EJBs are one example of this type of messaging. One application requests something from another application or sends a message to another application. The other application might be down or fail to receive the message for any reason, but the process does not fail. The other side receives the message or request whenever it is available, and then processes it. After completing the process, it informs the sender in the same way.

Figure 4.7 shows the basic architecture of asynchronous type messaging. It is very difficult to illustrate the asynchronous model in a figure. Therefore, I've tried to convey the asynchronous model by showing that the applications in a system connect to the system independently through a common element called a server. They communicate with each other, but they do not have to connect to the network at the same time. Any type of networking model such as a LAN, a WAN, an intranet, or the Internet can be used for connections, but applications are not connected directly. Another layer, such as a server, connects them to each other.

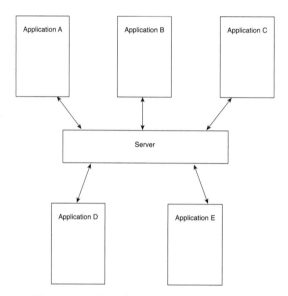

Figure 4.7 Asynchronous type messaging.

Asynchronous type messaging is the fundamental concept of MOM. Although messaging can be implemented in a synchronous way, it is not preferred because of some of its disadvantages.

Message–Sending Type Models

The sending type of messaging model can be classified into two types: *point-to-point* (also called p2p or PTP) and *publish-and-subscribe* (also called publish-subscribe, pub/sub).

Point-to-Point Type Messaging

In Figure 4.8, a sender sends the message to the receiver. The message goes from one application to another. It is not direct, but it can be assumed as direct because the message is sent from the sender to a virtual channel or buffered area, called a *queue*. The message is then requested by the receiver from the queue. It is not pushed to the receiver automatically.

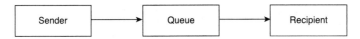

Figure 4.8   Point-to-point type messaging.

Some features of this p2p model are described in the following list:

- This model is called one-to-one model messaging because there is one sender and one receiver.
- Message transmitting can either be synchronous or asynchronous.
- The buffer area called a queue can have more than one receiver, but only one recipient can pull the message at a certain time. This feature is not defined in JMS specification 1.0.2. The implementation of this feature depends on JMS vendors' products.
- The recipient can see the contents of the queue via a queue browser before pulling it from the queue.

Publish-and-Subscribe Type Messaging

In the publish-and-subscribe model (see Figure 4.9), there is one sender (publisher) that can send a message to many recipients (subscribers). The *virtual channel* (queue in the p2p model) in the publish-and-subscribe model is called *topic*, and receivers subscribe to a topic. Any message sent to a given topic is delivered to all topic subscribers. Every receiver receives a copy of the message.

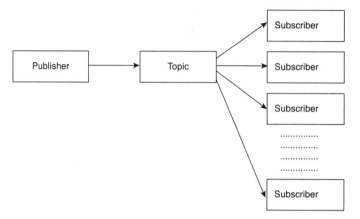

Figure 4.9   Publish-and-subscribe type messaging.

Unlike the p2p model, in the publish-and-subscribe model is a push-based model. Messages are delivered to the recipients automatically without them having to make a request. Some features of the publish-and-subscribe model are described in the following list:

- This model is called one-to-many messaging because there is one sender, but there are many receivers.
- Message transmitting can either be synchronous or asynchronous. It is mostly used for asynchronous messaging because the sender transmits the message independently from recipients.
- A subscriber can disconnect to receive the message from the topic, and later, it can reconnect to collect the messages published while it was disconnected. This feature is not defined in JMS Specification 1.0.2. Implementation of some messaging features depend on JMS vendors' products.

Summary

In this chapter, you learned about some basic concepts of MOM in addition to the history of middleware. TPM, RPC, ORB, in-house developed products, and MOM were examined in the history section. I provided some information about the networking feature of a MOM-based technology and the types of MOM architectures including centralized, decentralized, and hybrid architectures. The remainder of this chapter discussed the messaging types, such as synchronous, asynchronous, point-to-point, and publish-and-subscribe.

All the information provided in this chapter was centered around general concepts of MOM-based technologies and is not specific to JMS.

Questions and Answers

1. What is the difference between RPC and ORB, which seem the same?

They are based on the same model. Both are synchronous and point-to-point messaging types. They are not suitable for mission-critical applications because they rely heavily on the network. They do not work well for large applications because they do not scale well. The difference is that ORB is an object-oriented type of RPC.

2. For our company, we developed a middleware application using developers within the company at a lower cost than buying a middleware package. It has been working for years with no problem. Should we buy a middleware software package now?

It depends on your project and the structure of your company. If the organization and structure of your company (in terms of needs, configuration, consideration, and so on) does not change frequently, in-house development can be a good solution. You should make this decision based on certain parameters such as performance/benefit ratio, hidden costs, and so on. If you need a flexible and scalable product, an in-house product might cost more than you planned, and it takes time to develop with just a couple of developers. Don't forget to add in some of the hidden costs such as developing time, debugging time (which is the most important factor with in-house products), and the salaries of the developers.

3. Does the hybrid model eliminate the disadvantages of the centralized and decentralized architectures?

No. Centralized, decentralized, and hybrid models all have some advantages and disadvantages. Your model choice should depend on your project. The hybrid model does not eliminate any of the disadvantages of the two other architectures. It is just a combination of the two systems.

4. Can we say that synchronous messaging is point-to-point and asynchronous messaging is publish-and-subscribe?

No, both point-to-point and publish-and-subscribe messaging models can be used in either a synchronous or asynchronous model.

5

Concepts and Fundamentals of JMS Programming

IN THIS CHAPTER, YOU WILL LEARN the fundamentals and basic elements of Java Message Service (JMS) programming. In the next chapter, you will write three simple programs to help you understand how to develop a JMS application.

What Is a Messaging System or Service?

Messaging is a way or a mechanism that provides communication between software applications, programs, or objects on a distributed system. Remote Method Invocation (RMI) and socket programming are also types of messaging according to this definition. But, the focus of this book is on a message-based messaging system. As a simple definition, a message identifies the content transmitted between two or more applications or programs. One or more programs send a message, and the other one or more programs receive the message. You might think that a query from a SQL-based database using a graphical user interface (GUI) is a message. It is direct, one-to-one messaging, but a messaging system is more sophisticated than this simple example. It is more like using TCP/IP packets on a computer network. In a messaging system, there are clients that can send and receive messages. Each client connects to the messaging system, which provides a platform to create, send, and receive messages. A messaging system has three major features:

- A messaging system is loosely coupled. This is the most important feature of a messaging system and might be an advantage compared to other systems such as RMI. An application or program, called a *sender* or *publisher*, sends a message to a destination, not directly to another client. Another application or program, called a *receiver* or *subscriber*, receives the message from a destination. Senders and receivers do not have to be aware of each other.

- A messaging system isolates clients from each other. Neither sender nor receiver needs to know about each other. They only need to know the message format and destination.

- A messaging system allows decoupling. A sender and receiver use the system at different times. They do not have to be up and running at the same time. A sender sends the message to a destination, and the receiver takes the messages whenever it is ready. A sender does not need to wait for a response. It can process another task without being blocked. I refer to this feature as *asynchronous* messaging in the remainder of the book, which generally means that clients are able to use the system at different times, and they do not have to know whether other clients in the system are up and running.

Some developers consider email a part of a messaging system. Although email is a way of communication between people, and sometimes between people and software applications, a messaging system is different. It is used for communication between software applications or objects.

A messaging system is based on message-oriented middleware (MOM), which was explained in the previous chapter. MOM defines the rule of messaging as:

- How the message looks
- How a sender application sends the message
- How a receiver application receives the message
- How a receiver application reads the message

Advantages and Disadvantages of a Messaging System

In the messaging service (or system), there is a server, and clients connect to this server to communicate with each other (see Figure 5.1).

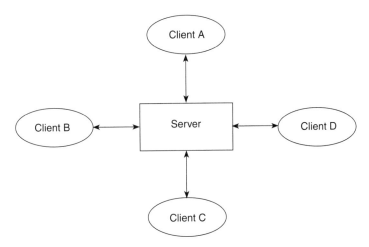

Figure 5.1   The messaging service architecture.

The server provides some essential services such as message persistence, load balancing, and security. The server provides asynchronous communication and guaranteed delivery from senders to receivers.

A messaging service is a great way for applications to communicate with each other, but it has some disadvantages:

- You have to send header and other information with the message content. Therefore, the total amount of information is larger than the message content itself, which might increase network traffic.

- Every message goes to the receivers through a server, which makes communication slower than a direct connection.

- Your messaging service provider (vendor) might not support all the JMS specifications defined by Sun Microsystems.

Before designing your JMS projects, you should compare the disadvantages such as network traffic, slower communication, and vendor-specific issues with the advantages such as loosely coupled or decoupled systems, portability, persistent messaging, and guaranteed delivery.

Briefly, if you only need to insert some new records into a local database and you have a very reliable network, you might not need to use a messaging system. Keep in mind that a messaging-based application consumes additional resources.

However, if you want to isolate networking problems in your client source code or if the database you want to access is in a different location, you might need to use a messaging service. A messaging service can ensure completion of transactions of an application properly such as manipulating data in a table of the database (for example, Insert, Delete, and Update statements), particularly if the database is unavailable (such as when using a laptop that is disconnected from the network). It will process the command (the message content) at a later time. Decoupling or loosely coupling is the best feature of a messaging service.

What Is the JMS API?

The JMS is a Java Application Programming Interface (API), which allows software applications, components, and objects to create, send, receive, and read messages. Sun Microsystems is a JMS vendor that markets an iPlanet product, but Sun designed and developed JMS specifications in collaboration with JMS vendors, not by itself. Sun also provides developers with reference implementations to test and apply specifications to your projects. In this book, I will use the JMS API Reference Implementation bundled with the Java 2 Platform Enterprise Edition (J2EE) version 1.3 or later to test sample applications instead of commercial JMS products. If you need more information about JMS products, refer to Appendix C, "Java Message Service (JMS) API Vendors." The JMS API enables communication that:

- Is loosely coupled
- Is asynchronous, which means that a JMS server delivers a message to the client, but the client does not have to read immediately
- Is reliable, which means that a JMS server ensures that a message is delivered once and only once

Point-to-Point and Publish-and-Subscribe Messaging

As mentioned in the previous chapter, there are two major messaging types: point-to-point (p2p or PTP) and publish-and-subscribe (pub/sub). They are the fundamentals of MOM and are supported by JMS specifications. (JMS vendors are not required to support both types of messaging, although many of them do.)

Recall that in p2p messaging, the domain (or destination) is called a queue (see Figure 5.2). The sender sends the message to the queue, and the receiver (recipient) takes (or reads) the message from the queue whenever it is ready. Although this seems like peer-to-peer, there can be two or more senders for the same queue.

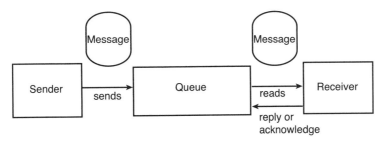

Figure 5.2 The p2p messaging service.

This queue is stored in the messaging server or in a relational database if data persistence is required. JMS does not ban using direct messaging, but it uses a queue for p2p messaging.

A human resource application that sends a message to the accounting application about annual salary increases for workers in a factory plant in Wisconsin is an example of p2p messaging.

In the pub/sub messaging type, a messaging domain (destination) is called a topic, a sender is called a publisher, and a receiver is called a subscriber (see Figure 5.3). Publishers send the message to a topic. Subscribers receive all of the messages sent to that topic as long as they subscribe to the topic. In this model, there are one or more publishers and receivers. If one publisher sends a message to the topic, all subscribers receive a copy of the same message. You might need to use this messaging model to notify a group of applications using the same message. An example of the pub/sub messaging model is when a production application sends a message to a *NewProduct* topic, and subscribers to the *NewProduct* topic, such as a sales application and a marketing application, receive this message.

This model supports multiple senders and receivers, and applications do not need to act together. Senders called publishers send (publish) their messages at different times, independently from other senders to the topic. Receivers called subscribers also read (subscribe) the messages from the topic, independently from other receivers.

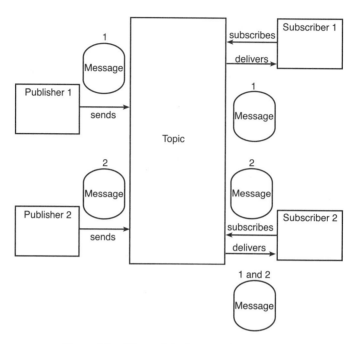

Figure 5.3 The pub/sub messaging service.

The JMS API and the J2EE Platform

Sun first released the JMS API in 1998. Its main purpose was to allow Java applications to work with MOM-based products. Because it was found very useful, many MOM vendors adopted and implemented the JMS API. In version 1.2 of the J2EE platform, vendors were not required to implement the JMS API. It was an add-on product, and vendors had to provide a JMS API interface. With version 1.3 of the J2EE platform, the JMS API is an integrated part of the platform. J2EE certified vendors, including Sun Microsystem's own application server product, "iPlanet," must support the JMS API. The JMS API in the J2EE platform version 1.3 has some valuable features:

- Enterprise JavaBeans (EJBs) or an enterprise Web component can create, send, and synchronously receive a message.

- Message-driven beans, which are new enterprise beans included with version 1.3 of the J2EE platform, allow asynchronous messaging.

- Messages that are sent and received can participate in Java Transaction API (JTA) transactions.

Additionally, EJB container architecture provides support for distributed transactions and allows for the concurrent consumption of messages.

The JMS API makes developing enterprise applications easier for developers and allows loosely coupled, synchronous and asynchronous, reliable communications and interactions between J2EE components and other applications capable of messaging. You can develop enterprise applications with new message-driven beans for specific business events in addition to the existing business events.

Another technology, the J2EE Connector, exists within the J2EE platform version 1.3, and it provides tight integration between Java enterprise applications and enterprise information systems (EIS). The JMS API is different from connector technology because it provides loosely coupled interaction between J2EE applications and database servers or information application servers (IAS).

Concepts of JMS Programming

In this section, I discuss some basic elements of JMS programming before providing you with some simple JMS examples and advanced applications.

JMS Architecture

Figure 5.4 shows the five main elements of the JMS architecture.

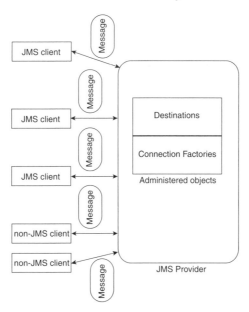

Figure 5.4 The five main elements of the JMS architecture.

Some brief information about each element follows, and more detailed information is provided in the remainder of the book.

- JMS provider—The JMS provider is like a container for the messaging system. It implements JMS interfaces, which are defined by the JMS specifications. It also provides some administrative features as well as some additional components, which are not required by the JMS specification, but are MOM-based technologies.

- JMS clients—The JMS clients are applications, components, or objects that produce and consume messages. They must be written in the Java language in order to be a JMS client.

- Non-JMS clients—Non-JMS clients are applications that use native client APIs instead of the JMS API.

- Administered objects—Administered objects are for client use, but are created by an administrator. There are two main administered objects— *destination* and *connection factories*—which are examined in subsequent sections.

- Message—The message is the heart of the messaging system. It is the object that provides information transfer between messaging system clients. If you do not have a message, there is no need to use a messaging system.

Message Consumption

One of the important concepts in the messaging system is message consumption, which is defined by timing properties of the system. Consuming a message means receiving the message, reading the message, or taking the message from the destination (queue or topic). A message is produced by a messaging client (sender or publisher), but the producing client is not interested in how the message will be consumed. This process is part of the receiving side, which is the target of the message.

The JMS specification defines two ways to consume a message:

- Synchronously—A receiver reads or takes the message from the destination by calling the `receive()` method. This `receive()` method blocks the application until a message arrives (blocking means that the receiver application waits for a message to arrive and does not perform any other transactions during this time). As a developer, you can specify a time limit to receive a message. If the message does not arrive within a specified time limit, it can time out, which releases the block.

- Asynchronously—A client can define a message listener (a mechanism similar to an event listener). Whenever a message arrives at its destination, a messaging server (JMS provider) delivers the message to the recipient (subscriber) by calling the `onMessage()` method. The client will not be blocked while waiting for the message.

Destinations

As one of two administered objects, a destination is the target of a message. The destination is where the message will be delivered. It is provider-independent. In the JMS specification, the Destination interface does not define a specific method. It is an administrative object, and its physical location on the server is chosen and handled by the provider. There are two types of destinations in the JMS specifications: queue and topic.

Recall from a previous section that the p2p messaging model uses a queue destination, and the pub/sub model uses a topic destination. The most important aspect and advantage of a destination is that its implementation is defined by the JMS provider. A sender sends the message to the destination by using the Destination interface, and the recipient receives the message from the Destination object. A recipient does not see the detail of the implementation. The messaging server, which in this case is the JMS provider, performs the implementation of the Destination object.

A destination is an administered object, and you can create it by using the Administrator tool in your application server, which is also included in the JMS server. Because J2EE Reference Implementation version 1.3 is used as the application server in this book, I will not use any vendor-specific features for this server. You will have to modify some commands or steps depending on your server.

If you want to create a queue for a p2p messaging model, you can type j2eeadmin at the command line as follows:

```
j2eeadmin -addJmsDestination <jndi_name_for_queue> queue
```

As an example, if you want to create a queue named levent_Boston, you can type it at the command line like this:

```
j2eeadmin -addJmsDestination levent_Boston queue
```

In JMS application client code, you usually need to look up a destination after you look up a connection factory. When you look up the levent_Boston queue, the line might look like the following in the code for lookup:

```
Queue erdQueue = (Queue) ctx.lookup("levent_Boston");
```

If you want to create a topic for a pub/sub messaging model, you can type j2eeadmin at the command line as follows:

```
j2eeadmin -addJmsDestination <jndi_name_for_topic> topic
```

As an example, if you want to create a topic named levent_Europe, you can type it at the command line like this:

```
j2eeadmin -addJmsDestination levent_Europe topic
```

In JMS application client code, you usually need to look up a destination after you look up a connection factory. When you look up the levent_Europe topic, the line might look like the following in the code for lookup:

```
Topic erdTopic = (Topic) ctx.lookup("levent_Europe");
```

A JMS application can use multiple queues and topics depending on your projects.

In addition to a permanent queue and topic, which are created by JMS administrators for the use of JMS clients, there are temporary queues and topics. These queues and topics are dynamic and are only created for the lifetime of the session. These temporary destinations:

- Are only used when a response is expected. A response can be specified by a JMSReplyTo message header when a message is sent.
- Are created by the current destination (queue or topic) and can only be accessed by this session and all other sessions that belong to the same connection.
- Are deleted automatically when the session is closed.

Connection Factory

A connection factory is another administered object. It is used to create a connection to the JMS provider by the client. It is similar to DriverManager in the Java Database Connectivity (JDBC) API, which hides the JDBC driver detail from the programmer. It encapsulates a series of connection configuration parameters and information. The host, which the JMS provider is running, or the port, which the JMS provider is listening to, is an example of the information that will be put into a connection factory. These types of configurations are the JMS administrator's responsibility, but they are needed by the client to create a proper connection to the JMS server.

A connection factory is defined in the JMS specification as an interface (javax.jms.ConnectionFactory) without a method. This is the root interface. In the client applications, you use two subtype interfaces—javax.jms. QueueConnectionFactory and javax.jms.TopicConnectionFactory—

depending on the messaging model (destination) used in your project. These subtype interfaces define the methods to create a connection to the server.

You can use two default connections, QueueConnectionFactory and TopicConnectionFactory, to create connections with the J2EE Reference Implementation version 1.3 if the JMS administrator did not create a connection factory. You can also create new connection factories as a JMS administrator.

The p2p Messaging Model for the Connection Factory

In the p2p messaging model, you can create a connection factory at the command line like this by typing the following:

```
j2eeadmin -addJmsFactory <jndi_name_for_conn_factory> queue
```

For example, if you name the connection factory conFactory_Montreal, the command will look like this:

```
j2eeadmin -addJmsFactory conFactory_Montreal queue
```

At the beginning of the JMS client application, you have to look up the connection factory after calling `InitialContext()`. For p2p messaging, the lines that contain calling the initial context and looking up the connection factory will look like this:

```
Context myContext = new InitialContext();
QueueConnectionFactory myQueueConnectionFactory =
    (QueueConnectionFactory) ctx.lookup("QueueConnectionFactory");
```

QueueConnectionFactory in the `ctx.lookup()` is the default connection factory preconfigured on the JMS server. If another is created and it needs to be used, you should substitute the default connection factory with the created one.

The pub/sub Messaging Model for the Connection Factory

In the pub/sub messaging model, you can create a connection factory at the command line like this by typing the following:

```
j2eeadmin -addJmsFactory <jndi_name_for_conn_factory> topic
```

For example, if you name the connection factory conFactory_SanDiego, the command will look like this:

```
j2eeadmin -addJmsFactory conFactory_SanDiego topic
```

At the beginning of the JMS client application, you have to look up the connection factory after calling `InitialContext()`. For pub/sub messaging, the lines that call the initial context and look up the connection factor, will look like this:

```
Context myContext = new InitialContext();
TopicConnectionFactory myTopicConnectionFactory =
    (TopicConnectionFactory) ctx.lookup("TopicConnectionFactory");
```

TopicConnectionFactory in the `ctx.lookup()` is the default connection factory preconfigured on the JMS server. If another is created and needs to be used, you should substitute the default connection factory with the created one.

In both messaging model examples, I used `InitialContext()` without parameters. This means that your code will search the jndi.properties file in the current CLASSPATH if it exists. This file contains vendor-specific information about the parameters to connect the JMS provider as well as other Java Naming Directory Interface (JNDI) parameters. If you need to, you can create a properties type variable and put these parameters into this properties variable. You can then provide this variable as a parameter in the `InitialContext()`, but you will lose portability of the client application. The parameters will specifically define the properties of the JMS vendor. If you want your application to be vendor-independent, use `InitialContext()` with no parameter.

Connections

A client application makes a connection after it completes configuring the administered objects, such as the connection factory object and the destination. It creates a virtual connection to the JMS provider, which is similar to an open TCP/IP socket between the client and the JMS provider.

Connections are created using factory methods from connection factories. If the client application has a connection factory, it can use this connection factory to create a connection. You can think of the connection as a communication channel between the application and the messaging server. You use a connection to create one or more sessions.

In the JMS specifications, methods of connections are defined in the javax.jms.Connection interface. Refer to Appendix D, "Overview of JMS Package Classes," for methods of the Connection interface.

Similar to connection factories, this interface has two subtype interfaces—javax.jms.QueueConnection and javax.jms.TopicConnection—depending on the messaging model. In the client code, you choose the methods from one of the interfaces depending the messaging model you are using.

The p2p Messaging Model for a Connection

In the client application of a p2p messaging model (queue type destination), you can create a connection like this:

```
QueueConnection myQueueConnection =
    myQueueConnectionFactory.createQueueConnection();
```

The myQueueConnectionFactory object should be created before creating the `QueueConnection` line by using the default or administrator-created ConnectionFactory object. Before the application consumes the message, you need to call this connection's `start()` method like this:

```
myQueueConnection.start();
```

When the application completes, you need to close any connection you created; otherwise, you will keep occupying the resource without using it. Closing a connection also closes its sessions, message producers, and message consumers. You can close the connection by calling the `close()` method like this:

```
myQueueConnection.close();
```

If you want to stop delivery of the messages without closing the connection, call the `stop()` method of the connection like this:

```
myQueueConnection.stop();
```

The pub/sub Messaging Model for a Connection

Similar steps are carried out when creating a connection using the topic (pub/sub) model as those carried out using the queue (p2p) model. Just substitute the word queue with the word topic. For consistency, I will explain them explicitly. You can create a connection for the pub/sub model like this:

```
TopicConnection myTopicConnection =
    myTopicConnectionFactory.createTopicConnection();
```

The myTopicConnectionFactory object should be created before creating the TopicConnection line by using the default or administrator created ConnectionFactory object. Before the application consumes the message, you need to call this connection's `start()` method like this:

```
myTopicConnection.start();
```

When the application completes, you need to close any connection you created; otherwise, you will keep occupying the resource without using it. Closing a connection also closes its sessions, message producers, and message consumers. You can close the connection by calling the `close()` method like this:

```
myTopicConnection.close();
```

If you want to stop delivery of the messages without closing the connection, call the stop() method of the connection like this:

```
myTopicConnection.stop();
```

When a connection is stopped by calling the stop() method temporarily, message delivery to this connection channel will be stopped. You must call the start() method to restart message delivery. Stopped mode prevents a client from receiving a message, but the client can still send a message.

Sessions

As defined in the JMS specification, a session is a single-threaded context used to produce and consume the messages in a messaging system. After creating a connection, you should create a session, which creates message producers, message consumers, and messages. Sessions allow the application to access the connection in order to send and receive messages. Sessions serialize the message, which is sent and received in a single-threaded model.

Let me explain the serialization in a single-threaded model. A messaging application (JMS client) acting as a sender produces *n* messages, but another application acting as a receiver will not receive these *n* messages at the same time. A JMS provider ensures that a receiver consumes the messages one by one.

As defined in the JMS specifications, a session provides a *transactional* context for the messaging. This means that the message is sent or received as a group in one unit. The context stores the messages for delivery until the messages are committed. For example, if the message has four parts, and if transacted messaging is chosen, these four messages are not delivered by the server (provider) until the transaction is committed. They are sent as a block.

Transactions are very important if you send a group of related information in different sessions. All of the transactions must be completed at once, such as in a banking transaction. For example, you might want to transfer an amount of money from one account to another. One of the sessions withdraws money from the first account, and the other transaction deposits the money into the second account. If you encounter a networking problem after you complete the first session, the money that you want to transfer from one account to another will disappear. Therefore, all related transactions should be put in one transaction unit and must be committed at the end of all successful transactions.

Another advantage of a transaction is that it gives you the chance to change your mind before completing the transaction by providing a *rollback* option. You can cancel all messages that are sent in one block using the rollback option.

A transaction is optional, and if it is *off-state* (meaning that no transaction is chosen), messages are delivered when they are sent. They are not stored for block delivery. If the session is without transactions, the recipient sends an acknowledgment when the message is received. If the sender client receives the acknowledgment, the message will not be sent to the client again.

There are three types of acknowledgment options:

- AUTO_ACKNOWLEDGE—An acknowledgment message is automatically sent to the sender whenever the delivery is complete.

- CLIENT_ ACKNOWLEDGE—The client must send the acknowledgment for each message programmatically.

- DUPS_OK_ ACKNOWLEDGE—The acknowledgment is not very strict and delivering the message again is possible if networking problems occur.

The basic methods for JMS sessions are specified in the javax.jms.Session interface. Refer to Appendix D for more information about the methods of a Session interface.

A Session interface, like a Connection interface, has two subtype interfaces—javax.jms.QueueSession and javax.jms.TopicSession—depending on the messaging model. I will explain how you can create a session in the client application in the following sections.

The p2p Messaging Model for a Session

In the p2p messaging model (queue type destination), you can create a session like this:

```
QueueSession myQueueSession =
     myQueueConnection.createQueueSession(false,
          Session.AUTO_ACKNOWLEDGE);
```

A queue session is created without a transaction (the first parameter is false in the `createQueueSession()` method) and the sender is acknowledged whenever the recipient receives the message (the second parameter is Session.AUTO_ACKNOWLEDGE in the `createQueueSession()` method). Do not forget to create the myQueueConnection object before this line.

The pub/sub Messaging Model for Session

Tasks in the pub/sub messaging model (topic type destination) are similar to the p2p model; you can create a session like this:

```
TopicSession myTopicSession =
     myTopicConnection.createTopicSession(true,
          Session.AUTO_ACKNOWLEDGE);
```

A topic session is created with a transaction (the first parameter is true in the `createTopicSession()` method) and the sender is acknowledged whenever the recipient receives the message (the second parameter is Session.AUTO_ACKNOWLEDGE in the `createTopicSession()` method). Do not forget to create the myTopicConnection object before this line.

A JMS connection can have one or more JMS sessions associated with this connection.

Message Producer

In the JMS specification, a message producer is defined as an object that is created by a session and is used to send a message to the destination. If you want to send a message in your code, you have to create a message producer through the session. Message-sending methods are implemented by the root javax.jms.MessageProducer interface. Refer to Appendix D for the methods of the MessageProducer interface. If the default values are valid for your application, you do not need to implement all the methods of MessageProducer. You most likely only need to create a message producer, send the created messages with the producer, and close it.

Like other interfaces, such as Session and Connection, this interface has two subtype interfaces: QueueSender and TopicPublisher. You should choose one of them in the client application depending on the messaging model you are using.

The p2p Messaging Model for a Message Producer

In the p2p messaging model (queue type destination), you can create a message producer object by using the QueueSender interface in the client code like this:

```
QueueSender myQueueSender =
    myQueueSession.createSender(myQueue);
```

The myQueueSender object is created for the myQueueSession session object to send a message to a queue type destination. Do not forget to create a queue session (myQueueSession object) before this line. myQueue is an administered object that specifies the queue name.

You can create an unidentified producer by specifying null as an argument in the `createSender()` method. In this case, you can wait until you send a message to specify the destination to send the message to.

After you create a message producer, your client application is ready to send the message if you created and prepared a message to send. In the p2p model, you can send the message by using the `send()` method like this:

```
myQueueSender.send(message);
```

If you created an unidentified producer, specify the destination as the first parameter in the `send()` method. The following lines show how to send a message to the myQueue queue:

```
QueueSender myQueueSender =
     myQueueSession.createSender(null);
     //other lines such as creating message
myQueueSender.send(myQueue, message);
```

The pub/sub Messaging Model for a Message Producer

Similarly, in the pub/sub messaging model (topic type destination), you can create a message producer object by using the TopicPublisher interface in the client code like this:

```
TopicPublisher myTopicPublisher =
     myTopicSession.createPublisher(myTopic);
```

The myTopicSender object is created for the myTopicSession session object to send a message to a topic type destination. Do not forget to create a topic session (myTopicSession object) before this line. myTopic is an administered object that specifies the topic name.

You can create an unidentified producer by specifying null as an argument in the `createPublisher()` method. In this case, you can wait until you send a message to specify the destination of the message.

After you create a message producer, your client application is ready to publish the message if you created and prepared a message to send. In the pub/sub model, you can send the message by using the `publish()` method like this:

```
myTopicPublisher.publish(message);
```

If you created an unidentified producer, specify the destination as the first parameter in the `publish()` method. The following lines show how to send a message to the myTopic topic:

```
TopicPublisher myTopicPublisher =
     myTopicSession.createPublisher(null);
     //other lines such as creating message
myTopicPublisher.publish(myTopic, message);
```

Message Consumer

If an application produces a message, it should be consumed by other applications. In the JMS specification, a message consumer is defined as an object that is created by a session and is used to receive a message that is sent to the destination. If you want to receive a message in your code, you have to create a message consumer through the session. Message-sending methods are implemented by the root javax.jms.MessageConsumer interface. Refer to Appendix D for the methods of the MessageConsumer interface.

Like other interfaces, such as Session and Connection, this interface has two subtype interfaces: QueueReceiver and TopicSubscriber. You should choose one of them in the client application depending on the messaging model you are using.

A message consumer allows the JMS client to register to a destination through a JMS provider, which handles and manages message delivery from the specified destination to the registered consumers for this destination.

Messages are consumed in two ways: synchronously and asynchronously for both messaging models. The following sections examine synchronous and asynchronous consuming for the p2p and pub/sub messaging models.

Synchronous Consuming for the p2p Messaging Model

In the synchronous p2p messaging model (queue type destination), you can create a message consumer object by using the QueueReceiver interface in the client code like this:

```
QueueReceiver myQueueReceiver =
    myQueueSession.createReciever(myQueue);
```

The myQueueReceiver object is created for the myQueueSession session object to receive a message that is sent to a queue type destination. Do not forget to create a queue session (myQueueSession object) before this line. myQueue is an administered object that specifies the queue name.

In the synchronous p2p messaging model, there is an additional receiving method: receiveNoWait(). This method is used when the message is immediately available. The difference between the receive() and receiveNoWait() methods is blocking. The receive() method blocks and waits until a message arrives if a timeout is not specified as a parameter. The receiveNoWait() method does not block a message consumer.

After you create a message consumer, your client application is ready to receive the message using the receive() method like this:

```
Message theMessageReceived = myQueueReceiver.receive();
```

If you want to set a timeout, specify the time in milliseconds as a parameter in the receive() method. You can use the receive() method at any time after calling the start() method of the queue connection. By adding the starting queue connection line, receiving lines listed in the preceding paragraph will look like this:

```
myQueueConnection.start();
Message theMessageReceived = myQueueReceiver.receive();
```

The myQueueConnection is the connection that was previously created.

After you receive the message, you can call the `close()` method to close the message consumer and release the resources dedicated to the message consumer.

Synchronous Consuming for the pub/sub Messaging Model

In the synchronous pub/sub messaging model (topic type destination), you can create a message consumer object by using the TopicSubscriber interface in the client code like this:

```
TopicSubscriber myTopicSubscriber =
    myTopicSession.createSubscriber(myTopic);
```

The myTopicSubscriber object is created for the myTopicSession session object to receive a message that is sent to a topic type destination. Do not forget to create a topic session (myTopicSession object) before this line. myTopic is an administered object that specifies the topic name.

In the synchronous pub/sub messaging model, there is an additional receiving method: `receiveNoWait()`. This method is used when the message is immediately available. The difference between the `receive()` and `receiveNoWait()` methods is blocking. The `receive()` method blocks and waits until a message arrives if a timeout is not specified as a parameter. The `receiveNoWait()` method does not block a message consumer.

After you create a message consumer, your client application is ready to receive the message using the `receive()` method like this:

```
Message theMessageReceived = myTopicReceiver.receive();
```

If you want to set a timeout, specify the time in milliseconds as a parameter in the `receive()` method. You can use the `receive()` method at any time after calling the `start()` method of a topic connection. By adding a starting topic connection line, the receiving lines listed in the preceding paragraph will look like this:

```
myTopicConnection.start();
Message theMessageReceived = myTopicReceiver.receive();
```

The myTopicConnection is the connection that was previously created.

After you receive the message, you can call the `close()` method to close the message consumer and release the resources dedicated to the message consumer.

A Message Listener for Asynchronous Messaging

Before providing you with information about asynchronous messaging, I need to explain the concept of a message listener. You will find more information about p2p and pub/sub messaging as well as sample code in the next two sections of this chapter.

As defined in the JMS specifications, a message listener is an object that acts as an asynchronous event handler for messages. There is one method in a message listener class that implements the MessageListener interface: onMessage(). In the onMessage() method, you define what should be done when a message arrives. From a developer's view, you develop a class that implements the MessageListener interface and overrides the onMessage() method in this class by putting proper codes in this method. The following sample code lines show you the structure of a developer created message listener class that can be used in an asynchronous receiver or publisher client application:

```
public class myListener implements MessageListener {
    // overriding onMessage method for your message type and format
    public void onMessage(Message parMessage) {
        // in the body of onMessage() method,
        // put the proper code lines what should
        //  be done when a message arrives
    } //end of onMessage method
} //end of class
```

One of the most important aspects of the message listener is that it is not specific to a particular destination type. The same listener can obtain messages from either a queue or a topic, depending on the messaging model, for example, p2p (QueueReceiver) or pub/sub (TopicSubscriber).

Another important aspect of the message listener is that a message listener usually expects a specific message type and format. You should define this message type in the onMessage() method. If the client application does not receive the proper message type, it must warn the client.

A message listener can reply to messages in two ways. First, it assumes a particular destination type specified in the code explicitly. Second, it can obtain the destination type of the message and create a producer for that destination type by using a temporary destination.

A message listener is serialized. The session that created the message consumer serializes the execution of all message listeners registered with the session. This means that only one of the current session's message listeners is running.

J2EE version 1.3 has a special bean that acts as a message listener: the message-driven bean. Message-driven beans are discussed in Chapter 10, "JMS and Web."

Asynchronous Consuming for the p2p Messaging Model

Asynchronous messaging is preferred in the pub/sub messaging model, but you can use it for both types of messaging models by using the MessageListener interface.

You should first register the message listener with the current QueueReceiver through the `setMessageListener` method for asynchronous messaging. For example, let's assume that you have developed a LevQueueListener class as a message listener that implements the MessageListener interface and overrides the `onMessage()` method. You can register the message listener like this:

```
LevQueueListener myQueueListener = new LevQueueListener();
myQueueReceiver.setMessageListener(myQueueListener);
```

The myQueueReceiver object is created for the myQueueSession session object to receive a message that is sent to a queue type destination. The myQueueListener object is a message listener object that listens to the channel whether the message arrives or not.

After you register the message listener, do not forget to call the `start()` method on the QueueConnection to begin message delivery. If you call the `start()` method before you register the message listener, you will miss messages.

Once message delivery begins, the message consumer automatically calls the message listener's `onMessage()` method whenever a message is delivered. The `onMessage()` method has a message type parameter. This parameter, which is a delivered message from the destination, will be cast as a proper message for the client. I will provide information about the message types in the next section.

Asynchronous Consuming for the pub/sub Messaging Model

Asynchronous messaging for the pub/sub messaging model is implemented by using a MessageListener interface similar to the one in the p2p model.

You should first register the message listener with the current TopicSubscriber through the `setMessageListener` method for asynchronous messaging. For example, let's assume that you have developed an ErdTopicListener class as a message listener that implements the MessageListener interface and overrides the `onMessage()` method. You can register the message listener like this:

```
ErdTopicListener myTopicListener = new ErdTopicListener ();
myTopicSubscriber.setMessageListener(myTopicListener);
```

The myTopicSubscriber object is created for the myTopicSession session object to receive a message that is sent to a topic type destination. The myTopicListener object is a message listener object that listens to the channel whether the message arrives or not.

After you register the message listener, do not forget to call the start() method on the TopicConnection to begin message delivery. If you call the start() method before you register the message listener, you will miss messages.

Similar to the p2p messaging model, once message delivery begins, the message consumer automatically calls the message listener's onMessage() method whenever a message is delivered. The onMessage() method has a message type parameter. This parameter, which is a delivered message from the destination, will be cast as a proper message for the client.

Messages

Earlier, I explained many concepts and techniques for a messaging system based on the JMS specifications. So far, I've discussed transferring a message from one application (client) to another application (client) or applications. This discussion about messages is the most important part of the chapter.

Technically, by transferring a message from one point to another you are actually producing a message in one software application and consuming that message in another software application. Even though the JMS message format is very simple, it still allows you to create compatible messages with other non-JMS applications on different types of platforms.

In other systems, such as Java RMI, Distributed Component Object Model (DCOM), or Common Object Request Broker Architecture (CORBA), message definition and usage is different from the JMS specification. In these systems, a message is a command to execute a method or procedure. In a JMS system, a message is not a command. It is a pure message that is transferred from one point to another. The message does not force the recipient to do something. The sender does not wait for a response.

As shown in Figure 5.5, a message object has three main parts: a message header, message properties, and a message body. Detailed information about the parts of a message object is provided in the following sections.

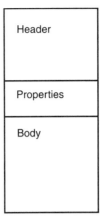

Figure 5.5   The three parts of a message structure.

The Header Part of the Message Object

A JMS message header contains some predefined fields. These fields are identifiers for a client and a provider. For example, every message has a unique id, time stamp, or priority. In addition to some optional fields, a message header must have certain fields such as a JMS destination. These accessor or mutator methods obey setJMS<HeaderName> and getJMS<HeaderName> syntax. A list of methods in a message header follows. If you need more information about properties methods, refer to Appendix D.

- getJMSDestination()
- setJMSDestination(Destination paramDestination)
- getJMSDeliveryMode()
- setJMSDeliveryMode(int deliveryMode)
- getJMSMessageID()
- setJMSMessageID(String ID)
- getJMSTimestamp()
- setJMSTimestamp(long timeStamp)
- getJMSExpiration()
- setJMSExpiration(long expiration)
- getJMSRedelivered()
- setJMSRedelivered(boolean redelivery)

- `getJMSPriority()`
- `setJMSPriority(int priority)`
- `getJMSReplyTo()`
- `setJMSReplyTo(Destination replyTo)`
- `getJMSCorrelationID()`
- `setJMSCorrelationID(String correlationValue)`
- `getJMSCorrelationIDAsBytes()`
- `setJMSCorrelationIDAsBytes(byte[] correlationValue)`
- `getJMSType()`
- `setJMSType(String type)`

Some of these fields are assigned by the client, some are assigned automatically when the message is delivered, and one field is assigned by a JMS provider (see Table 5.1).

Table 5.1   **Message Header Fields and How They Are Set**

Header Field	Set By
JMSDestination	Message Producer
JMSDeliveryMode	Message Producer
JMSExpiration	Message Producer
JMSPriority	Message Producer
JMSMessageID	Message Producer
JMSTimestamp	Message Producer
JMSRedelivered	JMS provider
JMSCorrelationID	Client
JMSReplyTo	Client
JMSType	Client

The Properties Part of the Message Object

Properties of a JMS message are like additional headers that are assigned to a message to provide information to the developer. These properties can be used to provide compatibility with other messaging systems. Properties can be used for message selectors, which are discussed later in this section.

Properties can either be predefined or user defined. They can be divided into three classes: application-specific properties, JMS-defined properties, and provider-specific properties.

For example, if you want to define a String type hostuserID property, you can define it by using the `setStringProperty()` accessor like this:

```
myTextMessage.setStringProperty("hostUserID", hostuserID);
```

The myTextMessage is the TextMessage type message created by using the `createTextMessage()` method. This hostUserID property is valid and meaningful only in the application. This kind of property specified in the property part of the message object is useful to filter messages using message selectors.

Most properties methods (accessor or mutator methods) of a message obey the set<DataType>Property and get<DataType>Property syntax. The properties methods list follows. If you need more information about properties methods, refer to Appendix D.

- `clearProperties()`
- `propertyExists(String name)`
- `getBooleanProperty(String name)`
- `getByteProperty(String name)`
- `getShortProperty(String name)`
- `getIntProperty(String name)`
- `getLongProperty(String name)`
- `getFloatProperty(String name)`
- `getDoubleProperty(String name)`
- `getStringProperty(String name)`
- `getObjectProperty(String name)`
- `getPropertyNames()`
- `setBooleanProperty(String name, boolean value)`
- `setByteProperty(String name, byte value)`
- `setShortProperty(String name, short value)`
- `setIntProperty(String name, int value)`
- `setLongProperty(String name, long value)`
- `setFloatProperty(String name, float value)`
- `setDoubleProperty(String name, double value)`
- `setStringProperty(String name, String value)`
- `setObjectProperty(String name, Object value)`

Message Selectors

In this section, I provide some brief information about message selectors, which are used in message headers and properties.

Another feature of a message consumer is to filter the message using message selectors. This process is like a SQL type query, and a message selector is a string that contains a criteria expression. You can filter a message with criteria from the message headers and the message properties. The message consumer only receives messages whose headers and properties match the criteria specified in the selector. A message selector cannot select messages based on the content of the message body.

For example, assume that there is an identifier named cityName in the JMS property of a message. You want to filter some cities when the message arrives. You can write a selector like this:

```
String mySelector = "cityName IN ('New York', 'Boston', 'Newark');
```

You can use this selector in the message receiver like this:

```
TopicSubscriber mySubscriber =
session.createSubscriber(topic, mySelector, false);
```

The selector sentence can be as complex as necessary. The identifier used in the selector sentence must always refer to the JMS property name or the JMS header name in the message.

The Body of the Message Object

In the JMS specifications, there are five different message body formats, which are also called message types: TextMessage, ObjectMessage, MapMessage, BytesMessage, and StreamMessage. Actually, these five message types are subinterfaces of the Message interface. JMS defines the Message interface, but it does not define its implementation. Vendors are free to implement and transfer the message in their own way. JMS tries to maintain standard interfaces for JMS developers. Vendors might ignore one message type and support their own message type in the Message interface.

Information about these five subinterfaces is provided in the following sections. You can find more information about subinterfaces of the Message interface and their methods in Appendix D.

TextMessage Interface

The TextMessage interface contains the java.lang.String type object. It is used when you need to transfer simple text messages. You can transfer more complicated messages such as XML documents as long as they are text-based. Before you send the message, you need to use the `createTextMessage()` and setText() methods. The setText() method takes a String type value or variable as a parameter. The following sample lines send a text message to a topic destination (pub/sub):

```
TextMessage messageOnBoard = session.createTextMessage();
messageOnBoard.setText("This is a text message");
myTopicPublisher.publish(messageOnBoard);
```

If the destination is a queue type (p2p), you only need to change the sender method as follows:

```
TextMessage messageOnBoard = session.createTextMessage();
messageOnBoard.setText("This is a text message");
myQueueSender.send(messageOnBoard);
```

When the message arrives at the consumer, it is extracted by the getText() method and is assigned a String variable. As an example, you can extract a text type message from the preceding example like this:

```
TextMessage recTextMessage = (TextMessage)message;
String recOnBoard = recTextMessage.getText();
```

ObjectMessage Interface

The ObjectMessage interface contains a serializable Java object. It is used when you need to transfer Java objects. Before you send the message, you need to use the createObjectMessage() and setObject() methods. The setObject() method takes a serializable object as a parameter. The following sample lines send an object message to a topic destination (pub/sub):

```
ObjectMessage theObjMessage =
session.createObjectMessage();
theObjMessage.setObj("This is an object message");
myTopicPublisher.publish(theObjMessage);
```

If the destination is a queue type (p2p), you only need to change the sender method as follows:

```
ObjectMessage theObjMessage =
session.createObjectMessage();
theObjMessage.setObj("This is an object message");
myQueueSender.send(theObjMessage);
```

When the message arrives at the consumer, it is extracted by the getObject() method and is assigned an Object variable. As an example, you can extract an object type message from the preceding example like this:

```
ObjectMessage recObjectMessage = (ObjectMessage)message;
Object recObjMessage = recObjectMessage.getObject();
```

MapMessage Interface

The MapMessage interface contains a set of name-value pairs. It is used when you need to transfer keyed data. This method takes a key-value pair as a parameter. Before you send the message, you need to use the `createMapMessage()` method and certain `setXXX()` methods depending on the value data type. The `setXXX()` methods are:

- `setInt()` for integer type value
- `setFloat()` for float type
- `setString()` for String type value
- `setObject()` for object type value
- `setBoolean()` for boolean type value
- `setBytes()` for byte type value
- `setShort()` for short type value
- `setChar()` for char type value
- `setLong()` for long type value
- `setDouble()` for double type value

The following sample lines send a map message to a topic destination (pub/sub):

```
MapMessage theMapMessage = session.createMapMessage();
theMapMessage.setString("HostName", "Montreal");
theMapMessage.setFloat("RAM", 512);
theMapMessage.setFloat("Disk", 80);
myTopicPublisher.publish(theMapMessage);
```

If the destination is a queue type (p2p), you only need to change the sender method as follows:

```
MapMessage theMapMessage = session.createMapMessage();
theMapMessage.setString("HostName", "Montreal");
theMapMessage.setFloat("RAM", 512);
theMapMessage.setInt("Disk", 80);
myQueueSender.send(theMapMessage);
```

When the message arrives at the consumer, it is extracted by the `getXXX()` methods and assigned to a proper type variable. As an example, you can extract the map type message from the preceding example like this:

```
MapMessage recMapMessage = (MapMessage)message;
String recHostName = recMapMessage.getString("HostName");
float recRAM = recMapMessage.getFloat("RAM");
int recDisk = recMapMessage.getInt("Disk");
```

BytesMessage Interface

The BytesMessage interface contains an array of primitive bytes. It is used when you need to transfer data in the application's native format, which might not be suitable for existing message types in the JMS specifications. You can transfer data between two applications regardless of its JMS status. Before you send the message, you need to use the `createBytesMessage()` method and certain `writeXXX()` methods depending on the value data type. The `writeXXX()` methods are:

- `writeByte(byte parValue)` for byte type value
- `writeBytes(byte[] parValue)` for array of byte value
- `writeBoolean(boolean parValue)` for boolean type value
- `writeChar(char parValue)` for char type value
- `writeShort(short parValue)` for short type value
- `writeInt(int parValue)` for integer type value
- `writeLong(long parValue)` for long type value
- `writeFloat(float parValue)` for float type value
- `writeDouble(double parValue)` for double type value
- `writeUTF(String parValue)` for String type value
- `writeObject(Object parValue)` for object type value

The BytesMessage interface is very similar to java.io.DataInputStream and java.io.DataOutputStream. The following sample lines send byte messages to a topic destination (pub/sub):

```
BytesMessage theBytesMessage =
session.createBytesMessage();
theBytesMessage.writeUTF("San Fransisco");
theBytesMessage.writeInt(120);
myTopicPublisher.publish(theBytesMessage);
```

If the destination is a queue type (p2p), you only need to change the sender method as follows:

```
BytesMessage theBytesMessage =
session.createBytesMessage();
theBytesMessage.writeUTF("San Fransisco");
theBytesMessage.writeInt(120);
myQueueSender.send(theBytesMessage);
```

When the message arrives at the consumer, it is extracted by the `readXXX()` methods and is assigned to a proper type variable. As an example, you can extract the bytes type message from the preceding example like this:

```
BytesMessage recBytesMessage = (BytesMessage)message;
String cityName = recBytesMessage.readUTF();
int carParking = recBytesMessage. readInt();
```

StreamMessage Interface

The StreamMessage interface contains a stream of primitive Java types such as int, char, double, boolean, and so on. Primitive types are read from the message in the same order they are written. The StreamMessage interface and its methods look like the BytesMessage, but they are not the same. StreamMessage keeps track of the order of written messages, and the message is then converted to the primitive type by following formal conversion rules.

Before you send the message, you need to use the `createStreamMessage()` and certain `writeXXX()` methods depending on the value data type. The `writeXXX()` methods are:

- `writeByte(byte parValue)` for byte type value
- `writeBytes(byte[] parValue)` for array of byte value
- `writeBoolean(boolean parValue)` for boolean type value
- `writeChar(char parValue)` for char type value
- `writeShort(short parValue)` for short type value
- `writeInt(int parValue)` for integer type value
- `writeLong(long parValue)` for long type value
- `writeFloat(float parValue)` for float type value
- `writeDouble(double parValue)` for double type value
- `writeString(String parValue)` for String type value
- `writeObject(Object parValue)` for object type value

You have to be careful when converting a message stream from a written format to a reading format. For example, you can write the message in long data type, and you can read it in long or String data type. Data type conversions are listed in Table 5.2.

Table 5.2 **StreamMessage Conversion Rules**

Written Message Type	Read Message Type
boolean	boolean, String
byte	byte, short, int, long, String
char	char, String
short	short, int, long, String

Written Message Type	Read Message Type
int	int, long, String
long	long, String
float	float, double, String
double	double, String
String	String, boolean, byte, short, int, long, float, double
byte[ ]	byte[ ]

The following sample lines send a stream message to a topic destination (pub/sub):

```
StreamMessage theStreamMessage =
session.createStreamMessage();
theStreamMessage.writeString("Alaska");
theStreamMessage.writeShort(49);
myTopicPublisher.publish(theStreamMessage);
```

If the destination is a queue type (p2p), you only need to change the sender method as follows:

```
StreamMessage theStreamMessage =
session.createStreamMessage();
theStreamMessage.writeString("Alaska");
theStreamMessage.writeShort(49);
myQueueSender.send(theStreamMessage);
```

When the message arrives at the consumer, it is extracted by the readXXX() methods and assigned to a proper type variable. As an example, you can extract the stream type message from the preceding example like this:

```
StreamMessage recStreamMessage = (StreamMessage)message;
String stateName = recStreamMessage.readString();
int stateNo = recStreamMessage. readShort();
```

Because some data types of the message written can be read in another data type by obeying formal conversion rules, the last line of the reading example can be written like this:

```
int stateNo = recStreamMessage. readInt();
```

or

```
int stateNo = recStreamMessage. readLong();
```

Summary

In this chapter, you learned the concepts of JMS programming and the basics of JMS API programming techniques. I started this chapter by explaining the definition of a messaging service and its major features. The messaging system is based on message-oriented middleware (MOM), which was explained in the previous chapter. Advantages and disadvantages of using a messaging system were then discussed prior to providing information about the JMS API.

The JMS API, which is built onto the J2EE 1.3 platform specifications, covers point-to-point and publish-and-subscriber messaging models used in MOM providers.

In this chapter, you learned the concepts of JMS programming including its architecture, message consumption, destination, connection factory, connection, session, message producer, message consumer, and message listener.

I also showed you how to create two administered objects, ConnectionFactory and Destination, and how to use them in JMS messaging applications.

I explained synchronous messaging and asynchronous messaging and compared the two models. You also learned about message structure and different message types in the JMS specifications.

Although I provided some information about JMS programming concepts and techniques, more details such as methods of some interfaces are discussed in Appendix D. Many concepts were explained using a few sample lines of code, but you can find complete and more valuable examples in the next chapter.

Questions and Answers

1. If there is no ConnectionFactory object created by the JMS provider administrator, what can I do?

A ConnectionFactory object is an administered object and must be created by the JMS provider administrator. If there is no ConnectionFactory object created, you can use the default ConnectionFactory object. You will learn more detailed information in the section, "Basic Steps to Write a JMS Application," in the next chapter.

2. If there is no Destination object created by the JMS provider administrator, what can I do?

A Destination object is an administered object like the ConnectionFactory object and must be created by the JMS provider administrator. If there is no Destination object created, you cannot use the JMS API for messaging. There is no default Destination object.

3. If I do not specify a value for the time-to-live method of the Message interface, what will happen to the message if the receiver is inactive?

If you do not specify a time for time-to-live, it means that the message will never expire. The message will be delivered whenever the receiver client is available, depending on the messaging model you are using.

4. Can I create two or more connections to send messages?

Yes, you can. Some advanced applications might use several connections. But a connection is a relatively heavyweight object. Therefore, only one connection is preferred. If you need to, you can create two or more sessions—which are lightweight JMS objects—and a number of message producers and consumers to send messages on different channels.

5. If I use transacted messaging and if the connection or session is closed in the middle of transmitting without an acknowledgment, what will happen to the message that is not sent to the destination?

In this case, the JMS provider will call the `rollback()` method, the messages that are not delivered will be deleted, and the messages already delivered to the destination will be removed from the destination by a JMS provider. The recipient will not receive any messages.

6. I want to filter some messages that should not be delivered to the consumer. How can I define a field in a message selector for some values in the message body?

A message selector only works with header and property fields. You cannot filter messages based on values in the message body.

7. In the message received, there is a ReplyTo field. If this destination is not created, how can I send a message to the destination specified in a ReplyTo field?

You can create a temporary destination dynamically. During the session, the connection is open, so you can send the message to this temporary destination. Whenever the connection is closed, this destination is removed along with the messages that have not yet been delivered.

JMS Programming Techniques with Examples

THUS FAR, YOU HAVE BEEN BOMBARDED with lots of concepts, classes, interfaces, methods, and sample lines of code. If you have not had previous message-based programming experience, you must be a little confused by some of the new concepts discussed. You might still have some questions in your mind, but they will be answered after you work with the samples I have provided later in this chapter. The examples in the chapter are aimed at making Java Message Service (JMS) programming techniques clearer for developers.

Basic Steps for Writing a JMS Application

Before looking at the sample JMS applications, I'll summarize the basic steps for writing JMS applications. If you need more detailed information on the fundamentals of the JMS API, refer to Chapter 5, "Concepts and Fundamentals of JMS Programming."

1. Obtain a ConnectionFactory through the Java Naming Directory Interface (JNDI), which is an administered JMS object. If a JMS administrator has not created a ConnectionFactory, you can use the default object (QueueConnectionFactory or TopicConnectionFactory depending on the messaging model you are using in the application you develop). If the messaging model is point-to-point (p2p), lookup lines in the application will look like this:

```
QueueConnectionFactory myQueueConnectionFactory = (QueueConnectionFactory)
ctx.lookup("QueueConnectionFactory");
```

If the messaging model is publish-and-subscribe (pub/sub), lookup lines in the application will look like this:

```
TopicConnectionFactory myTopicConnectionFactory = (TopicConnectionFactory)
➥ctx.lookup("TopicConnectionFactory");
```

2. Obtain the destinations from JNDI, which you will use to send and receive messages. Destinations are also administered and should be created by the JMS administrator.

For example, assume that a JMS administrator created a queue named queue_Asia for a p2p messaging model. The line in the application code for lookup might look like this:

```
Queue myQueue = (Queue) ctx.lookup("queue_Asia");
```

Or, assume that a JMS administrator created a topic named topic_GreenHouse for a pub/sub messaging model. The line in the application code for lookup might look like this:

```
Topic myTopic = (Topic) ctx.lookup("topic_GreenHouse");
```

3. Create a connection to the JMS provider by using the ConnectionFactory. It creates a virtual connection to the JMS provider.

You can create a connection for a p2p model like this:

```
QueueConnection myQueueConnection =
    myQueueConnectionFactory.createQueueConnection();
```

You can create a connection for a pub/sub model like this:

```
TopicConnection myTopicConnection =
    myTopicConnectionFactory.createTopicConnection();
```

4. Create a session by using the connection. A session is a single-threaded context to produce and consume the messages in a messaging system. After creating a connection, you should create a session that creates message producers, message consumers, and messages.

In a p2p messaging model, you can create a session like this:

```
QueueSession myQueueSession =
    myQueueConnection.createQueueSession(false,
        Session.AUTO_ACKNOWLEDGE);
```

In a pub/sub messaging model, you can create a session like this:

```
TopicSession myTopicSession =
    myTopicConnection.createTopicSession(false,
        Session.AUTO_ACKNOWLEDGE);
```

5. Create a message producer by using the session and destination objects for client applications to send the message.

   In a p2p messaging model, you can create a message producer object by using the QueueSender interface in the client code like this:

```
QueueSender myQueueSender =
    myQueueSession.createSender(myQueue);
```

   In a pub/sub messaging model, you can create a message producer object by using TopicPublisher interface in the client code like this:

```
TopicPublisher myTopicPublisher =
    myTopicSession.createPublisher(myTopic);
```

6. Create a message consumer by using the session and destination objects for client applications to receive the message synchronously.

   In a synchronous p2p messaging model, you can create a message consumer object by using QueueReceiver interface in the client code like this:

```
QueueReceiver myQueueReceiver =
    myQueueSession.createReceiver(myQueue);
```

   In a synchronous pub/sub messaging model, you can create a message consumer object by using TopicSubscriber interface in the client code like this:

```
TopicSubscriber myTopicSubscriber =
    myTopicSession.createSubscriber(myTopic);
```

7. Assign a message listener for asynchronous messages. A message listener is an object that acts as an asynchronous event handler for messages. There is one method, onMessage(), in a message listener class, which implements the MessageListener interface. Write a message listener class that contains the onMessage() method. Then, register the message listener with the current QueueReceiver or TopicSubscriber object through the setMessageListener() method for asynchronous messaging.

You can register the message listener for a queue type messaging model like this:

```
ClassQueueListener myQueueListener = new ClassQueueListener();
myQueueReceiver.setMessageListener(myQueueListener);
```

You can register the message listener for a topic type messaging model like this:

```
ClassTopicListener myTopicListener = new ClassTopicListener ();
myTopicSubscriber.setMessageListener(myTopicListener);
```

8. Create and send the message with the producer object. To send the message, use the `send()` method or `publish()` method as follows.

For a p2p model, you can send the message using the `send()` method like this:

```
myQueueSender.send(message);
```

For a pub/sub model, you can send the message using the `publish()` method like this:

```
myTopicPublisher.publish(message);
```

9. Receive and read the message with the consumer object. To receive the message, use the `receive()` method as follows.

For a p2p model, you can receive the message using the `receive()` method like this:

```
Message theMessageReceived = myQueueReceiver.receive();
```

For a pub/sub model, you can receive the message using the `receive()` method like this:

```
Message theMessageReceived = myTopicReceiver.receive();
```

Notice that the `receive()` method is used for receiving and reading messages for both the p2p and pub/sub models, unlike sender methods for sending the messages, which are `send()` and `publish()`.

A p2p Messaging Example

In this section, I provide an example for the p2p messaging model. This example shows you how to write a simple JMS application. It introduces you to the fundamentals of JMS programming techniques. You can develop a more sophisticated project by using this simple idea. A p2p JMS application has two parts: a *sender client application* and a *receiver client application*. You will learn about these applications in the next two sections.

The sender application, whose source code is provided in Listing 6.1, sends a text type message to the "queue_Montreal" queue type destination. The receiver application, whose source code is provided in Listing 6.2, reads the message from the "queue_Montreal" queue type destination and displays the received message on the screen.

A Sender-Client Application for the p2p Messaging Model

In this section, you learn how to write a sender application for a p2p messaging model step-by-step. I then provide the entire source code listing.

1. When you develop a JMS application regardless of the model you are using, you should create a JNDI context object. For example:

```
jndiContext = new InitialContext();
```

2. You then have to look up the connection factory and queue. Both are administered objects and are created by a JMS provider administrator. If a connection is not created, you can use the default connection factory, which is QueueConnectionFactory. You can use the following sample code lines in the JMS application. The variable cityQueueName represents the administered queue object. It must be given or defined before these lines in your application:

```
queueConnectionFactory = (QueueConnectionFactory)
    jndiContext.lookup("QueueConnectionFactory");
 queue = (Queue) jndiContext.lookup(cityQueueName);
```

3. You then need to create a connection and a session. For example:

```
queueConnection =
    queueConnectionFactory.createQueueConnection();
queueSession =
    queueConnection.createQueueSession(false,
        Session.AUTO_ACKNOWLEDGE);
```

In the preceding line, the session is not transacted, and the receiver will automatically acknowledge whenever it reads the message.

4. You need to create a sender and the message before sending the message. In this example, the message type is a text message, and it is set using the `setText()` method:

```
queueSender = queueSession.createSender(queue);
message = queueSession.createTextMessage();
message.setText("A message to demonstrate p2p model- LE");
```

5. You can send the message as follows:

```
queueSender.send(message);
```

6. You must send an end-of-stream message to finish sending the message. It can be nontext or an empty string message as in this example. The lines might look like this:

```
queueSender.send(queueSession.createMessage());
```

7. Close the session and connection to release the resources allocated for the application from the JMS provider like this:

```
queueConnection.close();
```

The entire source code is provided in Listing 6.1, which includes exception controls and other informative code lines. I explain how to run this application after I discuss the receiver application.

Listing 6.1   **Sender Application Source Code for a p2p Model**

```
1. import javax.jms.*;
2. import javax.naming.*;
3.
4. public class JMSBookQueueSender {
5.
6.   public static void main(String[] args) {
7.
8.   // Creating JMS object variables
9.   String   cityQueueName = "queue_Montreal";
10.  Context  jndiContext = null;
11.  QueueConnectionFactory  queueConnectionFactory = null;
12.  QueueConnection  queueConnection = null;
13.  QueueSession queueSession = null;
14.  Queue   queue = null;
15.  QueueSender  queueSender = null;
16.  TextMessage  message = null;
17.  System.out.println("Queue name is " + cityQueueName);
18.  // Creating a JNDI InitialContext object
19.   try {
20.       jndiContext = new InitialContext();
21.       } catch (NamingException e) {
22.       System.out.print("Error while creating JNDI ");
23.       System.out.println("context: " + e.toString());
24.       }
25.  // Looking up connection factory and queue
26.   try {
27.       queueConnectionFactory = (QueueConnectionFactory)
28.       jndiContext.lookup("QueueConnectionFactory");
29.       queue = (Queue)jndiContext.lookup(cityQueueName);
30.       } catch (NamingException e) {
31.       System.out.print("JNDI lookup queue failed: ");
32.       System.out.println(e.toString());
34.       }
35.  // Creating connection, session (not transacted)
36.   try {
37.       queueConnection =
```

```
38.          queueConnectionFactory.createQueueConnection();
39.      queueSession =
40.          queueConnection.createQueueSession(false,
41.          Session.AUTO_ACKNOWLEDGE);
42.  // Creating sender and text message
43.      queueSender = queueSession.createSender(queue);
44.      message = queueSession.createTextMessage();
45.      message.setText("A message to demonstrate p2p
46.          model- LE");
47.      System.out.print("Message to be sent: '");
48.      System.out.println(message.getText()+" '");
49.  // sending the message
50.      queueSender.send(message);
51.  // sending a non-text control message to end sending
52.      queueSender.send(queueSession.createMessage());
53.      System.out.print("Sending the message to ");
54.      System.out.println(cityQueueName + " is done");
55.      } catch (JMSException e) {
56.      System.out.print("Error while sending the ");
57.      System.out.println("message: " + e.toString());
58.      } finally {
59.  // closing the connection
60.          if (queueConnection != null) {
61.              try {
62.                  queueConnection.close();
63.                  } catch (JMSException e) {}
64.          } //end of if
65.      } //end of finally
66.  } //end of the main
67. } //end of class
```

A Receiver-Client Application for the p2p Messaging Model

In this section, you learn how to write a receiver application for the p2p messaging model step-by-step. I then provide the entire source code listing at the end of the section.

1. When you develop a JMS application regardless of the model you are using, you should create a JNDI context object as you do in the sender application. For example:

```
jndiContext = new InitialContext();
```

2. You then have to look up the connection factory and queue. Both are administered objects and are created by the JMS provider administrator. The variable cityQueueName represents the administered queue object, which must be given or defined before these lines in your application:

```
queueConnectionFactory = (QueueConnectionFactory)
    jndiContext.lookup("QueueConnectionFactory");
queue = (Queue) jndiContext.lookup(cityQueueName);
```

3. You need to create a connection and a session as follows:

```
queueConnection =
  queueConnectionFactory.createQueueConnection();
queueSession =
  queueConnection.createQueueSession(false,
    Session.AUTO_ACKNOWLEDGE);
```

In the preceding line, session is not transacted, and the receiver will automatically acknowledge whenever it reads the message.

4. You then create a receiver and start the message delivery. The lines might look like this:

```
queueReceiver = queueSession.createReceiver(queue);
queueConnection.start();
```

5. Once you receive the message, you assign it to a proper variable as follows:

```
Message myMessage = queueReceiver.receive();
message = (TextMessage) myMessage;
```

6. You then read an end-of-stream message to stop receiving the message. If you read a nontext or empty string message, you can stop reading by calling a break in an "if-else clause."

7. Close the session and connection to release the resources allocated for the application from the JMS provider like this:

```
queueConnection.close();
```

The entire source code is provided in Listing 6.2, which includes exception controls and other informative code lines. I explain how to run this client application with the sender application in the next section.

Listing 6.2 **Receiver Application Source Code for a p2p Model**

```
1. import javax.jms.*;
2. import javax.naming.*;
3.
4.  public class JMSBookQueueReceiver {
5.
6.  public static void main(String[] args) {
7.
8.  // Creating JMS object variables
9.  String   cityQueueName = "queue_Montreal";
10. Context  jndiContext = null;
11. QueueConnectionFactory  queueConnectionFactory = null;
12. QueueConnection  queueConnection = null;
13. QueueSession queueSession = null;
```

```
14.  Queue   queue = null;
15.  QueueSender  queueSender = null;
16.  TextMessage  message = null;
17.  System.out.println("Queue name is " + cityQueueName);
18.  // Creating a JNDI InitialContext object
19.   try {
20.       jndiContext = new InitialContext();
21.       } catch (NamingException e) {
22.       System.out.print("Error while creating JNDI ");
23.       System.out.println("context: " + e.toString());
24.       }
25.  // Looking up connection factory and queue
26.   try {
27.       queueConnectionFactory = (QueueConnectionFactory)
28.       jndiContext.lookup("QueueConnectionFactory");
29.       queue = (Queue)jndiContext.lookup(cityQueueName);
30.       } catch (NamingException e) {
31.       System.out.print("JNDI lookup queue failed: ");
32.       System.out.println(e.toString());
34.       }
35.  // Creating connection, session (not transacted)
36.   try {
37.     queueConnection =
38.       queueConnectionFactory.createQueueConnection();
39.     queueSession =
40.       queueConnection.createQueueSession(false,
41.       Session.AUTO_ACKNOWLEDGE);
42.  // Creating receiver, then starting message delivery
43.     queueReceiver = queueSession.createReceiver(queue);
44.     queueConnection.start();
45.     System.out.println("Ready to receive the message ");
46.       while (true) {
47.  // Receiving all text messages from the queue
48.         Message myMes = queueReceiver.receive();
49.           if (myMes != null) {
50.             if (myMes instanceof TextMessage) {
51.               message = (TextMessage) myMes;
52.               System.out.print("Reading message from : '");
53.               System.out.print(cityQueueName + "' ");
54.               System.out.println(message.getText());
55.             } else {
56.  // Stop receiving when the message
57.  // is end of stream from the queue
58.     System.out.println("Finished reading message ");
59.               break;
60.             } //end of if myMes instanceof
61.           } // end of if (myMes…)
62.         } //end of while
63.       } catch (JMSException e) {
64.       System.out.print("Error while receiving the ");
65.       System.out.println("message: " + e.toString());
```

continues

Listing 6.2   **Continued**

```
66.     } finally {
67. // closing the connection
68.   if (queueConnection != null) {
69.     try {
70.       queueConnection.close();
71.     } catch (JMSException e) {}
72.   } //end of finally
73. }
74.  } //end of main
75.} //end of class
```

Running p2p Client Applications

The final step is to run the p2p sender and receiver JMS applications. As you
know, JMS is part of the Java 2 Enterprise Edition (J2EE). Therefore, you
should first start the JMS provider. In this book, I show and test all applications
on the J2EE Reference Implementation provided by Sun. If you use this free
software, type **j2ee –verbose** at the command line to start J2EE and the JMS
server. If you see the following lines at the end of the command window, you
can run the JMS application as part of J2EE:

> Starting JMS service...

Initialization complete - waiting for client requests

..... // Other lines of command window of J2EE server

....

> J2EE server startup complete

The displayed messages might be different in your JMS provider, but you have
to make sure that J2EE and the JMS server are started properly.

You then need to create administered objects. For this example, you only
need to create a queue type destination. In both client applications, I used the
default connection factory, but the queue name "queue_Montreal" must be
created by the JMS administrator. In the J2EE Reference Implementation,
open a new command window and type the following:

j2eeadmin -addJmsDestination queue_Montreal queue

It will create a queue type destination named "queue_Montreal" (see
Figure 6.1). If this queue is successfully created, you will not receive any
error messages. If you want to see whether the destination is properly created,
you can check it by using j2eeadmin again.

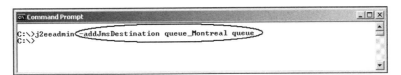

Figure 6.1   Starting J2EE and the JMS server.

Type the following in the command window (see Figure 6.2):

j2eeadmin –listJmsDestination

You will see the "queue_Montreal" destination in the destination list if it has
been properly created.

```
Command Prompt                                                    _ □ ×
C:\>j2eeadmin -addJmsDestination queue_Montreal queue
C:\>j2eeadmin -listJmsDestination
JmsDestination
------------
< JMS Destination : jms/Topic , javax.jms.Topic >
< JMS Destination : lev01 , javax.jms.Queue >
< JMS Destination : jms/Queue , javax.jms.Queue >
< JMS Destination : queue_Montreal , javax.jms.Queue >
C:\>_
```

Figure 6.2   Checking the destination by using the j2eeadmin command.

After you create the destination, open two additional command windows to
run the receiver and sender applications. Change the directory to the location
in which you compiled the sender application, which is
JMSBookQueueSender.class, and the receiver application, which is
JMSBookQueueReceiver.class. (This assumes that you wrote the source code
and compiled it without any syntax errors.)

   You can run the application in two ways. Let's run the sender and then the
receiver application. Type the following in the command window:

java JMSBookQueueSender

The application will send the message "A message to demonstrate p2p model-
LE" to the queue destination "queue_Montreal" (see Figure 6.3).

```
Command Prompt                                                    _ □ ×
C:\Javatest>java JMSBookQueueSender
Queue name is queue_Montreal
Java(TM) Message Service 1.0.2 Reference Implementation (build b14)
Message to be sent 'A message to demonstrate p2p model- LE '
Sending the message to queue_Montreal is done

C:\Javatest>
```

Figure 6.3   Running the sender JMS application in the first order.

To run the receiver application, type the following in the other command window:

java JMSBookQueueReceiver

The application will receive the message, "A message to demonstrate p2p model- LE," from the queue destination, "queue_Montreal" (see Figure 6.4).

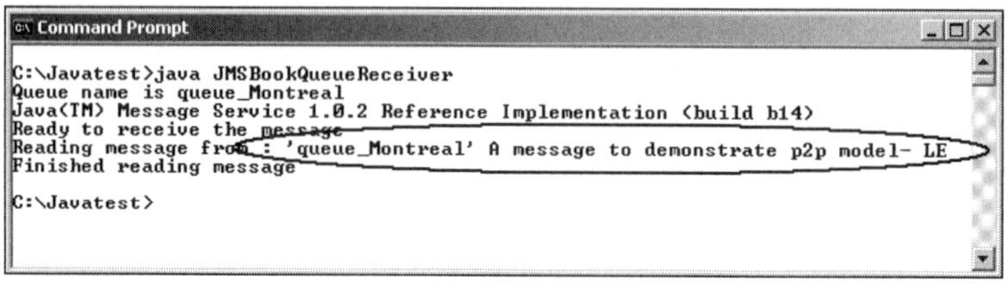

Figure 6.4   Running the receiver JMS application in the second order.

Because you sent the message and it is retained in the JMS server, the receiver reads the message whenever it is connected to the server. It does not wait. Now, let's change the running order. Run the receiver application as shown in Figure 6.5.

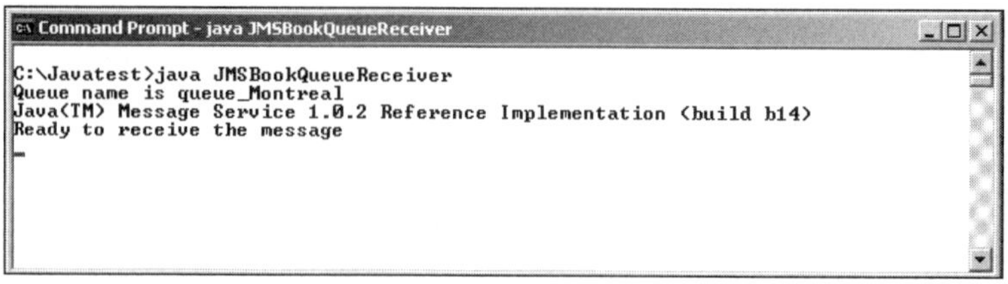

Figure 6.5   Running the receiver JMS application in the first order.

Notice that there is no message in the destination. The receiver is waiting for the message. Run the sender application as shown in Figure 6.6 to send a message to the destination.

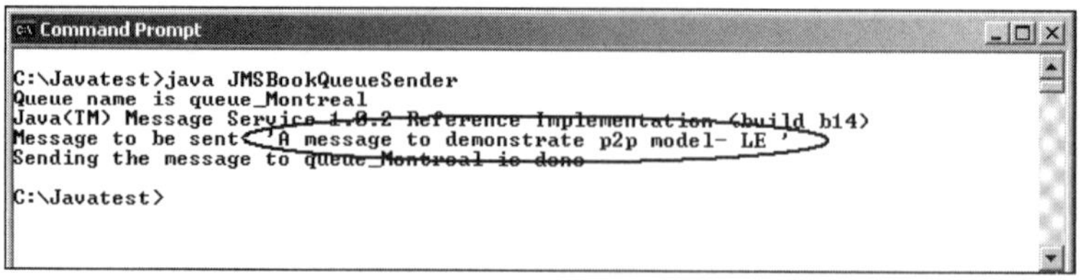

Figure 6.6   Running the sender JMS application in the second order.

Whenever you send the message from the sender application, the message is delivered to the receiver application. I recommend you try to run both applications in two separate windows at the same time, but first run the receiver, and then run the sender as in Figure 6.7.

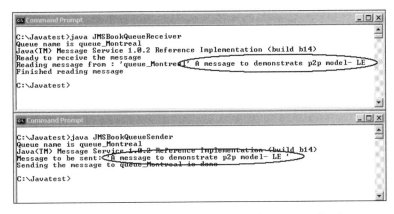

Figure 6.7   Running the receiver and sender JMS applications.

A pub/sub Messaging Example

In the previous section, a p2p messaging example was provided to help you understand the concepts and techniques of JMS programming. This section is aimed at making the JMS programming techniques clear for the developer as well. I provide an example for the asynchronous pub/sub messaging model. Again, this example shows how to write a simple JMS application. It introduces you to the fundamentals of JMS programming techniques. You can develop a more sophisticated project by using this simple idea.

An asynchronous pub/sub JMS application has three parts:

- MessageListener
- Publisher client application
- Subscriber client application

These applications are discussed in the following sections.

A MessageListener application, whose source code is provided in Listing 6.3, is a helper class for the subscriber application to receive and process a message. The subscriber application registers to the message listener class, and whenever a message arrives at the destination, the onMessage() method of the message listener class is invoked to read the message.

The publisher application, whose source code is provided in Listing 6.4, publishes a text type message to the "topic_Math" topic type destination.

The subscriber application, whose source code is provided in Listing 6.5, reads the message from the "topic_Math" topic type destination and displays the received message on the screen via the message listener's onMessage() method.

A Message Listener for a pub/sub Client Application

If you develop pub/sub messaging and you want it to be asynchronous, you need to use a message listener, which consists of the onMessage() method. Whenever the message is published to the topic, a JMS provider calls the consumer's onMessage() method to take the message from the topic. Basically, you have to process the message in this method. It should be in the same package or class directory as the subscriber client application. In the subscriber application, you need to create an instance from this helper class.

For the pub/sub example, the message listener source code is provided in Listing 6.3.

Listing 6.3   **Message Listener Source Code for a pub/sub Model**

```
1. import javax.jms.*;
2. public class JMSBookListener implements MessageListener {
3.
4.    // passing the message from the destination as a parameter
5.    public void onMessage(Message parMessage) {
6.      TextMessage myMessage = null;
7.      try {
8.      // check the message type is TextMessage
9.      if (parMessage instanceof TextMessage) {
10.     // if so, cast it into TextMessage variable
11.     myMessage = (TextMessage) parMessage;
12.     // reading and returning the message in Text format
13.     System.out.print("Message received from the topic: ");
14.     System.out.println(myMessage.getText());
15.     } else {
16.     // if not, warn the user
17.     System.out.println("Message of wrong type: " );
18.     System.out.println(parMessage.getClass().getName());
19.     }
20.     // throw the Exceptions if there are internal errors
21.   } catch (JMSException ejms) {
22.       System.out.print("JMSException in onMessage(): " );
23.       System.out.println(ejms.toString());
24.   } catch (Throwable tjms) {
25.       System.out.print("Exception in onMessage(): ");
```

```
26.      System.out.println(tjms.getMessage());
27.  } //end of try
28.  } //end of onMessage() method
29.  } //end of class
```

A Publisher Client Application for the pub/sub Messaging Model

In this section, you learn how to write a publisher application for a pub/sub messaging model step-by-step. Later in the section, the entire source code listing is provided.

1. When you develop a JMS application, regardless of the model you are using, you should create a JNDI context object. For example:

   ```
   jndiContext = new InitialContext();
   ```

2. You then have to look up the connection factory and topic. Both are administered objects and are created by a JMS provider administrator. If a connection factory is not created, you can use the default connection factory, which is TopicConnectionFactory. You can use the following code lines for your JMS application. The variable interestTopicName represents the administered topic object. It must be given or defined before these lines in your application:

   ```
   topicConnectionFactory = (TopicConnectionFactory)
     jndiContext.lookup("TopicConnectionFactory");
   topic = (Topic) jndiContext.lookup(interestTopicName);
   ```

3. You then need to create a connection and session as follows:

   ```
   topicConnection =
     topicConnectionFactory.createTopicConnection();
   topicSession =
     topicConnection.createTopicSession(false,
        Session.AUTO_ACKNOWLEDGE);
   ```

   In the preceding line, session is not transacted, and the subscriber automatically acknowledges whenever it reads the message.

4. You must create a publisher and the message before publishing the message. For this example, the message type is a text message, and it is set using the setText() method. The lines might look like this:

   ```
   topicPublisher = topicSession.createPublisher(topic);
   message = topicSession.createTextMessage();
   message.setText("A message to demonstrate pub/sub model- LE");
   ```

5. You publish the message as follows:

```
topicPublisher.publish(message);
```

6. Close the session and the connection to release the resources allocated for the application from the JMS provider like this:

```
topicConnection.close();
```

The entire source code is provided in Listing 6.4, which includes exception controls and other informative code lines. I explain how to run this application after I discuss the subscriber application.

Listing 6.4 Publisher Application Source Code for a pub/sub Model

```
1. import javax.jms.*;
2. import javax.naming.*;
3.
4. public class JMSBookTopicPublisher {
5.
6.  public static void main(String[] args) {
7.
8.   // Creating JMS object variables
9.   String           interestTopicName = "topic_Math";
10.  Context          jndiContext = null;
11.  TopicConnectionFactory  topicConnectionFactory = null;
12.  TopicConnection        topicConnection = null;
13.  TopicSession           topicSession = null;
14.  Topic                  topic = null;
15.  TopicPublisher         topicPublisher = null;
16.  TextMessage            message = null;
17.  System.out.println("Topic name is " + interestTopicName);
18.
19.  // Creating a JNDI InitialContext object
20.  try {
21.   jndiContext = new InitialContext();
22.  } catch (NamingException enaming) {
23.   System.out.print("Error while creating JNDI " );
24.   System.out.println("context: " + enaming.toString());
25.  }
26.
27.  // Looking up connection factory and queue
28.  try {
29.   topicConnectionFactory = (TopicConnectionFactory)
30.      jndiContext.lookup("TopicConnectionFactory");
31.   topic = (Topic)jndiContext.lookup(interestTopicName);
32.  } catch (NamingException enaming) {
33.   System.out.println("JNDI lookup topic failed: " );
34.   System.out.println(enaming.toString());
35.  }
```

```
36.
37.  try {
38.  // Creating connection, session (not transacted)
39.  topicConnection =
40.    topicConnectionFactory.createTopicConnection();
41.  topicSession =
42.    topicConnection.createTopicSession(false,
43.      Session.AUTO_ACKNOWLEDGE);
44.
45.  // Creating publisher and text message
46.  topicPublisher = topicSession.createPublisher(topic);
47.  message = topicSession.createTextMessage();
48.  message.setText("A message to demonstrate pub/sub model- LE");
49.
50.  System.out.print("Message to be published: '" );
51.  System.out.println(message.getText()+" '");
52.
53.  // publishing the message
54.  topicPublisher.publish(message);
55.  System.out.println("Publishing the message to " );
56.  System.out.println(interestTopicName + " is done");
57.
58.  } catch (JMSException ejms) {
59.    System.out.println("Error while publishing ");
60.    System.out.println("the message: " + ejms.toString());
61.  } finally {
62.    if (topicConnection != null) {
63.        try {
64.            topicConnection.close();
65.        } catch (JMSException ejms) {}
66.    }
67.  }
68.
69.  }  //end of the main
70. }  //end of class
```

A Subscriber Client Application for the pub/sub Messaging Model

In this section, you learn how to write a subscriber application for a pub/sub messaging model step-by-step. Later in the section, the entire source code listing is provided.

1. When you develop a JMS application, regardless of the model you are using, you should create a JNDI context object as you do in a publisher application. For example:

   ```
   jndiContext = new InitialContext();
   ```

2. You then have to look up a connection factory and topic. Both are administered objects and are created by a JMS provider administrator. If a connection factory is not created, you can use the default connection factory, which is TopicConnectionFactory. You can use the following lines in your JMS application. The variable interestTopicName represents the administered topic object. It must be given or defined before these lines in your application:

```
topicConnectionFactory = (TopicConnectionFactory)
    jndiContext.lookup("TopicConnectionFactory");
topic = (Topic) jndiContext.lookup(interestTopicName);
```

3. You then need to create a connection and a session as follows:

```
topicConnection =
    topicConnectionFactory.createTopicConnection();
topicSession =
    topicConnection.createTopicSession(false,
        Session.AUTO_ACKNOWLEDGE);
```

In the preceding line, a session is not transacted, and a subscriber automatically acknowledges whenever it reads the message.

4. You create a subscriber like this:

```
topicSubscriber =
                topicSession.createSubscriber(topic);
```

5. For asynchronous messaging, you need to register the message listener like this:

```
topicListener = new JMSBookListener();
topicSubscriber.setMessageListener(topicListener);
```

6. The lines to start the message delivery might look like this:

```
topicConnection.start();
```

7. The message listener will then take the message from the topic. You should keep the subscriber active to keep receiving the message. You can do this with a *while* loop like this:

```
inputStreamReader = new InputStreamReader(System.in);
    while (!(last == '*')) {
        last = (char) inputStreamReader.read();
    }
```

8. Close the session and the connection to release the resources allocated for the application from the JMS provider like this:

```
topicConnection.close();
```

The entire source code is provided in Listing 6.5, which includes exception controls and other informative code lines. I explain how to run this client application and the publisher application in the next section.

Listing 6.5 **Subscriber Application Source Code for a pub/sub Model**

```
1. import javax.jms.*;
2. import javax.naming.*;
3. import java.io.*;
4.
5. public class JMSBookTopicSubscriber {
6.
7.    public static void main(String[] args) {
8.    // Creating JMS object variables
9.    String            interestTopicName = "topic_Math";
10.   Context           jndiContext = null;
11.   TopicConnectionFactory  topicConnectionFactory = null;
12.   TopicConnection         topicConnection = null;
13.   TopicSession            topicSession = null;
14.   Topic                   topic = null;
15.   TopicSubscriber         topicSubscriber = null;
16.   JMSBookListener         topicListener = null;
17.   TextMessage             message = null;
18.   InputStreamReader       inputStreamReader = null;
19.   char                    last = '\0';
20.
21.     System.out.println("Topic name is " + interestTopicName);
22.
23.   // Creating a JNDI InitialContext object
24.   try {
25.       jndiContext = new InitialContext();
26.   } catch (NamingException enaming) {
27.       System.out.print("Error while creating JNDI ");
28.       System.out.println("context: " + enaming.toString());
29.   }
30.   // Looking up connection factory and queue
31.   try {
32.     topicConnectionFactory = (TopicConnectionFactory)
33.     jndiContext.lookup("TopicConnectionFactory");
34.     topic = (Topic)jndiContext.lookup(interestTopicName);
35.   } catch (NamingException enaming) {
36.     System.out.print("JNDI lookup topic failed: ");
37.     System.out.println(enaming.toString());
38.   }
39.
40.    try {
41.      // Creating connection, session (not transacted)
42.      topicConnection =
43.          topicConnectionFactory.createTopicConnection();
44.      topicSession =
```

Listing 6.5 **Continued**

```
45.          topicConnection.createTopicSession(false,
46.              Session.AUTO_ACKNOWLEDGE);
47.
48. // Creating subscriber
49.    topicSubscriber =
50.         topicSession.createSubscriber(topic);
51.
52. // Registering message listener with JMSBookListener helper class
53.    topicListener = new JMSBookListener();
54.    topicSubscriber.setMessageListener(topicListener);
55.
56. // Starting connection
57.    topicConnection.start();
58. // Control loop to end subscriber application
59. System.out.println("To end program, enter * and <return> key");
60.
61. inputStreamReader = new InputStreamReader(System.in);
62.    while (!(last == '*')) {
63.        try {
64.            last = (char) inputStreamReader.read();
65.        } catch (IOException eio) {
66.            System.out.print("I/O error occured: ");
67.            System.out.println(eio.toString());
68.        }
69.    } //end of while
70. } catch (JMSException ejms) {
71.     System.out.print("JMS Exception occurred: ");
72.     System.out.println(ejms.toString());
73. } finally {
74.     if (topicConnection != null) {
75.         try {
76.             topicConnection.close();
77.         } catch (JMSException ejms) {}
78.     } //end of if
79.    } //end of finally
80.
81.    } //end of the main
82. } //end of class
```

Running pub/sub Client Applications

The final step is to run the pub/sub publisher and subscriber JMS applications. As with a p2p application, you should type **j2ee –verbose** on the command line to start J2EE and the JMS server.

Make sure that J2EE and the JMS server are properly started. You then need to create administered objects for messaging. For this example, you only need to create a topic type destination. In both client applications, I used the default connection factory, but the topic name "topic_Math" must be created by the JMS administrator. Using the J2EE Reference Implementation, open a new command window and type the following line:

j2eeadmin –addJmsDestination topic_Math topic

If this topic is successfully created, you will not receive any error messages.

After you create the destination, open two additional command windows to run the publisher and subscriber applications. Change the directory to the location in which you located the sender application, which is JMSBookTopicPublisher.class, and the receiver application, which is JMSBookTopicSubscriber.class. (This assumes that you wrote the source code and compiled it without any syntax errors.) Do not forget to write and compile the JMSBookListener message listener Java file too. For this example, put the JMSBookListener.class in the same location as the publisher and subscriber.

Run the subscriber application first, and then run the publisher application. Type the following in the command window:

java JMSBookTopicSubscriber

The application will wait for a message that is sent to the topic "topic_Math." Run the subscriber application in two command windows to see whether the two subscriber applications will receive the same message from the publisher application (see Figure 6.8).

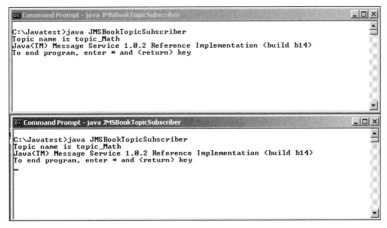

Figure 6.8   Running two subscriber JMS applications.

To run the publisher application, type the following in the other command window:

java JMSBookTopicSubscriber

The application will publish the message, "A message to demonstrate pub/sub model- LE," to the topic destination, "topic_Math." The other two subscribers will receive this message, as shown in Figure 6.9.

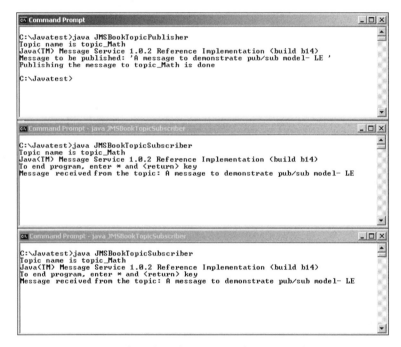

Figure 6.9   Running the subscriber JMS application in the second order.

Because a *while* loop was used, the subscriber application will keep waiting for the message from the topic. If you type "★" in the command window and press Enter, the subscriber application will be terminated.

A pub/sub Messaging Example with a Message Selector

In this section, you learn how to use the message selector and filter messages. Recall from Chapter 5, "Concepts and Fundamentals of JMS Programming," that you can filter messages before delivering them to a recipient by using criteria based on fields in the message header or message properties. In this example, I add a field to the message property and change it on different senders. I then filter this property in the receiver client application using a message selector. Recall that you cannot filter a message based on the message's content.

This example is built on the previous pub/sub example, whose source code is provided in Listings 6.3, 6.4, and 6.5. I will only show modified sections of the source code to save space.

A Message Listener for a pub/sub Client Application with a Message Selector

The source code for the message listener helper class discussed in this section is taken from Listing 6.3. In the subscriber application, if you use a message listener helper class with a different name, copy the message listener and save it with a new name in the location where the publisher and subscriber applications are. You should compile it, like any Java application, before using it with the subscriber application. If the name of the message listener helper class is changed, the subscriber class using the message listener helper class must reflect this new name. Otherwise, the subscriber class will use the old message listener helper class.

You can also modify the text to be displayed on the screen by rewriting code in the onMessage() method, although you do not need to change any lines in Listing 6.3.

A Publisher-Client Application for pub/sub with a Message Selector

For the pub/sub example with a message selector, you will modify the publisher client application source code in Listing 6.4. Because you need two publisher applications with different properties, copy this source code and save it using two different names. For this example, I will call one of the publisher applications "spring" and the other "summer." The entire source code for the application will not be repeated because of space considerations. Only the lines that are modified or added to the source code used in Listing 6.4 will be shown.

For this example, applications will publish and subscribe to a different topic named "FourSeason." Therefore, the first modification will be on line 9 of Listing 6.4 as follows:

```
String     interestTopicName = "FourSeason";
```

Do not forget to create the administered object "FourSeason" topic before running the applications. The displayed message to the user about the message content can be changed in line 48 of Listing 6.4. For the summer application, the line looks like this:

```
message.setText("Four Season Topic ** Season Name Property is Summer **");
```

For the spring application, the line looks like this:

```
message.setText("Four Season Topic ** Season Name Property is Spring **");
```

The last modification is to add a property to the source code. In the modified publisher applications, I will add a String type property called "SeasonName" to the message properties. In the spring application, its value will be "Spring," and in the summer application, its value will be "Summer." I will filter this property in the next section.

You can insert property lines after creating the message, but before sending the message. For this example, it is okay to add the lines before line 50 in Listing 6.4. For the summer application, the property line will look like this:

```
message.setStringProperty("SeasonName", "Summer");
```

For the spring application, the property line will look like this:

```
message.setStringProperty("SeasonName", "Spring");
```

After the modifications are made, save the files and compile them as you would any Java application. I will show you how to run these applications after providing information about the subscriber application.

A Subscriber Client Application for pub/sub with a Message Selector

For the pub/sub example with a message selector, you will modify the subscriber client application source code in Listing 6.5. Because you need two subscriber applications with different property filters, copy this source code and save it with two different names. I will name one subscriber application "spring" and the other "no_selector." I will not repeat the entire source code for the application. Instead, only the lines that have been modified or added to the source code in Listing 6.5 will be shown.

For this example, applications will publish and subscribe to a different topic named "FourSeason." Therefore, the first modification will be on line 9 of Listing 6.5 as follows:

```
String      interestTopicName = "FourSeason";
```

Do not forget to create an administered object "FourSeason" topic before running the application of it does not exist.

In the modified subscriber applications, I will add a message selector, which is a String type, and its content will filter a specific "SeasonName" property of the message. Because this selector will be used before creating a topic subscriber, you should add related lines before line 48 in Listing 6.5. For the spring subscriber application, a message selector line will look like this:

```
String springSelector = "SeasonName = 'Spring' ";
```

The no_selector application will not filter messages and will receive all messages delivered to the topic. Therefore, there is no need to create a message selector.

If you use a message selector, you need to modify the line for creating a subscriber for a topic session. For this example, you should rewrite line 50 in Listing 6.5 for the spring subscriber application as follows:

```
topicSession.createSubscriber(topic, springSelector, false);
```

You do not need to change this line for the no_selector subscriber application because a message selector is not used.

After the modifications are made, save the files, and then compile them as you would any Java application. I will show you how to run these applications in the next section.

Running pub/sub Client Applications with a Message Selector

To run the pub/sub publisher and subscriber JMS applications with a message selector, start the J2EE Reference Implementation by typing **j2ee –verbose** at the command line to start J2EE and the JMS server. Make sure that J2EE and the JMS server are properly started. You then need to create administered objects for messaging. For this example, you need to create a topic named "FourSeason."

After you create the destination, you need to open two command windows to run two publisher applications and open two additional command windows to run two subscriber applications. I will provide the order of running the applications to make the message selector usage clearer. Refer to the section "Running pub/sub Client Applications" for details on how to run the pub/sub applications. Only the results will be shown in this section.

Open two command windows to run the spring and no_selector subscriber applications, as shown in Figure 6.10.

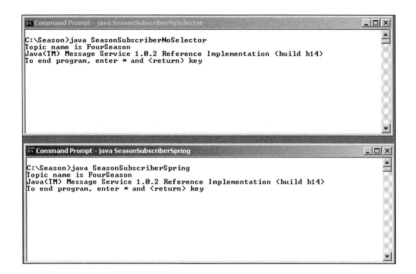

Figure 6.10   Running two subscriber JMS applications with a selector.

The subscriber applications are ready to read messages delivered to the "FourSeason" topic. Open two additional command windows to run the spring and summer publisher applications as shown in Figure 6.11.

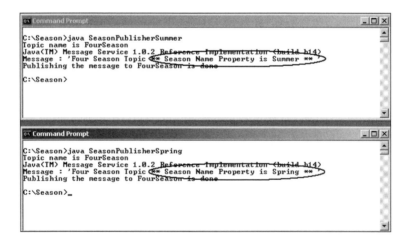

Figure 6.11   Running two publisher JMS applications with a selector.

The publisher applications send messages to the "FourSeason" topic, but because they have different values in their "SeasonName" property, they send different messages. This occurs even though their message content (message body) might be the same. In the example, I changed the message content to show that the messages are coming from different publishers. After publishing the message to the topic, the subscriber application windows will look like Figure 6.12.

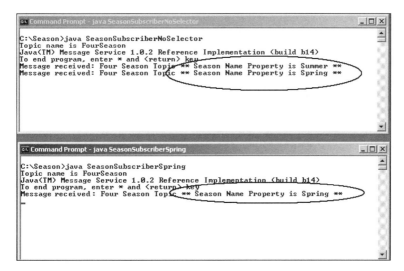

Figure 6.12   Subscriber JMS applications after publishing the message.

Notice that the spring subscriber application where the "SeasonName" property value is "Spring" has read only one message because of the message selector. The message, whose property "SeasonName" has a "Summer" value, is not delivered to the spring subscriber by means of a message selector. The no_selector subscriber has read both messages because there is no message selector on this application.

Summary

In this chapter, you were able to practice the concepts you learned in the previous chapter, and you learned how to apply programming techniques on a project using the JMS API. Four major topics were discussed in this chapter:

- I summarized the JMS programming steps for the p2p and pub/sub messaging models. Refer to section, "Basic Steps for Writing a JMS Application," whenever you need to remember these steps.

- I examined a simple p2p application. I explained the sender and receiver client applications step-by-step, provided entire source code listings of the applications, and showed you how to run them in two different orders.

- I examined a simple pub/sub application. I explained publisher and subscriber client applications step-by-step, provided entire source code listings of the applications, and showed you how to run them.

- I examined a pub/sub application with a message selector. I explained publisher and subscriber client applications step-by-step, provided the modified source code listings for the applications, and showed you how to run them.

The examples provided in this chapter are the simplest examples for a JMS project. You can develop more complicated (and useful) projects, but the skeleton of the applications will stay the same. You will find a more sophisticated application with source code and two application architectures without source code as final projects provided in Chapter 11, "Applications Using the JMS API."

Questions and Answers

1. Can two or more clients send a message to a queue type and a topic destination?

Yes. For a queue type destination, although it might seem like a peer-to-peer messaging model, one or more clients are able to send a message to the same queue. It is similar to many people sending a letter to one specific mailbox.

For a topic type destination, one or more clients are able to publish a message to the same topic. It is similar to many workers in a company putting a note on a board.

2. Can two or more clients receive a message from a queue type and a topic destination?

The answer is partially yes. For a topic type destination, one or more clients are able to subscribe to a message from the same topic. It's the nature of the pub/sub model. Many clients publish a message and many clients subscribe to the topic and read the message simultaneously. The messages are copies of the original message for each client.

For a queue type destination, many clients can receive the message, but a JMS server delivers the message to one client at a certain time. Each client receives a different message. Using a previous analogy, many people can send a letter to the same mailbox, but the owner of the mailbox must be the same person. Sometimes, two or more people can have identical keys for the same mailbox, but they visit the post office at different times. Only one of the key holders can pick up a particular letter, but the other owners cannot pick up the same letter because there is only one copy of the letter in the mailbox, and it has already been picked up by the other owner.

Java Message Service

7 JMS Realiability

8 JMS and XML

9 Message-Driven Beans

10 JMS and the Web

JMS Reliability

So FAR, YOU HAVE LEARNED THE BASIC CONCEPTS of JMS programming and how to write a simple JMS application. The most important goal of JMS is to properly deliver the message to the recipient. In this chapter, I will provide information about the level of reliability and performance for JMS applications.

What Is Reliability?

The first priority for JMS applications is to deliver the message once and only once. Many applications cannot tolerate dropped or duplicated messages. It is crucial that you not lose a message in the system for any reason because you will send the same message more than once. This issue is called *reliability*.

The most reliable way to produce a message is to send the message as a *persistent* message within a transaction. The most reliable way to consume a message is to receive the message from a durable subscription within a transaction. Additionally, you should not use a temporary queue to receive the message in a reliable way. Another aspect of the reliability issue is to set the priority level of the application.

Consider your project requirements when setting the reliability level because increasing the reliability level might not be as good for your project as you expect. The higher level of reliability, the more increased overhead and the less improved performance.

This chapter examines the reliability problem of the JMS API in two main topic areas: reliability supplied by software and reliability supplied by hardware. Software reliability is also considered the basic reliability mechanism and the advanced reliability mechanism. I will explain the reliability issues and other related considerations in detail throughout this chapter.

Basic Reliability Mechanisms

If you created a basic JMS application as discussed in the previous chapter, you probably applied the basic reliability mechanism to your project. These mechanisms can be examined in five subcategories:

- Message acknowledgment
- Message persistence
- Message priority level
- Message expiration
- Temporary destination

Some brief information about each category is provided in the following sections.

Message Acknowledgment

A message is consumed (received from a p2p client or a pub/sub client) by a JMS client, but the message is not considered consumed until the message has been acknowledged. A successful message consumption can be summarized as follows:

1. The JMS client reads the message (received from a p2p client or from a pub/sub client).

2. The JMS client processes the message properly.

3. The message is acknowledged. This acknowledgment can either be done by a JMS provider or by the JMS client. It depends on the session acknowledgment mode.

A JMS application and its sessions can be divided into two types according to the transaction type: *transacted sessions* and *nontransacted sessions*. An acknowledgment varies depending on the transaction type of the session.

If you have chosen a transacted session in your application, an acknowledgment will be done automatically when a transaction is committed. After all messages are received by the client, the entire message is acknowledged. If the transaction is rolled back, the message delivery will be stopped and all consumed messages are taken back from the recipient client. In this case, there is no acknowledgement because there is no properly delivered message.

If you have chosen a nontransacted session in your application, you have to specify how and when the message is acknowledged. Recall that you create a session for a p2p messaging model like this:

```
myQueueConnection.createQueueSession(param1, param2)
```

And you create a session for a pub/sub messaging model like this:

```
myTopicConnection.createTopicSession(param1, param2)
```

The myQueueConnection and myTopicConnection are connections that must be created before creating the sessions. Param1 is a boolean value that indicates whether the session is set to a transacted or nontransacted message delivery. If param1 value is true (transacted mode), the second parameter is ignored. If param1 value is false, the second parameter, param2, will define the acknowledgment mode. This parameter has three possible values:

- Session. AUTO_ACKNOWLEDGE—The session automatically acknowledges the message consumption. It can send the acknowledgment in two cases. First, it acknowledges whenever the client completes the `receive()` method call successfully. Second, it acknowledges whenever the MessageListener returns successfully after calling to process the message.

- Session. CLIENT_ACKNOWLEDGE—The client acknowledges the message by calling the message interface's `acknowledge()` method. This mode is a little different. Acknowledgment takes place on the session level. Whenever you use this method, you acknowledge all the messages that have been consumed by the client application session. For example, if a client consumes *n* messages and if this consumer acknowledges one of these *n* messages, all the *n* messages are acknowledged.

- Session. DUPS_OK_ACKNOWLEDGE—If you choose this value as an acknowledgment parameter, you allow a JMS provider to deliver some duplicated messages if the JMS provider fails. This option should only be used for consumers that can tolerate duplicate messages. The duplicate delivery option reduces session overhead because the session tries to prevent duplicate message delivery. (Do not forget to set the JMSRedelivered message header to true if you want the JMS provider to redeliver a message.)

Refer to Appendix D, "Overview of JMS Package Classes," for the methods used for acknowledgments, such as `receive()` or `acknowledge()`.

What Happens When the Session Terminates?

Before the message or messages are acknowledged, a session might terminate for some reason. The system behaves differently depending on the messaging model used.

If you use a p2p messaging model and the session (QueueSession) terminates, the JMS provider retains the messages that have been received, but not acknowledged by the consumer and redelivers them whenever the consumer accesses the queue.

If you use a pub/sub messaging model and the session (TopicSession) terminates, the JMS provider retains the messages that have been received, but not acknowledged by the consumer and redelivers them as long as the topic subscribing has been chosen as a *durable subscribe type*. If you have chosen *nondurable subscribing*, unacknowledged messages are dropped when the session terminates for any reason.

If you use queue or durable subscription, you should use the `recover()` method of the Session interface. Calling this method stops a nontransacted session and restarts the session with its first unacknowledged message. It does have one disadvantage, however. The pointer is reset to the point after its last acknowledged message. But the messages in the queue or topic might be different from the messages that were originally delivered. For example, some messages might be expired, or higher priority messages might have arrived.

Message Persistence

In a JMS application, you can specify the message persistence mode. The JMS API supports two delivery modes, which are described in the following list. Choose one of them depending on your project requirements.

- PERSISTENT—This delivery mode is the default delivery mode. In this mode, the JMS provider ensures that the message will not be lost during transmission to the client if the JMS provider fails for any reason. A message is stored in a storage area (a relational database or a flat file) when it is sent. The provider keeps the message in the storage area until the message is read by the client application. If the provider detects that the message is lost, it sends the message again unless it has received an acknowledgment from the receiver.

- NON_PERSISTENT—In this mode, the JMS provider is not obligated to save the message in a storage area for guaranteed delivery. If the JMS provider fails while transmitting the message to the recipient, there is no guarantee that the message is saved. It might be lost. You can increase performance with this mode because the server does not allocate additional resources to guarantee message delivery.

You can specify the delivery mode in two ways. First, you can use the `setDeliveryMode()` method of the MessageProducer interface. In your application, you can use a line like this:

```
setDeliveryMode(DeliveryMode.NON_PERSISTENT);
```

or

```
setDeliveryMode(DeliveryMode.PERSISTENT);
```

This method sets the producer's default delivery mode, which is PERSISTENT by default. It means that it will affect all messages sent by this producer.

Secondly, you can put the delivery mode into the `send()` or `publish()` method. For example, you might have a line like the following in your source code:

```
myQueueSender.send(myQueue, myMessage, DeliveryMode.NON_PERSISTENT, 6, 5000);
```

In this line, you send a message (myMessage) to a queue (myQueue), and you specify its delivery mode as NON_PERSISTENT with a priority level of 6 and a time to live parameter of 5000 milliseconds. (You will learn about priority levels and time to live in the following sections.) This line only affects this message, not all the messages.

If you do not need the lost message, you can choose NON_PERSISTENT as the delivery mode because it reduces the storage area needs and overhead, and improves performance. If you cannot afford the missing message, you should definitely choose the PERSISTENT mode.

Message Priority Level

In a JMS application, a priority level changes the order of delivery from a JMS provider to the consumer client. A provider delivers the messages with a higher priority level first. There are 10 levels of priority. Level 0 is the lowest level; level 9 is the highest. The default level is 4, and if you do not specify a priority level, the message is delivered with this priority level.

There are two ways to set a priority level. First, you can do it in the `send()` or `publish()` method. For example, in your source code, you might have a line like this:

```
myQueueSender.send(myQueue, myMessage, DeliveryMode.NON_PERSISTENT, 6, 5000);
```

In this line, the third parameter, which is 6, is the priority level. This priority level is for this message only. It does not affect other messages sent by the MessageProducer.

Secondly, you can use the `setPriority()` method of the MessageProducer interface. Calling this method affects all the messages sent by this message producer because it sets the default priority level of the message producer.

Message Expiration

In a JMS application, you can set an expiration time for the messages that will be delivered to the consumer. Messages have a default time to live value of zero if you do not specify an expiration value. A message that has a zero default value will never expire. If you set an expiration value, the message will be obsolete after the specified time. An obsolete message will be removed from the JMS provider and will not be delivered.

You can set an expiration value in two ways. First, you can provide this value in the `send()` or `publish()` method as the fourth parameter. For example, in your source code, you might have a line like this:

```
myQueueSender.send(myQueue, myMessage, DeliveryMode.NON_PERSISTENT, 6, 5000);
```

In this line, the fourth parameter, which is the time to live value, is set to 5000 milliseconds. This expiration time is for this message only. It does not affect other messages sent by the MessageProducer.

Secondly, you can use the `setTimeToLive()` method of the MessageProducer interface. Calling this method affects all messages that are sent by this message producer because it sets the default expiration time of the message producer. The value is given as a parameter in the method.

If the message does not have a chance to be delivered before the expiration time, it will be dropped and will not be delivered.

Temporary Destinations

As you learned in previous chapters, queue type or topic type destinations must be created by JMS administrators using the administrator tools of the JMS provider. Creating destinations programmatically is not recommended. These types of administratively created destinations are long-lasting destinations and can be used by any JMS client as long as the client adheres to some rules defined by the provider and the JMS API specifications.

In addition to the long-lasting destinations, the JMS API allows you to create temporary destinations that only last as long as the connection in which they are created. These temporary destinations are created using the `createTemporaryQueue()` method of the QueueSession interface or the `createTemporaryTopic ()` method of the TopicSession interface.

Temporary destinations can be used by other objects that are created by the same connection. For example, any session created by the connection that created the temporary destination can use this destination and can create consumers for it. Sessions that are created by other connections cannot use this temporary destination.

Temporary destinations live while the connection is alive. Whenever a connection is closed, its temporary destinations are closed as well. After closing, their content is lost.

Why Do You Need Temporary Destinations?

Temporary destinations are used to implement a simple request/reply mechanism. For example, you might receive a message that has a JMSReplyTo header. If so, you need to send a reply to the destination given in this header value. In this case, you create a temporary destination with a name specifying the value of the JMSReplyTo message header field. The consumer of the message uses this JMSReplyTo field as a destination and can send a reply.

Advanced Reliability Mechanisms

In addition to the basic reliability mechanism, there are two advanced reliability mechanisms used to deliver messages: *local transaction* and *durable subscription*. Some brief information about each mechanism is provided in the following sections.

Using Local Transactions

As defined, *transaction* means that you group a series of operations together as one operation and complete them together. There are two concepts for transactions: *committing* and *rolling back*. After completing a group of operations successfully, you commit the transaction. After committing the transaction, the system acknowledges the creator of the operations. If one transaction of this group fails, you roll back all the transactions. Transactions that have been completed are returned to their original state (before the transactions started). If you need to implement this group of transactions again, the group of transactions restarts from the beginning.

A general sense of a transaction as explained in the preceding paragraph can be applied to JMS applications.

A JMS client can use local transactions to group messages for sending and receiving. A Session interface of the JMS API consists of `commit()` and `rollback()` methods for committing and rolling back a transaction. A transaction commit means that all produced messages are sent, and all consumed messages are acknowledged. A transaction rollback means that all produced messages are destroyed, and all consumed messages are recovered and redelivered (if they have not expired).

If you choose transacted messaging in your application, sessions will always be in a transaction. After you call a `commit()` or `rollback()` method, you will end one session and start another session. If you close a transacted session, it rolls back the transaction in progress. It will not process any message produced and consumed.

This type of transaction is a local transaction and cannot be used in a distributed application. If you use Enterprise JavaBeans components, which are part of a distributed application, you cannot use the `commit()` and `rollback()` methods of a Session interface.

Specifying a Transaction

A transaction is specified when you create a session by using the first parameter of the `createQueueSession()` method of the QueueConnection interface or the `createTopicSession()` method of the TopicConnection interface, depending on your messaging model. This parameter is a boolean type value. If it has a value of true, the session will be transacted; if it has a value of false, the session will not be transacted. In the case of the transacted mode, the second parameter of the method, which specifies acknowledgment type, will be ignored.

For example, for a transacted session in the p2p messaging model, your source code might contain a line that looks like this:

```
myQueueSession = queueConnection. createQueueSession(true,0);
```

For a transacted session in a pub/sub messaging model, your source code might have a line that looks like this:

```
myTopicSession = topicConnection. createTopicSession(true,0);
```

In both cases, a second argument has been chosen as 0 because it will be ignored in a transacted session.

A Combination of Processes in a Single Transaction

You can group several sending and several receiving processes in a single trans-action. However, it is not recommended that you combine sending and receiv-ing in a transaction. If you need to combine them, you should organize their order carefully. For example, when you use a request-reply mechanism in a combined transaction, the program will not work properly if you send a mes-sage and wait for a reply to the message sent in the same transaction. The sending cannot be committed until you receive a reply, and you cannot get a reply until it is committed. This causes the system to hang. Due to this kind of risk, combined transactions are not preferred.

Another important point concerning messages and transactions is that a message can travel in more than one transaction. In the JMS application shown in Figure 7.1, a message does not go directly from a sender application to a receiver application. There is no interaction between two client applications. The message first goes to the JMS server from the sender, and then it goes to the receiver from the JMS server. Transactions take place between an applica-tion and a server, not two applications. Therefore, a message sent by a sender is one transaction, and a message received is another transaction.

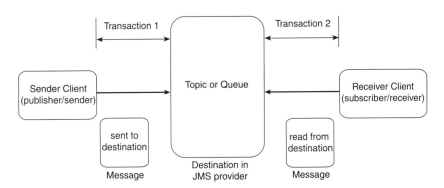

Figure 7.1   Local transaction structure.

Producing and consuming messages can occur in a session. In this case, pro-ducing (sending) the message and consuming (receiving) the message can be transactional. If they belong to a different session, they cannot be transactional because messaging across different sessions cannot be transactional.

The `commit()` and `rollback()` methods for local transactions are associated with a session. You should not combine queue and topic related operations in a single transaction. For example, if you receive a message from a queue, you cannot publish this message to a topic in the same transaction. A QueueReceiver object and a TopicPublisher object belong to different interfaces.

You can receive a message from a queue and send this message to another queue in the same transaction as long as you use the same queue session to create queue receiver and queue sender objects.

If you need to send and receive a message using the same session for asynchronous messaging, you must pass the client application's session to the message listener's constructor function. It creates a message producer for this session.

Durable Subscription

When discussing message acknowledgment earlier, I mentioned that you cannot recover lost messages for a nondurable subscription in the a pub/sub messaging model. You should define a delivery mode in the publisher application as PERSISTENT and the subscription type as a durable subscription if you want to make sure that a pub/sub application receives all published messages. (As previously explained, you can choose delivery mode as NON_PERSISTENT, but you risk losing the message to increase performance or allocate less resources).

As you know, you can create a nondurable subscriber by using the createSubscriber() method of the TopicSession interface. A nondurable subscriber can receive the message while it is active. When it is inactive, it cannot receive the message, and it will miss the message. This is not the same for queue type messaging delivery. A queue type client can consume the message even when it is inactive. It can receive messages that were sent while it was inactive, whenever it accesses the queue.

You need to use a durable subscriber for a topic type messaging model to receive a message even if the client is inactive, which is similar to the case in a queue type messaging model. It causes a higher overhead, but guarantees message delivery.

A durable subscriber registers a durable subscription with a unique ID, which is kept by the JMS provider. Subsequent subscriber objects with the same identity resume the same subscription, which the previous subscriber left. If there is no active subscriber for a durable subscription, the JMS provider saves the messages for this subscription and delivers them whenever a subscriber becomes active. There is one active subscriber for a durable subscription at a time.

Messages that have expired before delivery will not be delivered even with a durable subscription.

To create a durable subscription, you need to establish the unique ID of a durable subscriber by setting a client ID for the connection and a topic and subscription name for the subscriber.

Comparing Durable and Nondurable Subscriptions

In a nondurable subscription, you can receive a message after you create a subscriber until you close it, as shown in Figure 7.2. You can create the subscriber by calling the `createSubscriber()` method of the TopicSession interface. You can close this subscriber by calling the `close()` method of the MessageConsumer interface.

You can also create a subscription between the create and close period of a subscriber. This means the subscriber period is equal to the subscription period because a subscriber is identical to a subscription for a nondurable pub/sub messaging model. You can receive messages between the create and close period for a nondurable subscription. You will miss the message after you close the subscriber until you create the subscriber once again. A JMS provider will not retain the messages while the subscriber is inactive.

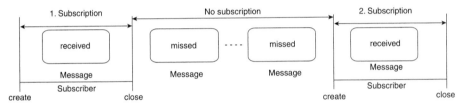

Figure 7.2   Nondurable subscription structure.

In the durable subscription shown in Figure 7.3, a subscriber and a subscription are separate concepts: They are not identical. A subscription starts Calling the `createDurableSubscriber()` method of the TopicSession interface. Creating a durable subscriber by calling this method, you can also create the first subscriber as long as a subscriber registers a durable subscription with a unique identity. You can stop a durable subscription by calling the `unsubscribe()` method of the TopicSession interface. After you call the `createDurableSubscriber()` method, you can close and re-create the same durable subscriber until you call the `unsubscribe()` method for the subscription. A subscriber in a durable subscription is closed by calling the `close()` method of the MessageConsumer interface.

As is the nature of a JMS system, you can definitely receive messages between the create and close period of a subscriber. As long as a subscriber is registered to a subscription and this subscription is active, a subscriber can receive the missing messages at a later time even it is inactive, which is the period between the close and the next create.

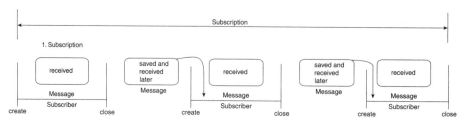

Figure 7.3   Durable subscription structure.

Creating a Durable Subscription

You cannot use a default connection factory to create a durable subscription. You should create a connection factory administratively that specifies a unique client ID for the client. Generally, for the J2EE Reference Implementation, you can create a connection factory with some properties by typing in a command line like this:

```
j2eeadmin -addJmsFactory <CFname> (queue|topic) [-props (<name>=<value>)+]
```

You can modify this general syntax to easily create a durable subscription connection factory. As an example, if you want to create a connection factory named MY_MATH_FAC for a topic destination with a clientID value of ID32, you can use the following at the command line:

```
j2eeadmin -addJmsFactory MY_MATH_FAC topic -props clientID= ID32
```

Changes will be done in the subscriber application. You do not need to change anything in the publisher application in terms of the connection factory or other durable subscription requirements. You do not need to change anything on the message listener either because it does not use the connection factory directly.

In the subscriber application, you should first change the connection factory line. Instead of using the default connection factory, you should substitute it with the connection factory that is created by the JMS administrator and includes a unique client ID.

After modifying the connection factory line, you create a durable subscriber by using the `createDurableSubscriber(topic, sub_name)` method. In this method, the first parameter is the topic name you subscribe to; the second parameter is the subscription name. Every time you reactivate your subscription, you use the *sub_name* parameter to subscribe to the same session in order to catch the missing messages while the subscriber is inactive. As an example, your source code for creating a durable subscriber might look like this:

```
String mySubscriber = "FinalExams";
TopicSubscriber myTopicSubscriber =
topicSession.createDurableSubscriber(topicExams, mySubscriber);
```

A subscriber becomes active when you start the topic connection. If you need to close the subscriber, which makes it inactive, you might use a line like this in your source code:

```
myTopicSubscriber.close();
```

The messages published to the topic destination will not be delivered to the subscriber and will be held in the JMS server with its unique ID. Whenever it is reactivated, the waiting messages will be delivered.

If you close the subscription (not the subscriber), you will use the `unsubscribe()` method. In your source code, unsubscribe lines might look like this:

```
myTopicSubscriber.close();
topicSession.unsubscribe(mySubscriber);
```

Writing a Durable Subscription Application

Recall from Chapter 6, "JMS Programming Techniques with Examples," when you developed simple JMS applications for a p2p messaging model, that you ran the client applications in two different orders. First, you ran the sender and then you ran the receiver. In this case, the receiver successfully read the messages sent by the sender. Secondly, you tried to run the receiver and then the sender. In this case, the receiver waited until the sender sent the message. In this mode, the receiver read the messages sent by the sender as well.

Unfortunately, you did not get the same result when using the pub/sub messaging model. When the subscriber (receiver) was not active, it missed the messages sent by the publisher (sender) because you developed a nondurable subscription.

Now try running the pub/sub application, which was described in the pub/sub model sample application in Chapter 6, and change the sequence in which the publisher and receiver applications are executed before running the durable subscription example. This should be done in order to understand that messages can be lost if a nondurable subscription model is used for writing a pub/sub model application, and the receiver (subscriber) is not active.

To clarify any questions you might have concerning a durable subscription, I'll provide a sample application in this section. Actually, it is not an entirely new application. I'll modify the nondurable pub/sub application developed in the section "A pub/sub Messaging Example" in Chapter 6 (see Listing 6.3 for message listener source code, Listing 6.4 for publisher application source code, and Listing 6.5 for subscriber application source code).

For the durable subscription example, you do not need to change anything in the publisher client application (see Listing 6.4) and message listener (see Listing 6.3) for asynchronous messaging. In the durable subscription application example, I'll modify and add some lines to the publisher application source code in Listing 6.4 to better display the output message. All changes are just cosmetic changes and are not essential. Therefore, I will not provide the publisher application and message listener source code again.

I'll modify the subscriber application (see Listing 6.5) in order to convert it from a nondurable application to a durable application. Only the modified or added lines will be provided. I'll also change the name of the application to JMSDurableSubscriber, which is not really necessary for the example. I noted this change to avoid any confusion because you will see the application names in the sample display output.

To make the modifications, follow these steps:

1. Add the following line just after line 19 of Listing 6.5:

```
String                duraSubName = "MathDurableSub";
```

This variable will be used as a parameter in the method of creating a durable subscription.

2. Change line 33 of Listing 6.5 to the following to use the connection factory created by the JMS administrator:

```
jndiContext.lookup("MY_LEVCON_FAC");
```

In this connection factory, you add the clientID for the server to hold the messages while the subscriber is inactive.

3. Change line 50 of Listing 6.5 to the following to create a durable subscriber:

```
topicSession.createDurableSubscriber(topic, duraSubName);
```

In this line, you give the subscription a name, which you defined in Step 1, as the second parameter.

4. You can add a few lines between line 60 and 61 of Listing 6.5 (these
   lines are not vital for this example) to display user-friendly output like
   this:

```
System.out.println("    ");
System.out.println("There may be some messages while subscriber is
➥inactive");
System.out.println("###################################");
System.out.println("    ");
```

These lines will help the user distinguish received messages while the
subscriber is active or inactive.

5. You can add a few lines between line 73 and 74 of Listing 6.5 (these
   lines are not vital for this example) to display user-friendly output
   like this:

```
System.out.println(" Subscriber is closed, subscription unsubscribed.");
System.out.println("    ");
```

These lines will help the user distinguish the received messages while the
subscriber is active or inactive.

Running a Nondurable Subscription

After typing and saving the source code files, compile them and make sure
there are no syntax errors. One more important point before running the
subscriber application is to create a connection factory named MY_LEV-
CON_FAC with a unique client ID. To create this connection factory using
the J2EE Reference Implementation administrator tool, type the following at
the command line:

```
j2eeadmin -addJmsFactory MY_LEVCON_FAC topic -props clientID= ID32
```

To show you some durable subscription concepts, I'll display several different
executions of the application in the remainder of this section. To follow along,
start the J2EE Reference Implementation by typing **j2ee –verbose** at the
command line, and then open two additional command-line windows.
Arrange them to fit the same screen to see what happens during the
message publishing and subscribing. Then, follow these steps to produce the
desired results:

1. In the first command window, run the publisher application twice, and
   send two different messages to the topic. Do not run the subscriber
   application yet. This means the subscriber does not exist to consume the
   message from the topic (see Figure 7.4).

Figure 7.4   No subscriber exists.

2. After publishing the messages to the topic, run the subscriber application in the second window. Although you do not publish any new messages, the subscriber receives some messages. They are the messages that were sent to the topic when there was no subscriber. The JMS provider saves the messages and delivers them whenever a subscriber is connected to the provider (see Figure 7.5).

Figure 7.5   Subscriber is activated.

3. Now publish (send) some messages to the topic while both clients are active. The subscriber will immediately receive the messages (see Figure 7.6).

Figure 7.6   Both client applications are running.

4. Stop the subscriber application to make it inactive. Closing the connection automatically closes the subscriber because closing the connection closes the session. Publish (send) some messages to the topic again. The subscriber cannot receive these messages because its connection is closed to the JMS provider (see Figure 7.7).

Figure 7.7   Stopping the subscriber application.

5. Start the subscriber application to reactivate the subscriber. As you can see in Figure 7.8, the subscriber application again receives the messages published (sent) by the publisher to the topic.

Figure 7.8 Reactivating the subscriber application.

Clustering for Reliability

In previous sections of this chapter, I provided some information about software reliability mechanisms. There is one more reliability mechanism: *clustering*. It is a hardware approach to reliability, not a software issue. Clustering is an extensive subject. In this section, I will just briefly discuss clustering.

As defined, clustering combines multiple physical computers to serve as one logical, single computer (see Figure 7.9). By using clustering, you can increase the capacity and availability of the messaging application more than you can with a single computer. For example, you can serve a limited number of clients at a time with a single computer. If you need to serve a large number of clients, you usually need several computers. You cannot connect numerous computers randomly. They must be connected to each other and must act as a single computer for the clients.

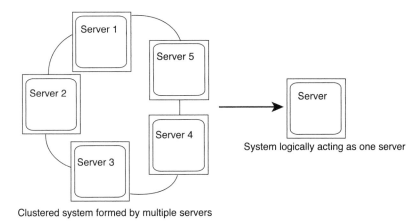

Clustered system formed by multiple servers

Figure 7.9 Clustering structure.

As an example, let's consider some Web-based email sites such as Yahoo.com, Hotmail.com, and so on. Because they have millions of users, they cannot possibly store all users' information in one computer. However, when you connect to their web sites to check your email, you do not need to know which computer is responsible for your account. You just connect and use their facilities with one name. You think you are connecting to the same server from any location.

The JMS system is based on a central JMS server. It handles and manages the messaging system, and controls the coming and going of messages. If your messaging traffic increases, you might want to consider clustering. Cluster systems can be divided into two categories: *parallel computation clustering* and *service clustering*. JMS clustering is in the service clustering category because it is a server that is designed to serve messaging clients.

Distinct physical locations force some organizations to establish multiple computer systems. In a perfect environment, all computers would be in the same room or location, connected to each other by a local area network (LAN). In this scenario, it is very easy to manage them. Unfortunately, this is a dream for some companies. Computers are usually in different buildings, cities, and even countries. However, you can create a system that acts as a single computer to the user or client. This system can be formed using different computers in different physical locations. They can be connected in a wide area network (WAN) or a similar type of network. With this kind of architecture, you might need clustering, but clustering might not work properly on a computer network if computers are located in different locations. Or at the very least, it might cost more (in terms of additional network devices, administrator staff, manageability, and so on) than a LAN type network because of the lower bandwidth. Clustered computers must be designed to address certain problems, such as increasing performance, increasing efficiency, and decreasing the possibility of failure.

You need clustering for two reasons: capacity and availability.

Clustering increases the capacity of a JMS system when you need to process more messages (or bytes) per second, need to process more persistent (or non-persistent) storage areas, or need more simultaneous connections for more network-intensive operations.

Increasing the capacity with clustering for a JMS system also helps load balancing, which might be a problem at the connection level. Each client is connected to one and only one node of the clustering system. There are different approaches for load balancing such as assigning a new client to the next node of the clustering system, assigning a new client to the least loaded node, reassigning a client to the nodes to keep the system balanced, and so on.

The important factor in JMS clustering that makes it different from other systems is that a JMS system does not have one server. You should consider that a JMS system might have a messaging server and separate persistent storage. You can increase the number of messaging servers, but you cannot get sufficient increased performance if every messaging server is connected to the same persistent storage server. You should design the clustering architecture carefully. Increasing the number of certain types of computers might not improve the performance as you might expect.

Availability is a vital problem for a tightly coupled system. Although a JMS system is loosely coupled, availability is very important. Producer clients and consumer clients do not have to be available at the same time to interact because they are loosely coupled, but clients must have interaction with the JMS server. They will send to and receive from this server. Therefore, the JMS server must have high availability. Another reason to have a JMS server with high availability for client/server interactions is that some clients might only have a chance to connect to the system at a certain time (not continuously), or a producer might need a reply from the consumer within a certain time range. In these cases, JMS server availability is vital. Using clustering in a JMS system will increase its availability.

There is no one type of architecture in which to build the clustering system. It varies depending on your messaging system, networking structure, database server structure, and your requirements. Sometimes, efficiency can decrease when the capacity is increased. And sometimes, improving availability can cost much more than what you actually get from the system.

Summary

In this chapter, you learned how to increase the reliability of a JMS system. Reliability of a JMS system means that a message produced by a client must be consumed by the target client once and only once. It should not be lost on the way from its producer to the consumer, and it should not be delivered more than once.

You can improve reliability by using both software mechanisms and hardware mechanisms. Software reliability mechanisms can be divided into two categories: basic and advanced. Basic reliability mechanisms can be classified into five subcategories: message acknowledgment, message persistence, message priority level, message expiration, and temporary destination.

You also learned about advanced reliability mechanisms to deliver messages. They include local transaction and durable subscription.

In this chapter, I also provided some brief information about clustering, which is a hardware approach for reliability. You can combine multiple computers in the system and have them act as one computer to the clients. You can increase the capacity, efficiency, and reliability of a messaging system with clustering.

Questions and Answers

1. If I use durable subscription for a pub/sub messaging model in the subscriber application, should I use the same connection factory that I created for the publisher application?

No. Because they are loosely coupled, the publisher and subscriber applications do not have to know each other. Their connection to the JMS provider can be different. They have a right to choose different connection factories. A durable subscriber application must use its own connection factory because a JMS provider assigns a unique client ID to keep its messages while it is inactive. It is not a publisher issue.

2. Does the JMS provider keep the expired messages while a durable subscription is inactive?

No. The expired messages will not be delivered to the consumer regardless of whether it is durable or nondurable.

3. In a transacted mode, what will happen if I choose DUPS_OK_ACKNOWLEDGE as the acknowledgment?

Nothing. If you specify the transacted mode parameter (the first parameter) of `createQueueSession()` or `createTopicSession()` as true, the second parameter will be ignored. In a transacted mode, the sender will be acknowledged automatically whenever the transaction is committed.

4. I receive messages in a transaction from a queue, and I want to publish them to a topic. How can I do this?

It is not that simple. You cannot send and receive messages from different destinations in the same transactions because transactions belong to a session. One session is used for one type of destination. For your purpose, receive the messages from a queue in one session, keep the messages in a temporary storage area, and publish them to a topic in another session.

5. If I use clustering for a JMS system, such as mirroring of the JMS provider and its data storage, can I avoid software reliability issues? Because software reliability increases the size of the message as a result of increasing the message header, I want to prevent this from happening.

Your solution sounds fine. Clustering is a very good hardware approach to increase reliability. But, it is recommended that you use a software reliability approach as well. Hardware and software reliability approaches complement each other. You cannot sacrifice one of them if you choose the other.

8

JMS and XML

IN THIS CHAPTER, I WILL DISCUSS HOW Extensible Markup Language (XML) and Java Message Service (JMS) work together. The JMS specification does not specify any mechanism for how to carry an XML-formatted message body, but XML payloads can still be transferred via JMS systems. Because XML is text-based, it can be treated programmatically as a Text type message by a JMS client application developer.

Sun released the Java XML Pack to enable developers to use XML in Java-based applications. This pack combines several of the key industry standards for XML such as Simple API for XML Parsing (SAX), Document Object Model (DOM), XML Stylesheet Language Transformation (XSLT), Simple Object Access Protocol (SOAP), Universal Description Discovery and Integration (UDDI), Electronic Business XML (ebXML), and Web Services Description Language (WSDL). In this pack, there are four XML APIs:

- Java API for XML Processing (JAXP)
- Java API for XML Messaging (JAXM)
- Java API for XML Registries (JAXR)
- Java API for XML-based RPC (JAX-RPC)

The JAXM API allows developers to do XML messaging using the Java platform. But it is not directly related to JMS technology. It is used to send and receive document-oriented XML messages using a pure Java API. Unfortunately, it is not part of JMS. It is included with the Java Web Services Developer Pack (WSDP). You can write JAXM applications either on a Java 2 Platform Standard Edition (J2SE) platform or a Java 2 Platform Enterprise Edition (J2EE) platform. These applications do not have to be deployed as distributed applications, for example, in a servlet container or a J2EE container. JAXM implements SOAP 1.1 with attachments. As a developer, you can focus on building, sending, receiving, and decomposing messages. The programming of low-level XML communications is the responsibility of the JAXM implementation or a provider. Detailed information on the JAXM API is beyond the scope of this book.

JAXP is the API that deals with the processing of XML documents and files. Developers use to send and receive messages using the JAXP API in conjunction with the JMS API, although JAXP has nothing to do with the JMS API directly. This chapter will provide a sample application using JAXP.

Before I demonstrate how to use XML with JMS, I'll provide some brief information about XML using a simple example as infrastructure. You can find information about web technologies including XML at `http://www.w3.org`, which is the World Wide Web Consortium's (W3C) official web site. On the `http://www.xml.org` web portal, which is supported by the open source group Organization for Advancement of Structured Information Standards (OASIS), there are some very helpful discussions and valuable information for XML developers. When writing this chapter, I found lots of useful information from the articles on this web site.

What Is XML?

XML is a markup language like HTML. Actually, XML is beyond a markup language: It is a language for constructing other customized markup languages. For example, you can use XML to create a markup language to describe mathematical data. The markup languages that are created by XML are officially called XML applications, but many developers are not used to using this definition.

XML is derived from Standard Generalized Markup Language (SGML), which was also an ancestor of HTML. Developers can use XML and SGML to develop self-describing documents. XML is a simplified version of SGML and is more suitable for use with web applications. Both languages use text-based markups, called tags, to describe data, and other applications or tools to process this information correctly.

HTML or XML?

Many developers think that XML will replace HMTL's role in web applications in the near future. It is true that XML is needed because of the weaknesses of HMTL. HTML is limited in terms of formatting and dynamic content. XML is a solution for the limitations of HTML, but HTML technology will exist along with XML for a long time to come. HTML, which is also an SGML application like XML, is a very simple language in which to develop web pages. Today, many web developers are able to create web applications without high-level programming experience using HMTL. XML is more sophisticated than HTML, and some web developers avoid using it.

Unfortunately, XML technology is not supported by all web browsers. Internet Explorer started to support XML with version 5, whereas Netscape started to support XML with version 6. The more important contrast to draw is that HTML is a language for creating web pages, whereas XML is a language for exchanging data. HTML will evolve into XML-compliant XHTML, but it is not going away in favor of XML anytime soon.

XML Syntax

Unlike HTML, XML is case-sensitive. XML is not flexible in its use of quotation marks and closing tags. An XML document must be well formed. For example, you definitely have to use quotation marks for an attribute and close the open tag of an element. Let's look at a simple line of an XML document:

```
<headquarter continent="America">Toronto</headquarter>
```

In this line, <headquarter> is a tag, which is similar to a tag in an HTML document such as <title> or <body>. This tag is called an element in XML, and its value is "Toronto" in this sample line. The tag can contain a composed text value, another tag, or nothing, depending on your document design and specification. An open tag in an XML document must be closed. In this line, the </headquarter> tag closes the open tag. An element can have attributes in addition to its value, which is "continent" in this example. An attribute of an element provides additional information about the data as well as the element's value.

Because XML is case-sensitive, you should be careful when you type tags and attributes. For example, for the preceding sample line, if you close the <headquarter> tag with </Headquarter>, the document is not a well-formed XML document because the opening and closing tags do not match (due to the difference in the case of the letter H).

An XML Document Structure

A well-formed XML document consists of one root element called the *document element* and its child elements. Child elements must be nested properly within each other. For example, if an element is a child of a parent element, the child element must have its opening and closing tags inside its parent's opening and closing tags. Lines in Listing 8.1 demonstrate the properly nested lines of a well-formed document. In the listing, "department" is the parent element and "section_name," "location," and "population" are child elements of "department."

Listing 8.1 **Properly Nested Elements**

```
<department>
    <section_name>Production</section_name>
    <location>New York</location>
    <population>45</population>
</department>
```

Listing 8.2 shows improperly nested elements in an XML document. The "name" and "location" elements do not have closing tags within their parent "department" element. Therefore, this document is not well formed and is not valid.

Listing 8.2 **Improperly Nested Elements**

```
<department>
    <section_name>Production
    <location>New York
    <population>45</population>
</department>
</section_name></location>
```

An XML document must be written using a hierarchical organization similar to a company's organizational chart. Therefore, I will convert a simple organizational chart, illustrated in Figure 8.1, into an XML document (see Listing 8.3) to explain how to properly create an XML document.

In this example, the company is defined using specific properties: company title, its size, its sector, its CEO's name and hire date, location of its headquarters as city and continent, departments with department names, the vice president's name, department location, and number of the department worker.

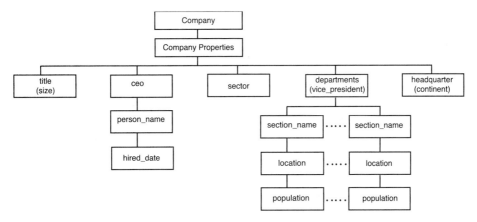

Figure 8.1 A company's organizational chart.

Listing 8.3 **XML Document of a Company's Organizational Chart**

```xml
<?xml version="1.0" ?>
<company>
 <company_properties>
  <title size="medium">Niagara Falls Water Regulation Inc.</title>
  <sector>water process and regulation</sector>
  <headquarter continent="America">Toronto</headquarter>
  <ceo>
     <person_name>Janet Waterboy</person_name>
     <hired_date>12 May 2001</hired_date>
  </ceo>
  <departments vice_president="Tony River">
    <department>
      <section_name>Production</section_name>
      <location>New York</location>
      <population>45</population>
    </department>
     <department>
      <section_name>Sales and Marketing</section_name>
      <location>Toronto</location>
      <population>25</population>
    </department>

    <department>
      <section_name >Accounting</section_name >
      <location>Toronto</location>
      <population>12</population>
    </department>
  </departments>
 </company_properties>
</company>
```

> **Tools to Write an XML File**
>
> XML can be written using any text editor or word processor, even Notepad. You must save the file as a text file with the .xml extension.

All XML documents must start with the following line:

```
<?xml ?>
```

In this <> symbol pair, you can put an XML version number or other information such as a character set, whether you are referring to an external document or not. If the version is added as in the first line of Listing 8.3, the line will look like this:

```
<?xml version="1.0" ?>
```

After starting the preceding XML definition tag, every XML document must contain one root element that contains all of the other elements in the document. In Listing 8.3, the root element is <company>. All other elements such as <company_properties> or <ceo> must be located within the root element tag. The XML document must end with a closing tag root element, which is </company> in this example.

Be sure to pay close attention when you supply values for attributes. You should definitely enclose the attribute values in quotation marks. If you forget the quotation marks in an HTML file, a web browser will not produce an error, and it will display the value. If an XML file is missing its quotation marks or has other syntax errors, the user will receive an error message instead of the XML data.

Listing 8.3 proves that it is not difficult to write a valid XML document. It is very similar to an HTML file, which contains tags and some textual data. Both use the same markup language syntax to define open and close tags and attributes. The HTML language can be thought of as a special form of XML because elements and their behaviors are predefined. Using this approach, an HTML document can be defined as an SGML application with self-contained information about its elements. Web browsers, which are used to process and display HTML documents, are programmed to handle each element in a specific way.

In other words, HTML provides a universal way to create a user interface, whereas XML provides a universal way to describe data and its structure to process it. Primarily, an XML file is not used to display data in a web browser. It is designed to describe and organize a collection of data for a specific field or purpose. Different fields have different XML language elements. For example, if you develop an XML application for a mathematics project, you might have <plus>, <minus>, <add>, or <subtract> element tags. For a geographic project, the XML document might have <altitude>, <location>, <longitude>, <air_pressure>, and so on.

Processing an XML Document

If you have experience developing HMTL documents, it is not difficult to understand XML syntax. Once you understand the basics, you must decide how you want your XML documents to be processed by the applications you write. You should be able to process an XML file programmatically, using the data to query databases, generate messages, and perform other tasks. To process XML data, you will need a software module called an *XML processor*, which is specified by the W3C. You can read the XML document and access its content and structure by using an XML processor. Developers do not write their own processor. It is usually included with some products. For example, in Internet Explorer version 5 and later, there is a built-in processor called Microsoft XML (MSXML).

With an XML processor, developers can read any well-formed XML document and access any element as well as its value and attribute(s). The platform on which you produce an XML file is not important. You can create it in a mainframe environment, and you can process and read it on a Windows or UNIX environment. So, you can use XML technology to transfer data and information between applications that are created in different environments. Therefore, XML is becoming an important technology in JMS applications because JMS provides interaction between applications created on totally different environments. If you can combine these two platform-independent technologies in a project, you might get an increased benefit of communicating and connecting applications using different technologies.

Validation of XML

The previous section demonstrated that it is very easy to write a well-formed XML document. However, it is too easy to write an XML document that causes an application-level problem, even though it is technically well-formed. I will address this application-level problem using a sample XML document shown in Listing 8.4. This XML file is a summarized version of the XML file in Listing 8.3.

Listing 8.4 **An XML Document Causing an Application-Level Problem**

```
<?xml version="1.0" ?>
<company>
 <company_properties>
  <ceo>
     <person_name>Janet Waterboy</person_name>
     <hired_date>12 May 2001</hired_date>
  </ceo>
  <departments vice_president="Tony River">
    <department>
      <section_name>Production</section_name>
      <location>New York</location>
    </department>
      <departments vice_president="Rock Mountain">
        <department>
          <section_name>Sales and Marketing</section_name>
          <location>Toronto</location>
        </department>
      </departments >
  </departments>
 </company_properties>
</company>
```

In the example, everything looks fine at a glance. All open tags are closed, but there is a "departments" element within a "departments" element. It is theoretically acceptable XML syntax, but it might be a problem at runtime. You should always catch and rectify these problems. There are some validating mechanisms that can be used to check the XML document against some set of predefined rules, which is generally called a *schema*. Schemas are important tools for document consistency. There are two main schemas: Document Type Definition (DTD) and XML Schema. Some brief information about schemas is provided in the next section.

Another confusing point of this well-formed XML is that the document might have the same element name for different nodes. For example, instead of using the "person_name" and "section_name" words, you would use only the "name" word for both elements. It is again theoretically acceptable XML syntax, but if you only perform a search on the "name" element, you will not be able to determine the specific "name" element you are looking for. This is because the well-formed XML in the XML document has a "name" element for different nodes. As a developer, you should avoid using the same node element names to prevent these kinds of conflicts.

You also need to know whether your XML document is valid or not. You can check an XML document's validity with an XML validator. XML validators are packages that check the XML file and return errors and warnings about its validity. There are some XML validators on the Web. Please refer to appropriate web sites and books to obtain up-to-date information about XML validators.

Schemas and DTD

A schema is a set of predefined rules for describing a given XML document. A schema defines the elements in the XML document and the attributes associated with these elements. In the definition, you specify a parent and child relationship between elements as well as the number and the sequence of the child elements. You can also define the element content, but you only have two options: *empty* or *text*. You also do not have as many variable type choices as in other programming languages.

DTDs are used to describe XML document schemas. In this section, I'll briefly discuss how to use DTDs to ensure well-formed XML documents.

The DTD language was not originally designed for XML. It is a language used to define validation rules for SGML documents. It can be used to define XML validation because XML is an SGML application (or a subset of SGML). When you run the XML application, the XML processor uses the DTD for validation of the XML file.

A DTD file can either be separate from the XML file or inserted in the XML document directly. In Listing 8.5, I'll create a DTD file separately and reference it from the XML document shown in Listing 8.3. In Listing 8.6, I'll put the DTD information directly into the XML document shown in Listing 8.3. In the listings, I will not repeat the lines after embedding the DTD information (as a file name or directly) in order to save space.

Listing 8.5 **Inserting DTD File Name (With the .dtd Extension) Information into an XML File**

```
<?xml version="1.0" standalone="no" ?>
<!DOCTYPE company SYSTEM "company.dtd">
<company>
//Other lines can be seen in Listing 8.3
</company>
```

Listing 8.6 **Inserting DTD Information Directly into an XML File**

```
<?xml version="1.0" standalone="no" ?>
<!DOCTYPE company [
// All lines from DTD file are shown in Listing 8.7
]>
<company>
//Other lines can be seen in Listing 8.3
</company>
```

The complete source code for the DTD file named company.dtd is shown in Listing 8.7. I'll first explain the rules and syntax of creating DTD files.

Start by changing the first line in the XML file like this:

```
<?xml version="1.0" standalone="no" ?>
```

The parameter stand-alone with a "no" value indicates that the XML document will work with an external file, which is a DTD file in this example.

In the second line of Listing 8.5, there is an additional line:

```
<!DOCTYPE company SYSTEM "company.dtd">
```

The DOCTYPE declaration must start with a <!DOCTYPE (recall that it is case-sensitive) followed by the root element, which is "company" in this example. After the root element, you must type SYSTEM (again it is case-sensitive). It shows that this DTD has been created by you; it is not public. It is designed for your own application. If you use a public DTD for validation, you have to write PUBLIC after the root element.

In this case, you can check your XML document validity against a DTD file created by someone else and located in any other location. If you use a public DTD, you have to obey some specific rules, which are not covered in this book. Before closing the tag, you need to provide a DTD URL (relative or absolute) that indicates the location of the DTD file. For this example, I'll save the file in the same directory as the XML file. Therefore, I only need to use the file name. If you located the file in another network location, you should provide the complete URL. A DTD file tag finishes with a '>' symbol.

Because DTD is very broad subject, I will not focus on the DTD syntax. Refer to the books or web sites recommended at the beginning of this chapter for more information. Listing 8.7 contains the content of the DTD file you used in the XML file shown in Listings 8.5 and 8.6. This XML document is validated against a validator at `http://www.stg.brown.edu/service/xmlvalid`. This validator checks validity of both online (that is, located in any place on the Internet) and local (that is, located in any place on your local computer or local network) XML documents.

Listing 8.7   **The DTD File for the "Company" Document Type**

```
<!ELEMENT company (company_properties)*>
 <!ELEMENT company_properties (title?, sector, headquarter, ceo?,
departments)>
 <!ELEMENT title (#PCDATA)> <!ATTLIST title size (small ¦ medium ¦ big)
#REQUIRED>
<!ELEMENT sector (#PCDATA)>
 <!ELEMENT headquarter (#PCDATA)>
  <!ATTLIST headquarter continent (America ¦ Europe)  #REQUIRED>
```

```
<!ELEMENT ceo (person_name, hired_date)>
  <!ELEMENT person_name (#PCDATA)>
  <!ELEMENT hired_date (#PCDATA)>
<!ELEMENT departments (department)+>
<!ATTLIST departments vice_president CDATA #IMPLIED>
  <!ELEMENT department (section_name, location, population)>
  <!ELEMENT section_name (#PCDATA)>
   <!ELEMENT location (#PCDATA)>
   <!ELEMENT population (#PCDATA)>
```

XML Namespace

In an HTML document, tags are predefined and understood by the browser. Because XML documents are flexible and can be freely created by developers, the same tag name can be used in a different application or in the same application in a different location using a different meaning. The XML namespace is used to distinguish these identical tags.

Namespaces are specified in the root element tag, which is <company> in the example. Listing 8.8 shows what the syntax for a namespace might look like if a namespace is needed.

Listing 8.8 **Namespace Syntax for an XML File**

```
<company
  xmlns:tagname1 = "someURL"
  xmlns:tagname2 = "anotherURL"
// specify  all other namespaces
>
```

As an XML developer, you cannot control other applications using XML technology; therefore, you might need namespaces to resolve any potential ambiguity. However, your application is under your control. Try to avoid using identical tag names in the same application as much as possible to simplify your XML documents.

Processing Technologies

An XML processor, also called a *parser*, is a software module that is able to read XML documents and allows developers to access their content and structure. This process is also called *parsing* the XML document. As a developer, you will select an XML parser according to your implementation considerations (such as the platform you are running on and the functionality you need). For Java-based applications, you can use JAXP. The current version, 1.1.3, and an earlier access version, 1.2, are both available at the time of this writing. (In the previous version, JAXP represented Java API for XML Parsing instead of Processing.)

JAXP enables applications to parse and transform XML documents. JAXP version 1.1 supports the latest XML standards: DOM, SAX, and XSLT. DOM and SAX are explained in the following sections. XSLT is also briefly described in the following section. JAXP provides namespace support to work with DTDs to avoid naming conflicts.

The main JAXP APIs are defined in the javax.xml.parser package, which contains two vendor-neutral factory classes: SAXParserFactory and DocumentBuilderFactory. They provide SAXParser and DocumentBuilder classes. The JAXP API provides a common interface for different vendors' SAX and DOM parsers.

Other packages available in addition to the javax.xml.parser are as follows:

- org.w3c.dom defines the Document class (a DOM) as well as classes for all of the components of a DOM. The DOM allows you to read XML documents into a hierarchical tree and manipulate their content and structure. In addition, the DOM makes it easy to build XML documents "from scratch."

- org.xml.sax defines the basic SAX APIs. SAX allows you to define your own event-driven XML parsers. SAX is handy when you want to have different actions take place as an XML document is sequentially parsed.

- javax.xml.transform defines the XSLT APIs that let you transform XML into other forms.

DOM Technology

The DOM is based on a tree model, and the XML document is represented as a tree structure in memory. Figure 8.1 shows a type of tree model. DOM has a programming interface to reach the nodes of the tree and access the elements as well as their values and attributes. The DOM API is easy to use. It represents XML in a tree structure of objects, and developers can use it to manipulate the hierarchy of application objects. Because it is in memory, you can access and manipulate the elements easily.

Its disadvantage is that DOM uses huge amounts of system memory for very large XML files. If you transfer large amounts of XML data over a network or the Internet, the application must wait until the whole XML file finishes loading. The DOM interface inspects each node of the tree, alters its contents, obtains its child nodes, removes nodes, and appends nodes as requested by the application. All components are node objects that occupy memory. Therefore, if you develop server-side applications, using a SAX API might be a better approach if the XML document is not broken up and cannot be partially processed.

If you use the DOM API to parse an XML document, your application might contain the lines shown in Listing 8.9.

Listing 8.9   **Some Lines in an Application Using DOM to Parse the XML File**

```
DocumentBuilderFactory dbf = DocumentBuilderFactory.newInstance();
DocumentBuilder db = dbf.newDocumentBuilder();
Document myDoc = db.parse(new File("companyIn.xml"));
```

At the end of this chapter, in the section, "A Sample Application Using the JAXP API in JMS," (see Listings 8.11 and 8.12), I provide a sample application in which a DOM API is used to parse an XML document.

SAX Technology

Unlike DOM, SAX is an event-driven XML parsing API. It does not require the entire file to be loaded into memory, making it faster than DOM. The XML processor finishes reading the XML element and calls the document into one of its custom event handlers, which can be designed by the developer. Because it does not have a tree structure, the SAX model does not have any objects in memory.

Its disadvantage is that you cannot access the document randomly as you can with the DOM model. Appropriate uses of the SAX API are with server-side applications and data filters because they do not require an in-memory representation of the XML document, preferring instead to process the XML document one piece at a time.

If you use the SAX API to parse an XML document, your application might contain the same lines shown in Listing 8.10.

Listing 8.10   **Some Lines in an Application Using SAX to Parse the XML File**

```
SAXParserFactory sbf = SAXParserFactory.newInstance();
XMLReader myXmlReader = spf.newSAXParser().getXMLReader();
xmlReader.parse(new File("companyIn.xml"), DefaultHandler dh);
```

Transformation Technologies

An XML document is a way of representing and transferring data. After you create and deliver it, the XML document must be read, accessed, and transformed to a meaningful form for users. In this section, I will provide some brief information on how to transform an XML document into another readable form. XML documents are usually converted to an HTML document, which can then be displayed in a browser.

It is quite difficult to convert an XML file into an HTML file using DOM because using DOM is unscalable and memory-intensive. For example, if you want to display departments that belong to a specific vice president and their associated data, you must manually navigate the tree to find these elements and create the output strings for the HMTL table. Even for a few departments, this is a very complicated process. Therefore, another language was created to transform an XML document into an HTML file; that language is Extensible Stylesheet Language (XSL) whose specification is defined by W3C. XSL provides a less memory-intensive way to transform XML data to HTML. The stylesheets created can be used by applications written by any XML-capable language on any platform (not just Java). A simple query language called XPath is also used with XSL.

Because XSL and XPath are very sophisticated subjects and are not necessary for JMS applications, I will not provide detailed information about them. If you need more information about these topics, please refer to the books recommended at the beginning of this chapter.

A Sample Application Using the JAXP API in JMS

XML and the combination of XML and JMS are quite complex subjects for one chapter. Therefore, instead of providing more details, I prefer to provide a real-world example to demonstrate how XML technology can be used in a JMS application.

Using the p2p messaging model in the sample application, I'll transmit an XML file from a sender client to a receiver client through a queue type destination named "queue_Company," which must be created administratively. I'll use the XML document represented in Figure 8.1. Because of space considerations, I will not repeat the XML document in the code listing. The basic XML file is provided in Listing 8.3. In the example, the XML file containing DTD information will be used as provided in Listing 8.6. (The DTD information is in Listing 8.7.) The sender and receiver application code listings are modified versions of the examples examined in Chapter 6. The sender application is similar to the source code in Listing 6.1. I modified the queue name and the message content. I will only explain the changed or added lines instead of providing the complete source code.

I created a new queue type destination named "queue_Company." Therefore, you should create this queue as an administrative object in your JMS provider and change line 9 of Listing 6.1 as follows:

```
String    myQueueName = "queue_Company";
```

If you changed the queue name as I did (myQueueName for this example), you must update other lines containing this variable throughout the entire source code.

The main change on the sender application is to read an XML document and convert it to a proper message type for JMS. For the example in Listing 8.11, you need to read the "companyIn.xml" file line by line, add the "\n" character at the end of every line you read, and append this combined line to a StringBuffer.

After you finish reading all lines in the XML document, convert the StringBuffer type value to a Text type value. This conversion must be performed so you can transfer a Text type value as a message via JMS, not a StringBuffer type value. The lines implementing the XML document and converting it into a proper type are provided in Listing 8.11. Insert these lines between lines 16 and 17 of Listing 6.1.

I added some cosmetic changes to properly display some messages as well, but they are not very important and do not affect the function of the application. I will explain how the sender application works after discussing the receiver application in the following section.

Listing 8.11   Added Lines of Sender Application Source Code Transmitting an XML Document Through the p2p Model

```
1.  String       XMLText ;
2.
3.  //preparing XML document as string
4.  File fileComp = new File("companyIn.xml");
5.  StringBuffer fileCompText = new StringBuffer();
6.  try {
7.  FileReader fileCompReader = new FileReader(fileComp);
8.  BufferedReader bufferedCompReader =
9.          new BufferedReader(fileCompReader);
10.  String lineComp;
11.  while (( lineComp = bufferedCompReader.readLine()) != null ) {
12.      fileCompText.append(lineComp);
13.      fileCompText.append("\n");
```

```
14.   } // end of while
15.   } catch (FileNotFoundException NoFileExc) {
16.     System.out.println("Error finding XML file " +
17.         NoFileExc.toString());
18.   } catch (IOException ioExc) {
19.     System.out.println("Error reading XML file " +
20.         ioExc.toString()) ;
21.   } // end of try
22. XMLText = fileCompText.toString();
```

The receiver application is similar to the source code in Listing 6.2. It is based on a p2p type messaging consumer. Because I modified the original source code to read and process the transmitted XML data using more than a few lines, the entire source code of the receiver application for this example is provided in Listing 8.12. I will explain how it works in the following section.

Listing 8.12   **Receiver Application Source Code Reading and Processing an XML Document Through the p2p Model**

```
1. import javax.jms.*;
2. import javax.naming.*;
3. import java.io.*;
3.
4. //JAXP
5. import javax.xml.parsers.DocumentBuilderFactory;
6. import javax.xml.parsers.DocumentBuilder;
7.
8. //DOM API
9. import org.w3c.dom.Document;
10. import org.w3c.dom.Element;
11. import org.w3c.dom.Node;
12. import org.w3c.dom.NodeList;
13.
14. //SAX API
15. import org.xml.sax.InputSource;
16. import org.xml.sax.SAXException;
17.
18. public class CompanyReceiverDOM {
19.
20. public static void main(String[] args) {
21.   // Creating JMS object variables
22.   String   myQueueName = "queue_Company";
23.   Context jndiContext = null;
24.   QueueConnectionFactory  queueConnectionFactory = null;
25.   QueueConnection  queueConnection = null;
26.   QueueSession queueSession = null;
27.   Queue   queue = null;
28.   QueueReceiver  queueReceiver = null;
29.   TextMessage  message = null;
30.
```

```
31.    System.out.println("Queue name is " + myQueueName);
32.    // Creating a JNDI InitialContext object
33.    try {
34.        jndiContext = new InitialContext();
35.        } catch (NamingException e) {
36.        System.out.println("Error while creating JNDI " +
37.            "context: " + e.toString());
38.        }
39.    // Looking up connection factory and queue
40.    try {
41.        queueConnectionFactory = (QueueConnectionFactory)
42.            jndiContext.lookup("QueueConnectionFactory");
43.        queue = (Queue)jndiContext.lookup(myQueueName);
44.        } catch (NamingException e) {
45.        System.out.println("JNDI lookup queue failed: " +
46.            e.toString());
47.        }
48.    // Creating connection, session (not transacted)
49.    try {
50.      queueConnection = queueConnectionFactory.createQueueConnection();
52.      queueSession =  queueConnection.createQueueSession(false,
53.            Session.AUTO_ACKNOWLEDGE);
54.    // Creating receiver, then starting message delivery
55.      queueReceiver = queueSession.createReceiver(queue);
56.      queueConnection.start();
57.      System.out.println("Ready to receive XML document as a message ");
58.        while (true) {
59.    // Receiving XML in text messages from the queue
60.          Message myMes = queueReceiver.receive();
61.          if (myMes != null) {
62.              if (myMes instanceof TextMessage) {
63.                  message = (TextMessage) myMes;
64.                  System.out.println("Reading the document from : '" +
65.                      myQueueName + "' ");
66.                  System.out.println("***##***##***###");
67.                  System.out.println(" ");
68.                  getTheNode(message.getText(), args[0]) ;
69.                  System.out.println("***##***##***###");
70.                  System.out.println(" ");
71.              } else {
72.    // Stop receiving when the message
73.    // is end of stream from the queue
74.                  System.out.println("Finished reading the XML
75.                      document as a message ");
76.                  break;
77.              } //end of if myMes instanceof
78.          } // end of if (myMes != null)
79.        } //end of while
80.      } catch (JMSException e) {
81.        System.out.println("Error while receiving the message: " +
82.            e.toString());
```

continues

Listing 8.12 **Continued**

```
83.     } finally {
84.  // closing the connection
85.   if (queueConnection != null) {
86.      try {
87.         queueConnection.close();
88.      } catch (JMSException e) {}
89.    } //end of finally
90.  }
91.  } //end of main
92.
93. public static void getTheNode(String messageText, String myNode) {
94.
95. try {
96.   // creating a stream from text type XML message
97.   StringReader myReader = new StringReader(messageText);
98.
99.   // creating a SAX InputSource for the stream
100.   InputSource companySrc = new InputSource(myReader);
101.   // implementing JAXP document builder
102.   DocumentBuilderFactory myDbf =
103.         DocumentBuilderFactory.newInstance();
104.   DocumentBuilder myDb = myDbf.newDocumentBuilder();
105.   // parsing the XML and generate a DOM
106.   Document doc = myDb.parse(companySrc);
107.   // get the contents of the nodes
108.   org.w3c.dom.NodeList findingNodes = null;
109.   findingNodes = doc.getElementsByTagName(myNode);
110.   System.out.println("node number of \"" + myNode + "\" element : "
111.         + findingNodes.getLength());
112.    for (int i=0; i<= findingNodes.getLength()-1; i++) {
113.   System.out.println((i+1) + ". node value of \"" + myNode
114.         + "\" element : " +
115.   findingNodes.item(i).getFirstChild().getNodeValue() );
116.   System.out.println((i+1) + ". node attribute of \"" + myNode
117.         + "\" element : " +
118.   findingNodes.item(i).getAttributes() );
119.   } //end of for
120.  } catch (javax.xml.parsers.ParserConfigurationException DbfExc) {
121.    System.out.println("Error at getTheNode : "
122.         + DbfExc.toString());
123.  } catch (org.xml.sax.SAXException parser) {
124.    System.out.println("Error at getTheNode : "
125.         + parser.toString());
126.  } catch (java.io.IOException ioExc) {
127.    System.out.println("Error at getTheNode : "
128.         + ioExc.toString());
129.  } //end of try
130. } //end of getTheNode
131.
132. } //end of class
```

Running the Sender and Receiver Applications

After typing the source code as shown in the previous section, compile the code and correct any syntax errors.

A sender application reads the XML document and prepares it to send as a Text type message to the queue type destination. To run the sender application named "CompanySender" at the command prompt, type **java CompanySender**. A window shown in Figure 8.2 is displayed, which indicates that the "companyIn.xml" XML file has been sent to the destination.

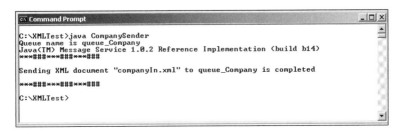

Figure 8.2   Running the sender application.

The receiver application then reads the Text type message from the queue type destination. To run the receiver application named "CompanyReceiverDOM" at the new command prompt, type **java CompanyReceiverDOM**.

The heart of the receiver application is the `getTheNode()` method. It takes the Text type message that was read from the queue named "queue_Company" as a parameter. It converts it into a stream and InputSource type to be used in JAXP to create an XML DOM Document. After this process is complete, you can access the values and attributes of each node in the structure. You have to provide the node names (elements in an XML document) as parameters in the command line when you run the receiver application.

I will run it with different node names, such as "headquarter," "location," and "person_name." Do not forget to run the sender application to send the XML document because the receiver application consumes the message at every running. Otherwise, you will not get any results on the screen. The screen will only display some cosmetic outputs and an empty line.

I first run the receiver application with the "headquarter" parameter as illustrated in Figure 8.3. The application displays the headquarter element value, which is Toronto in this example and its attribute, which is continent="America."

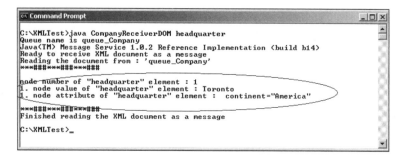

Figure 8.3   Running the receiver application with the headquarter parameter.

Then, I run the receiver application with the "location" parameter as illustrated in Figure 8.4. The application displays the location element values and its attributes. Because there are three location elements belonging to the same parent, the application displays all three. In this example, the location elements only have values, they do not have attributes. Therefore, the attribute lines are empty.

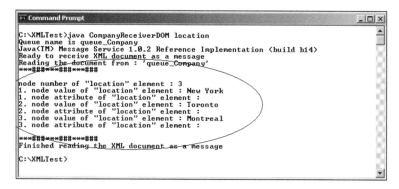

Figure 8.4   Running the receiver application with the location parameter.

When you run the receiver application with the "name" parameter, as illustrated in Figure 8.5, the application displays that the node does not exist because there is no "name" element. There are two element tags that have a similar purpose, but they are different tags, and they have different names: "person_name" and "section_name." Therefore, you have to run the application with the "person_name" and "section_name."

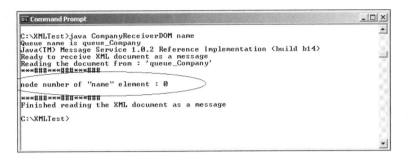

Figure 8.5   Running the receiver application with the name parameter.

When you run the receiver application with the "person_name" and "section_name" parameters, the application displays node values and attributes as illustrated in Figures 8.6 and 8.7, respectively.

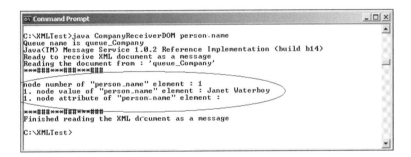

Figure 8.6   Running the receiver application with the person_name parameter.

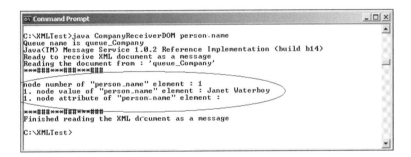

Figure 8.7   Running the receiver application with the section_name parameter.

As you can see from the outputs, DOM allows you to access the element values and attributes of an XML document transmitted via a JMS destination.

The example I provided in this section shows how to send and receive an XML-based document in applications using JMS API. It is hard to understand how XML technology is important in JMS-based applications with one sample application. You will understand its practical importance when you need to transfer XML messages in JMS applications.

Summary

In this chapter, you learned how to combine XML and JMS technologies in your Java messaging applications. Once you harness the power of XML, you can easily use it on any platform just like Java language-based technologies. XML and JMS leverage the performance and success of your messaging projects because XML works with almost all platforms, operating systems, and languages.

I also discussed how to use XML in message payloads and the basic functionality of Sun's XML APIs. The section was divided into three main subsections: the fundamentals of XML, JAXP, and a demonstration application.

In the section on XML fundamentals, I provided some XML history, differences and similarities between HTML and XML, XML syntax, and XML document structure. I also mentioned XML processing, XML transformation, and the validation of an XML document.

In the section on JAXP, I showed how you could use XML technology and XML documents in a Java application. Parsing using DOM, SAX, and XLST transformation was provided in this section with some sample code.

In the example section, I developed a p2p messaging application and transmitted an XML document via a JMS system. I provided source code for the sender and receiver applications. I also provided their outputs.

Questions and Answers

1. In the Java API for XML pack, JAXM is included to send and receive messages. Does it replace the role of JMS in messaging applications?

JAXM is not directly related to the JMS technology, nor is it part of JMS. It is included with the Java Web Services Developer Pack (WSDP) and is used to send and receive document-oriented XML messages using a pure Java API. You can write JAXM applications either on the J2SE platform or the J2EE platform.

2. Which parsing model is better, DOM or SAX?

It depends on your XML document. DOM is a tree structure and is easy to use, but if the document is very large, it is difficult to handle because you have to write how to access the nodes programmatically. In addition, a DOM tree is represented in memory. The larger the file, the more memory space is allocated. In the SAX model, you do not have to finish reading all of the nodes into memory, but you cannot access the nodes randomly, and your SAX application will have no sense of the structure of the XML document.

3. XML is an exceptionally verbose format in which the number of bytes used for the tags themselves often exceed the number of bytes used for data. However, XML is becoming increasingly important despite its inefficiencies and verbosity. Why?

There is no method or model you can use without any disadvantages. In a JMS application, it becomes harder to work with an XML document, but the XML files are text-based and can be used on and with any platform, operating system, and language. Powerful related technology such as XPath for querying XML data and XSLT for transforming XML into other formats make XML especially appealing. As a result, XML is becoming accepted as an industry standard for vendors, developers, and users.

4. In the JMS Message interface, there are five subinterfaces for transmitting a message: ByteMessage, MapMessage, ObjectMessage, StreamMessage, and TextMessage. However, there appears to be no subinterface for handling XML data. Why? Will this change soon?

You are right. The JMS specification 1.0.2 does not have integrated support for XML-based documents. In the future, it is likely that XML support will be added because it is needed by many developers. With the current specifications, you can convert XML data into a Text type message and then consume it.

5. Are there tools available for writing XML documents, DTDs, schemas, and other XML-related files?

XML files are pure text files. You can write them in any text editor or word processor as long as you save them as a text file with a .xml extension. But, XML technology is not only used to write XML files, it is also used to apply different technologies to text files such as parsing, transforming, and so on. Therefore, you might need some special tools. You can find many community-driven XML tools at `http://www.w3.org/XML`. In addition, I highly recommend XML Spy by Altova, an XML Integrated Development Environment (IDE) available from `http://www.altova.com`.

9

Message-Driven Beans

I N CHAPTER 2, "ENTERPRISE JAVABEANS (EJB)," I provided information about EJB, but it was limited to the two commonly used beans: the session bean and the entity bean. They make up the skeleton of an enterprise application because they allow you to design and develop distributed applications. Although you can use session beans and entity beans to produce and consume messages with JMS, they can only be used for consuming messages synchronously. Sun Microsystems introduced another bean for asynchronous messaging with EJB 2.0: the message-driven bean. In this chapter, I will discuss the message-driven bean and provide a simple example to show how you can use it in your JMS application.

What Is a Message-Driven Bean?

A message-driven bean is an enterprise bean used to process messages in a JMS system asynchronously. You can produce messages by using an entity or a session bean, and you can consume messages by using an entity or a session bean synchronously in addition to using them in their primary role handling transactional tasks or database tasks. However, they block the server resources in synchronous mode. A message-driven bean is only designed to be used in a messaging system as a consumer for asynchronous messaging. It acts as a JMS message listener, which is similar to an event listener. The only difference is that it receives messages instead of events.

Messages can be sent to the system by any Java 2 Platform Enterprise Edition (J2EE) component such as a stand-alone application, another enterprise bean, or a web component (JavaServer Pages [JSP] or Java servlet). Messages can also be produced by a JMS application or an application that does not use J2EE. As long as the message is received by a JMS provider, it can be processed by a message-driven bean.

At the time of this writing, message-driven beans only work with JMS messages. However, the Sun web site states that in the future, they might process other types of messages as well.

There is a major difference between a message-driven bean and the other two enterprise beans. It does not have a remote or a home interface. It only has a bean class. Clients cannot access message-driven beans through interfaces. Therefore, it is better to use a message-driven bean in conjunction with a session or an entity bean to access an EJB container. A message-driven bean has at least one business method—onMessage()—in the bean class. Whenever a message is received by a JMS provider, this method is called by the container, similar to how a message listener is triggered. A message-driven bean casts the message to one of five JMS message types and processes the message in this method, or there can be other helper methods in the class that can be called by the onMessage() method.

A message-driven bean is very similar to a stateless session bean because it does not retain any information or state about the client. All instances of the message-driven bean are equivalent. A container puts a number of them in a pool and assigns a received message to any instance in the pool.

If you need to handle states across client messages, you can use instance variables to hold references to stateful client data such as connections to a JMS provider, an open database connection, references to other beans, and so on.

In the onMessage() method of a message-driven bean, you can also invoke other beans to help process the received message.

All operations within the onMessage() method are part of a single transaction. If message delivery fails at any point in the process, the transaction will be rolled back, and the message will be redelivered.

Architecture of a Message-Driven Bean

As illustrated in Figure 9.1, a message-driven bean resides in an EJB container of a J2EE server, and it connects to a JMS destination (queue or topic type). Any JMS client application can send a message to a destination via the JMS provider. The provider interacts with the EJB container, and the container assigns a message-driven bean from the instance pool to process the message.

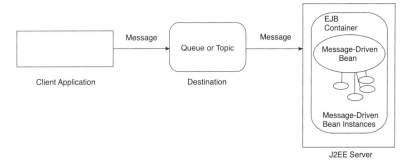

Figure 9.1   Architecture of a message-driven bean.

Life Cycle of a Message-Driven Bean

A message-driven bean is similar to a stateless session in terms of its life cycle. Because it is never passivated, its life cycle has two stages: *nonexistent* and *ready* (for the onMessage() method and other helper methods if they exist). Figure 9.2 illustrates the stages of a message-driven bean. An EJB container on the J2EE server creates a pool for message-driven bean instances. A container calls two methods when the message-driven bean instance is taken to the pool. The setMessageDrivenContext() method is called to pass the context object to the instance, and then the ejbCreate() method is called. At the end of the life cycle, the container calls the ejbRemove() method. After calling the ejbRemove() method, the instance is ready for garbage collection.

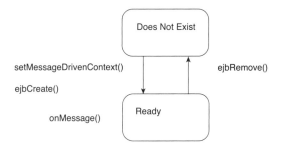

Figure 9.2   Life cycle of a message-driven bean.

The Message-Driven Bean Class

As mentioned earlier, a message-driven bean does not have a remote or a home interface, unlike an entity bean or a session bean. It only has a bean class. In this section, I will briefly describe the structure of a message-driven bean.

The message-driven bean class:

- Must implement the MessageDrivenBean and MessageListener interfaces. The message-driven bean class is similar to a message listener bean.
- Must be defined as public and cannot be abstract or final.
- Must consist of one `onMessage()` method to process the message.
- Might consist of some helper methods to process a message called by the `onMessage()` method.
- Must consist of one `ejbCreate()` method, one `setMessageDrivenContext()` method, and one `ejbRemove()` method, even if they are empty.
- Might contain a public constructor with no argument.
- Cannot define a `finalize()` method.

The `onMessage()` method acts like a message listener—similar to the one you developed in a simple application in Chapter 6, "JMS Programming Techniques with Examples" (see Listing 6.3). In a message-driven bean, the `onMessage()` method code lines in the bean class might look like those in Listing 9.1.

Listing 9.1 **Some Lines From the *onMessage( )* Method of a Message-Driven Bean**

```
public void onMessage(Message parMessage) {
    TextMessage myMessage = null;
    try {
        if (parMessage instanceof TextMessage) {
            myMessage = (TextMessage) parMessage;
            System.out.print("MESSAGE BEAN: Message ");
            System.out.println("received from the topic: ");
            System.out.println("=" + myMessage.getText()+ "=" );
// other helper methods can be called here
// if defined in the bean class
        } else {
            System.out.println("Message of wrong type: " +
                parMessage.getClass().getName());
        }
```

```
    } catch (JMSException ejms) {
        System.out.println("JMSException in onMessage(): " +
            ejms.toString());
    } catch (Throwable tjms) {
        System.out.println("Exception in onMessage():" +
            tjms.getMessage());
    } //end of try
} //end of onMessage() method
```

Combining a Message-Driven Bean with Session and Entity Beans

There is no interface for client applications to access the message-driven bean business methods (`onMessage()` and other helper methods). Your application uses other beans' business methods (session and entity beans) to use a message-driven bean and its methods. The `onMessage()` method of the message-driven bean is called when a message arrives at a JMS provider. This method then processes the message. You call other beans' business methods via helper methods of the message-driven bean to process the arrived message in the other beans or classes of the application. A message-driven bean can be defined as an inner bean. It must be combined with other types of beans to process the message properly.

There is no specific structure or architecture used to combine a message-driven bean with session or entity beans. Figure 9.3 and 9.4 illustrate two examples of these combinations.

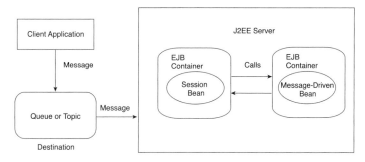

Figure 9.3   An example of combining a message-driven bean with a session bean.

In Figure 9.3, a session bean interacts with a message-driven bean. A client application might send a message to a destination via a JMS provider. The onMessage() method of the message-driven bean is called, and then a business method of the session bean can be called by a helper class in the message-driven bean.

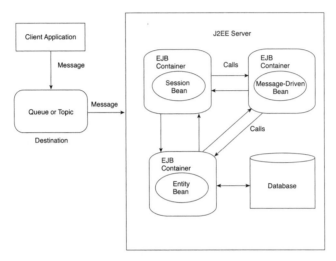

Figure 9.4 An example of combining a message-driven bean with an entity bean.

In Figure 9.4, a session bean and an entity bean interact with a message-driven bean. The entity bean also has a connection with a database to manipulate some data from the database in the application. Messages can be sent by an application to a destination via a JMS provider. The onMessage() method of a message-driven bean is called to process the message, and it might also call the other helper methods in the message-driven bean class. These helper methods can interact with the entity bean to implement a database task or interact with the session bean to complete some transactional tasks.

You can design your message producers or consumers using session or entity beans. A message-driven bean allows the application to consume the message asynchronously.

A Message-Driven Bean Example

As the preceding information proves, a message-driven bean is not very difficult to understand if you have moderate experience using session and entity beans. Its structure is quite clear and simple. At first glance, simple things can sometimes look more complicated than they actually are. Message-driven beans are very simple to work with. To understand how they work, let's develop a sample application. In this section, I will provide a simple source code example that deploys the bean and demonstrates what it does.

The publisher source code for this example is similar to the publisher application source code in Listing 6.4. However, the entire source code listing will not be repeated. You'll need to change line 9 in Listing 6.4 as follows because the topic named "topic_MDB" will be used as a destination in the application to publish and subscribe the message:

```
String                    interestTopicName = "topic_MDB";
```

This topic type destination should be created administratively. To create a topic, start the J2EE server by typing **j2ee –verbose**. After the server starts successfully, type the following at the command prompt:

j2eeadmin –addJmsDestination topic_MDB topic.

Lines 48 through 51 of Listing 6.4 are rearranged to display the message as illustrated in Listing 9.2. These cosmetic changes are not very important and do not affect the functionality of the publisher application.

Listing 9.2 **Changed Lines of Listing 6.4**

```
48.     message.setText("A message to demonstrate pub/sub
49.           with MessageDriven Bean- LE");
50.     System.out.print("Message to be published: '");
51.     System.out.print("message.getText()+" '");
```

In Listing 9.3, the bean class and its message-driven bean methods are listed. This listing is very similar to the message listener source code in the JMS application in Listing 6.3. I will provide the entire source code of the bean class even though it is similar because there are some important differences in terms of implementing a bean. There are also important differences implementing a JMS consumer application as a message-driven bean vis-à-vis a normal JMS consumer Java application. A message-driven bean is designed as an enterprise bean, and it contains methods such as `onMessage()`, `setMessageDrivenContext()`, `ejbCreate()`, and `ejbRemove()`.

Listing 9.3   **Source Code of the Bean Class for a Message-Driven Bean**

```
1. import javax.ejb.*;
2. import javax.naming.*;
3. import javax.jms.*;
4.
5. public class MessageBean implements MessageDrivenBean,
6.       MessageListener {
7.
8.   private transient MessageDrivenContext mdc = null;
9.   private Context context;
10.
11.   public void setMessageDrivenContext(MessageDrivenContext mdc)
12.   {
13.     System.out.println("In MessageBean.setMessageDriveContext() ");
14.     this.mdc = mdc;
15.   }
16.
17.   public void ejbCreate() {
18.   }
19.   // passing the message from the destination as a parameter
20.   public void onMessage(Message parMessage) {
21.       TextMessage myMessage = null;
22.
23.       try {
24.           // check the message type is TextMessage
25.           if (parMessage instanceof TextMessage) {
26.               // if so, cast it into TextMessage variable
27.               myMessage = (TextMessage) parMessage;
28.               // reading and returning the message in Text format
29.               System.out.print("MESSAGE BEAN: Message ");
30.               System.out.println("received from the topic: ");
31.               System.out.println("=" + myMessage.getText()+ "=" );
32.           } else {
33.               // if not, warn the user
34.               System.out.println("Message of wrong type: " +
35.                   parMessage.getClass().getName());
36.           }
37.       // throw the Exceptions if there are internal errors
38.       } catch (JMSException ejms) {
39.           System.out.println("JMSException in onMessage(): " +
40.               ejms.toString());
41.       } catch (Throwable tjms) {
42.           System.out.println("Exception in onMessage():" +
43.               tjms.getMessage());
44.       } //end of try
45.   } //end of onMessage() method46.    public void ejbRemove() {
47.   }
48. } //end of class
```

You can write the bean class source code using Forte for Java Community Edition(FFJ CE). Refer to Appendix A, "J2SE and J2EE Settings," for an explanation on where to download and how to set up FFJ. The FFJ CE software for developing Java applications is free of charge. In the working directory of FFJ, create a new package for the message-driven bean application, and then create the bean class in this package. You will need a properly created package in the FFJ working directory to deploy your application. You can use the deployment tool in the J2EE Reference Implementation to deploy your application.

Deploying the Bean Class

Before viewing the result of running an application containing a message-driven bean, let's discuss how to deploy a message-driven bean. Appendix B, "Application Deployment Tool," explains how to deploy a bean in more detail, but a message-driven bean has some specific steps. These steps are explained in this section. If you need more information about creating and deploying an enterprise application in a general sense, refer to Appendix B.

While developing this simple message-driven bean example, I'll use the FFJ Development Tool, the J2EE Reference Implementation, and the Sun Reference Deployment Tool as explained in Appendix A. If you need more information on where to download these tools and how to set them up on your computer, refer to Appendix A.

Start by running the FFJ Development Tool and creating a new package under the working directory. For this example, I named the new package MDBExample and saved it in the c:\ffjDevelopment working directory. Figure 9.5 illustrates the source code for the MessageBean and PublisherClient classes developed in the FFJ Development Tool.

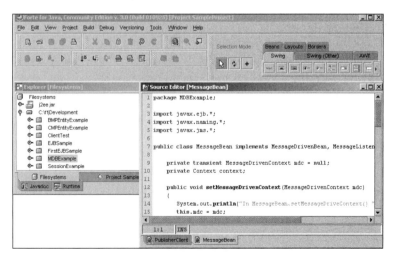

Figure 9.5   Source code for a message-driven bean application
in the FFJ Development Tool.

From the command prompt on your system, run the deployment tool of the J2EE Reference Implementation Deployment Tool by typing **deploytool**.

Figure 9.6 shows a deployed application named FirstHello. Refer to Appendix B for information on how this application is deployed.

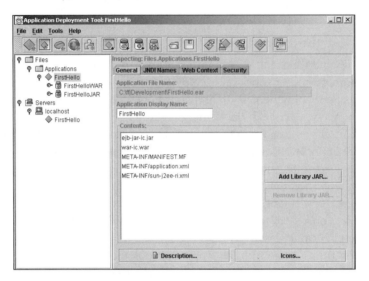

Figure 9.6   The Application Deployment Tool graphical user interface.

Let's deploy another application containing a message–driven bean as another example. To create a new application to deploy, highlight Application in the left pane, click File, select New, and then select Application. A dialog box appears containing two text fields for entering an application file and a display name. I entered C:\ffjDevelopment\FirstMessage.ear in the Application File Name text field and FirstMessage in the Application Display Name text field (see Figure 9.7).

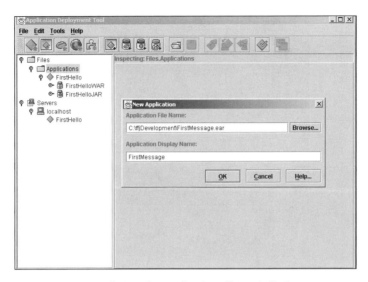

Figure 9.7   Defining the application file and display name.

To add a new component to the application, highlight the FirstMessage application in the left pane, click File, select New, and then select Enterprise Bean.
The New Enterprise Bean Wizard appears. The following steps guide you
through the wizard:

1. The Wizard starts with an Introduction page, which provides some brief
    information about deploying a bean. Click Next to continue.

2. You should provide a JAR file name for this application and add class
    files for the JAR file content. I provided FirstMessageJAR as the JAR file
    name. To add class files, click the Edit button on the Content window of
    the dialog box. The Edit Contents of FirstMessageJAR dialog box
    appears. Make sure the starting directory is the same working directory
    in which you developed the application with the Development Tool
    (c:\ffjDevelopment for this example). Explore the files in the
    MDBExample directory under the Available Files window. Highlight
    the MessageBean.class and PublisherClient.class files and add them to the
    Contents of the FirstMessageJAR window (see Figure 9.8). Click OK to
    return to the EJB JAR dialog box. Figure 9.9 shows the JAR file name
    and the class files that were added to the content of the JAR file pro-
    vided. Click Next to continue.

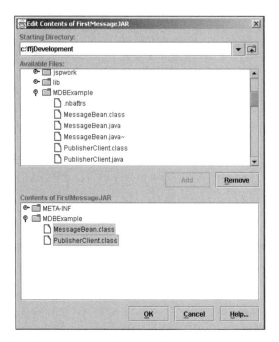

Figure 9.8   The Edit Contents dialog box for the EJB JAR page of the wizard.

Figure 9.9   The EJB JAR page of the wizard.

3. The General page of the wizard allows you to define the kind of bean you will add to the application. Choose the Message-Driven Bean option. After you've made this choice, the Local Interfaces and Remote Interfaces sections will be grayed out, and you will not be able to provide information for these fields. However, you must provide information for the Enterprise Bean Class. For this example, enter **MDBExample.MessageBean** for the Enterprise Bean Class and **MessageBean** for the Enterprise Bean Name. (See Figure 9.10.) Click Next to continue.

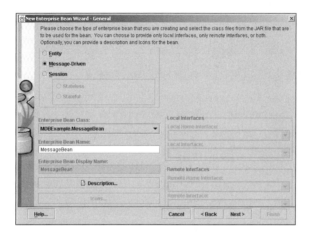

Figure 9.10   The General page of the wizard.

4. On the Transaction Management page, choose Container-Managed for this example. The wizard then displays the `onMessage()` method. Choose Required as the Transaction attribute (see Figure 9.11), and click Next to continue.

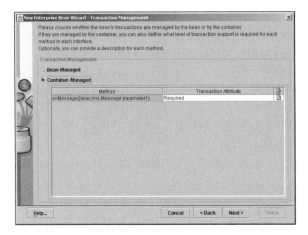

Figure 9.11   The Transaction Management page of the wizard.

5. On the Message-Driven Bean Settings page, specify the administrative objects for the application such as the destination type, the destination name, and the connection factory. For this example, choose the Topic type destination, and enter **topic_MDB** for the destination and **TopicConnectionFactory** for the connection factory (see Figure 9.12). Click Next to continue.

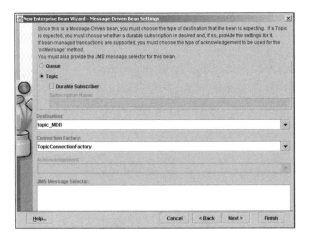

Figure 9.12   The Message-Driven Bean Settings page of the wizard.

6. Do not add or change anything on the Environment Entries page of the wizard. Click Next to continue.

7. Do not add or change anything on the Enterprise Bean References page of the wizard. Click Next to continue.

8. Do not add or change anything on the Resource References page of the wizard. Click Next to continue.

9. Do not add or change anything on the Resource Environment References page of the wizard. Click Next to continue.

10. Do not add or change anything on the Security page of the wizard. Click Next to continue.

11. After you have completed each preceding page of the wizard, the Review Settings page appears, as illustrated in Figure 9.13. If all settings are satisfactory, click Finish to complete the wizard and add the new message-driven bean to the application.

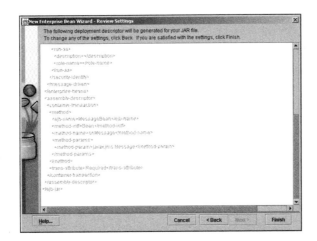

Figure 9.13 The Review Settings page of the wizard.

After creating a new application and adding an enterprise bean, you will deploy the application. To deploy the application, highlight the FirstMessage application, click Tools, and then select Deploy. The Deploy Wizard appears. The following steps guide you through the wizard:

1. The first page of the wizard is the Introduction. Choose FirstMessage as the Object to Deploy and localhost as the Target Server (see Figure 9.14). Do not forget to select the Return Client Jar check box. Click Next to continue.

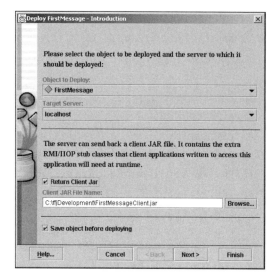

Figure 9.14   The Introduction page of the wizard.

2. On the JNDI Names page of the wizard, enter **topic_MDB** as the JNDI Name of the MessageBean component as illustrated in Figure 9.15. For the message-driven beans, JNDI names must be used as the destination name. This destination name must be the same name specified in the Message-Driven Bean Settings page of Adding a New Component to an Enterprise Application (see Figure 9.12). Click Next to continue.

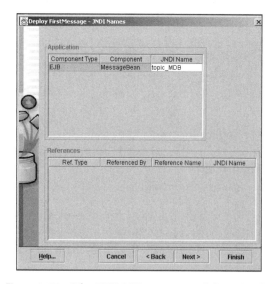

Figure 9.15   The JNDI Names page of the wizard.

3. The deployment progress bar displays the progress of the deployment. If there is a problem during deployment, error or warning messages will appear in addition to the progress information. If everything goes well, the deployment will finish and the Cancel button will change to an OK button. Click OK after the deployment of the application is complete.

Once deployment is complete, the Application Deployment Tool should look similar to Figure 9.16. In the figure, two applications have been deployed— one of them is FirstMessage.

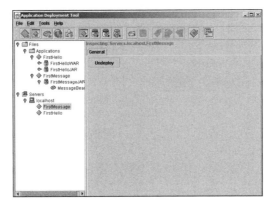

Figure 9.16 The Application Deployment Tool showing the FirstMessage application.

Running the Message-Driven Bean Application

Prior to running the message-driven bean application, you should publish a message to the topic to see what will happen when you run the message-driven bean application. For this example, you can publish a message to the topic_MDB destination by using the PublisherClient. Let's run the sample application on FFJ.

1. Run FFJ on you computer system if it is not already running.
2. Expand the MDBExample package under the c:\ffjDevelopment directory.
3. Highlight PublisherClient.
4. Right-click and choose Execute, as illustrated in Figure 9.17.

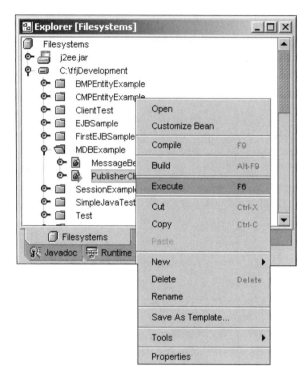

Figure 9.17   Executing the PublisherClient application.

After executing the PublisherClient application, the FFJ Output Window will display some messages from the client application as designed in your source code (see Figure 9.18). As mentioned earlier, a message-driven bean is an inner bean, and it does not contain remote or local interfaces. Clients cannot access this bean directly. The processed message can be used by the EJB container and other beans. You cannot display the result directly on the screen. You can display what the message-driven bean produces by starting the J2EE Reference Implementation server in a Command Prompt window. I recommend that you run J2EE with the "–verbose" parameter to see EJB container messages in the J2EE Reference Implementation Command Prompt window. Otherwise, you cannot see what the message-driven bean does when it receives the message. The result of the message-driven bean receiving a message from the PublisherClient application is illustrated in Figure 9.19.

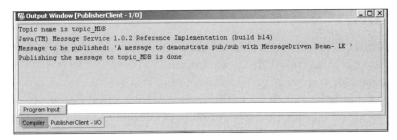

Figure 9.18   The FFJ Output Window after executing the PublisherClient application.

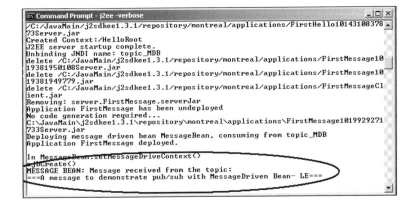

Figure 9.19   The result of typing **j2ee –verbose** at the command prompt.

After you publish a message to the topic, the JMS provider calls the
onMessage() method in the message-driven bean. Because there is no client
application for the message-driven bean, the result will only be displayed in
the Reference Implementation command window, which is **j2ee –verbose**
for this example. The onMessage() method of the message-driven bean receives
the message, casts it to a Text type message, and sends the Text type message to
a display unit with some additional user-friendly strings.

Summary

This chapter provided detailed information about message-driven beans, which are an integral part of the EJB 2.0 specification.

A message-driven bean is an enterprise bean that processes messages in a JMS system asynchronously. You can produce messages using an entity or a session bean and consume messages using an entity or a session bean synchronously. You need a message-driven bean to consume messages in a messaging system asynchronously. It acts as a JMS message listener, which is similar to an event listener.

When compared to the other two enterprise beans, a message-driven bean has one major difference. It does not have a remote or a home interface. It only has a bean class. Clients cannot access message-driven beans through interfaces. A message-driven bean has at least one business method—onMessage()—in the bean class to process a message. A message-driven bean class contains the setMessageDrivenContext() method, the ejbCreate() method, and the ejbRemove() methods in addition to the onMessage() method.

A message-driven bean resides in an EJB container of a J2EE server, and it connects to a JMS destination (queue or topic type). Any JMS client application can send a message to a destination via the JMS provider. A message-driven bean application can consume this message asynchronously.

A message-driven bean is similar to a stateless session bean in terms of its life cycle. Because it is never passivated, its life cycle has two stages: nonexistent and ready. A message-driven bean is an inner bean, and it is not accessed by the client application directly through a remote or home interface. It can have contact with other beans in the EJB container to process a message.

The remainder of the chapter focused on a simple example demonstrating how to develop, deploy, and run an application containing a message-driven bean.

Questions and Answers

1. When I send several separate messages to a topic, how many message-driven beans will be assigned to these messages to process them: one or a quantity of beans equal to the number messages?

Message-driven bean instances are created and put into a pool by the container. Whenever a message arrives at the destination, a JMS provider informs the EJB container to call the onMessage() method and process the message. An EJB container assigns an idle message-driven bean instance for each message that arrives. Therefore, every message can be handled by a different message-driven bean instance. It also means that a message-driven bean can process messages from multiple clients.

2. I can use an entity or a session bean to produce and consume messages. Can I also use a message-driven bean to produce and consume messages?

No. A message-driven bean is only designed to consume messages asynchronously. It cannot produce a message. You can use any JMS application, J2EE, or a non-J2EE application to produce messages.

3. A message-driven bean is similar to a stateless session bean. If I need to save some conversational information between a client and a bean, is there a message-driven bean similar to a stateful session bean?

No. Message-driven bean instances do not retain data or conversational state for a specific client. There is no corresponding stateful session bean for a message-driven bean. However, objects assigned to instance variables of the message-driven bean will be visible across the handling of multiple client messages.

10

JMS and the Web

IN THIS CHAPTER, I WILL DISCUSS how you can use the JMS API with web applications. You have already learned the concepts concerning JMS throughout this book, so you only need to learn how to combine these concepts with web components. I will assume that you have had some experience developing applications using web components. If you need more information about Java and web components, refer to Budi Kurniawan's *Java for the Web with Servlets, JSP, and EJB: A Developer's Guide to J2EE Solutions* (New Riders, 2002).

Architectures of a JMS Provider and a Web Client

A web component for Java-based applications is a Java servlet or a JavaServer Page (JSP). Using JMS with a web component means sending a message to a destination or receiving a message from a destination through a web client using either a Java servlet or a JSP. I will discuss the combined use of the JMS API and a web component for two different architectures: the *two-tier architecture and the three-tier architecture*. Some brief details about these two architectures are provided in the following sections.

JMS and the Web in a Two-Tier Architecture

In a two-tier model, a web client application, which is contained by a web server in addition to other services like Java Message Service (JMS) or Java Database Connectivity (JDBC), consists of the presentation layer and the business layer. Web components (Java servlets or JSP files) on a web server are accessed by a web client through a web browser. The J2EE Reference Implementation server is used as the JMS server and the web server for this book. It might seem as though all projects must be three-tier when you run a J2EE server. In fact, a web server can run without a J2EE server. Therefore, I classify it as a two-tier architecture if you use a JMS provider directly from a web component, even though a JMS server is part of the J2EE server, which is the basis of the three-tier model. A JMS server can be thought of as a server providing a message service. Figure 10.1 illustrates the JMS and web architecture in a two-tier model.

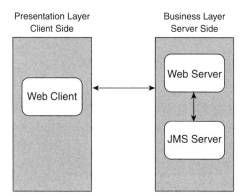

Figure 10.1   The architecture of a two-tier model with JMS and a web application.

In the web components, you can write source code to access (send or receive messages to) a JMS provider. These components reside in the web server, and web clients can call these components. A web server provides a connection between a web client and a JMS provider. If the web client is a producer client, a message is delivered to the destination created in the JMS provider. If the web client is a consumer client, a message is delivered to the client from the destination in the JMS provider.

In the section, "A Sample Application Using JMS through a Web Client," I provide a sample web client application as well as the source code.

JMS and the Web in a Three-Tier Architecture

In Chapter 2, "Enterprise Java Beans (EJB)," you explored the Java 2 Enterprise Edition (J2EE); therefore, the details of J2EE and its fundamental technology, EJB, will not be repeated in this section. Figure 10.2 illustrates the general structure of a three-tier architecture containing a web server and a JMS server in addition to an EJB container and other services that build an enterprise application.

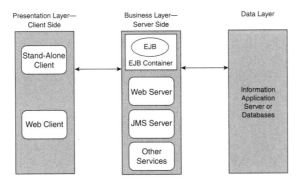

Figure 10.2   The architecture of a three-tier model for a J2EE server.

A J2EE server manages the interaction between an EJB container, a web server, a JMS server, and other enterprise services. Figure 10.3 depicts the necessary parts of the architecture illustrated in Figure 10.2. I'll explain the JMS and web component combination functionality in the J2EE server shown in this figure.

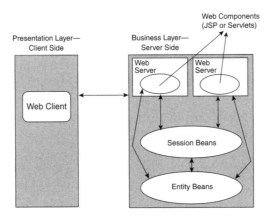

Figure 10.3   The architecture of a three-tier model containing only the JMS and web server components.

In a three-tier architecture, a web client, which can be any web browser, talks with the web server using the HTTP protocol and accesses server-side resources and applications through web components like Java servlets, JSP, EJBs (session or entity), and so on. These web components reside in the web server. A web component calls the business methods of EJBs for messaging. The web server contacts the EJB container to access these EJBs, which consist of business methods for sending messages to a destination or consuming messages from a destination in the JMS provider. If the web client is designed to send a message to a destination in the JMS provider, it must call a business method, which is written to send or publish a message through a home and remote interface of the EJB. A message is sent to the destination through a web server and an EJB container. Consuming a message from a destination has the same methodology. A web component must call a business method, which is written to receive or subscribe to a message through a home and remote interface of the EJB. A message is taken from the destination through a web server and an EJB container.

As an example, you can modify and adapt the two-tier sample application, which is provided in the next section, to a three-tier JMS Web application. You only need to add JMS-related code in the JSP file to the enterprise bean class file as a business method. You then call this business method from the JSP file through a home and remote interface of this EJB (either session or entity beans). Because a web client cannot consume messages asynchronously, you cannot use message-driven beans in a web application.

A Sample Application Using JMS through a Web Client

A web client that uses the JMS API does the same thing as a stand-alone client except it does it in a different way. Stand-alone clients can produce messages and consume messages synchronously or asynchronously. The J2EE Platform Specification does not define how web components implement JMS messages and interact with a JMS provider. Web components (either Java servlets or JSPs) can produce messages and consume messages synchronously. The only difference between a web client and a stand-alone client is how they consume messages. Web components cannot consume messages asynchronously.

Synchronous consuming blocks the server and ties up server resources. Therefore, you should avoid using the `receive()` method call in a web component while consuming messages. Instead, you should use the `receive()` method with a time parameter, such as the `receive(long parTimeOut)` method, to avoid blocking server resources.

In the next two sections, I provide two sample JMS applications accessed by a web client. One is a message producer, and the other is a message consumer.

A Web Client Application That Produces a Message to a JMS Destination

A web producer client works like the stand-alone client you learned about in the examples in Chapter 6, "JMS Programming Techniques with Examples." It can send a message to a queue or publish a message to a topic. I'll modify the sender client application example for a p2p model in Chapter 6 (Listing 6.1) to create a web producer client. The source code is shown in Listing 10.1.

Listing 10.1 **The Sender Web Client Source Code**

```
1. <%@page contentType="text/html"%>
2. <%@ page import="javax.naming.*, javax.rmi.*, java.util.*, javax.jms.*"%>
3. <html>
4. <head><title>
5. This JSP Page sends a message to the queue without using a bean
6. </title></head>
7. <body>
8. <%
10.    out.println("This JavaServer Page as a web component SENDS a message
to a queue");
11.    out.println("<BR>");
12.    out.println("to demonstrate how you can combine JMS with web
components");
13.    out.println("<BR>");
14.    out.println("<BR>");
15.
16.    // Creating JMS object variables
17.    String              cityQueueName = "queue_Montreal";
18.    Context             jndiContext = null;
19.    QueueConnectionFactory  queueConnectionFactory = null;
20.    QueueConnection     queueConnection = null;
21.    QueueSession        queueSession = null;
22.    Queue               queue = null;
23.    QueueSender         queueSender = null;
24.    TextMessage         message = null;
25.
26.    out.println("Queue name is " + cityQueueName);
27.    out.println("<BR>");
28.
29.    // Creating a JNDI InitialContext object
30.    try {
31.      jndiContext = new InitialContext();
32.    } catch (NamingException e) {
33.      out.println("Error while creating JNDI " + "context: " + e.toString());
34.    }
```

continues

Listing 10.1 **Continued**

```
35.
36.    // Looking up connection factory and queue
37.    try {
38.      queueConnectionFactory = (QueueConnectionFactory)
39.      jndiContext.lookup("QueueConnectionFactory");
40.      queue = (Queue) jndiContext.lookup(cityQueueName);
41.    } catch (NamingException e) {
42.      out.println("JNDI lookup queue failed: " + e.toString());
43.    }
44.
45.    // Creating connection, session (not transacted)
46.    try {
47.      queueConnection =
48.        queueConnectionFactory.createQueueConnection();
49.      queueSession =
50.      queueConnection.createQueueSession(false,
51.        Session.AUTO_ACKNOWLEDGE);
52.
53.      // Creating sender and text message
54.      queueSender = queueSession.createSender(queue);
54.      message = queueSession.createTextMessage();
55.      message.setText("**SENDING A MESSAGE TO DEMONSTRATE USING JMS FROM
          ➡WEB CLIENT**");
56.      out.println("Message to be sent by regular JSP client: ");
57.      out.println("<BR>");
58.      out.println(message.getText());
59.      out.println("<BR>");
60.
61.      // sending the message
62.      queueSender.send(message);
63.      // sending a non-text control message to end sending
64.      queueSender.send(queueSession.createMessage());
65.      out.println("Sending the message to " + cityQueueName + " by a web
          ➡client is done");
66.      out.println("<BR>");
67.
68.    } catch (JMSException e) {
69.      out.println("Error while sending the message: " + e.toString());
70.    } finally {
71.
72.      // closing the connection
73.      if (queueConnection != null) {
74.          try {
75.              queueConnection.close();
76.          } catch (JMSException e) {}
77.      }
78.    }
80. %>
81. </body>
82. </html>
```

When you run the web client in Listing 10.1, the JSP file sends a message to the queue type destination, "queue_Montreal," and displays some informative messages about the progress of sending the message. In the JSP file, there are some cosmetic lines in the source code in addition to JMS-related code. If you need more information about JMS concepts and examples, refer to Chapter 5, "Concepts and Fundamentals of JMS Programming," and Chapter 6.

Running a Web Client Sending a Message

To run a JSP file on the JMS server side, you must start the JMS server, and the queue type destination ("queue_Montreal" for this example) must be created administratively. To start the server, type **j2ee –verbose** at the command prompt. After the J2EE server startup is complete, you are ready to run the JMS client. If you did not create the destination, type the following at another command prompt:

j2eeadmin –addJmsDestination queue_Montreal queue

Once you have started the JMS provider and have created the destination successfully, you can call the sample JSP file provided in Listing 10.1 from a web browser on your computer. The web component in Listing 10.1 is a very simple JSP file. It immediately sends a message to the destination whenever your browser calls the JSP on the web server. This example is for demonstration purposes only. Depending on your project, you can modify and enhance this sample application. For example, you might need to present the user with a JSP page containing an HTML form to capture the message that the user wants to send. When the user submits the form, the JSP page captures this input data in the `doPost()` (or `doGet()` wherever applicable) method. The user's input data is then sent by the JSP to the destination as a JMS message. Figure 10.4 illustrates the result of calling the sample web producing client application.

To run a JSP file, you need a web server that supports Java servlets and JSP technology. A J2EE server has a built-in web server that runs JSP files. If you use a different JMS provider that does not have a proper web server to run JSP files, refer to Appendix A, "J2SE and J2EE Settings," to download Tomcat, which is a free add-on product for the Apache Web Server. If you do not want to use the Apache Web Server with Tomcat, the Tomcat server itself contains a built-in internal web server.

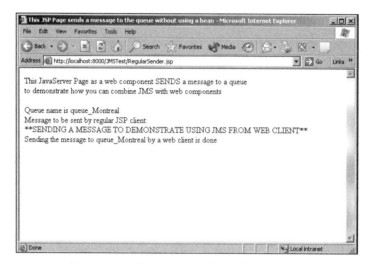

Figure 10.4 Running a web producer client.

A Web Client Application That Consumes a Message from a JMS Destination

A web consumer client works like a stand-alone client, which you learned about in the examples in Chapter 6. It can receive a message from a queue or subscribe to a message from a topic. In Listing 10.2, I modify the receiver client application example for the p2p model in Chapter 6 (Listing 6.2) to create a web consumer client.

Listing 10.2 **The Receiver Web Client Source Code**

```
1. <%@page contentType="text/html"%>
2. <%@ page import="javax.naming.*, javax.rmi.*, java.util.*, javax.jms.*"%>
3. <html>
4. <head><title>
5. This JSP Page receives a message from the queue without using a bean
6. </title></head>
7. <body>
8. <%
9.    out.println("This JavaServer Page as a web component RECEIVES a
message from a queue");
10.   out.println("<BR>");
11.   out.println("to demonstrate how you can combine JMS with web
components");
12.   out.println("<BR>");
13.   out.println("<BR>");
```

```
14.
15.    // Creating JMS object variables
16.    String                   cityQueueName = "queue_Montreal";
17.    Context                  jndiContext = null;
18.    QueueConnectionFactory   queueConnectionFactory = null;
19.    QueueConnection          queueConnection = null;
20.    QueueSession             queueSession = null;
21.    Queue                    queue = null;
22.    QueueReceiver            queueReceiver = null;
23.    TextMessage              message = null;
24.
25.    out.println("Queue name is " + cityQueueName);
26.    out.println("<BR>");
27.
28.    // Creating a JNDI InitialContext object
29.    try {
30.      jndiContext = new InitialContext();
31.    } catch (NamingException e) {
32.      out.println("Error while creating JNDI context: " + e.toString());
33.    }
34.
35.    // Looking up connection factory and queue
36.    try {
37.      queueConnectionFactory = (QueueConnectionFactory)
38.        jndiContext.lookup("QueueConnectionFactory");
39.      queue = (Queue) jndiContext.lookup(cityQueueName);
40.    } catch (NamingException e) {
41.      out.println("JNDI lookup queue failed: " + e.toString());
42.    }
43.
44.    // Creating connection, session (not transacted)
45.    try {
46.      queueConnection =
47.        queueConnectionFactory.createQueueConnection();
48.      queueSession =
49.        queueConnection.createQueueSession(false,
50.          Session.AUTO_ACKNOWLEDGE);
51.    // Creating receiver, then starting message delivery
52.      queueReceiver = queueSession.createReceiver(queue);
53.      queueConnection.start();
54.      out.println("Ready to receive the message ");
55.      out.println("<BR>");
56.
57.      // Receiving all text messages from the queue
58.      Message m = queueReceiver.receiveNoWait();
59.        if (m instanceof TextMessage) {
60.          message = (TextMessage) m;
61.          out.println("Reading message from : '" + cityQueueName + "' ");
62.          out.println("<BR>");
63.          out.println(message.getText());
```

continues

Listing 10.2   **Continued**

```
64.            out.println("<BR>");
65.            out.println("Finished reading message ");
66.        } else {
67.
68.        // Stop receiving when the message is end of stream from the queue
69.            out.println("There is no proper message from the queue");
70.            out.println("<BR>");
71.            out.println("Finished reading message ");
72.            out.println("<BR>");
73.        }
74.    } catch (JMSException e) {
75.      System.out.println("Error while receiving the message: " + e.toString());
76.    } finally {
77.
78.    // closing the connection
79.    if (queueConnection != null) {
80.        try {
81.            queueConnection.close();
82.        } catch (JMSException e) {}
83.    } //end of if
84.    } //end of finally
85. %>
86. </body>
87. </html>
```

When you run the web client in Listing 10.2, the JSP file will read the message from the queue type destination "queue_Montreal" and display some informative messages about the progress of receiving the message. In the JSP file, there are some cosmetic lines in the source code in addition to JMS-related code.

Running a Web Client Receiving a Message

To run the JSP file on the JMS server side, you must start your JMS server. Refer to the section, "Running a Web Client Sending a Message," to obtain information on starting the JMS server. The queue type destination ("queue_Montreal" for this example) must have already been created administratively while sending the message. For a receiver application, you do not need to re-create the destination.

Once you have successfully started the JMS server, you can call the JSP file from a web browser on your computer. The JSP file provided in Listing 10.2 is a very simple file. It immediately reads a message from the destination whenever you call the JSP on the web server. It waits for a message for 5000 milliseconds to avoid blocking the server's resources. This example is for demonstration purposes only. Depending on your project, you can modify and enhance this sample application.

Figure 10.5 illustrates the result of calling the sample web consumer client application if there is a message in the queue. If there is no message in the queue, calling the JSP file will display some informative messages as illustrated in Figure 10.6.

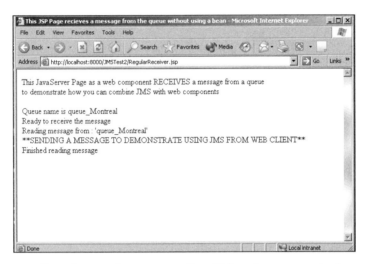

Figure 10.5 Running a web consumer client if there is a message in the queue.

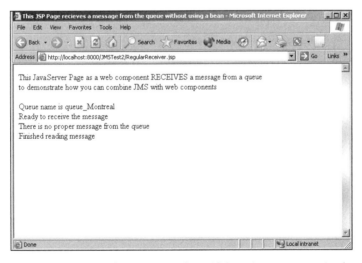

Figure 10.6 Running a web consumer client if there is no message in the queue.

Summary

In this chapter, you learned how to use the JMS API with web components and how to apply the JMS concepts you have learned about to web applications.

Using JMS with a web component means that you can send a message to a destination or receive a message from a destination through a web client by using either a Java servlet or a JSP. The JMS API and a web component can work together in two different architectures: a two-tier architecture and a three-tier architecture.

Sample web client applications (a message producer and a message consumer) and their source code were provided as well as the results of running these web applications.

Questions and Answers

1. Can I use a message-driven bean to send or receive messages with web components?

No. You can use session or entity beans for synchronous messaging in web components, but you cannot use message-driven beans because they are designed for asynchronous messaging. Web client applications cannot consume messages asynchronously.

2. What is the difference between the `receive()`, `receive(long timeout)`, and `receiveNoWait()` methods in web components?

In a web consumer client for JMS applications, you should avoid using the `receive()` method because it blocks the server's resources. Instead, you should use the `receive()` method with a time parameter or the `receiveNoWait()` method.

3. Should I handle sending or receiving a message from a web component directly or put it into a business method of a bean and call this business method from the web component?

This problem is not related to JMS. It is a two-tier or three-tier architecture modeling issue. Using JMS through web components is possible for both architectures. The selection of the two-tier or three-tier architecture totally depends on your project requirements.

IV

Java Message Service Applications

11   Developing Applications Using the JMS API

Developing Applications Using the JMS API

THIS CHAPTER IS DEDICATED TO SAMPLE APPLICATIONS and design layouts. I introduce a JMS application, provide its source code, and demonstrate how it runs. In addition to a sample application with source code, I discuss two JMS application scenarios (or design layouts) that you can apply to your real-world projects.

The sample JMS application and scenarios are not part of a real-world project. They are written to show how you can use the JMS API in your projects. (The source code for a real-world project would consume half the pages in this book.) In this chapter, I want to complete as much of the puzzle we tried to solve in the previous 10 chapters as possible. The sample application is aimed at answering the remaining questions you might have. You can optimize and rewrite this application in a better way, depending on your project considerations. I have kept it as simple as possible. You can also develop more complicated projects using JMS.

The Design Layout of the "Ask Advance Payment" Application

Let me first explain the problem definition of the "Ask Advance Payment" application. In a typical company, there are times when employees might need to request an advance payment for a particular reason. Normally, an employee would fill out a form and submit it to a manager or another department, such as the accounting department in the company. A manager or another authority would then decide whether to grant the request based on certain criteria. These criteria can include the ratio between the advance payment amount and the employee's salary, the employee's grade, the employee's position, and so on.

The example that I will implement in this chapter is designed to solve this kind of problem using a JMS application. There are two types of clients in the example: a "PaymentAsker" who asks for an advance payment and a "Decider" who decides whether to grant the request. As is the nature of JMS applications, there are two topics and a message listener. The functionality of this sample application is explained in more detail in the "What Does the Application Do?" section.

In Figure 11.1, there are N number of clients publishing messages to a topic type destination named "AskPayment." Messages of client applications named "PaymentAsker" contain PersonID, Grade, Advance Payment Request Amount, and Monthly Gross Income Amount information. The diagram in Figure 11.1 shows the relationship between the entities of the JMS application. (This diagram might not conform to the standard diagrams with which you are familiar.) Figure 11.2 illustrates the contents of the message.

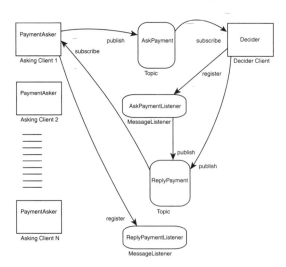

Figure 11.1 Layout of the application design.

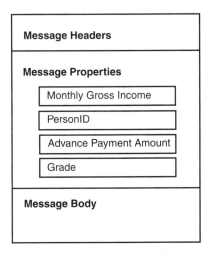

Figure 11.2 Message structure sent by the "PaymentAsker" client.

The "PaymentAsker" source code is provided in Listing 11.1. Another client application named "Decider," whose source code is provided in Listing 11.2, subscribes to the "AskPayment" topic. It registers the AskPaymentListener message listener, whose source code is provided in Listing 11.3. The "Decider" application reads the message from the topic via a message listener. The onMessage() method of the AskPaymentListener processes the message and publishes the processed message to the topic, "ReplyPayment," using the helper method decideAndReply().

In this helper method, the advance payment request is accepted or rejected based on the information from the message received from the topic, "AskPayment." Publisher clients "PaymentAsker" also subscribe to the topic "ReplyPayment," and register the ReplyPaymentListener to a message listener whose source code is provided in Listing 11.4. Whenever the replied message from a "Decider" client arrives at the topic, "ReplyPayment," the onMessage() method of the ReplyPaymentListener is invoked, and the message is processed for the "PaymentAsker" client.

Source Code for the Applications

In this section, I provide the source code for the client applications and the topics' message listeners.

Listing 11.1   **Source Code for the "PaymentAsker" Client Application**

```
1. import javax.jms.*;
2. import javax.naming.*;
3. import java.io.*;
4.
5. public class PaymentAsker {
6.
7.     public static void main(String[] args) {
8.
9.         // Creating JMS object variables for publish topic
10.        String                  interestTopicName = "AskPayment";
11.        Context                 jndiContext = null;
12.        TopicConnectionFactory  topicConnectionFactory = null;
13.        TopicConnection         topicConnection = null;
14.        TopicSession            topicSession = null;
15.        Topic                   topic = null;
16.        TopicPublisher          topicPublisher = null;
17.        TextMessage             message = null;
18.
19.        double  payment = Double.parseDouble(args[0]);
20.        String  personID = args[1];
21.        byte    grade   = Byte.parseByte(args[2]);
22.        double  income  = Double.parseDouble(args[3]);
23.
24.        PaymentAsker  myPaymentAsker = new PaymentAsker();
25.
26.        // Creating a JNDI InitialContext object
27.        try {
28.            jndiContext = new InitialContext();
29.        } catch (NamingException enaming) {
30.            System.out.println("Error while creating JNDI " +
31.                "context: " + enaming.toString());
32.        }
33.
34.        // Looking up connection factory and queue
35.        try {
36.            topicConnectionFactory = (TopicConnectionFactory)
37.                jndiContext.lookup("TopicConnectionFactory");
38.            topic = (Topic) jndiContext.lookup(interestTopicName);
39.        } catch (NamingException enaming) {
40.            System.out.println("JNDI lookup topic failed: " +
41.                enaming.toString());
42.        }
43.
44.        try {
45.        // Creating connection, session (not transacted)
46.         topicConnection =
47.             topicConnectionFactory.createTopicConnection();
48.         topicSession =
49.             topicConnection.createTopicSession(false,
50.                 Session.AUTO_ACKNOWLEDGE);
51.
```

Listing 11.1 **Continued**

```
52.        // Creating publisher and text message
53.        topicPublisher = topicSession.createPublisher(topic);
54.        message = topicSession.createTextMessage();
55.        message.setText("** Asking Advance Payment **");
56.
57.        // Specifying properties for the message
58.        message.setDoubleProperty("AskAdvPayment", payment);
59.        message.setStringProperty("PersonID", personID);
60.        message.setByteProperty("Grade", grade);
61.        message.setDoubleProperty("Income", income);
62.
63.        System.out.println("   ");
64.        System.out.print("Topic name for asking advance ") ;
65. .      System.out.println("payment:   " + interestTopicName);
66.        System.out.println("Message : '" + message.getText()+" '");
67.        System.out.println("***  Message properties *** ");
68.        System.out.println(" Advance Payment = " + payment);
69.        System.out.println(" PersonID = " + personID);
70.        System.out.println(" Grade = " + grade);
71.        System.out.println(" Income = " + income);
72.        System.out.println(" ");
73.
74.        // publishing the message
75.        topicPublisher.publish(message);
76.        System.out.print("Publishing the message to ");
77.        System.out.println(" interestTopicName + " is done");
78.        System.out.println("****************************");
79.
80.      } catch (JMSException ejms) {
81.       System.out.print("Error while publishing the message: ");
82.       System.out.println(ejms.toString());
83.      } finally {
84.      if (topicConnection != null) {
85.            try {
86.                topicConnection.close();
87.            } catch (JMSException ejms) {}
88.      }
89.      }
90.
91.    myPaymentAsker.getTheReply(personID, "ReplyPayment");
92.
93.  }  //end of the main() method
94.
95.    public void getTheReply(String parPersonID,
96.         String parReplyTopic) {
97.
98.        // Creating JMS object variables for reply topic
99.        String                interestTopicNameR = parReplyTopic;
100.       Context               jndiContextR = null;
101.       TopicConnectionFactory  topicConnectionFactoryR = null;
```

continues

Listing 11.1 **Continued**

```
102.        TopicConnection        topicConnectionR = null;
103.        TopicSession           topicSessionR = null;
104.        Topic                  topicR = null;
105.        TopicSubscriber        topicSubscriberR = null;
106.        ReplyPaymentListener   topicListenerR = null;
107.        TextMessage            paymentMessage = null;
108.        InputStreamReader      inputStreamReader = null;
109.
110.        System.out.println("   ");
111.        System.out.print("Topic name for replied message:  ");
112.        System.out.println(interestTopicNameR);
113.
114.        // Creating a JNDI InitialContext object
115.        try {
116.            jndiContextR = new InitialContext();
117.        } catch (NamingException enaming) {
118.            System.out.print("Error while creating JNDI " );
119.            System.out.println("context: " + enaming.toString());
120.        }
121.
122.        // Looking up connection factory and queue
113.        try {
114.            topicConnectionFactoryR = (TopicConnectionFactory)
115.                jndiContextR.lookup("TopicConnectionFactory");
116.            topicR = (Topic)
117.                jndiContextR.lookup(interestTopicNameR);
118.        } catch (NamingException enaming) {
119.            System.out.print("JNDI lookup topic failed: ");
120.            System.out.println(enaming.toString());
121.        }
122.
123.        try {
124.        // Creating connection, session (not transacted)
125.            topicConnectionR =
126.                topicConnectionFactoryR.createTopicConnection();
127.            topicSessionR =
128.                topicConnectionR.createTopicSession(false,
129.                    Session.AUTO_ACKNOWLEDGE);
130.
131.        // Defining message selector for specified PersonID
132.         String PersonSelector = "PersonID = '" + parPersonID +"' ";
133.
134.        // Creating subscriber with message selector
135.            topicSubscriberR =
136.                topicSessionR.createSubscriber(topicR,
137.                    PersonSelector , false);
138.        // Registering message listener with
139.        // ReplyPaymentListener helper class
140.         topicListenerR = new ReplyPaymentListener();
141.
```

```
142.        // Creating subscriber
143.        topicSubscriberR.setMessageListener(topicListenerR);
144.
145.        // Starting connection
146.        topicConnectionR.start();
147.
148.        // Control loop to end subscriber application
149.        inputStreamReader = new InputStreamReader(System.in);
150.            while (!(topicListenerR.checkAnswer)) {
151.            }
152.
153.        } catch (JMSException ejms) {
154.            System.out.print("JMS Exception occurred: ");
155.            System.out.println(ejms.toString());
156.        } finally {
157.            if (topicConnectionR != null) {
158.                try {
159.                    topicConnectionR.close();
160.                } catch (JMSException ejms) {}
161.            }
162.        }
163.
164.    } //end of getTheReply() method
165.
166. }  //end of class
```

The "PaymentAsker" client application in Listing 11.1 is written to send the
message to the "AskPayment" topic. This application includes lines to create a
connection to the JMS server, which is similar to all JMS applications. It has
an additional method to the main() method, which is getTheReply(). It subscribes to the ReplyPayment topic via "parReplyTopic" parameter and reads
the reply message using the message listener ReplyPaymentListener. In the
design structure, only the client who sends the advance payment request must
receive his/her own request response. Therefore, the getTheReply() method
uses a message selector. Notice that the message contains some properties in
addition to the message body. A "Decider" application reads and filters out
these properties in order to decide whether to grant the advance payment
request.

Listing 11.2 **Source Code for the "Decider" Client Application**

```
1. import javax.jms.*;
2. import javax.naming.*;
3. import java.io.*;
4.
```

continues

Listing 11.2 **Continued**

```
5. public class Decider {
6.
7.    public static void main(String[] args) {
8.        // Creating JMS object variables
9.        String                interestTopicName = "AskPayment";
10.       Context               jndiContext = null;
11.       TopicConnectionFactory topicConnectionFactory = null;
12.       TopicConnection       topicConnection = null;
13.       TopicSession          topicSession = null;
14.       Topic                 topic = null;
15.       TopicSubscriber       topicSubscriber = null;
16.       AskPaymentListener    topicListener = null;
17.       TextMessage           paymentMessage = null;
18.       InputStreamReader     inputStreamReader = null;
19.       char                  last = '\0';
20.
21.        // Creating a JNDI InitialContext object
22.        try {
23.            jndiContext = new InitialContext();
24.        } catch (NamingException enaming) {
25.            System.out.print("Error while creating JNDI " ); +
26.            System.out.println("context: " + enaming.toString());
27.        }
28.
29.        // Looking up connection factory and queue
30.        try {
31.            topicConnectionFactory = (TopicConnectionFactory)
32.                jndiContext.lookup("TopicConnectionFactory");
33.            topic = (Topic) jndiContext.lookup(interestTopicName);
34.        } catch (NamingException enaming) {
35.            System.out.print("JNDI lookup topic failed: ");
36.            System.out.println(enaming.toString());
37.        }
38.
39.        try {
40.        // Creating connection, session (not transacted)
41.            topicConnection =
42.                topicConnectionFactory.createTopicConnection();
43.            topicSession =
44.                topicConnection.createTopicSession(false,
45.                    Session.AUTO_ACKNOWLEDGE);
46.
47.        // Creating subscriber with message selector for Decider1
48.            topicSubscriber =
49.                topicSession.createSubscriber(topic);
50.
51.        // Registering message listener with
52.        // AskPaymentListener helper class
53.            topicListener = new AskPaymentListener();
54.            topicSubscriber.setMessageListener(topicListener);
```

```
55.
56.          // Starting connection
57.             topicConnection.start();
58.             paymentMessage = topicListener.myMessage;
59.
60.          System.out.println("Topic name is " + interestTopicName);
61.
62.          // Control loop to end subscriber application
63.          System.out.println(" ");
64.          System.out.println("To end program, enter * and <return>");
65.          System.out.println(" ");
66.          inputStreamReader = new InputStreamReader(System.in);
67.           while (!(last == '*')) {
68.             try {
69.                 last = (char) inputStreamReader.read();
70.             } catch (IOException eio) {
71.               System.out.print("I/O error occured: ");
72.               System.out.println(eio.toString());
73.             }
74.           }  //end of while
75.
76.        } catch (JMSException ejms) {
77.             System.out.print("JMS Exception occurred: ");
78.             System.out.println(ejms.toString());
79.        } finally {
80.             if (topicConnection != null) {
81.                 try {
82.                     topicConnection.close();
83.                 } catch (JMSException ejms) {}
84.             }
85.        }
86.
87.    }  //end of the main() method
88.
89. }  //end of class
```

The "Decider" client application in Listing 11.2 is written to read the message from the "AskPayment" topic. This application includes lines to create a connection to the JMS server, which is similar to all JMS applications. It reads the message via the message listener helper class AskPaymentListener. This helper class contains an additional method decideAndReply(), which decides whether to grant the advance payment request. This method sends its decision to the topic, "ReplyPayment."

Listing 11.3 **Source Code for the AskPaymentListener Message Listener**

```
1. import javax.jms.*;
2. import javax.naming.*;
3. import java.io.*;
4.
5.
6. public class AskPaymentListener implements MessageListener {
7.
8.      public TextMessage myMessage = null;
10.      public String deciderID ;
11.
12.    // passing the message from the destination as a parameter
13.    public void onMessage(Message parMessage) {
14.
15.        try {
16.         // check the message type is TextMessage
17.         if (parMessage instanceof TextMessage) {
18.          // if so, cast it into TextMessage variable
19.           myMessage = (TextMessage) parMessage;
20.          // reading and returning the message in Text format
21.           System.out.print("Message received from the topic: ");
22.           System.out.println(myMessage.getText());
23.           decideAndReply(myMessage);
24.         } else {
25.         // if not, warn the user
26.           System.out.println("Message of wrong type: ");
27.           System.out.println(parMessage.getClass().getName());
28.         }
29.        // throw the Exceptions if there are internal errors
30.        } catch (JMSException ejms) {
31.           System.out.println("JMSException in onMessage(): ");
32.           System.out.println(ejms.toString());
33.        } catch (Throwable tjms) {
34.           System.out.println("Exception in onMessage(): ");
35.           System.out.println(tjms.getMessage());
36.        } //end of try
37.    } //end of onMessage() method
38.
39.    public void decideAndReply(Message parMessage) {
40.
41.        // Creating JMS object variables
42.        String                  interestTopicName = "ReplyPayment";
43.        Context                 jndiContext = null;
44.        TopicConnectionFactory  topicConnectionFactory = null;
45.        TopicConnection         topicConnection = null;
46.        TopicSession            topicSession = null;
47.        Topic                   topic = null;
48.        TopicPublisher          topicPublisher = null;
49.        TextMessage             decidedMessage = null;
50.
```

```
51.         // Creating helper variables
52.         double    payment = 0  ;
53.         String  personID = "" ;
54.         byte    grade   = 0  ;
55.         double  income  = 0 ;
56.         String  answer = "rejected";
57.
58.         // Properties of the received message
59.         try {
60.         payment   = parMessage.getDoubleProperty("AskAdvPayment");
61.         System.out.print("  AskAdvPayment: " + payment + " ** ");
62.         personID  = parMessage.getStringProperty("PersonID");
63.         System.out.println(" PersonID: " + personID);
64.         grade =  parMessage.getByteProperty("Grade");
65.         System.out.print("  Grade: " + grade+ " ** ");
66.         income =  parMessage.getDoubleProperty("Income");
67.         System.out.println("Income: " + income);
68.         System.out.println("  ");
69.
70.         // Deciding accept or reject
71.         if ((grade> 2) &&  (grade<= 5) && (payment<=income/8))
72.             answer = "accepted"; else answer = "rejected";
73.         if ((grade> 5) &&  (grade<= 7) && (payment<=income/6))
74.             answer = "accepted"; else answer = "rejected";
75.         if ((grade> 7) &&  (grade<= 9) && (payment<=income/4))
76.             answer = "accepted"; else answer = "rejected";
77.         System.out.println("  Advance payment will be " + answer );
78.         } catch (JMSException ejms) {
79.         System.out.print("JMSException in decide(): ");
80.         System.out.println(ejms.toString());
81.         }
82.
83.         System.out.print(" Topic name for reply of advance ");
84.         System.out.println("payment request: " + interestTopicName);
85.
86.         // Creating a JNDI InitialContext object
87.         try {
88.             jndiContext = new InitialContext();
89.         } catch (NamingException enaming) {
90.             System.out.print("Error while creating JNDI ");
91.             System.out.println("context: " + enaming.toString());
92.         }
93.
94.         // Looking up connection factory and queue
95.         try {
96.             topicConnectionFactory = (TopicConnectionFactory)
97.                 jndiContext.lookup("TopicConnectionFactory");
98.             topic = (Topic) jndiContext.lookup(interestTopicName);
99.         } catch (NamingException enaming) {
100.            System.out.println("JNDI lookup topic failed: ");
101.            System.out.println("enaming.toString());
```

continues

Listing 11.3   **Continued**

```
102.        }
103.
104.        try {
105.        // Creating connection, session (not transacted)
106.            topicConnection =
107.                topicConnectionFactory.createTopicConnection();
108.            topicSession =
109.                topicConnection.createTopicSession(false,
110.                    Session.AUTO_ACKNOWLEDGE);
111.
112.        // Creating publisher and text message
113.        topicPublisher = topicSession.createPublisher(topic);
114.        decidedMessage= topicSession.createTextMessage();
115.        decidedMessage.setText("** Replying of AdvancePayment
116.                Request for " + personID +" **");
117.
118.        // Specifying properties for the message
119.        decidedMessage.setDoubleProperty("AskAdvPayment", payment);
120.        decidedMessage.setStringProperty("PersonID", personID);
121.        decidedMessage.setByteProperty("Grade", grade);
122.        decidedMessage.setDoubleProperty("Income", income);
123.        decidedMessage.setStringProperty("Answer", answer);
124.
125.        // publishing the replied message
126.        topicPublisher.publish(decidedMessage);
127.        System.out.print("Publishing the message to ");
128.        System.out.println(interestTopicName + " is done");
129.        System.out.println("********************************");
130.        System.out.println("   ");
131.
132.        } catch (JMSException ejms) {
133.          System.out.print("Error while publishing the message: ");
134.          System.out.println(ejms.toString());
135.        } finally {
136.          if (topicConnection != null) {
137.                try {
138.                    topicConnection.close();
139.                } catch (JMSException ejms) {}
140.          }
141.        }
142.
143.    } //end of decideAndReply() method
144.
145. } //end of class
```

The AskPaymentListener message listener helper class in Listing 11.3 is written to help read the message from the "AskPayment" topic and process the message for the "Decider" client application. This message listener consists of the onMessage() method, which reads the message from the topic, just like all JMS message listener classes. It contains an additional helper method: decideAndReply(). This helper method decides whether to accept or reject the advance payment request. This method also contains some lines to create a connection to the "ReplyPayment" topic. The result of the decision is sent to the "ReplyPayment" topic using the decideAndReply() helper method.

Listing 11.4   **Source Code for the ReplyPaymentListener Message Listener**

```
1. import javax.jms.*;
2. import javax.naming.*;
3. import java.io.*;
4.
5.  public class ReplyPaymentListener implements MessageListener {
6.
7.      public TextMessage replyMessage = null;
8.      boolean checkAnswer = false;
9.
10.     // passing the message from the destination as a parameter
11.     public void onMessage(Message parMessage) {
12.
13.        try {
14.           // check that the message type is TextMessage
15.           if (parMessage instanceof TextMessage) {
16.            // if so, cast it into TextMessage variable
17.            replyMessage = (TextMessage) parMessage;
18.            // reading and returning the message in Text format
19.            System.out.println("Message received from Reply Topic ");
20.            System.out.println(replyMessage.getText());
21.            checkAnswer = false;
22.            paymentStatus(replyMessage);
23.
24.           } else {
25.            // if not, warn the user
26.            System.out.println("Message of wrong type: ");
27.            System.out.println(parMessage.getClass().getName());
28.            }
29.            // throw the Exceptions if there are internal errors
30.        } catch (JMSException ejms) {
31.            System.out.println("JMSException in onMessage(): ");
32.            System.out.println(ejms.toString());
33.        } catch (Throwable tjms) {
34.            System.out.println("Exception in onMessage(): ");
35.            System.out.println(tjms.getMessage());
36.        } //end of try
37.     } //end of onMessage() method
38.
39.     public void paymentStatus(Message parMessage) {
40.        // Creating helper variables
41.        double     payment = 0  ;
```

continues

Listing 11.4 **Continued**

```
42.         String  personID = "" ;
43.         byte    grade   = 0 ;
44.         double  income  = 0 ;
45.         String  answer = "";
46.
47.         // Properties of the received message
48.         try {
49.         System.out.println("*************************************");
50.         payment   = parMessage.getDoubleProperty("AskAdvPayment");
51.         System.out.print("  AskAdvPayment: " + payment + " ** ");
52.         if (payment>0) checkAnswer = true; else checkAnswer = false;
53.
54.         personID   = parMessage.getStringProperty("PersonID");
55.         System.out.println("  PersonID: " + personID);
56.         grade      = parMessage.getByteProperty("Grade");
57.         System.out.print("  Grade: " + grade + " ** ");
58.         income     = parMessage.getDoubleProperty("Income");
59.         System.out.println("  Income: " + income);
60.         System.out.println("   ");
61.
62.         answer =  parMessage.getStringProperty("Answer");
63.         System.out.println("Answer: " + answer );
64.         System.out.print("!!! The advance payment " + payment);
65.         System.out.print(" for " + personID + " is ");
66.         System.out.println(answer + " !!!");
67.
68.         } catch (JMSException ejms) {
69.             System.out.println("JMSException in onMessage(): ");
70.             System.out.println(ejms.toString());
71.         } //end of try
72.
73.     } //end of paymentStatus() method
74.
75. } //end of class
```

The ReplyPaymentListener message listener helper class in Listing 11.4 is written to help read the message from the "ReplyPayment" topic and process the message for the "PaymentAsker" client application. This message listener contains the onMessage() method, which reads the message from the topic, just like all JMS message listener classes. It consists of an additional helper method: paymentStatus(). This helper method displays the status of the decision sent by the "Decider."

What Does the Application Do?

In the first section of this chapter, "The Design Layout of the 'Ask Advance Payment' Application," I briefly explained the function of the application and what you should expect when you run the application's class files. In this section, I will provide more details.

This application is designed for an employee to ask for an advance payment via a JMS system. The employee publishes the advance payment request by running the "PaymentAsker" client application. The "PaymentAsker" sends this request to the "AskPayment" topic as a message. The "Decider" application subscribes to this topic to read the messages that arrive. Whenever the message arrives at the topic, the onMessage() method of AskPaymentListener is invoked to process the message. It casts the message to the proper type. This onMessage() method calls a helper method to accept or reject the request. This helper method publishes the message containing the answer to the "ReplyPayment" topic. The publisher application of the advance payment request subscribes to the "ReplyPayment" topic and registers the ReplyPaymentListener. Whenever a message arrives at this topic, the message is processed and is then read by the "PaymentAsker" client.

There is also a message selector for the "PaymentAsker" when it reads the message from the "ReplyPayment" topic. The topic filters the message based on the PersonID and delivers the message to the client who previously requested the advance payment. In response, a JMS client asks for an advance payment. This request is accepted or rejected and an answer is returned to the client who requested it.

In the next section, I explain how to run the application as well as describe what you will see on the screen when the application runs.

Running the Application

You should first properly compile the source code for the client applications and message listeners after you write them. Then, run the J2EE Reference Implementation by entering **j2ee −verbose.** If you see the message "J2EE server startup complete" at the command prompt, you can run the JMS applications.

Because topics are administrative objects, the topics "AskPayment" and "ReplyPayment" must be created using j2eeadmin at another command prompt as follows:

j2eeadmin –addJmsDestination AskPayment topic

and

j2eeadmin –addJmsDestination ReplyPayment topic

I will demonstrate how this application works step-by-step. Open a command prompt and run the "Decider" application, as illustrated in Figure 11.3. It will wait for a message, which will arrive at the "AskPayment" topic.

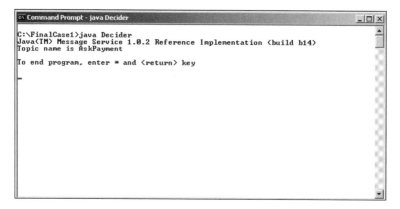

Figure 11.3　The "Decider" application.

Open another command prompt to run the publisher application "PaymentAsker." One or more "PaymentAsker" applications will publish the request message using the same class file with different arguments. The first argument is the amount of the advance payment request, the second argument is the PersonID of the employee, the third argument is the grade of the employee, and the fourth argument is the monthly gross income of the employee. For example, Figure 11.4 illustrates a "PaymentAsker" with a request of 170 dollar advance payment for an employee with a PersonID of LE2, a grade of 5, and a monthly income of 2345.

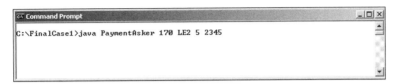

Figure 11.4 A "PaymentAsker" application with the argument values of 170, LE2, 5, and 2345.

After you run the "PaymentAsker" illustrated in Figure 11.4, you will see a screen similar to the one in Figure 11.5. It displays the header property of the message and the answer for the advance payment request, which is a rejection for the example that uses the argument values of 170, LE2, 5, and 2345. It also displays that the message with the answer header property is published to the "ReplyPayment" topic.

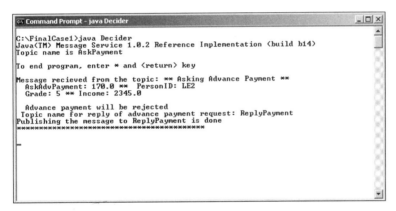

Figure 11.5 The "Decider" application after receiving the message with the 170, LE2, 5, and 2345 header property values.

The message and answer are received by the publisher client as illustrated in Figure 11.6. The answer is a rejection for this example.

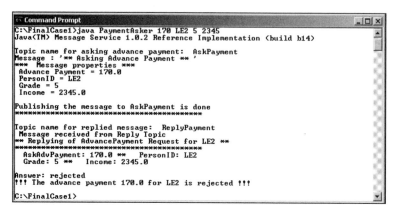

Figure 11.6 The "PaymentAsker" application receives the answer.

Run the same application, but change the grade number to 9 instead of 5. The message will be received by the "Decider" application as illustrated in Figure 11.7. This figure displays the header property of the message and the answer for the advance payment request, which is an acceptance for this example using the 170, LE2, 9, and 2345 argument values. It also displays that the message with an answer header property is published to the "ReplyPayment" topic.

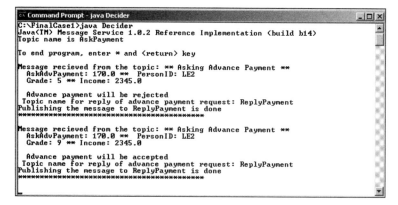

Figure 11.7 The "Decider" application after receiving the message with the 170, LE2, 9, and 2345 header property values.

The message containing a grade of 9 is received by the publisher client as illustrated in Figure 11.8. The answer is an acceptance based on the new argument values.

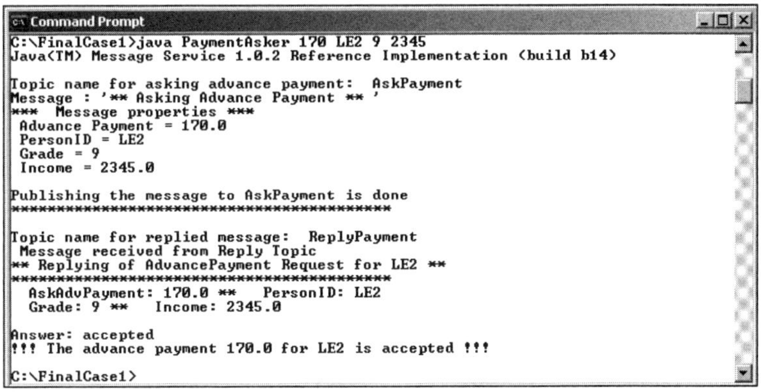

```
C:\FinalCase1>java PaymentAsker 170 LE2 9 2345
Java(TM) Message Service 1.0.2 Reference Implementation (build b14)

Topic name for asking advance payment:  AskPayment
Message : '** Asking Advance Payment ** '
*** Message properties ***
 Advance Payment = 170.0
 PersonID = LE2
 Grade = 9
 Income = 2345.0

Publishing the message to AskPayment is done
********************************************

Topic name for replied message:  ReplyPayment
 Message received from Reply Topic
** Replying of AdvancePayment Request for LE2 **
********************************************
    AskAdvPayment: 170.0 **    PersonID: LE2
    Grade: 9 **    Income: 2345.0
Answer: accepted
!!! The advance payment 170.0 for LE2 is accepted !!!

C:\FinalCase1>
```

Figure 11.8 The "PaymentAsker" application with a grade of 9 receives the answer.

Try this JMS application with different argument values, and run the publisher application on more than one command prompt window for different PersonID values to see how the message selector works.

Modify the source code according to your real or potentially real project considerations. Enhance and optimize the applications. For example, separate some functions into individual methods for reusability or modify the application to a web-based JMS application to collect user input through web forms. As discussed earlier, this example is designed to provide a model for your real JMS applications. Try to apply the idea and design structure of the example to other applications regardless of whether they are simpler or more sophisticated.

Design Samples of JMS Applications

In this section, I provide two design architectures for two applications using JMS and Java 2 enterprise beans (session, entity, and message-driven beans). Only their function is discussed; their source code is not provided. In these examples, diagrams are not standard graphics nor diagrams you have worked with before while developing software projects. Their purpose is only to illustrate the relationship between components and entities of the applications. Although these design layouts are only examples to help you with your real-world JMS projects, as you study the sample architecture, you'll agree that JMS is a key technology in J2EE, and it will find broad use in J2EE applications.

The "Promoting" Application

Before explaining the structure of the application using Java enterprise beans, I'd like to provide the problem to be solved using the JMS API.

In many companies, staff members are promoted to upper-level positions from time to time, depending on their success. A responsible person, such as a president or vice president, informs the proper department to implement the promotions in the company records. This JMS application provides a new approach to manage this procedure by using the JMS API and Java enterprise beans.

Briefly, in this application, the vice president publishes a message to a topic about the promotion. Human Resources and the office manager subscribe to this topic, read the message, store the promotion in a database, and send the response to a queue. The vice president reads the progress about the promotion sent to him or her from this queue. The technical detail of the sample application design structure follows.

In this sample application, which uses message-driven and entity beans, the Vice_President client publishes a newly promoted manager to the "Promote_To_Manager" topic. The HR_director and Office_Setup message-driven beans subscribe to this topic and process the message using the onMessage() method in their own class as well as the Personal_Info and Office_Info entity beans. These entity beans map Personal_Info and Office_Info data in the database.

The request from the topic is processed. The resulting information is updated in the database and is then sent to the Promoting_Done queue by entity beans. The publisher client Vice_President also connects to this queue and reads the result from the queue. The design layout for this example is illustrated in Figure 11.9.

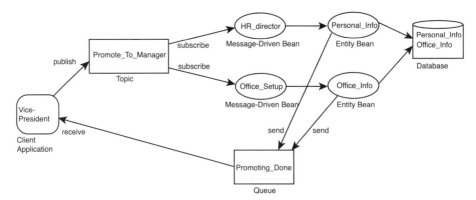

Figure 11.9   The "Promoting" application design layout.

The "New Product" Application

Before explaining the structure of the application, I'd like to provide the problem to be solved using the JMS API.

From time to time, production companies bring a new product to the market. Certain departments related to production handle some steps before manufacturing the new product. This JMS application provides a new approach to manage this procedure using the JMS API and Java enterprise beans.

In this application, in terms of the internal process, the production department contacts the production planning department and the sales department before producing the new product. To do this, the production client publishes information about the new product to a topic. The production planning department and sales department subscribe to this topic and read the message. These departments handle certain internal processes for the new product and take the necessary steps to manufacture it using Java enterprise beans and an enterprise information server or a database. While these steps are being taken, another message is sent to another topic. This message can contain information about the product such as cost, price, and technical specifications. Everyone in the company who subscribes to this topic can read the message about the new product. The technical detail of the sample application design structure is explained as follows.

In this example application, which uses message-driven, session, and entity beans, the Production client publishes a newly planned product to the "New_Product_Planning" topic. The Production_Planning and Sales message-driven beans subscribe to this topic and process the message using the `onMessage()` method in their own class as well as the Plan Supply Material, and Calculate Cost and Price session beans. These session beans call the Supply_Chain_Info and Cost_Info entity beans, which provide a connection to an enterprise information server containing supply chain information for product planning and cost information.

The Cost and Planning request for a new product is processed by session beans. The result is updated by entity beans in the database and is sent to the "New_Product" topic using session beans. Other clients subscribe to the "New_Product" topic to read information about the new product, which contains its cost and supply material information. The design layout for this example is illustrated in Figure 11.10.

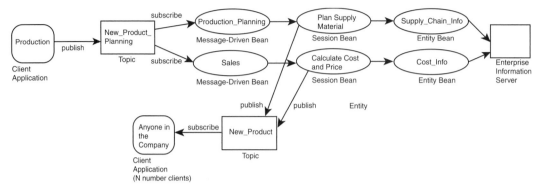

Figure 11.10   The "New Product" design layout.

Summary

In the previous 10 chapters, you learned about JMS related concepts, theory, and technologies. You applied the JMS theory to simple examples. This chapter focused on sample applications similar to a final project in a course.

The first JMS application is based on an automatic decision mechanism of an advance payment request. This application contains four Java classes; their source code is provided in the chapter. The design layout of the application was explained as was the structure of the source code and the functionality of the application. The results of running the application were also provided.

The second JMS application demonstrated the design layout of the "Promoting" application. The third JMS application demonstrated the design layout of the "New Product" application. Both applications used enterprise beans (session, entity, and message-driven beans). What you can do with the JMS API and how you can use enterprise beans in JMS applications was also explained.

V

Appendixes

A   J2SE and J2EE Settings

B   Application Deployment Tool

C   Java Message Service (JMS) API Vendors

D   Overview of JMS Package Classes

J2SE and J2EE Settings

JAVA MESSAGE SERVICE (JMS) IS PART of the Java 2 Platform Enterprise Edition (J2EE), which is an extension of the Java 2 Standard Edition (J2SE). In this appendix, I will explain which software application you need as well as how to install and configure the software on your computer. All the software packages used in the book are Windows versions. Particularly, applications are written and tested on Windows XP. If you develop your project on UNIX (HP-UNIX, Sun Solaris, or Linux) or any other operating system, you might need to consult your operating system vendor or the Sun web site at http://java.sun.com for Java related issues. Because Java is a platform independent technology, the code listings of the applications in this book will work on any platform regardless of which platform you use to write the code listings.

Before I provide detailed information about the software packages needed, let's briefly review the items you will need to run and develop Java enterprise applications:

- J2SE
- J2EE
- A development tool
- A deployment tool

The first three elements will be examined in this appendix. The deployment tool will be explained in Appendix B, "Application Deployment Tool.". In addition to these items, you will need the following items to run the examples in this book:

- A web server that supports servlets and JavaServer Pages (JSP). A web server will probably be included with your application server. It is J2EE for this book.
- A database (MS Access is used for the examples in this book).
- A Java Database Connectivity (JDBC) driver for the chosen database if possible (a JDBC-ODBC bridge is used for the examples in this book).

Web server requirements will also be examined in this appendix. Database and JDBC driver requirements are beyond the scope of this book.

J2SE

Although you can write Java source code in any Integrated Development Environment (IDE), to compile and run a Java application, you must at least install J2SE. JMS is part of J2EE, but you have to start everything with J2SE. All other Java technologies, even J2EE, are an extension of the J2SE Software Development Kit (SDK). In this section, you will learn how to obtain, install, and configure J2SE on your computer.

Downloading the J2SE SDK

You should first download J2SE from Sun's Java web site at `http://java.sun.com` unless you acquire it from your vendor. At the time of this writing, version 1.4 Beta 3 is available, but the book is based on version 1.3.1. To download the proper J2SE file, follow these steps:

1. Go to `http://java.sun.com`. Because everything changes with the speed of thought in the Internet world, you might find that the dedicated Sun Java web site URL is not valid. If so, check the updated site address through Sun's commercial web site at `http://www.sun.com` or contact your vendor.
2. Find the latest version of J2SE (1.3.1 for this book) on this page.
3. Select the proper file depending on your operating system. The Windows version was chosen for this book.
4. You can download the file by using FTP or HTTP. You can also download the entire file at once or download the file in smaller pieces depending on your Internet connection.

It is beyond the scope of this book to provide information about how to use J2SE. If you need more information about using the program, go to `http://java.sun.com/j2se/1.3/docs`. If you want more general information, go to `http://developer.java.sun.com/developer/infodocs`, and click the link that you need on this page. It will take you to another page from which you can download some training materials and a starting guide.

Setting Up J2SE

Next, you need to install the J2SE SDK file. In Windows Explorer, find the location of the file you downloaded as shown in Figure A.1.

Figure A.1 Finding the J2SE file on your system.

When you double-click the icon that represents the installation file, setup will start unpacking the file.

The setup process for the J2SE SDK is very similar to the installation of other applications on a Windows operating system. The following steps describe the process:

1. A Welcome dialog box appears and provides generic information about the installation process.

2. A Software License Agreement appears. If you want to install the J2SE SDK, you must accept the agreement.

3. Choose the destination location. In this book the location used is C:\JavaMain\j2sdkse1.3.1.

4. The next step is very important in the setup process. Figure A.2 shows the selection of the five components of the Java SDK:

   - Program Files—Contains the libraries and executables for the J2SE SDK.

   - Native Interface Header—Contains the C header files for the Java Native Interface and the Java Virtual Machine Debugger Interface.

   - Old Native Interface—Contains the C header files for the old Native Method Interface.

   - Demos—Contains small applets and applications with their source code to show Java's language ability.

   - Java Sources—Contains source code for all classes in the core J2SE packages.

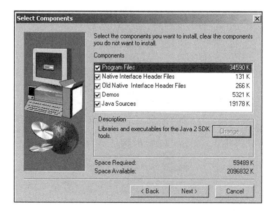

Figure A.2   Select Components step of the setup process.

The most important component is the Program Files component. You can clear the check box of the components that you do not want to install, but it is recommended that you install all the components if you have enough space on your hard disk.

Verifying the Installation of the J2SE SDK

Now that you have installed J2SE, let's talk about what it does. What is the difference between before and after the installation? The easiest way to test J2SE is to use the command prompt (known as the MS-DOS prompt on some Windows operating systems such as Windows 95/98/ME). You can select the command prompt by clicking Start, Accessories. You can also access the command prompt by clicking Start, Run and typing **cmd**. At the command prompt, go to the bin directory under the J2SE directory, which you installed previously, and type **java −version**.

If you receive a message in the command prompt dialog box similar to Figure A.3, it means that your setup has been completed properly. If not, your setup did not finish properly. It is recommended that you uninstall, deleting all the files in the destination location, restart the computer, and reinstall the setup file. Make sure you have downloaded the proper file for your system.

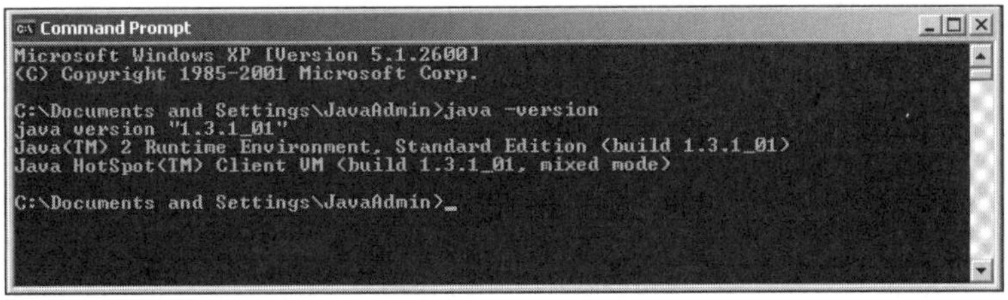

Figure A.3   Testing the installation at the command prompt.

The message java version "1.3.1_01" in Figure A.3 means you have installed J2SE properly. Does it mean that any Java source code in which there is no syntax error will work on your system? Let's test it by using the Hello World example in Listing A.1.

Listing A.1.   **Hello World Example to Test the Installation**

```
class HelloJavaUser{

    public static void main (String[] arguments){
        System.out.println("Hello Java User! ");
    }

} //end of the HelloJavaUser class
```

Save this code in any location on your system except in the location in which you installed the J2SE SDK. You can type and save this file in any text editor such as Notepad. Don't forget to make its extension .java; otherwise, you might encounter problems when you compile.

Then, go to command prompt on your system and change your working directory to the directory in which you saved the file (see Figure A.4).

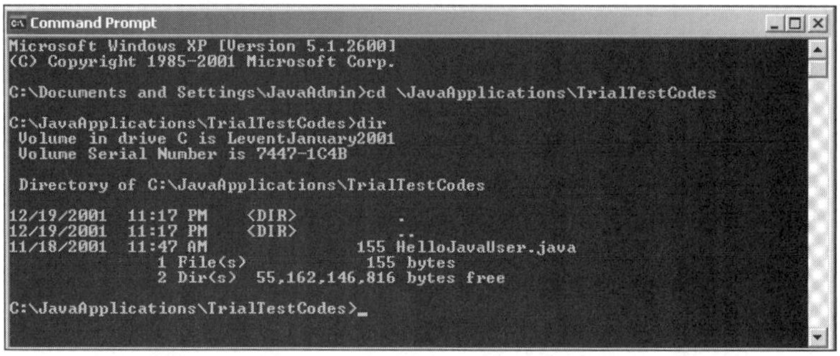

Figure A.4   Saving the simple Java code in a directory.

To compile the source file, type **javac HelloJavaUser.java** at the command prompt. You should immediately receive an error message stating that the source code could not be compiled (see Figure A.5).

Figure A.5   Trying to compile the simple Java code.

Actually, nothing is wrong with your source code. Your system just did not recognize the javac command. Where is javac? It is in the directory named bin under the J2SE installation directory. Type this directory path definition before calling javac (just in front of the command as shown in Figure A.6) and compile again. You should not receive an error message. When you check the files in the directory, you should see the HelloJavaUser.class file, which means it has compiled properly (see Figure A.6).

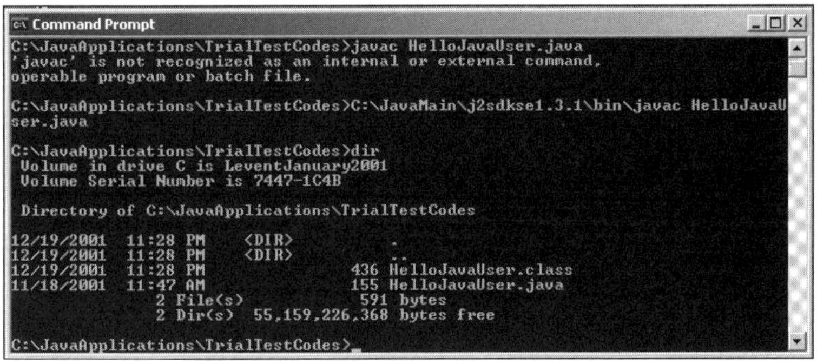

Figure A.6 Successful compiling of the simple Java code in a directory.

You then need to configure your system to run the Java compiler and call the Java standard classes anywhere on your system.

Configuring J2SE on Your System

The most important step after setting up the J2SE SDK is to configure it for your system. This configuration depends on your operating system and its version. In this section, the Windows NT/2000/XP configurations are explained. Because of its architecture, J2EE is not available for Windows 95/98/ME; therefore, any kind of installation and configuration for these operating systems are excluded from this chapter, although J2SE is available. You should consult your system administrator for different operating systems, although the main concept is the same for many operating systems.

If you develop Java applications and run them on Windows NT/2000/XP, or similar operating systems, configuring the PATH and CLASSPATH variables is a little different from Windows 95/98/ME operating systems. There is no autoexec.bat file. PATH and CLASSPATH variables can be reached from System Properties in Administrative Tools (the location might change slightly depending on the variety of Windows operating systems you use). You need to change or assign certain values to these variables in the Environment Variables dialog box as shown in Figure A.7.

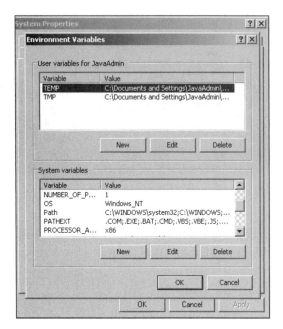

Figure A.7 The Environment Variables dialog box to configure the PATH and
CLASSPATH variables.

Configuring the PATH Variable for J2SE

If you want to compile and run your Java source code in any location on the
system, you should add the directory of the Java compiler executable file in
this PATH listing. You can place the directory name directly into the PATH
System Variables listing, but this is not recommended. A better way is to create
a system variable named JAVA_HOME first, and then build all your configuration on it. This will not only prevent you from having to type the same directory name many times, but it also allows you to update version changes by
updating only one variable. You will use this Java Home directory content at
least twice in the PATH variable and once in CLASSPATH. Also, if you don't
have to type it many times, you will not mistype it. Additionally, Java comes
with almost with same directory structure. If you install a new version with a
different Home directory name, subdirectory names will stay the same. You can
change the Java Home directory and still be able to use other system variables
without any problem.

To create a Java Home variable, click the New button in the Environment
Variables dialog box. A New System Variable dialog box appears. Enter
JAVA_HOME into the Variable Name box, and then enter the directory path,
which is the Java installation directory on your system, into the Variable Value

box as shown in Figure A.8. This directory is C:\JavaMain\j2sdkse1.3.1 for this book. Substitute the name of your directory if it is different from the directory used in the book. Be careful, this must be the topmost directory of the J2SE SDK.

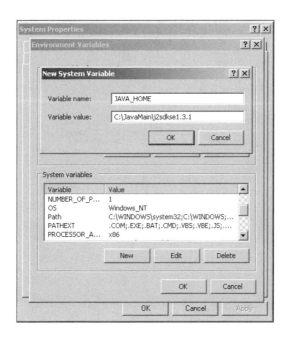

Figure A.8   The New System Variable dialog box to create the JAVA_HOME variable.

You can use this variable in any other system variables such as PATH and CLASSPATH. System or user variable values are not case sensitive in Windows operating systems.

To add the Java compiler executable file directory in the PATH listing, select Path from the System Variables listing and click the Edit button. The Edit System Variable dialog box opens. Do not change the Variable Name; in the Variable Value box, add **%JAVA_HOME%** and **%JAVA_HOME%\bin** at the end of the existing list by using a semicolon (;) separator between items (see Figure A.9). The PATH variable value is not case sensitive in Windows like other system variables.

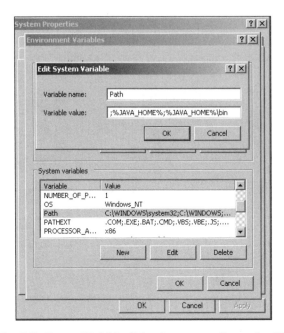

Figure A.9   The Edit System Variable dialog box to configure the PATH variable.

If There Is No PATH Variable

Although putting only the %JAVA_HOME%\bin value in the PATH variable is enough to run Java applications, it is recommended that you also put the %JAVA_HOME% value in PATH variable to make sure that you can run any Java executable file under the topmost directory of the installed Java program.

If you don't see a PATH System Variable, which is rare (for example, you might have a newly built computer, or you might have reformatted your hard disk and only installed the operating system), you should create it just as you created the New System Variable and enter the proper values into it. The steps are exactly the same as when creating the Java Home variable.

Configuring the CLASSPATH Variable for J2SE

After configuring the PATH variable, you should configure the CLASSPATH variable to find proper class files for your applications. Java looks for the tools.jar file, which contains all the Java standard class libraries. This file is used to compile and run Java programs. You should indicate where the tools.jar file is on your system. Otherwise, you could receive a Class not Found error. This error occurs if your Java application cannot find the class that was inherited into your application. (Actually, you might see this error message if the file name is not spelled or capitalized correctly, or a folder does not contain the source code.)

The J2SE SDK searches the tools.jar file first in the CLASSPATH settings; it then looks for java.exe and uses this file's location to determine where tools.jar is. This file is usually located in the lib subdirectory in the J2SE installation directory on your system. You can add this directory name into the CLASSPATH System Variable.

If that variable does not exist on your System Variables listing, you can create it by clicking New on the Environment Properties dialog box. The steps are exactly the same as when creating the Java Home variable. The only difference is the variable name and its value. Enter **CLASSPATH** as the name, and enter the entire directory path from the root directory of the tools.jar file. You can provide this value directly, but providing it with the Java Home variable is highly recommended. So, you can enter **%JAVA_HOME%\lib\tools.jar** in the Variable Value box (see Figure A.10). If it is created for the first time, do not forget to put a period (.) before this value, and then separate it with a semicolon (;). The period means that the current directory will also be used when the compiler and runtime look for class files.

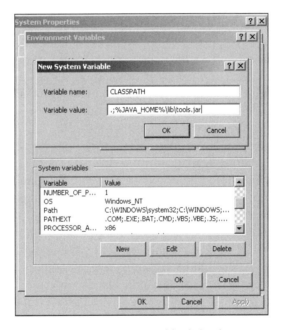

Figure A.10   The New System Variable dialog box to create the CLASSPATH variable.

If the variable exists in your System Variables listing, you can select the CLASSPATH variable from the System Variables listing by clicking Edit. Add the tools.jar file (with its directory path starting from the root directory) at the end of the CLASSPATH variable. Do not forget to use the semicolon (;) separator between the listing items in the CLASSPATH variable. For example, enter **%JAVA_HOME%\lib\tools.jar** at the end of the CLASSPATH Variable Value box. Like other system variables, the CLASSPATH variable value is not case sensitive in Windows.

If you need classes that you developed or any other developer created for the project separately, their directory names must be referenced in the CLASSPATH variable. If there is no special class file directory in CLASSPATH variable, the J2SE SDK looks for the default java\lib directory on your system or current working directory. As an example, if you have classes in C:\Javatest\Project_Class, you should put this directory information in the CLASSPATH variable if you want to reach the class files in C:\Javatest\Project_Class from any location on your computer. In this case, add **C:\Javatest\Project_Class** to the end of the CLASSPATH variable by separating the listing items with a semicolon (;).

Similarly, if you have .jar files to be reached by any other Java application, you should put the file names with their entire directory information in the CLASSPATH variable. For example, if you have FirstSteps.jar in the directory C:\Javatest\Special_Gate, add **C:\Javatest\Special_Gate\FirstSteps.jar** to the end of the CLASSPATH variable by separating the listing items with a semicolon (;).

You should have administrative privileges for Windows NT and Windows 2000 or similar operating systems to make changes to PATH and CLASS-PATH. Windows XP Home Edition does not require administrative privileges to make changes to system variables despite the fact that the configuration steps are similar to Windows NT.

Although only the Windows installation and configuration are explained in this section of the book, the steps and key concepts are very similar for other operating systems, such as UNIX or Linux. You can configure these system variables in the proper files such as a .sh script file or a .profile file. You'll need read/execute permission to the directory where J2SE is installed.

J2EE

As a language, Java has three different versions. Besides J2SE, it has two more editions: the Micro Edition and J2EE. J2EE has already been introduced in the book because JMS is part of J2EE.

In this section, you will learn how to install J2EE on your system. J2EE is an extension of J2SE; therefore, you must install J2SE before you install J2EE.

Downloading the J2EE SDK

Start by downloading J2EE from the Sun Java web site at `http://java.sun.com` unless you acquire it from your vendor. As of this writing, version v 1.3 is available. To download the proper J2EE file, follow these steps:

1. Go to `http://java.sun.com`. As mentioned earlier, be sure to check the updated site address via Sun's commercial web site at `http://www.sun.com` or contact your vendor for a possible web address change.

2. Select the latest version of J2EE (for this book it is version 1.3) on this page.

3. Select the proper J2EE SDK file to download depending on your operating system. The Windows version was chosen for this book. At the time of this writing, only the Windows NT/2000 version is available, but the examples and sample application designed for this book works with Windows XP as well.

4. You can download the file by using FTP or HTTP. You can also download the entire file at once or download the file in smaller pieces depending on your Internet connection.

It is beyond the scope of this book to provide information about how to use J2EE. If you need more information about using the program, go to `http://java.sun.com/j2ee/docs.html`. If you want more general information, go to `http://developer.java.sun.com/developer/infodocs`, and click the link that you need on this page. It will take you to another page from which you can download some training materials and a starting guide.

Setting Up J2EE

Install the J2EE file. In Windows Explorer, find the location of the file you downloaded as shown in Figure A.11.

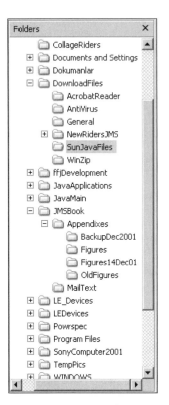

Figure A.11   Finding the J2EE file on your system.

The setup process for the J2EE SDK is very similar to the installation of other applications on a Windows operating system. The following steps describe the process:

1. A Welcome dialog box appears, which provides generic information about the installation process.

2. The Software License Agreement appears. If you want to install the J2EE SDK, you must accept the agreement.

3. Choose the destination location. For this book, the location used is C:\JavaMain\j2sdkee1.3.1.

4. Select a Component of the Java Development Kit. This screen is a little different from J2SE. There is only one component in J2EE: Program Files, which includes libraries and executables for the J2EE SDK.

Usually, you can clear the check box of the component if you do not want to install it, but in this case you do not have a choice.

Verifying the Installation of the J2EE SDK

As with J2SE, you can test J2EE to see whether it is installed properly before using it with applications. Go to the command prompt of your operating system and type **j2ee.bat**.

You will probably receive an error message such as "'j2ee.bat' is not recognized as an internal or external command, operable program, or batch file."

This message informs you that the j2ee.bat file was not found. This file must be in the J2EE installation directory's bin directory. Let's put this directory information in front of j2ee.bat, like this:

```
c:\JavaMain\j2sdkee1.3.1\bin\j2ee.bat
```

You probably received another error message such as "ERROR: Set J2EE_HOME before running this script."

Your installation is okay, but you need to configure something on your system. Both error messages are shown in Figure A.12. In the next section, you will see how to configure Java 2 Enterprise Edition. After the configuration, you can verify the installation again.

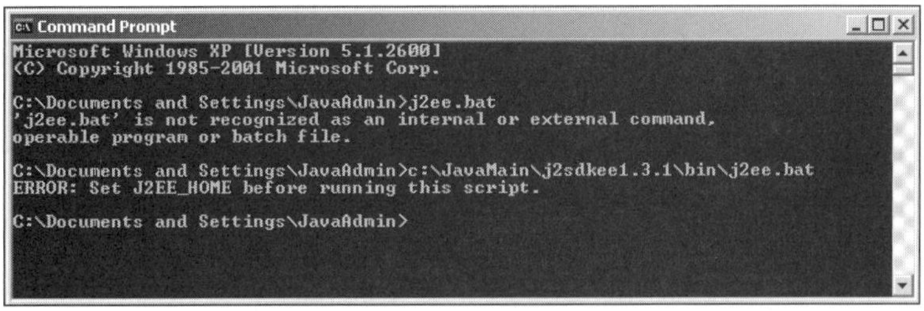

Figure A.12   Testing the J2EE SDK installation.

Configuring J2EE on Your System

As with J2SE, you should introduce the J2EE class files and executable files' directory into your system. This can be done in the PATH and CLASSPATH variables. Your system must know where the j2ee.jar file is as well as the \bin directory of the J2EE installation. You should first create the J2EE Home variable and put other information associated with the J2EE Home variable into the PATH and CLASSPATH variables.

Configuring the PATH Variable for J2EE

If you want to run Java enterprise applications from any location on your system, you should add the directory containing the Java enterprise executable batch files to the PATH listing. You have to create a J2EE Home directory variable, and then build your configuration on it.

To create a J2EE Home variable, click the New button in the Environment Variables dialog box. The New System Variable dialog box opens. Enter J2EE_HOME into the Variable Name box, and then enter the directory path into the Variable Value box. This directory is the Java installation directory on your system (see Figure A.13), which is C:\JavaMain\j2sdkee1.3.1 in this book. Substitute your directory name if it is different from the directory name used in the book. Be careful, this must be the topmost directory of the J2EE SDK.

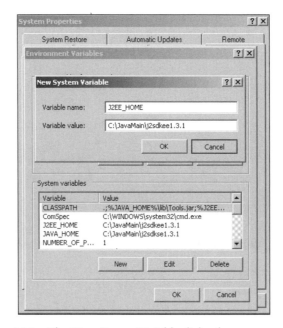

Figure A.13   The New System Variable dialog box to create the J2EE_HOME variable.

To add the Java Enterprise executable batch files directory to the PATH listing, select Path from the System Variables listing and click the Edit button. The Edit System Variable dialog box opens. Do not change the Variable Name; in the Variable Value box, add **%J2EE_HOME%** and **%J2EE_HOME%\bin** to the end of the existing list by putting a semicolon (;) separator between the items (see Figure A.14). Like other system variables, the PATH variable value is not case sensitive in Windows.

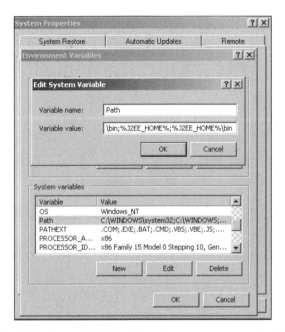

Figure A.14   The Edit System Variable dialog box to configure the PATH variable.

Although putting only the %J2EE_HOME%\bin value into the PATH variable is enough to run Java enterprise applications, it is recommended that you put the %J2EE_HOME% value in the PATH variable as well.

Configuring the CLASSPATH Variable for J2EE

After configuring the PATH variable, you should also configure the CLASSPATH variable to find proper class files for your enterprise applications. Java looks for the j2ee.jar file for enterprise applications, which contains all the Java enterprise class libraries. This file is used to run Java enterprise programs. You should indicate to your system where the j2ee.jar file resides.

  This file is usually located in the lib subdirectory in the J2EE SDK installation directory on your system. You can add this directory name to the CLASSPATH system variable.

If you have installed J2SE—which you must do in order to run J2EE—the PATH and CLASSPATH system variables should already exist. Therefore, you can select the CLASSPATH variable from the System Variables listing by clicking Edit. Add the j2ee.jar file with its entire directory path from the root directory to the end of the CLASSPATH variable. Do not forget to use the semicolon (;) separator between the listing items. Add **%J2EE_HOME%\lib\j2ee.jar** to the end of the CLASSPATH Variable Value box. Like other system variables, the CLASSPATH variable value is not case sensitive in Windows (see Figure A.15).

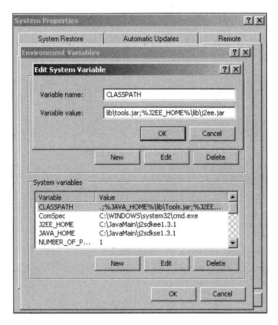

Figure A.15   The Edit System Variable dialog box to configure the CLASSPATH variable.

You should have administrative privileges to make changes to PATH and CLASSPATH in Windows NT and Windows 2000 or in similar operating systems. Windows XP Home Edition does not require administrative privileges to make changes to the system variables despite the fact that the configuration steps are similar to Windows NT.

You can now test the installation. Type **j2ee** at the command prompt. If you receive output similar to Figure A.16, you can get relax because this indicates that the installation has completed properly.

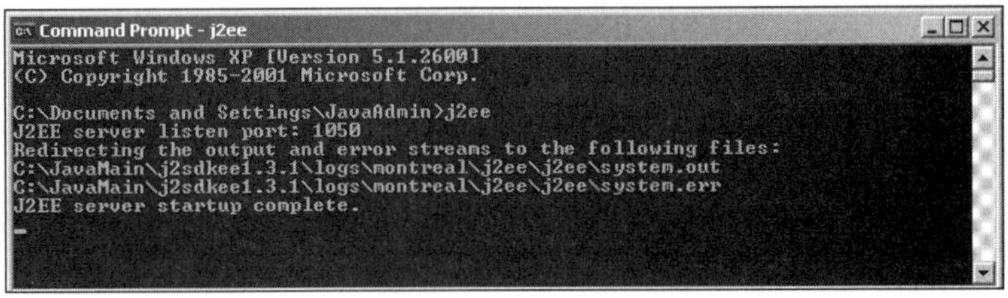

Figure A.16 Testing the Enterprise Edition installation after configuring the system.

Forte for Java Community Edition

Although you can write Java source code in any text editor, as a developer, if you want to make your life a little easier, you should use a professional Java editor—particularly one that supports enterprise applications and Web Services. You have many choices, for example, Forte for Java, Visual Café, JBuilder, JDeveloper, and CodeWarrior. In this book, Forte for Java Community Edition was used because it is free for developers. If you buy its professional version or purchase one of the other products, you might get additional benefits, but the free version is sufficient for now.

In this section, I'll show you how to obtain, install, and configure the Forte for Java Community Edition.

Downloading the Forte for Java Community Edition

You can get the Forte for Java file from the Sun Microsystems web site at `http://www.sun.com/forte/ffj`.

This page provides general information about Forte Tools including Java tools. Under Forte for Java, click the Get the Software link. It will take you to another page from which you can order or download Forte for Java tools free of charge or those with a fee. Go to the Community Edition section of this page to download the proper Forte for Java Community Edition file.

You can save the file in a directory to install at a later time. For the Windows operating system, Forte for Java version 3.0 is available at the time of this writing. The file size is almost 30 MB.

Setting Up the Forte for Java Community Edition

To run Forte for Java version 3.0 on your system, you must have J2SE version 1.3.1, which you already have because you have J2EE. If you need to run Forte for Java on any other computer, make sure J2SE is installed on your system.

To install Forte for Java version 3.0, find the file you saved during the download, which is named ffj30_ce_ml.exe for this book (see Figure A.17).

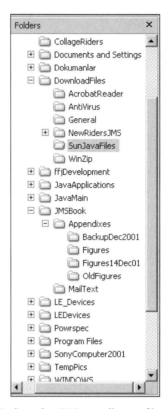

Figure A.17   Finding the FFC installation file on your system.

After you double-click the file, it will start to extract the installation files and will ask you to choose a language to setup. Your choices in the list box are English or Japanese. Choose the appropriate language, which is English for this book. When you click OK, the Setup Wizard will appear and guide you through the following process:

1. The Welcome screen appears, which provides some information about the product.
2. As usual, you will confirm the license agreement. For free software, you must accept the agreement. It is just a legal procedure.

3. After you confirm the agreement, the Setup Wizard will search for J2SE on your system. Forte for Java version 3.0 is only tested on J2SE version 1.3.1. Although it is not tested on earlier versions, you can still use J2SE version 1.3, but there is no guarantee that it will work properly. Use it at your own risk (see Figure A.18). You might encounter some unusual and unexpected problems while developing or running Java applications.

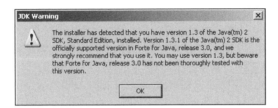

Figure A.18 J2SE version warning for Forte for Java.

4. The Setup Wizard then searches compatible Java Virtual Machine directories (J2SE's bin directory) and displays them in the dialog box. For some reason, if you installed J2SE on more than one location on your system, it shows all the directories. You have to choose one of them.

5. The next step shows the components you can install. If you do not want to install a component, clear the component's check box. It is recommended that you select all components. In this dialog box, you can change the Forte for Java installation directory. By default, it is C:\forte4j.

6. The next step associates .java and .nbm (NetBeans module) extension files with the Forte for Java IDE. Select both check boxes.

After all selections are made, the Setup Wizard installs Forte for Java on your system. Click Finish to complete the installation.

Testing the Forte for Java Community Edition

If the installation is successful, the Setup Wizard places a Forte for Java CE (FFJ CE) icon on the Programs list of your system (see Figure A.19). Choose Forte for Java CE from the list to run the program.

Figure A.19   Forte for Java CE icon on the Programs list.

If the program is being run for the first time, the Setup Wizard continues to help you make some settings complete. At anytime, you can click the Finish button and run the IDE directly. If you need to run the Setup Wizard later on, choose Tools, Setup Wizard on the FFJ IDE menu bar.

Follow these steps to continue setting up FFJ CE:

1. Before running FFJ CE, choose or create a working or development directory for FFJ CE because a dialog box will appear asking for this development directory.

2. FFJ CE will ask you to configure some settings from previous versions of FFJ CE installed on your system. You can skip this step if there is no previous installation.

3. FFJ CE works with iPlanet Web Server (the latest version of iPlanet Web Server can be downloaded from `http://www.iplanet.com`). If you have iPlanet Web Server on your system, provide its installation directory information to the Setup Wizard. If you do not have it, click the Cancel button.

4. Set the general settings for FFJ. If you are behind a firewall, you can set up a Proxy server as well.

5. Select a set of modules to install. There are three options: Basic, Complete, Custom. The Complete Set of Modules is the recommended setting.

6. That should be it. If you click the Next button, you can set up two additional advanced settings. If you click the Finish button, the FFJ CE IDE will start (see Figure A.20).

It is beyond the scope of this book to provide information about how to use FFJ CE. If you need more information about the program, go to `http://www.sun.com/forte/ffj`.

This web page provides general information about Forte Tools including Java tools. Click the Documentation link under Forte for Java on this page. It will take you to another page from which you can download some training materials and a starting guide.

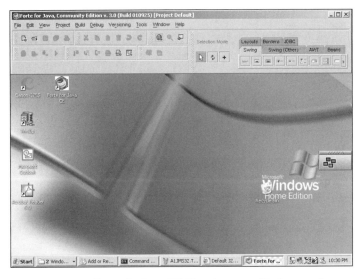

Figure A.20   Forte for Java CE Development Tool menu bar.

Web Server for J2EE Applications

To develop and run J2EE, you need a web server installed on your system. But it must support Java technologies such as the JSP engine. If you develop enterprise applications professionally, most likely you have a J2EE compliant application server, such as iPlanet, WebSphere, BEAWebLogic and so on. Each application server includes its own web server, which supports J2EE web-related technologies.

   The idea behind this book is to recommend free software during the learning phase that is not based on a specific application server. In this regard, you are fortunate. The J2EE SDK comes with a web server too! When you run the J2EE server from a command prompt using the "-verbose" parameter to see which products are included with J2EE, you will see that a web server at port 8000 is running (see Figure A.21) in addition to other programs, such as JMS or a secure web server at port 7000.

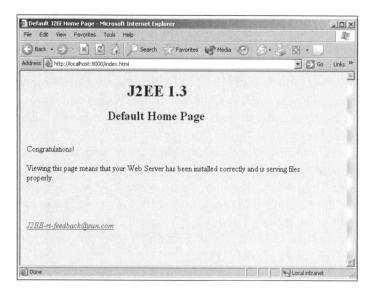

Figure A.21 j2ee –verbose display.

When you browse to `http://localhost:8000` after starting the J2EE server, you will see a page similar to the one shown in Figure A.22.

Figure A.22 J2EE Web Server.

You can use the built-in version of Tomcat that is bundled with FFJ CE. More information about Tomcat can be found at `http://jakarta.apache.org/tomcat/index.html`.

Tomcat is a free add-on product that belongs to the Apache Web Server, which also contains an internal web server. If you do not have J2EE or FFJ installed on your system and you need them; go to `http://java.sun.com/products` or `http://jakarta.apache.org/tomcat/index.html` for free downloads.

You can download the installation guide and training documents as well from the preceding web sites.

B

Application Deployment Tool

IN THIS APPENDIX, YOU WILL LEARN how to deploy a component of an enterprise application such as a bean or a web component like a JavaServer Page (JSP).

The deployment tool can vary depending on your application server. In this book, I use the Java 1.3 Reference Implementation as an application server and Forte for Java as a development tool to develop components of an enterprise application.

Starting the Deployment Tool

The Java 1.3 Reference Implementation has its own user-friendly deployment tool with a graphical user interface. After you write your application using a development tool and you need to run the deployment tool, you should first start the Java 2 Enterprise Edition (J2EE) application server. Type **j2ee –verbose** at the command line to start the J2EE Reference Implementation Server. The parameter verbose is recommended so you can see what is going on during server startup while deploying the application. It is a very good way to see problems that can occur. After you see the following line at the command prompt, you can work with the application server.

```
J2EE server startup complete.
```

You then need to type **deploytool** at another command prompt to run the deployment tool (see Figure B.1).

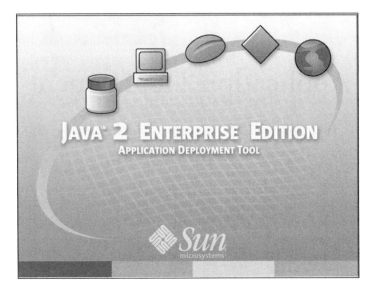

Figure B.1 Starting the Application Deployment Tool.

The Application Deployment Tool's main menu, which contains four menu commands—File, Edit, Tools, and Help— is displayed. (See Figure B.2.)

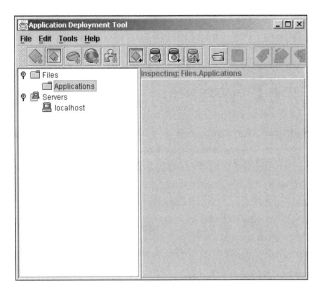

Figure B.2 The Application Deployment Tool's graphical user interface.

Unfortunately, there is no sample application provided to demonstrate the deployment tool. As a result, you need to write a very simple enterprise application to see how the deployment tool works, for example, a session bean that says "Hello." To write a simple enterprise application, follow these steps:

1. Run Forte for Java to write the application.

2. Create a new package called EJBSample under the FFJ development directory, which is C:\ffjDevelopment for this book.

3. Write a home interface, remote interface, and bean class under this package (see their source code in Listings B.1, B.2, and B.3).

4. Compile the source code and correct any syntax errors if needed.

Listing B.1 **Bean Class Source Code Named FirstEJB**

```
1. package EJBSample;
2.
3. import javax.ejb.*;
4. public class FirstEJB implements SessionBean {
5.
6.     public FirstEJB() {  }
7.
8.     public String saySomething() {
9.         return "-Hello Hello Hello-";
10.    } //end of saySomething()
11.
12.     public void ejbCreate() throws CreateException { }
13.     public void setSessionContext(SessionContext sc) { }
14.     public void ejbRemove()  { }
15.     public void ejbActivate() { }
16.     public void ejbPassivate() {  }
17.
18. } //end of class FirstEJB
```

Listing B.2 **Remote Interface Source Code Named First**

```
1. package EJBSample;
2.
3. import java.rmi.RemoteException;
4. import javax.ejb.*;
5.
6. public interface First extends EJBObject {
7.
8.     public String saySomething() throws RemoteException;
9.
10. } //end of interface First
```

Listing B.3   **Home Interface Source Code Named FirstHome**

```
1. package EJBSample;
2.
3. import java.io.Serializable;
4. import java.rmi.RemoteException;
5. import javax.ejb.*;
6.
7. public interface FirstHome extends EJBHome {
8.
9.    public First create() throws
                 RemoteException, CreateException;
10.
11. } //end of interface FirstHome
```

Adding a New Application

After you finish writing the sample enterprise application on the development tool, which is a session bean saying Hello, go to the Application Deployment Tool again. You will see two panes under the menu commands as well as icons. In the left pane, there are two main items: files and servers. The server for this example is localhost, to which you do not need to give the name explicitly. You need to add the enterprise applications to the Application folder, which is one level below the Files folder.

Highlight Files or Applications in the left pane, and then select the File command from the menu bar. Choose New, and then choose Application (see Figure B.3) to add a new application.

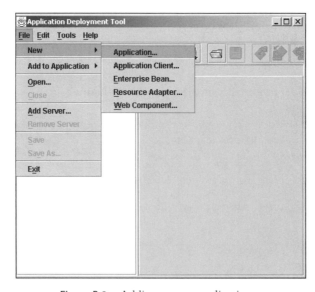

Figure B.3   Adding a new application.

The New Application dialog box appears. Figure B.4 shows two text fields that must be filled in. The first text field requires the application file name, which will be saved to disk and must use the extension .ear. The second text field is for the application display name, which will be used to display the application on the deployment tool. Using the same name is recommended for both boxes. The application file must be in the FFJ development directory. For this example, I have chosen FirstHello as the name of the application (see Figure B.5).

Figure B.4   New application dialog box.

Figure B.5   New application dialog box containing file names.

After you add a new application, the application deployment tool user interface looks like the illustration in Figure B.6. You then need to add enterprise components, such as a bean, a JSP, or a Java servlet.

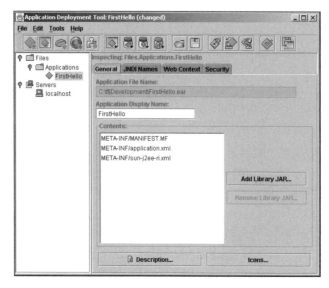

Figure B.6   Deployment tool user interface after adding an application.

Adding an Enterprise Bean to the Application

To add an enterprise bean to the FirstHello application, follow these steps:

1. Highlight the application name.

2. Select the File menu command, choose New, and then select Enterprise Bean.

3. The New Enterprise Bean Wizard-Introduction page is displayed (see Figure B.7). This wizard will help you create a new enterprise bean. As you can see on the page, there are three required steps: identifying an EJB JAR file, selecting the bean type, and identifying a bean class and its interfaces. There are also some optional steps. Click Next to continue.

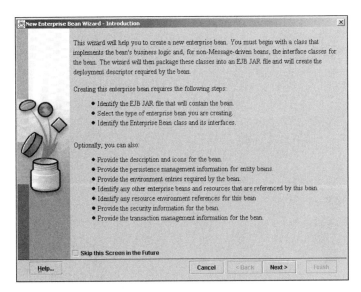

Figure B.7 EJB JAR Wizard introduction page.

Note

You can obtain more information about each step of the wizard by clicking the Help button on the left side of wizard dialog box. You can also find some experimental help and information about the deployment tool from J2EE developers at the http://developer.java.sun.com/developer.

4. Identify the JAR file, bean class, and the bean home and remote interface (see Figure B.8) on this page.

 a. A JAR file is required to contain the enterprise bean. You can create a new JAR file within an existing application or use an existing JAR file. I will create a new one for this example and enter FirstHelloJAR as its name in the JAR Display Name Box.

 b. Click the Edit button to add a bean class and its interfaces to the JAR file. Another dialog box called Edit Contents is displayed. In this dialog box, you have to select the bean class and its interfaces in the FFJ development directory. (For this development tool, the starting directory must remain as the FFJ development directory, which is C:\ffjDevelopment for this example. Do not change it to your application directory.) Select the class and interfaces under the Available Files window. Click the Add button to add the contents of the FirstHelloJAR window. They are then added to the JAR file of your application (see Figure B.9). Click OK to return to the previous dialog box, which is EJB JAR as illustrated in Figure B.8. After you return to the EJB JAR dialog box of the wizard, click Next.

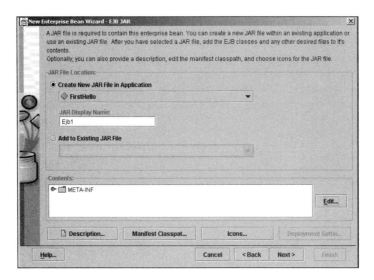

Figure B.8   EJB JAR dialog box.

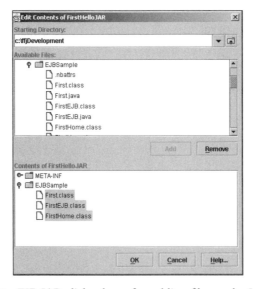

Figure B.9   EJB JAR dialog box after adding files to the JAR file.

5. After you have created the JAR file and have added a bean class and its interfaces to that file, you need to identify the type of bean and identify which added files are the bean class, home interface, and remote interface (see Figure B.10). This identification is essential for the application server to appropriately determine what the added file represents. There are three types of beans: entity beans, session beans, and message-driven beans. For this sample application, the bean will be a stateless session bean.

Figure B.10   General dialog box for the bean.

a. You then have to identify the bean class under the Enterprise Bean Class drop-down menu. In this example, the bean class is the FirstEJB object (shown in Listing B.1), which belongs to the EJBSample package. After you identify the bean class, bean name, and the bean display name, the class name (FirstEJB) will automatically be written under the Enterprise Bean Name and the Enterprise Bean Display name. It is not recommended that you change these names.

b. You then have to fill in the Remote Interfaces section of the dialog box. Select the FirstHome object (shown in Listing B.3), which belongs to the EJBSample package, as the Remote Home Interface. Then, select the First object (shown in Listing B.2), which belongs to the EJBSample package, as the Home Interface. Click Next after completing these entries.

6. Choose the Transaction Management type. For this example, it is Container-Managed (see Figure B.11). Whenever you choose the container-managed type, it will show remote and home interface methods. For this example, I only have one method in the remote interface: saySomething(). Its transaction attribute is required. You can change the transaction attribute by clicking its box and defining another attribute that the method needs. Click Next.

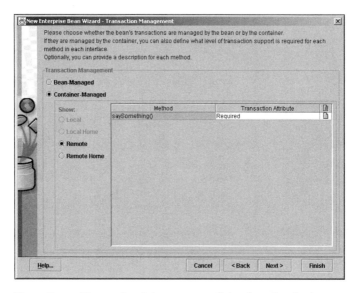

Figure B.11 Transaction Management dialog box for the bean.

7. After selecting the Transaction Management type, you need to complete the Environment Entries dialog box, which allows you to list any environment entries that are referenced in the code of the enterprise bean. I will not add any environment entries for this sample application. Click Next.

8. After defining Environment Entries, you need to define Enterprise Bean References, which allow you list any enterprise beans that are referenced in the code of this bean. I will not add any enterprise bean references for this sample application. Click Next.

9. After you define Enterprise Bean References, you must define Resource References, which allow you to list any resource factories referenced in the code of this enterprise bean. I will not add any resource factories references for this sample application. Click Next.

10. After defining Resource References, define Resource Environment References, which allow you to list any resource environment references in the code of this enterprise bean. I will not add any resource environment references for this sample application. Click Next.

11. After defining Resource Environment References, define Security, which will not be changed from the default selection for this sample application. Click Next.

12. The final step is to review the Settings dialog box (see Figure B.12). The deployment descriptor in the window, which is an XML file, will be generated for the JAR file. This file can be used for any other application server that uses an XML descriptor to deploy an enterprise application. To change any of the settings, click Back. If you are satisfied with the settings, click Finish.

Figure B.12 Review Settings dialog box for the bean.

After you add a new enterprise bean to the JAR file of the application, the Application Deployment Tool user interface will look like Figure B.13. You see a JAR file whose display name is FirstHelloJAR under your application, which is FirstHello. The JAR file contains an enterprise bean, which in this example is FirstEJB.

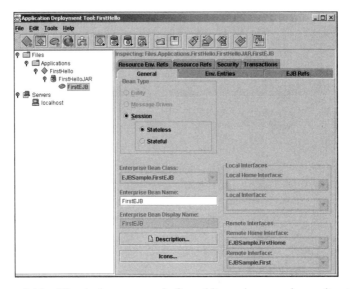

Figure B.13   The deployment tool after adding a bean to the application.

Deploying the Application

After you have created the application and have identified its enterprise bean component, you need to deploy it as an enterprise application. These steps are explained as follows:

1. Select Tools and choose Deploy (see Figure B.14).

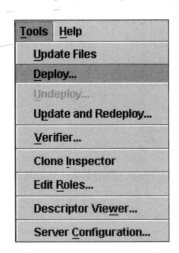

Figure B.14   Deploy command on the Tools menu.

2. The Introduction dialog box of the Deploy Wizard, as shown in Figure B.15, is displayed. Select the object to be deployed, which is FirstHello, and the server to which it should be deployed. Do not forget to select the Return Client Jar check box.

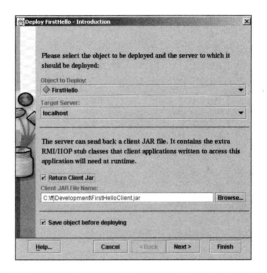

Figure B.15 Introduction dialog box of the Deploy Wizard.

3. Provide Java Naming Directory Interface (JNDI) names for the EJB and References. In this example, you only have one EJB class. I will provide JNDIofFirstEJB as the JNDI name for the bean class (see Figure B.16).

Figure B.16 JNDI Names dialog box in the Deploy Wizard.

4. Review the dialog box of the Deploy Wizard before starting the deployment. It states that the bean class is ready to be deployed to the selected server. Click Finish to start deploying.

The Deployment Progress dialog box shows the status of the application's deployment to the selected server. You can see warnings and errors during the deployment. If everything goes well, deployment will be completed successfully and the Cancel button, which you see during deployment, will change to an OK button (see Figure B.17). Click OK to return to the Deployment Tool user interface if the deployment is successful.

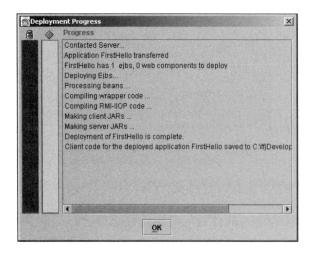

Figure B.17 Deployment Progress box.

The deployment tool will add the FirstHello.ear and FirstHelloClient.jar files to the FFJ development directory, which in this case is ffjDevelopment (see Figure B.18).

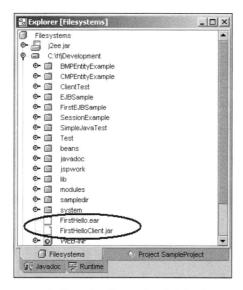

Figure B.18   .ear and client .jar file under the development directory.

If you need to access an enterprise bean from a client application, you have to mount the client JAR file, which is FirstHelloClient.jar, into the Filesystems. If you use a different development tool than I used or if the client application is executed as a stand-alone application at the command prompt, the client JAR file (FirstHelloClient.jar) must be added to CLASSPATH of the tool or command prompt environment.

Adding a Web Component to the Application

In this section, you will learn how to add a web component to the application, deploy it, and run the web component as a client. A web component such as a JSP or a Java servlet is a client application for an enterprise application, but it runs in a client web browser, such as Internet Explorer or Netscape, and has contact with an EJB container and its components through a web server. You can call a method in the bean class from the JSP file in your web browser.

For this example, I will add a JSP file to the application (see its source code in Listing B.4). Create a new component as a JSP element in the development tool and type the source code provided in Listing B.4. This JSP file will behave like a client of the enterprise application and will run in a browser such as Netscape or Internet Explorer.

Listing B.4   **JSP Component Source Code Named FirstClientWEB**

```
1.  <%@page contentType="text/html"%>
2.  <%@ page import="javax.naming.*,
             javax.rmi.*, EJBSample.*, java.util.*"%>
3.  <html>
4.  <head><title>JSP Component added to FirstHello
           Enterprise Application</title></head>
5.  <body>
6.
7.  <%
8.    out.println("Hello for deployment demonstration
             for JMS book-LE");
9.    out.println("<BR>");
10.   Context leContext = new InitialContext();
11.   out.println("Context done: ");
12.   out.println("<BR>");
13.   Object leResult = leContext.lookup("JNDIofFirstEJB");
14.   out.println("lookup done ");
15.   out.println("<BR>");
16.
17.   FirstHome leHome =
18.   (FirstHome)javax.rmi.PortableRemoteObject.narrow(
           leResult, FirstHome.class);
19.   out.println("narrow done ");
20.   out.println("<BR>");
21.   First leRemote = leHome.create();
22.   out.println("remote done ");
23.   out.println("<BR>");
24.   out.println("You have a message from server : "
             + leRemote.saySomething());
25.   out.println("<BR>");
26.   leRemote.remove();
27.
28.   %>
29.   </body>
30.   </html>
```

Follow these steps to add a web component:

1. Select File and choose New. Then select Web Component, as shown in Figure B.19.

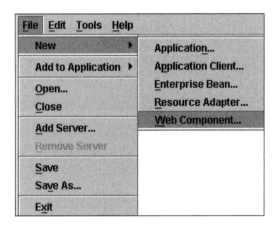

Figure B.19 Adding a web component to the application.

2. The Introduction page of the New Component Web Wizard appears, as illustrated in Figure B.20. This wizard will help you create a new web component (a servlet class or a JSP file). The wizard will then package the selected files into a Web ARchive (WAR) file. In addition to some optional steps, there are two required steps: selecting the WAR file to contain the component and identifying the servlet class or JSP file. Click Next to continue.

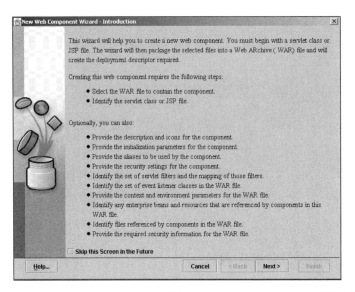

Figure B.20   Introduction page of the New Web Component Wizard.

3. The wizard displays the content of the WAR file (see Figure B.21). In this step, you can identify the WAR file and enterprise bean JSP file.

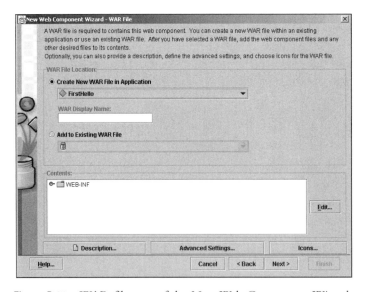

Figure B.21   WAR file step of the New Web Component Wizard.

   a. Identify the WAR file for the component. You can create a new WAR file within an existing application or use an existing WAR file. For this example, create a new WAR file whose display name is FirstHelloWAR.

   b. You then need to add a web component to the file by clicking the Edit button. An Edit dialog box appears. Find the JSP file and add it to the content (see Figure B.22). After clicking the OK button, you will return to the WAR File step of the Wizard, illustrated in Figure B.21. Click Next.

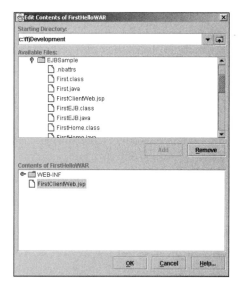

Figure B.22   Adding a JSP file to the content of the WAR file.

4. Choose the Component Type and identify the type of web component. Choose JSP for this example. Click Next.

5. In the Component General Properties dialog box, choose the JSP file or servlet class and provide a name for it. For this example, the JSP file name must be FirstClientWeb.jsp. Click Next.

6. The Component Initialization Parameters and Aliases dialog boxes allows you to list any initialization parameters referenced in the code. I will not add any initialization parameter for this example. Click Next.

7. The Aliases dialog boxes allows you to provide the aliases for this web component. I will not add any component aliases for this example. Click Next.

8. The Component Security dialog box will remain as the default for this example. Click Next.

9. The WAR File Environment dialog box allows you to list any environment entries that are referenced in the code of the components. I will not add any environment entries for this example. Click Next.

10. The Context Parameters dialog box allows you to list any context parameters that are referenced in the code of the components. I will not add any context parameters for this example. Click Next.

11. The Enterprise Bean References dialog box allows you to list any enterprise beans that are referenced in the code of the components. I will not add any enterprise beans for this example. Click Next.

12. The Resource References dialog box allows you to list any resource factories that are referenced in the code of the components. I will not add any resource factories for this example. Click Next.

13. The Resource Environment References dialog box allows you to list any resource environment entries that are referenced in the code of the components. I will not add any resource environment reference for this example. Click Next.

14. The File References dialog box allows you to provide a list of the welcome files used by your WAR file. I will not add any file for this example. Click Next.

15. The Component Security dialog box allows you to choose the method to be used to authenticate users of this WAR file. You can also define the security constraints that define which users are authorized to access the content of the WAR file. I will not add any user authentication method or security constraints for this example. Click Next.

16. In the final dialog box before deployment, you will see the Review Settings screen as in Figure B.23. It is the deployment descriptor that will be generated for the WAR file. To change any of the settings, click Back. If you are satisfied with the settings, click Finish.

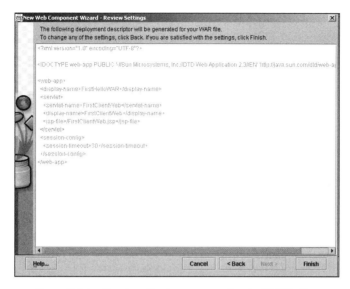

Figure B.23   Review Settings screen for the WAR file.

As you can see in Figure B.24, a web component is added to the application.

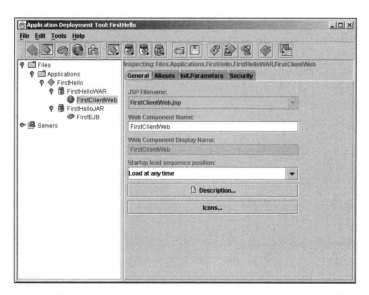

Figure B.24   A new web component is added to the enterprise application.

After adding a new component, you have to redeploy the application with its new component (the JSP file). There are two ways to do this:

- Highlight the application name (FirstHello) under the localhost server, and click the Undeploy button in the window on the right, or choose the Undeploy command under the Tools menu. Then highlight the application name again (FirstHello) under the Applications folder on the left pane (see Figure B.25). Select Tools, and choose the Deploy command. (If you changed any file's source code in the application, do not forget to choose the Update Files command under Tools before redeploying; otherwise, the changes will not be effective.)

- Highlight the application name (FirstHello) in the Applications folder in the left pane (see Figure B.25). Select Tools, choose Update, and then select Redeploy. (This way is simpler than the preceding approach.)

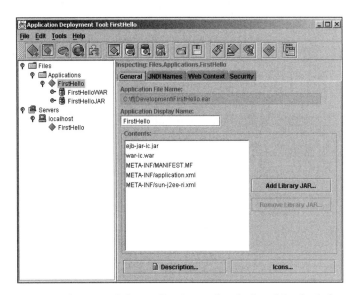

Figure B.25   Selection of the application to be deployed in the left pane.

Both methods will redeploy the application. These steps are similar to the steps you performed in the "Deploying the Application" section. The only difference is an additional dialog box called .WAR File Context, which is displayed after the JNDI Names dialog box. In the .WAR File Context box, enter a context root for the WAR file FirstHelloWAR. For this example, I will enter HelloRoot in the Context Root box (see Figure B.26).

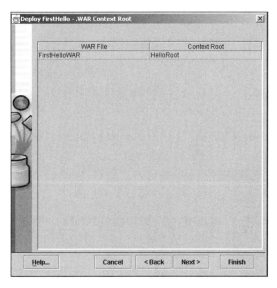

Figure B.26 Providing the Context Root name for the WAR file.

After completing the deployment of the application, you will see a
Deployment Progress dialog box like the one shown in Figure B.27. If the
deployment succeeds, click OK.

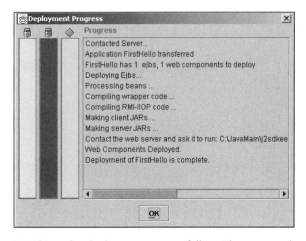

Figure B.27 Finishing the deployment successfully with a new web component.

You can call this JSP file in a web browser. Recall that the J2EE server has a built-in Tomcat web server, which supports servlet technology and JSP. Tomcat runs on a socket 8000 as the default for the J2EE Reference Implementation Server. When you need to run the sample JSP file, which is added to the application, it must be called in the browser like this:

```
http://localhost:8000/HelloRoot/FirstClientWeb.jsp
```

The web server root is `http://localhost:8000`, HelloRoot is the Context Root you provided during the deployment, and FirstClientWeb.jsp is a web component within the application. Figure B.28 shows the web page after you call this JSP file.

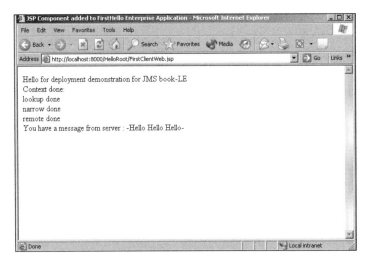

Figure B.28 Running the client web component in a browser.

C

Java Message Service (JMS) API Vendors

JAVA MESSAGE SERVICE (JMS), WHICH IS a standard part of the Java 2 Platform Enterprise Edition (J2EE) version 1.3, is an API rather than a product offered by Sun Microsystems. A JMS server runs on a J2EE server, but Sun does not intend to be a JMS vendor. Sun created the JMS API for developers to connect to a message server.

Even though Sun Microsystems has defined the JMS API specification, and its iPlanet application server supports the JMS API, the primary goal of Sun Microsystems is not to be a vendor of the JMS API. Sun provides the API, which facilitates communication with a JMS server, but leaves creation of these servers to other vendors. JMS and the JMS classes are created by Sun in collaboration with major JMS vendors.

In this appendix, you will find some brief information about the JMS vendors and their message server products, which can be classified depending on their license status from Sun Microsystems.

Licensed servers by Sun Microsystems include:

- BEA (WebLogic Server)
- IBM (MQSeries)
- iPlanet ([formerly Sun Microsystems] JMQ or iMQ)
- Talarian/TIBCO (SmartSockets for JMS)
- Progress (SonicMQ)
- Macromedia (JRun)

Nonlicensed servers by Sun Microsystems include:

- Fiorano (FioranoMQ)
- Softwired (iBus)

Reference implementation and open source servers include:

- ExoLab (OpenJMS)
- Sun Microsystems (J2EE 1.3 Reference Implementation Server)

Unfortunately, all of the vendors and products cannot be covered in this appendix. If you want to see a full list of message service vendors that are licensed or not licensed by Sun, visit `http://java.sun.com/products/jms/licensees.html` for licensed servers and `http://java.sun.com/products/jms/nonlicensedvendors.html` for nonlicensed servers.

Information provided about the vendors in this book was obtained from vendors' manuals, programs, training materials, and web sites at the time this book was written. For updated product information, visit each vendor's web site.

In the following sections, I provide a criteria list to help you choose the proper JMS vendor for the application you are developing as well as brief information about some of the JMS vendors and their products.

Criteria to Choose an Appropriate JMS Vendor

In this section, I provide you with questions to consider when you need to choose a JMS provider. Collecting the answers to these questions from candidate providers will help you find the right product. Answers to these questions depend on the project, and answers will vary from project to project. The criteria list provides a good way to compare different products on the same level before making your decision.

Criteria List to Help You Choose the Appropriate JMS Vendor

- What is the latest version of the message server product?
- Is it fully compliant with the JMS specifications? If so, what version of the JMS specifications?
- Which platforms does it support on the client and server sides?
- Which languages does it support in addition to Java?
- Which version of Java Virtual Machine (JVM) does it support for a client and a server?
- Which operating systems does it support?
- Does it support HTTP firewall tunneling?
- Does it integrate with other message vendors' products?
- What kind of messaging mechanism does it support (point-to-point or publish-and-subscribe or both)?
- Does it have additional features beyond the JMS specification such as fault tolerance, scalability, additional message type support, guaranteed delivery, and so on?
- What kind of networking protocols does it support?
- What kind of security protocols does it support?
- Does it support clustering architecture?
- Does it support guaranteed message delivery?
- Does it support message-driven beans and other Enterprise JavaBeans (EJBs)?
- How does it support persistence?
- How does it implement naming and directory services?
- What kind of administration tool does it provide? Does it allow remote administration?
- Does it support Lightweight Directory Access Protocol (LDAP) to store JMS administered objects on an LDAP server?

BEA Systems Inc. (WebLogic Server)

Because WebLogic has a sizeable share in the enterprise application server market, it is a very well-known (maybe the most common in addition to IBM) JMS vendor as well. The BEA WebLogic Server is certified as J2EE-compliant by Sun. It fully supports the JMS 1.0.2 specifications. The WebLogic Server supports the leading UNIX, Linux, and mainframe operating systems in addition to Windows NT/2000/XP.

The WebLogic Server's JMS API implementation supports both point-to-point and publish-and-subscribe messaging. The JVM must be version 1.2 or later on the client side and version 1.3 or later on the server side.

WebLogic Server provides a very user-friendly GUI to configure JMS administered objects.

The WebLogic JMS service supports synchronous and asynchronous message consumers. WebLogic recommends the use of asynchronous messaging as much as possible because application server resources are not locked up or waiting as in a synchronous messaging architecture.

WebLogic Server supports either multicast or TCP/IP transport protocols. The multicast JMS option is only available for the publish-and-subscribe model, and durable subscriptions are not supported. The multicast option only supports asynchronous message listeners.

When using WebLogic in your JMS applications, you have two options: transacted sessions and integration with the WebLogic Server's Java Transaction API (JTA) transaction service. Many JMS applications require transactional messaging. Transacted sessions provide a convenient means to use transactions within JMS, but other components such as EJBs or Java Database Connectivity (JDBC) access cannot participate in these transactions.

WebLogic JMS can directly access all of the WebLogic Server services, such as message-driven EJBs, in addition to session and entity EJBs.

BEA WebLogic Server clusters are designed to deliver scalable and highly available applications in a way that is completely transparent to the application. It supports Domain Name Service (DNS), Java Naming and Directory Interface (JNDI), and Remote Method Invocation (RMI).

Security uses cryptography-based privacy and user authentication. Encryption, authentication, and authorization are based on Secure Socket Layer (SSL). All WebLogic Server services including JMS are securely available through firewalls via tunneling through HTTP or HTTPS.

The latest version of WebLogic is 7.0. For updated product information about WebLogic, visit `http://www.bea.com`. With version 7.0, BEA WebLogic introduced its new product, BEA WebLogic Workshop, to develop, test, and deploy enterprise-class web service applications rapidly on the BEA WebLogic Enterprise Platforms. WebLogic Workshop leverages messaging architecture by using JMS control. Visit `http://www.bea.com/products` for more information about WebLogic Workshop and other related products.

IBM (MQSeries)

Another leader in the enterprise application market is IBM, which has been offering a message service since the beginning of JMS history. The MQSeries JMS implementation supports point-to-point and publish-and-subscribe messaging. IBM supports the JMS 1.0.2 specifications by providing its own Java classes. MQSeries classes for JMS are a set of Java classes that implement Sun Microsystem's JMS specification.

The IBM JMS implementation uses J2EE Connector Architecture. Sun provided a .jar file with the J2EE Connector classes prior to version 5.2. This new version of the MQSeries JMS classes eliminates the need for the J2EE Connector classes, so you do not need to download this file. It is already in the server.

MQSeries provides two types of communications from a Java program to a queue manager: *bind* and *client*. These communication types are called transport types in MQSeries.

With the new version, MQSeries supports the EJB 2.0 specification, which allows developers to use message-driven beans that can be configured to asynchronously receive messages. If your version of MQSeries does not provide support for message-driven beans, an object outside the EJB container is required to listen to asynchronous messages and pass them to an enterprise bean. MQSeries version 5.3 offers added security using SSL.

The MQSeries server is supported by many operating systems including IBM platforms, UNIX platforms, and Windows platforms. Visit IBM's web site for detailed and updated information.

The latest version of MQSeries is 5.3. For updated product information about MQSeries, visit `http://www.ibm.com`.

iPlanet (JMQ or iMQ)

Java Message Queue (JMQ) was introduced to the JMS market by Sun. After the iPlanet products were released to market by the Sun-Netscape Alliance, JMQ joined the iPlanet E-Commerce Solutions family and its name became iPlanet Message Queue (iMQ) for Java 2.0. In March 2002, Sun officially concluded its original alliance agreement with AOL. iPlanet is now a division of Sun and is a core component of the Sun Open Net Environment.

iPlanet is fully compliant with J2EE and the JMS 1.0.2 specification. It provides high performance and reliable messaging for the publish-and-subscribe and point-to-point models.

Because it supports the EJB 2.0 specification, it supports message-driven EJBs in addition to session and entity EJBs in JMS applications.

It supports Windows NT/2000/XP, Windows 98/ME, Sun Solaris, and Linux operating systems. It requires Java 2 Standard Edition (J2SE) version 1.3.0 or later (version 1.4 is available at the time of this writing) for administration tools. Client applications are supported on JDK 1.1.8 and Java 2 SDK Standard Edition version 1.2.2 and later.

iPlanet provides both command-line and GUI tools for an iMQ message service and manages application-specific aspects of messaging.

iPlanet provides access to JMS administered objects through JNDI. It also supports LDAP and file system service. It has the ability to communicate with an iMQ message service over a number of different transports including TCP and HTTP, and uses SSL connections. It supports HTTP tunneling for firewalls.

The latest version of iMQ is 2.0. For updated product information about iMQ, visit `http://www.iplanet.com`.

Sun Microsystems (J2EE 1.3 Reference Server)

iMQ is a member of the iPlanet product family. With J2EE version 1.3, the JMS server comes with the standard ability to develop JMS applications, including message-driven beans. Sun provides this as a "reference implementation" for developers. It is free with all other products of J2EE.

This version of the J2EE Reference Implementation supports EJB 2.0, Java Servlet 2.3, JavaServer Pages (JSP) 1.2, JMS 1.0.2, Connector 1.0, JDBC Standard Extension 2.0, JTA 1.0, JavaMail 1.2, and Java API for XML Processing (JAXP) 1.1.

The J2EE Reference Implementation is fully compliant with the JMS 1.0.2 specifications and supports the point-to-point and publish-and-subscribe messaging models. It provides access to JMS administered objects through JNDI. It also supports LDAP and file system service.

The administration tool is a command-line utility. You can use it by running j2eeadmin.bat.

The JMS Reference Implementation is available for Windows NT/2000/XP, Linux, and UNIX operating systems. The J2EE SDK does not support Windows 95/98/ME; therefore, the Reference Implementation cannot work on them. The JMS client can run on either Windows 95/98/ME or Windows NT/2000/XP.

The latest version of J2EE is 1.3.1. For updated product information about J2EE, visit `http://java.sun.com/j2ee` or `http://java.sun.com/products/jms`.

TIBCO/Talarian (SmartSockets for JMS)

Talarian was a JMS vendor before it was acquired by TIBCO software. Its product, SmartSockets, is now a member of the TIBCO product family. SmartSockets for JMS supports the publish-and-subscribe and point-to-point models. The publish-and-subscribe implementation runs on Talarian's underlying RTserver and MQserver products. RTserver sends messages to and receives messages from other RTservers asynchronously as well synchronously.

SmartSockets for JMS allows C, C++, and other non-Java clients as well as Java to access JMS services (both send and receive). It supports any J2EE certified application server including IBM's WebSphere and BEA's WebLogic.

SmartSockets for JMS supports the JMS 1.0.2 specifications and requires JVM version 1.2 or later for the client and server side.

SmartSockets for JMS uses a standard SSL protocol and supports firewall tunneling for maximum security.

You can use SmartSockets on UNIX (including Solaris, HP-UX, AIX, DEC UNIX, Compaq Tru64, and IRIX); Windows XP, Windows NT, and Windows 2000; VxWorks, IBM OS/390, and Linux. Additionally, client platforms can be Windows 95/98/ME.

The latest version of SmartSockets for JMS is 1.1. For updated product information about SmartSockets, visit `http://www.talarian.com` or `http://www.tibco.com`.

Progress (SonicMQ)

SonicMQ is Progress's JMS product, which is fully compatible with J2EE 1.3 and the JMS 1.0.2 specifications. With version 3.0, SonicMQ fully supports the point-to-point and publish-and-subscribe models. The client and server side must be running on a JVM (JDK 1.1.8 or later).

With version 4.0, SonicMQ supports message-driven beans. It provides guaranteed message persistence over the Internet. It has a built-in XML parser, which provides an interface called XMLMessage. Although the JMS specification does not support an XML type message, you can easily parse the XML type message wrapped in a text type message.

Dynamic Routing Architecture (DRA) is the most important aspect of SonicMQ. DRA allows for exchanging messages between the client and the server of the SonicMQ product dynamically through a single server. It also provides clustering message servers.

SonicMQ provides a direct connection between Internet/HTTP-based messages and JMS queues. It enables seamless, secure integration between external Internet messages and the internal JMS messaging bus.

Client-side persistence of SonicMQ allows JMS clients to continue to operate in the event they become disconnected from the JMS server.

The SonicMQ HTTP/HTTPS feature allows the more efficient combination of firewall-friendly HTTP and the fault-tolerance, security, and performance of JMS for distributed application integration.

It has many valuable features for JMS developers such as guaranteed delivery via durable subscriptions, a dead message queue, duplicate message detection, and XML message type support in addition to five basic JMS message types.

It provides GUI and command-line tools for configuring and monitoring administered objects.

The latest version of SonicMQ is 4.0. For updated product information about SonicMQ, visit `http://www.progress.com` or `http://www.sonicsoft-ware.com`.

Fiorano (FioranoMQ)

Since 1995, Fiorano has been working on innovative infrastructure solutions to reduce the complexity of composing, deploying, debugging, and extending business processes. Its name sounds Italian, but it is located in the United States.

FioranoMQ, a product of Fiorano, was developed as a Java Message Server. Fiorano previously had two different JMS products: FioranoMQ Multicast and FioranoMQ Enterprise. Both are now combined into one product.

FioranoMQ is compliant with the JMS 1.0.2 specifications. It supports the point-to-point and publish-and-subscribe messaging models. Client and server applications must be running on a JVM (JDK 1.1 or later).

It provides command-line and GUI tools for configuring administered objects. It also supports JNDI and LDAP for naming and directory services. The FioranoMQ file-based data store delivers guaranteed messages significantly faster than many other JMS implementations.

FioranoMQ supports both 40-bit and 128-bit message encryption on multiple platforms. It provides communication between the client and server using HTTP as well as the HTTPS protocol.

FioranoMQ centralizes user authentication sources by combining users, groups, permissions, and access control lists, and provides integration with security on Windows NT and UNIX platforms. It also allows you to store and access directory information and services on a standard LDAP server.

FioranoMQ provides for bridges to other JMS providers like IBM MQSeries and non-JMS message servers like Microsoft Message Queue (MSMQ).

As of this writing, FioranoMQ has not been certified by Sun, but it fully supports the JMS 1.0.2 specifications.

The latest version of FioranoMQ is 5.2. For updated product information about FioranoMQ, visit `http://www.fiorano.com`.

Softwired (iBus)

Softwired offers three editions of its JMS product: iBus//MessageServer, iBus//MessageBus, and iBus//Mobile. They can be used separately or in combination.

iBus products support JNDI and LDAP for naming and directory services. They have built-in integration with an XML parser and support XML type messaging in addition to five basic JMS messaging types.

iBus//MessageServer, which is defined as an Enterprise Quality Messaging Infrastructure on Softwired's web site, is a JMS implementation and is compliant with the JMS 1.0.2 specifications.

It is a robust and highly scalable JMS server. It supports the point-to-point and publish-and-subscribe messaging models. One of its most important features is guaranteed, once and only once, secure, reliable messaging.

The client and server side applications must be running on JVM 1.1.6 or later on the client side and JVM 1.2 or later on the server side. It supports firewall tunneling using 128-bit SSL and HTTP.

iBus//MessageServer is fully tested and supported on Solaris, Windows 2000, Windows NT, and Linux. It is expected to work on AIX, HP UNIX, IRIX, and AS/400.

iBus//MessageBus is designed for a distributed architecture. It is compliant with the JMS 1.0.2 specifications and supports the JMS publish-and-subscribe messaging model. It also supports HTTP tunneling, only between two dedicated JMS clients.

According to Softwired's web site, "iBus//MessageBus is a versatile pure Java messaging middleware product that supports the instantaneous delivery of message objects via IP multicast, TCP, SSL, and other protocols such as satellite communication and infrared. It offers a unique solution for a wide range of applications, such as electronic business, client/server applications, enterprise application integration, clustering products for load sharing and fault-tolerance, groupware applications, and information distribution among embedded systems."

iBus/Mobile offers support for wireless JMS clients. It uses a Java API for the client side, which is similar to JMS, but a lightweight version of the product for mobile devices.

iBus//Mobile clients connect to an iBus//MessageServer through a special proxy. iBus//Mobile handles all the issues associated with unreliable networks. It connects to the full spectrum of wireless devices.

On the device side, iBus//Mobile supports the Java 2 Micro Edition (J2ME) standard and PersonalJava as well as J2SE. On the server side, iBus//Mobile plugs directly into various stand-alone JMS providers including the iBus//MessageServer.

iBus//Mobile security is based on user authentication, JMS access control, and data encryption through SSL. It also supports HTTP tunneling.

IBus JMS products are not licensed by Sun as of yet, but they fully support the JMS 1.0.2 specifications.

The latest versions of these products are iBus//MessageBus 4.1.2, iBus//MessageServer 4.5, and iBus//Mobile 3.0. For updated product information about iBus products, visit `http://www.softwired-inc.com`.

ExoLab (OpenJMS)

OpenJMS, which is funded by ExoLab, is based on the JMS 1.0.2 specifications. It is an open-source implementation of the JMS API specification. It supports the point-to-point and publish-and-subscribe messaging models. Its source is open to developers and can be used for testing and learning about JMS.

The server and client side must be running on a JVM 1.2 or higher. OpenJMS supports the point-to-point and publish-and-subscribe messaging models, guaranteed delivery of messages, and synchronous and asynchronous message delivery. OpenJMS uses JDBC for persistence. Some other features of OpenJMS include an administration GUI, XML-based configuration files, applet support, integration with servlet containers such as Jakarta Tomcat, support for RMI, TCP, HTTP, and SSL protocol stacks, support for large numbers of destination subscribers, automatic client disconnect detection, local transactions, and message filtering using SQL92-like selectors.

The latest version of OpenJMS is 0.7.2. For updated product information about OpenJMS, visit `http://openjms.exolab.org`.

Macromedia (JRun)

JRun Server, currently owned by Macromedia (which acquired Allaire, the original maker), is designed for developing and running Java applications. Before version 4.0, JRun Server had three different products: JRun Professional, Advanced, and Enterprise. JRun is now released as one product that combines all existing, new, and enhanced features. JRun 4 is fully compliant with J2EE version 1.3, and it has a JMS implementation, which supports the JMS API 1.0.2 specifications. JRun 4 runs on all the major operating systems: Windows (95/98/NT/2000/XP), Solaris, Linux, IBM AIX, HP-UX, and Compaq Tru64.

The JRun 4 message server is used for deploying enterprise applications with full support for distributed messaging and message-oriented middleware (MOM) application architectures.

JRun 4 supports the point-to-point and publish-and-subscribe messaging models asynchronously and synchronously. You can specify messages as persistent, which prevents lost messages in a server shutdown.

Durable subscriptions are available with publish-and-subscribe type messaging, which guarantees that a client will receive all messages that are generated, even when the client is inactive.

Messaging support is fully transacted. You can use bean-managed persistence (BMP) and container-managed persistence (CMP) type EJBs for message persistence logging. JRun 4 supports the EJB 2.0 specifications including message-driven beans. JRun did not support message-driven beans for JMS applications in version 3.1 and earlier versions.

JRun 4 will also integrate with leading Java Integrated Development Environments (IDEs) to enable you to develop your applications using your favorite development environment in addition to its own editing tool Dreamweaver MX.

JRun supports JNDI for naming and directory services.
The latest version of JRun is 4.0. For updated product information about JRun, visit `http://www.macromedia.com`.

Overview of JMS
Package Classes

IN THIS APPENDIX, I PROVIDE INFORMATION about the interfaces and methods of the javax.jms package. You do not need to know every method in the JMS package that is specified in the Java Message Service (JMS) specification until you need them to use in your projects. But it is good to know which interfaces and methods are available and what you can do with them. The JMS package information provided in this appendix is based on the Java web site of Sun Microsystems. You can find more detailed and up-to-date information by visiting this web site at http://java.sun.com/j2ee.

Class Hierarchy for the javax.jms Package

Like all other packages, javax.jms classes inherit from the java.lang.Object. There are three main classes in the javax.jms class tree that extend the Object class:

- class javax.jms.QueueRequestor
- class javax.jms.TopicRequestor
- class java.lang.Throwable

Figure D.1 illustrates the class hierarchy of the javax.jms package. Information about these three classes is provided in the following sections.

```
•class java.lang.Object
        •class javax.jms.QueueRequestor
    • class javax.jms.TopicRequestor
    • class java.lang.Throwable
        •class java.lang.Exception
            • class javax.jms.JMSException
            •class javax.jms.IllegalStateException
            •class javax.jms.InvalidClientIDException
            •class javax.jms.InvalidDestinationException
            •class javax.jms.InvalidSelectorException
            •class javax.jms.JMSSecurityException
            •class javax.jms.MessageEOFException
            •class javax.jms.MessageFormatException
            • class javax.jms.MessageNotReadableException
            •class javax.jms.MessageNotWriteableException
            •class javax.jms.ResourceAllocationException
            •class javax.jms.TransactionInProgressException
            •class javax.jms.TransactionRolledBackException
```

Figure D.1   Class hierarchy of the javax.jms package.

class javax.jms.QueueRequester

The QueueRequestor constructor is used for a nontransacted QueueSession and a destination Queue. When a sender sends a message and waits for a reply, the request() method of the QueueRequestor is used. It creates a TemporaryQueue for the responses.

Its constructor looks like this:

```
public QueueRequestor(QueueSession session, Queue queue)
        throws JMSException
```

The QueueSession type session parameter is the session to which the queue will belong. The Queue type parameter is the queue type destination to which the reply will be sent.

The QueueRequestor throws a JMSException if the JMS provider fails to create the QueueRequestor because of some internal errors. It often throws an exception because of an invalid destination.

In this class implementation, session parameters are nontransacted, and their delivery mode is either AUTO_ACKNOWLEDGE or DUPS_OK_ACKNOWLEDGE.

This class has two methods: request() and close().

The Message type request() method looks like this:

```
public Message request (Message message) throws JMSException
```

The `request()` method takes a Message type parameter and throws a JMSException if there is an internal error. It sends a request and waits for a reply. Only one reply per request is expected. The parameter message is the message that is sent.

The `close()` method closes the QueueRequester and its session. After closing the session, resources allocated for the queue are released. The `close()` method throws a JMSException if there is problem while closing the QueueRequester.

class javax.jms.TopicRequester

The TopicRequestor constructor is used for a nontransacted TopicSession and a destination topic. When a sender sends a message and waits for a reply, the `request()` method of the TopicRequestor is used. It creates a TemporaryTopic for the responses.

Its constructor looks like this:

```
public TopicRequestor(TopicSession session, Topic topic)
        throws JMSException
```

The TopicSession type session parameter is the session to which the topic will belong. A topic type topic parameter is the topic type destination to which the reply will be sent.

The `TopicRequestor()` constructor throws a JMSException if the JMS provider fails to create the TopicRequestor because of some internal errors. It often throws an exception because of an invalid destination.

In this class implementation, session parameters are nontransacted, and their delivery mode is either AUTO_ACKNOWLEDGE or DUPS_OK_ACKNOWLEDGE.

This class has two methods: `request()` and `close()`.

The Message type `request()` method looks like this:

```
public Message request (Message message) throws JMSException
```

It takes a Message type parameter and throws a JMSException if there is an internal error. It sends a request and waits for a reply. Only one reply per request is expected. The parameter message is the message that is sent.

The `close()` method closes the TopicRequestor and its session. After closing the session, resources allocated for the topic are released. The `close()` method throws a JMSException if there is problem while closing the TopicRequestor.

class java.lang.Throwable

The class java.lang.Throwable extends the Object class, and the Throwable class is the superclass of all errors and exceptions in the Java language. It contains one class (class java.lang.Exception), which contains class javax.jms.JMSException in addition to other Exception classes.

The JMSException class is the root class of all JMS API exceptions, and it has 12 subclasses to throw when there is an internal error:

- class javax.jms.IllegalStateException
- class javax.jms.InvalidClientIDException
- class javax.jms.InvalidDestinationException
- class javax.jms.InvalidSelectorException
- class javax.jms.JMSSecurityException
- class javax.jms.MessageEOFException
- class javax.jms.MessageFormatException
- class javax.jms.MessageNotReadableException
- class javax.jms.MessageNotWritableException
- class javax.jms.ResourceAllocationException
- class javax.jms.TransactionInProgressException
- class javax.jms.TransactionRolledBackException

Figure D.1 also illustrates all of the JMS API exceptions, which inherit the JMSException class.

In this book, I focus on the details of the interfaces in the javax.jms package.

Interface Hierarchy for the javax.jms Package

The javax.jms package consists of 17 interfaces to implement the messaging system between software applications. These interfaces also have subinterfaces. The main interfaces in the javax.jms package are as follows:

- interface javax.jms.ConnectionFactory
- interface javax.jms.Connection
- interface javax.jms.ConnectionMetaData
- interface javax.jms.ConnectionConsumer
- interface javax.jms.DeliveryMode

- interface javax.jms.Destination
- interface javax.jms.Message
- interface javax.jms.MessageConsumer
- interface javax.jms.MessageListener
- interface javax.jms.MessageProducer
- interface javax.jms.ExceptionListener
- interface javax.jms.QueueBrowser
- interface java.lang.Runnable
- interface javax.jms.ServerSession
- interface javax.jms.ServerSessionPool
- interface javax.jms.XAConnection
- interface javax.jms.XAConnectionFactory

Figure D.2 illustrates the most commonly used interfaces of the javax.jms package. I will provide some information about the most important and commonly used interfaces in the following sections.

```
·interface javax.jms.Connection
        ·interface javax.jms.QueueConnection
        ·interface javax.jms.TopicConnection
·interface javax.jms.ConnectionConsumer
·interface javax.jms.ConnectionFactory
        ·interface javax.jms.QueueConnectionFactory
        ·interface javax.jms.TopicConnectionFactory
·interface javax.jms.Destination
        ·interface javax.jms.Queue
        ·interface javax.jms.Topic
·interface javax.jms.Message
        ·interface javax.jms.BytesMessage
        ·interface javax.jms.MapMessage
        ·interface javax.jms.ObjectMessage
        ·interface javax.jms.StreamMessage
        ·interface javax. jms.TextMessage
·interface javax.jms.MessageConsumer
        ·interface javax.jms.QueueReceiver
        ·interface javax.jms.TopicSubscriber
·interface javax.jms.MessageListener
·interface javax.jms.MessageProducer
        ·interface javax.jms.QueueSender
        ·interface javax.jms.TopicPublisher
·interface javax.jms.QueueBrowser
·Interface javax.jms.Session
        ·interface javax.jms.QueueSession
        ·interface javax.jms.TopicSession
        ·interface javax.jms.XASession
```

Figure D.2 The most commonly used interfaces of the javax.jms package.

The javax.jms.ConnectionFactory Interface

A ConnectionFactory object hides connection configuration parameters from the client. An administrator defines these parameters by using the administration tool of the JMS provider. A ConnectionFactory object is a JMS administered object. The client only uses this object to create a connection with a JMS provider.

The ConnectionFactory interface and the object implementing the interface do not depend on a Java Naming Directory Interface (JNDI) API, but JMS clients find the ConnectionFactory object by looking up the ConnectionFactory object in a JNDI namespace. The administrator can place an administered object anywhere in a namespace. The JMS API does not define a naming policy. JMS providers usually provide tools for administrators to create and configure administered objects in a JNDI namespace.

A ConnectionFactory interface has two subinterfaces for two different messaging models, which you'll read about in the following sections.

The javax.jms.QueueConnectionFactory Interface

If the messaging model is point-to-point (p2p), a client uses a QueueConnectionFactory object to create QueueConnection objects. This interface has two methods:

- createQueueConnection()—Creates a queue connection with the default user identity. The connection is created in stopped mode. Before starting message delivery, you first have to call the start() method of a Connection interface.

- createQueueConnection(*String userID, String userPassword*)—Acts like the createQueueConnection() method. It also authenticates the user with a userID and password.

Both methods throw a JMSException. If client authentication fails due to an invalid userID or password, the method also throws a JMSSecurityException.

The javax.jms.TopicConnectionFactory Interface

In the publish-and-subscribe (pub/sub) messaging model, a client uses the TopicConnectionFactory object to create TopicConnection objects. This interface has two methods:

- createTopicConnection()—Creates a topic connection with the default user identity. The connection is created in stopped mode. You must call the start() method of a Connection interface to start message delivery.

- createTopicConnection(*String userID, String userPassword*)—Acts like the createQueueConnection() method. It also authenticates the user with a userID and password.

Both methods throw a JMSException. If client authentication fails due to an invalid userID or password, it also throws a JMSSecurityException.

The javax.jms.Connection Interface

A JMS client creates a client's active connection to its JMS provider via a Connection object. It typically allocates provider resources outside the Java Virtual Machine (JVM).

A Connection object hides an open connection to a JMS provider. The connection is an open TCP/IP socket between a client and a provider service daemon.

JMS client connection creation is implemented where client authentication takes place. It can specify a unique client identifier, provide a ConnectionMetaData, and support an optional ExceptionListener object.

Most clients will do all their messaging with a single connection because a connection is a relatively heavyweight (network-intensive) object due to the authentication and communication setup. Some advanced applications might use several connections.

A JMS client creates a connection, one or more sessions if needed, and a number of message producers and consumers. When a connection is created, it is in stopped mode. That means that no messages can be delivered until you call the start() method explicitly.

After all message consumers have been created, the client calls the connection's start() method, and messages begin arriving at the connection's consumers. It is better to leave the connection in stopped mode until communication setup is complete. A connection can be started immediately, and then the message consumers can finish processing. The clients should be prepared to handle asynchronous message delivery while they are still in the process of setting up.

A message producer can send messages while a connection is stopped.

The following list contains the eight methods of the Connection interface and a brief description of each:

- getClientID()—Gets the client identifier from the provider, which is set by the factory when the connection is created. This value is specific to the JMS provider. It is either preconfigured by an administrator in a ConnectionFactory object or assigned dynamically by the application by calling the setClientID() method.

- `setClientID(String ID)`—Sets the client identifier. The ID given in the parameter list should be a valid provider-specific string.
- `ConnectionMetaData()`—Returns an object that contains information about the connection and the provider for this connection.
- `getExceptionListener()`—Gets the exception listener object for the current connection.
- `setExceptionListener()`—Sets the exception listener for the current connection.
- `start()`—Starts (or restarts) a connection's delivery of incoming messages. Calling the `start()` method on a connection that has already been started is ignored.
- `stop()`—Temporarily stops a connection's delivery of incoming messages. Delivery can be restarted using the connection's `start()` method. When the connection is stopped, delivery to all the connection's message consumers is inhibited: blocks received synchronously and messages are not delivered to message listeners.
- `close()`—Closes the connection and releases the resources allocated by the JMS provider. There is no need to close the sessions, producers, and consumers of a closed connection. Closing a connection causes all temporary destinations to be deleted and causes any of its sessions' transactions in progress to be rolled back. Closing a connection does not force an acknowledgment of client-acknowledged sessions.

Methods of the Connection interface throw the following exceptions:

- JMSException if the JMS provider fails due to some internal error
- InvalidClientIDException if the JMS client specifies an invalid or duplicate client ID
- IllegalStateException if the JMS client attempts to set a connection's client ID at the wrong time or when it has been administratively configured

The Connection interface has two subinterfaces for two different messaging models, as you'll discover in the following sections.

The javax.jms.QueueConnection Interface

The QueueConnection object is an active connection to a JMS provider for a p2p messaging model. A client creates QueueSession objects (which I will examine in the following sections) by using a QueueConnection object, and it creates objects for producing and consuming messages. This interface has two methods:

- createQueueSession(*boolean transacted, int acknowledgeMode*)—
  Creates a QueueSession object. A boolean type transacted
  parameter defines whether the session is transacted. An Integer
  type acknowledgeMode indicates whether the consumer will
  acknowledge any messages it receives. Valid values are
  Session.AUTO_ACKNOWLEDGE, Session.CLIENT_
  ACKNOWLEDGE, and Session.DUPS_OK_ACKNOWLEDGE.
  This parameter is ignored if the session is transacted.

- createConnectionConsumer(*Queue parQueue, String messageSelector,*
  ServerSessionPool, parServerSessionPool, int maxMessages)—Creates
  a connection consumer for this connection. This is an optional operation.
  It is for an expert facility, not for regular JMS clients.

Both methods throw a JMSException. The `CreateConnectionConsumer()`
method also throws an InvalidDestinationException and an
InvalidSelectorException.

The javax.jms.TopicConnection Interface

The TopicConnection object is an active connection to a JMS provider for the
pub/sub messaging model. A client creates TopicSession objects by using the
TopicConnection object, and it creates objects for producing and consuming
messages. This interface has three methods:

- createTopicSession(*boolean transacted, int acknowledgeMode*)—
  Creates a TopicSession object. A Boolean type transacted parameter
  defines whether the session is transacted. An Integer type
  acknowledgeMode indicates whether the consumer will acknowledge
  any messages it receives. Valid values are Session.AUTO_
  ACKNOWLEDGE, Session.CLIENT_ACKNOWLEDGE, and
  Session.DUPS_OK_ACKNOWLEDGE. This parameter is ignored
  if the session is transacted.

- createConnectionConsumer(*Topic parTopic, String messageSelector,*
  ServerSessionPool parServerSessionPool, int maxMessages)—Creates a
  connection consumer for this connection. The
  `createConnectionConsumer()` method is an optional operation. It is for an
  expert facility, not for regular JMS clients.

- createDurableConnectionConsumer(*Topic parTopic, String*
  subscriptionName, String messageSelector, ServerSessionPool
  parServerSessionPool, int maxMessages)—Creates a durable connection
  consumer for this connection. This is an optional operation. It is for
  expert facility, not for regular JMS clients.

All methods throw a JMSException. The `createConnectionConsumer()` and `createDurableConnectionConsumer()` methods also throw an InvalidDestinationException and an InvalidSelectorException.

The javax.jms.ConnectionConsumer Interface

The messages that are consumed by client applications are specified by a destination object (queue or topic). You can also filter the message by using a message selector. For application servers, Connection objects optionally provide a special facility for creating a ConnectionConsumer, which must be given a ServerSessionPool to use for processing its messages.

Normally, when network traffic is off peak, a ConnectionConsumer gets a ServerSession from its pool, loads it with a single message, and starts it. During peak traffic times, messages can back up. If this happens, a ConnectionConsumer can load each ServerSession with more than one message. This reduces the thread context switches and minimizes resource use at the expense of some serialization of message processing.

The ConnectionConsumer interface has two methods:

- `getServerSessionPool()`—Gets the ServerSession pool associated with the connection consumer and returns the ServerSession pool used by this connection consumer.

- `close()`—Closes the connection consumer and releases the resources that the JMS provider allocated but no longer needs.

Both methods throw a JMSException.

The javax.jms.Destination Interface

A Destination object hides a provider-specific address to send or receive a message. The JMS API does not define a standard address syntax because existing message-oriented middleware (MOM) products have own their address syntax types, which are different from each other. Therefore, it is hard to bridge MOM products with a common single syntax.

Destination is an administered object that is specified by a JMS provider administrator. There is no default value as in a ConnectionFactory if the administrator has not defined the object using an admin tool. It might also contain provider-specific configuration information in addition to its address because it is an administered object.

The JMS API also supports a client's use of provider-specific address names. A Destination interface and its object do not depend on a JNDI API, but JMS clients find it by looking it up in a JNDI namespace. The administrator can place an administered object anywhere in a namespace. The JMS API does not define a naming policy. JMS providers usually provide tools for administrators to create and configure administered objects in a JNDI namespace.

JMS provider implementations of administered objects should implement the javax.naming.Referenceable and java.io.Serializable interfaces so that they can be stored in all JNDI naming contexts. In addition, it is recommended that these implementations follow the JavaBeans design patterns.

The Destination interface has two subinterfaces for the two different messaging models, as you'll discover in the following sections.

The javax.jms.Queue Interface

A Queue object hides a provider-specific queue name. Using a Queue object is the way a client specifies the identity of a queue to JMS API methods.

The actual length of time that messages are held by a queue and the consequences of resource overflow are not defined by the JMS API.

The javax.jms.Queue interface has two methods:

- `getQueueName()`—Gets the name of the queue. It throws a JMSException if the JMS provider implementation of Queue fails to return the queue name due to some internal error.

- `toString()`—Returns a string representation of the object.

The javax.jms.Queue interface has one subinterface: TemporaryQueue, which is a unique Queue object created for the duration of a QueueConnection. It is a system-defined queue that can be consumed only by the QueueConnection that created it.

The TemporaryQueue interface has one method: `delete()`. This method deletes the temporary queue. If there are existing receivers still using it, a JMSException is thrown.

The javax.jms.Topic Interface

A Topic object hides a provider-specific topic name. It is the way a client specifies the identity of a topic to JMS API methods.

The actual length of time that messages are held by a queue and the consequences of resource overflow are not defined by the JMS API.

Many pub/sub providers group topics into hierarchies and provide various options for subscribing to parts of the hierarchy. The JMS API places no restriction on what a Topic object represents. It can be a leaf in a topic hierarchy, or it can be a larger part of the hierarchy.

The javax.jms.Topic interface has two methods:

- `getTopicName()`—Gets the name of the topic. It throws a JMSException if the JMS provider implementation of Topic fails to return the topic name due to some internal error.
- `toString()`—Returns a string representation of the object.

The javax.jms.Topic interface has one subinterface: TemporaryTopic, which is a unique Topic object created for the duration of a TopicConnection. It is a system-defined queue that can be consumed only by the TopicConnection that created it.

The TemporaryTopic interface has one method: `delete()`. This method deletes the temporary topic. If there are existing subscribers still using it, a JMSException is thrown.

The javax.jms.Session Interface

A Session object is a single-threaded context for producing and consuming messages. It is considered a lightweight JMS object. A session is a factory for its message producers and consumers. It supports a single series of transactions and combines the producers and consumers into atomic units. A session keeps the message until the session has been acknowledged, and it serializes execution of message listeners registered with its message consumers. It can create and service multiple message producers and consumers.

One typical use of a session is to have a thread block on a synchronous MessageConsumer until a message arrives. The thread can then use one or more of the Session's MessageProducers. If a client application wants to have one thread produce messages while others consume them, the client should use a separate session for its producing thread in addition to its consuming thread.

The `close()` method is the only session method that can be called while another session method is being executed in another thread.

A session can be specified as transacted. Each transacted session supports a single series of transactions. When a transaction commits, its atomic unit of input is acknowledged, and its associated atomic unit of output is sent. If a transaction rollback is done, the transaction's sent messages are destroyed, and the session's input is automatically recovered. A transaction is completed using either its session's `commit()` method or its session's `rollback()` method.

A Session interface has 16 methods:

- `createBytesMessage()`—Creates byte-type messages that are used to communicate with non-JMS clients. A BytesMessage object is used to send a message containing a stream of uninterpreted bytes.

- `createMapMessage()`—Creates a message that stores key-value pairs. In the MapMessage interface, names are String objects and values are primitive values in the Java programming language.

- `createMessage()`—Creates a message with no body information. A Message object holds all the standard message header information. It can be sent when a message containing only header information is sufficient.

- `createObjectMessage()`—Creates a message that contains a single, serializable object.

- `createObjectMessage(Serializable myObject)`—Creates a message that contains a single, serializable object given in the parameter list.

- `createStreamMessage()`—Creates a message that contains a stream of self-defining data. It is similar to a BytesMessage and is used to communicate with a non-JMS client.

- `createTextMessage()`—Creates a message that contains a string.

- `createTextMessage(StringBuffer myString)`—Creates a message that contains a string given in the parameter list.

- `getTransacted()`—A boolean method that returns true if the session is transacted; false if the session is not using transaction.

- `commit()`—If the session is transacted, commit sends any waiting messages in the transaction store area and sends an acknowledgment for received messages. It releases any locks currently held.

- `rollback()`—If the session is transacted, rollback removes all the messages in the transaction store area and cancels the message sending. It releases any locks currently held.

- `close()`—Closes the session and releases the resources that are used for the Session object. There is no need to close the producers and consumers of a closed session. Closing a transacted session must roll back the transaction in progress.

- `recover()`—Tells the session to redeliver the messages that have not been acknowledged by the recipient. New messages will not be affected and will continue to be delivered normally.

- `getMessageListener()`—Returns this session's message listener if a message listener is assigned.

- setMessageListener()—Assigns a message listener to the session.
- run()—An optional operation that is intended to be used only by application servers, not by ordinary JMS clients.

Methods of the Session interface throw the following exceptions:

- JMSException if the JMS provider fails due to an internal error
- IllegalStateException if the method is called by a transacted session
- TransactionRolledBackException if the transaction is rolled back due to some error during commit

The javax.jms.QueueSession Interface

A QueueSession object provides methods to send and receive messages with QueueReceiver, QueueSender, QueueBrowser, and TemporaryQueue objects.

QueueSession prevents you from losing a message because of a session termination. Some messages might be received by the client, but not acknowledged. When a QueueSession terminates for some reason, these messages will be retained and redelivered when a consumer next accesses the queue.

The javax.jms.QueueSession interface has seven methods:

- createQueue(*String queueName*)—Creates a queue identity given a name as a parameter. This method is not used very frequently. It is provided where clients need to dynamically manipulate queue identity. You can create a queue identity with a provider-specific name. By doing this, a client loses its portability advantage.

  This method is not used to create a physical queue. A Queue object is an administered object and is not initiated by the JMS API. The only exception is the creation of temporary queues, which is accomplished with the createTemporaryQueue() method.

  The createQueue() method throws a JMSException.

- createReceiver(*Queue queue*)—Creates a QueueReceiver object to receive messages from the specified queue as the parameter. It throws a JMSException and an InvalidDestinationException.

- createReceiver(*Queue queue, String messageSelector*)—Creates a QueueReceiver object to receive messages from the specified queue by using a message selector.

  You can only deliver messages with properties or a header that match the message selector expression. If there is no message selector for the message consumer, there must be a value of null or an empty string.

The `createReceiver()` method throws a JMSException, an InvalidDestinationException, and an InvalidSelectorException.

- `createSender(Queue queue)`—Creates a QueueSender object to send messages to the specified queue as the parameter. It throws a JMSException and an InvalidDestinationException.

- `createBrowser(Queue queue)`— Creates a QueueBrowser object to peek at the messages on the specified queue in the parameter list. It throws a JMSException and an InvalidDestinationException.

- `createBrowser(Queue queue, String messageSelector)`—Creates a QueueBrowser object to peek at the messages on the specified queue using a message selector. Similar to the `createReceiver()` method, you can only deliver messages with properties or headers that match the message selector expression. If there is no message selector for the message consumer, there must be a value of null or an empty string.

  The `createBrowser()` method throws a JMSException, an InvalidDestinationException, and an InvalidSelectorException.

- `createTemporaryQueue()`—Creates a TemporaryQueue object, which is a temporary queue identity to send and receive messages. It exists as long as a QueueConnection exists. You can delete it before a QueueConnection is closed. It throws a JMSException.

The javax.jms.TopicSession Interface

A TopicSession object provides methods to send and receive messages with TopicSubscriber, TopicPublisher, and TemporaryTopic objects. It also provides a method for deleting its client's durable subscribers.

The javax.jms.TopicSession interface has eight methods:

- `createTopic(String topicName)`—Creates a topic identity given a name as the parameter. This method is not used very frequently. It is provided where clients need to dynamically manipulate topic identity. You can create a topic identity with a provider-specific name. By doing this, the client loses its portability advantage.

  This method is not used to create a physical topic. A Topic object is an administered object and is not initiated by the JMS API. The only exception is the creation of temporary topics, which is accomplished with the `createTemporaryTopic()` method.

  The `createTopic()` method throws a JMSException.

- `createSubscriber(Topic topic)`—Creates a nondurable subscriber to the specified topic. A client uses a TopicSubscriber object to receive messages that have been published to a topic. Regular TopicSubscriber objects are not durable. This means that they only receive messages that are published while they are active.

  The `createSubscriber()` method throws a JMSException and an InvalidDestinationException.

- `createSubscriber(Topic topic, String messageSelector, boolean noLocal)`—Creates a nondurable subscriber to the specified topic. Nondurable clients only receive messages that are published while they are active. Using a message selector will filter out the message, which will not be delivered to the consumer. Setting the noLocal parameter to true inhibits the delivery of messages published by its own connection.

  A client uses a TopicSubscriber object to receive messages that have been published to a topic. Regular TopicSubscriber objects are not durable. This means that they only receive messages that are published while they are active.

  Messages are filtered based on the criteria in a message selector, and filtered messages are not delivered to the client. Only messages with properties or headers that match the message selector expression will be delivered. If there is no message selector for the message consumer, there must be a value of null or an empty string.

  In some cases, a connection can publish *and* subscribe to a topic. The subscriber NoLocal attribute allows a subscriber to inhibit the delivery of messages published by its own connection. The default value for this attribute is false.

  The `createSubscriber()` method throws a JMSException, an InvalidDestinationException, and an InvalidSelectorException.

- `createDurableSubscriber(Topic topic, String name)`—Creates a durable subscriber to the specified topic. If a client needs to receive all the messages published to the topic, even when the subscriber is inactive, this client uses a durable TopicSubscriber object to receive messages that have been published to a topic. The JMS provider retains a record of this durable subscription and ensures that all messages from the topic's publishers are retained until this durable subscriber acknowledges them. Messages for a durable subscriber can expire before they are delivered to the client or are acknowledged by the client.

The `createDurableSubscriber()` method throws a JMSException and an InvalidDestinationException.

- `createDurableSubscriber(Topic topic, String name, String messageSelector, boolean noLocal)`—Creates a durable subscriber to the specified topic. A durable client receives messages that are published even when it is inactive. A JMS provider retains a record of this durable subscription and ensures that all messages from the topic's publishers are retained until they are either acknowledged by this durable subscriber or they have expired. Using a message selector will filter out the message, which will not be delivered to the consumer. Setting the noLocal parameter to true inhibits the delivery of messages published by its own connection.

If a client needs to receive all the messages published to the topic, even when the subscriber is inactive, this client uses a durable TopicSubscriber object to receive messages that have been published to a topic. The JMS provider retains a record of this durable subscription and ensures that all messages from the topic's publishers are retained until this durable subscriber acknowledges them. Messages for a durable subscriber can expire before they are delivered to the client or acknowledged by the client.

Messages are filtered based on the criteria in a message selector, and filtered messaged are not delivered to the client. Only messages with properties or headers that match the message selector expression will be delivered. If there is no message selector for the message consumer, there must be a value of null or an empty string.

In some cases, a connection can publish *and* subscribe to a topic. The subscriber NoLocal attribute allows a subscriber to inhibit the delivery of messages published by its own connection. The default value for this attribute is false.

Sessions with durable subscribers must always provide the same client identifier. Only one session at a time can have a TopicSubscriber for a particular durable subscription. A client can change an existing durable subscription by creating a durable TopicSubscriber with the same name and a new topic and/or message selector.

The `createDurableSubscriber()` method throws a JMSException, an InvalidDestinationException, and an InvalidSelectorException.

- createPublisher(*Topic topic*)—Creates a publisher for the specified topic. This method returns a TopicPublisher object. A client uses a TopicPublisher object to publish messages on a topic. Each time a client creates a TopicPublisher on a topic, it defines a new sequence of messages that have no ordering relationship with the messages it has previously sent.

  The createDurablePublisher() method throws a JMSException and an InvalidDestinationException.

- createTemporaryTopic()—Creates a TemporaryTopic object, which is a temporary topic identity for sending and receiving messages. It exists as long as a TopicConnection exists. You can delete it before the TopicConnection closes. It throws a JMSException.

- unsubscribe(*String name*)—Unsubscribes a durable subscription that has been created by a client. This method deletes the state being maintained on behalf of the subscriber by its provider. The client should not delete a durable subscription while there is an active TopicSubscriber for the subscription or a consumed message has not yet been acknowledged in the session. It throws a JMSException and an InvalidDestinationException.

The javax.jms.XASession Interface

The optional XASession interface extends the capability of a session by adding access to a JMS provider's support for the Java Transaction API (JTA). This support takes the form of a javax.jms.XAResource object. The functionality of this object closely resembles that defined by the standard X/Open XA Resource interface. I will not focus on this optional interface. Refer to Sun's web site for more detailed information.

The javax.jms.MessageProducer Interface

A client uses a MessageProducer object to send messages to a destination. MessageProducer is the parent interface for all message producers.

A client can also create a message producer without supplying a destination. In this case, a destination must be provided in the send operation while sending the message. A typical use for this kind of message producer is to send replies. A destination is provided in the JMSReplyTo part of the message.

The MessageProducer interface has 11 methods:

- setDisableMessageID(*boolean value*)—Sets whether message IDs are disabled, which are enabled by default. Because MessageID increases the message size, some JMS providers allow clients to disable the MessageID to optimize the header by using the setDisableMessageID() method if the application does not need this ID.

- `getDisableMessageID()`—Gets an indication of whether message IDs are disabled.

- `setDisableMessageTimestamp(boolean value)`—Sets whether message timestamps are disabled, which are enabled by default. Because a timestamp increases the message size, some JMS providers allow clients to disable the timestamps to optimize the header by using the `setDisableMessageTimestamp()` method if the application does not need this timestamp.

- `getDisableMessageTimestamp(boolean value)`—Gets an indication of whether timestamps are disabled.

- `setDeliveryMode(int deliveryMode)`—Sets the producer's default delivery mode, which is PERSISTENT by default. The delivery modes are DeliveryMode.NON_PERSISTENT or DeliveryMode.PERSISTENT.

- `getDeliveryMode()`—Gets the producer's default delivery mode.

- `setPriority(int defaultPriority)`—Sets the producer's default priority. The JMS specifications define 10 levels of priority value from 0 (the lowest) to 9 (the highest). It is set to 4 by default. Normal priority level is between 0 and 4, and expedited priority is between 5 and 9.

- `getPriority()`—Gets the producer's default priority.

- `setTimeToLive(long timeToLive)`—Sets the default length of time in milliseconds from its dispatch time that a produced message should be retained by the message system before delivering it to the consumer. The default value is zero, which means the message will stay in the message system until it is delivered to the consumer.

- `getTimeToLive()`—Gets the default length of time in milliseconds from its dispatch time that a produced message should be retained by the message system.

- `close()`—Closes the message producer and releases resources that are allocated by the provider.

All the methods in the MessageProducer interface throw a JMSException if the JMS provider fails due to some internal error.

Two subinterfaces of the MessageProducer interface are discussed in the following sections.

The javax.jms.QueueSender Interface

The QueueSender object is used to send messages to a queue destination. The Queue (p2p destination) is specified when a QueueSender is created. If you attempt to use the `send()` method for an unidentified QueueSender, an UnsupportedOperationException will be thrown.

While the message is being sent, other threads within the client must not change the message. If the message is modified, the result of the `send()` is undefined. After sending a message, the client can modify the message without affecting the message that was sent previously. The same message object can be sent multiple times.

JMSDestination, JMSDeliverMode, JMSExpiration, JMSPriority, JMSMessageID, and JMSTimeStamp are message headers as part of the message.

The QueueSender interface has five methods:

- `getQueue()`—Gets the queue associated with the QueueSender.
- `send(Message message)`—Sends the message to the queue with the default delivery mode, priority, and time to live attribute values.
- `send(Message message, int deliveryMode, int priority, long timeToLive)`—Sends the message to the queue by specifying a delivery mode, priority, and time to live value as parameters of the method.
- `send(Queue queue, Message message)`—Sends the message to the queue for an unidentified message producer with a default delivery mode, priority, and time to live value. Normally, a queue must be given when the message producer is created, but JMS supports unidentified message producers. If there is no predefined queue, the queue must be supplied every time a message is sent.
- `send(Queue queue, Message message, int deliveryMode, int priority, long timeToLive)`—Sends the message to the queue for an unidentified message producer by specifying a delivery mode, priority, and time to live value as parameters of the method. Normally, a queue must be given when the message producer is created, but JMS supports unidentified message producers. In this case, the queue must be supplied every time a message is sent.

Methods of the QueueSender interface throw the following exceptions:

- JMSException if the JMS provider fails due to some internal error
- MessageFormatException if an invalid message is specified
- InvalidDestination if a client uses the method with an invalid queue
- java.lang.UnsupportedOperationException if the client did not specify a queue at creation time

The javax.jms.TopicPublisher Interface

A TopicPublisher object is used to publish messages to a topic destination. The topic (pub/sub destination) is specified when a TopicPublisher is created. If you attempt to use the `publish()` method for an unidentified TopicPublisher, an UnsupportedOperationException will be thrown.

While the message is being published, other threads within the client must not change the message. If the message is modified, the result of the `publish()` method is undefined. After publishing a message, the client can modify the message without affecting the message that was published previously. The same message object can be published multiple times.

JMSDestination, JMSDeliverMode, JMSExpiration, JMSPriority, JMSMessageID, and JMSTimeStamp are message headers as part of the message.

The TopicPublisher interface has five methods:

- `getTopic()`—Gets the topic associated with the TopicPublisher.

- `publish(Message message)`—Publishes the message to the topic with a default delivery mode, priority, and time to live value.

- `publish(Message message, int deliveryMode, int priority, long timeToLive)`—Publishes the message to the topic by specifying a delivery mode, priority, and time to live value as parameters of the method.

- `publish(Topic topic, Message message)`—Publishes the message to the topic for an unidentified message producer with a default delivery mode, priority, and time to live value. Normally, a topic must be given when the message producer is created, but JMS supports unidentified message producers. In this case, the topic must be supplied every time a message is published.

- `publish(Topic topic, Message message, int deliveryMode, int priority, long timeToLive)`—Publishes the message to the topic for an unidentified message producer by specifying a delivery mode, priority, and time to live value as parameters of the method. Normally, a topic must be given when the message producer is created, but JMS supports unidentified message producers. In this case, the topic must be supplied every time a message is published.

Methods of the TopicPublisher interface throw the following exceptions:

- JMSException if the JMS provider fails due to some internal error

- MessageFormatException if an invalid message is specified

- InvalidDestination if a client uses the method with an invalid topic
- java.lang.UnsupportedOperationException if the client did not specify a topic at creation time

The javax.jms.MessageConsumer Interface

A client uses a MessageConsumer object to receive messages from a destination. MessageConsumer is the parent interface for all message consumers.

A message selector can create a message consumer. The message selector filters the messages that will be delivered to the message consumer based on criteria in the selector.

A client can either synchronously receive a message consumer's messages or have the consumer asynchronously deliver them as they arrive.

For synchronous receivers, a client can read the messages by using one of its `receive()` methods. There are several variations of `receive()` methods that allow a client to poll or wait for the next message.

For asynchronous delivery, a client can register a MessageListener object with a message consumer. Whenever messages arrive at the message consumer, a MessageConsumer object delivers them by calling the `onMessage()` method in the MessageListener object. The MessageListener throws an exception if there is a programming error on the client application.

The MessageConsumer interface has seven methods:

- `getMessageSelector()`—Gets the message consumer's message selector expression. If no message selector exists for the message consumer, it returns a null value.

- `getMessageListener()`—Gets the message consumer's MessageListener. If there is no listener set, it returns a null value.

- `setMessageListener(MessageListener listener)`—Sets the message consumer's MessageListener. With this method, the listener is the message listener to which the messages are to be delivered.

  If you want to disable the message listener for the message consumer, you have to set the message listener to null. You cannot call the `setMessageListener()` method while messages are being consumed by an existing listener or the consumer is being used to consume messages synchronously.

- `receive()`—Receives the next message that arrives at the message consumer. Because there is no timeout period specified, calling this method blocks indefinitely until a message arrives or until the message consumer is closed. If the message is sent within a transaction, the consumer keeps the message until the transaction is committed.

- `receive(long timeout)`—Receives the next message that arrives at the message consumer within the specified timeout interval. Calling this method blocks until a message arrives, the timeout expires (if there is timeout period specified) or the message consumer is closed. If the timeout is specified as zero, it means it will not expire and calling the method will block indefinitely.
- `receiveNoWait()`—Receives the next message if one arrives immediately at the message consumer.
- `close()`—Closes the message consumer and releases the resources allocated from the JMS provider.

All methods of the MessageConsumer interface throw a JMSException if the JMS provider fails due to some internal error.

In the following sections, I discuss two subinterfaces of the MessageConsumer interface.

The javax.jms.QueueReceiver Interface

The QueueReceiver object is used to receive messages delivered to a queue destination. The queue (p2p destination) is specified when a QueueReceiver is created.

It is possible to have multiple QueueReceivers for the same queue. The JMS API does not define how messages are distributed between the QueueReceivers.

If there is a message selector specified, messages remain on the queue if they are selected from the receiver. A message selector allows a QueueReceiver to skip messages. This means that when the skipped messages are eventually read, the total ordering of the reads does not retain the partial order defined by each message producer. Only a QueueReceiver without a message selector will read messages in message producer order.

The QueueReceiver interface has one method: `getQueue()`. It gets the queue associated with the QueueSender. It throws a JMSException if the JMS provider fails due to some internal error.

The javax.jms.TopicSubscriber Interface

The TopicSubscriber object is used to receive messages that have been published to a topic destination. The topic (pub/sub destination) is specified when a TopicSubscriber is created.

It is possible to have multiple TopicSubscribers for the same topic. TopicQueue will deliver each message for a topic to each subscriber if they are eligible to receive the message. Each copy of the message is treated as a completely separate message. Work done on one copy has no effect on the others.

Acknowledging one does not acknowledge the others. One message can be delivered immediately, whereas another waits for its subscriber to process messages ahead of it.

Regular TopicSubscriber objects are not durable. They only receive messages that are published while they are active. They miss the message if they are inactive or closed.

If a client needs to receive all the messages published on a topic, including the ones published while the subscriber is inactive, it must use a durable TopicSubscriber. In this case, all messages from the topic's publishers are retained until this durable subscriber acknowledges them or they have expired. TopicSessions provide the `unsubscribe()` method to delete a durable subscription created by their client.

Filtered messages by a message selector will never be delivered to a subscriber.

In some cases, a connection can publish *and* subscribe to a topic. The subscriber NoLocal attribute allows a subscriber to inhibit the delivery of messages published by its own connection.

The TopicPublisher interface has two methods:

- `getTopic()`—Gets the topic associated with the TopicPublisher.
- `getNoLocal()`—Gets the NoLocal attribute for the subscriber. The default value for this attribute is false.

Both methods throw a JMSException if the JMS provider fails due to some internal error.

The javax.jms.MessageListener Interface

A MessageListener object is used to receive delivered messages asynchronously.

Each session must ensure that it serially passes messages to the listener. A listener is assigned to one or more consumers of the same session. This listener can assume that the `onMessage()` method is not called by the next message. It waits until the session has completed the last call.

The MessageListener interface has one method: `onMessage(Message message)`. It passes the message, which is given as a parameter, to the listener. It does not throw an exception.

The javax.jms.Message Interface

You need the javax.jms.Message interface if you work with message systems because the Message interface is the root interface of all JMS messages. It defines the message header and the acknowledge method used for all messages.

Most MOM products treat messages as lightweight entities that consist of a header, properties, and a body (which is sometimes called a *payload*). The header and properties contain fields used for message routing and identification; the body contains the application data that will be sent.

The JMS API cannot support all of the message models because the definition of the message varies significantly across vendors. The goals of the JMS message model can be summarized as follows:

- Provide a single and unified message API

- Provide an API to create messages that are suitable for the format used by provider-native messaging applications

- Support application development on different platforms including operating systems, machine architectures, and computer languages

- Support messages containing objects in the Java programming language and Extensible Markup Language (XML) documents

The JMS API provides a set of message interfaces to define the JMS message model, but it does not provide implementations of these interfaces. Each JMS provider supplies a set of message factories with its Session object for creating instances of messages. In this way, the provider designs and uses message implementations according to its specific needs.

A JMS provider should accept message implementations different from its own implementation. Efficiency might be less than you expect, but messages definitely must be handled. The only exception for this support is to handle foreign message implementation. If the foreign message implementation contains a JMSReplyTo header field that is set to a foreign destination implementation, the provider is not required to handle or preserve the value of this header field.

If you need to filter messages, the JMS API provides you with a message selector. A consumer client can specify which message it wants to receive based on the criteria of the header field references and property references by using a JMS message selector. Message selectors cannot reference message body values.

A message selector is a String whose syntax is based on a subset of the SQL92 conditional expression syntax. If the value of a message selector is an empty string, the value is treated as a null, which indicates that there is no message selector for the message consumer. A message selector contains literals, identifiers, white space, expressions, standard bracketing (), logical operators, comparison operators, and arithmetic operators.

A Message interface has three fields for default values:

- DEFAULT_DELIVERY_MODE—The message producer's default delivery mode is PERSISTENT.
- DEFAULT_PRIORITY—The message producer's default priority is 4.
- DEFAULT_TIME_TO_LIVE—The message producer's default time to live is unlimited; the message never expires.

The Message interface has 45 methods:

- `getJMSMessageID()`—Gets the message ID.
- `setJMSMessageID(String ID)`—Sets the message ID.
- `getJMSTimestamp()`—Gets the message timestamp.
- `setJMSTimestamp(long timestamp)`—Sets the message timestamp.
- `getJMSCorrelationIDAsBytes()`—Gets the correlation ID as an array of bytes for the message.
- `setJMSCorrelationIDAsBytes(byte[] correlationID)`—Sets the correlation ID as an array of bytes for the message.
- `getJMSCorrelationID()`—Gets the correlation ID for the message.
- `setJMSCorrelationID(String correlationID)`—Sets the correlation ID for the message.
- `getJMSReplyTo()`—Gets the Destination object to which a reply to the message should be sent.
- `setJMSReplyTo(Destination replyTo)`—Sets the Destination object to which a reply to the message should be sent.
- `getJMSDestination()`—Gets the Destination object for the message.
- `setJMSDestination(Destination destination)`—Sets the Destination object for the message.
- `getJMSDeliveryMode()`—Gets the DeliveryMode value specified for the message.
- `setJMSDeliveryMode(int deliveryMode)`—Sets the DeliveryMode value for the message.
- `getJMSRedelivered()`—Gets an indication of whether this message is being redelivered.
- `setJMSRedelivered(boolean redelivered)`—Specifies whether this message is being redelivered.

- `getJMSType()`—Gets the message type identifier supplied by the client when the message was sent.
- `setJMSType(String type)`—Sets the message type.
- `getJMSExpiration()`—Gets the message's expiration value.
- `setJMSExpiration(long expiration)`—Sets the message's expiration value.
- `getJMSPriority()`—Gets the message priority level.
- `setJMSPriority(int priority)`—Sets the priority level for the message.
- `clearProperties()`—Clears a message's properties.
- `propertyExists(String name)`—Indicates whether a property value exists.
- `getBooleanProperty(String name)`—Returns the value of the boolean property with the specified name.
- `getByteProperty(String name)`—Returns the value of the byte property with the specified name.
- `getShortProperty(String name)`—Returns the value of the short property with the specified name.
- `getIntProperty(String name)`—Returns the value of the int property with the specified name.
- `getLongProperty(String name)`—Returns the value of the long property with the specified name.
- `getFloatProperty(String name)`—Returns the value of the float property with the specified name.
- `getDoubleProperty(String name)`—Returns the value of the double property with the specified name.
- `getStringProperty(String name)`—Returns the value of the String property with the specified name.
- `getObjectProperty(String name)`—Returns the value of the Java object property with the specified name.
- `getPropertyNames()`—Returns an enumeration of all the property names.
- `setBooleanProperty(String name, boolean value)`—Sets a boolean property value with the specified name into the message.
- `setByteProperty(String name, byte value)`—Sets a byte property value with the specified name into the message.

- setShortProperty(*String name, short value*)—Sets a short property value with the specified name into the message.
- setIntProperty(*String name, int value*)—Sets an int property value with the specified name into the message.
- setLongProperty(*String name, long value*)—Sets a long property value with the specified name into the message.
- setFloatProperty(*String name, float value*)—Sets a float property value with the specified name into the message.
- setDoubleProperty(*String name, double value*)—Sets a double property value with the specified name into the message.
- setStringProperty(*String name, String value*)—Sets a String property value with the specified name into the message.
- setObjectProperty(*String name, Object value*)—Sets a Java object property value with the specified name into the message.
- acknowledge()—Acknowledges all consumed messages of the session of the consumed message. All consumed JMS messages support the acknowledge() method for use when a client has specified that its JMS session's consumed messages are to be explicitly acknowledged. By invoking acknowledge() on a consumed message, a client acknowledges all messages consumed by the session that the message was delivered to.
- clearBody()—Clears out the message body. Clearing a message's body does not clear its header values or property entries. If the message body is read-only, calling this method leaves the message body in the same state as an empty body in a newly created message.

Methods of the Message interface throw the following exceptions:

- JMSException if the JMS provider fails due to some internal error
- MessageFormatException if the type of conversion or object is invalid
- MessageNotWriteableException if properties are read-only
- IllegalStateException if the method is called on a closed session

JMS messages are formed by three parts:

- Header—Header fields have values that identify and route the message. Both the client and the provider use them. All messages support the same set of header fields.
- Properties—You can define application-specific values in the properties part of the message. Each message contains a built-in facility to support application-defined properties. Application-defined message filtering is implemented by a mechanism provided by the properties.

- Body—The JMS API defines several types of message body, which cover many of the messaging styles and types that are used by major messaging vendors. It has five subinterfaces based on the message types. I provide some information about them in the following sections.

The javax.jms.BytesMessage Interface

A BytesMessage object is used to send a message containing a stream of uninterpreted bytes. It inherits from the Message interface and adds a message body that contains bytes. The receiver of the message supplies the interpretation of the bytes. Its methods are based largely on those found in java.io.DataInputStream and java.io.DataOutputStream.

This message type is available for client encoding of existing message formats. Try to use one of the other self-defining message types specified by the JMS API if possible.

Although the JMS API allows the use of message properties with byte messages, they are typically not used because the inclusion of properties can affect the format.

When the message is first created and when `clearBody()` is called, the body of the message is in write-only mode. After the first call to reset has been made, the message body is in read-only mode. If `clearBody()` is called on a message in read-only mode, the message body is cleared, and the message is in write-only mode.

The BytesMessage interface has 26 methods:

- `readBoolean()`—Reads a boolean from the bytes message stream.

- `readByte()`—Reads a signed 8-bit value from the bytes message stream.

- `readUnsignedByte()`—Reads an unsigned 8-bit number from the bytes message stream.

- `readShort()`—Reads a signed 16-bit number from the bytes message stream.

- `readUnsignedShort()`—Reads an unsigned 16-bit number from the bytes message stream.

- `readChar()`—Reads a Unicode character value from the bytes message stream.

- `readInt()`—Reads a signed 32-bit integer from the bytes message stream.

- `readLong()`—Reads a signed 64-bit integer from the bytes message stream.

- `readFloat()`—Reads a float from the bytes message stream.
- `readDouble()`—Reads a double from the bytes message stream.
- `readUTF()`—Reads a string that has been encoded using a modified UTF-8 format from the bytes message stream.
- `readBytes(byte[] value)`—Reads a byte array from the bytes message stream. In this method, the parameter value is the buffer into which the data is read.
- `readBytes(byte[] value, int length)`—Reads a portion of the bytes message stream. In this method, the parameter value is the buffer into which the data is read, and the parameter length is the number of bytes to read, which must be less than or equal to value.length.
- `writeBoolean(boolean value)`—Writes a boolean to the bytes message stream as a 1-byte value. The value true is written as the value (byte)1; the value false is written as the value (byte)0.
- `writeByte(byte value)`—Writes a byte to the bytes message stream as a 1-byte value.
- `writeShort(short value)`—Writes a short to the bytes message stream as two bytes, high byte first.
- `writeChar(char value)`—Writes a char to the bytes message stream as a 2-byte value, high byte first.
- `writeInt(int value)`—Writes an int to the bytes message stream as four bytes, high byte first.
- `writeLong(long value)`—Writes a long to the bytes message stream as eight bytes, high byte first.
- `writeFloat(float value)`—Writes the float value to the bytes message stream as a 4-byte quantity (high byte first) by converting the float argument to an int.
- `writeDouble(double value)`—Writes the double value to the bytes message stream as an 8-byte quantity (high byte first) by converting the double argument to a long.
- `writeUTF(String value)`—Writes a string to the bytes message stream using UTF-8 encoding in a machine-independent manner.
- `writeBytes(byte[] value)`—Writes a byte array to the bytes message stream.

- `writeBytes(byte[] value, int offset, int length)`—Writes a portion of a byte array to the bytes message stream. In this method, the parameter value is the byte array value to be written, the parameter offset is the initial offset within the byte array, and the parameter length is the number of bytes to use.
- `writeObject(Object value)`—Writes an object to the bytes message stream. This method only works for the objectified primitive object types (Integer, Double, Long, and so on), String objects, and byte arrays.
- `reset()`—Puts the message body in read-only mode and repositions the stream of bytes to the >beginning.

Methods of the BytesMessage interface throw the following exceptions:

- JMSException if the JMS provider fails due to some internal error
- MessageEOFException if an unexpected end of bytes stream has been reached
- MessageFormatException if the object is of invalid type
- MessageNotWriteableException if properties are read-only
- MessageNotReadableException if properties are write-only

The `writeObject()` method also throws a NullPointerException if the parameter value is null.

The javax.jms.MapMessage Interface

A MapMessage object is used to send a set of name-value pairs. The names are String objects, and the values are primitive data types in the Java programming language. The entries can be accessed sequentially or randomly by name. The order of the entries is undefined.

When a client receives a MapMessage, it is in read-only mode. If a client attempts to write to the message at this point, a MessageNotWriteableException is thrown. If `clearBody()` is called, the message can then be read from *and* written to.

MapMessage objects support the conversion table in Table D.1. A value written as the row type can be read as the column type. The marked cases must be supported. The unmarked cases must throw a JMSException. The String-to-primitive conversions can throw a runtime exception if the primitive's `valueOf()` method does not accept it as a valid String representation of the primitive.

Table D.1.   **Conversion Table of Data Types**

	boolean	byte	short	char	int	long	float	double	string	byte[]
boolean	X								X	
byte		X	X		X	X			X	
short			X		X	X			X	
char				X					X	
int					X	X			X	
long						X			X	
float							X	X	X	
double								X	X	
String	X	X	X		X	X	X	X	X	
byte[]										X

The MapMessage interface has 25 methods:

- getBoolean(*String name*)—Returns a boolean value with the specified name.

- getByte(*String name*)—Returns the byte value with the specified name.

- getShort(*String name*)—Returns the short value with the specified name.

- getChar(*String name*)—Returns the Unicode character value with the specified name.

- getInt(*String name*)—Returns the int value with the specified name.

- getLong(*String name*)—Returns the long value with the specified name.

- getFloat(*String name*)—Returns the float value with the specified name.

- getDouble(*String name*)—Returns the double value with the specified name.

- getString(*String name*)—Returns the String value with the specified name.

- getBytes(*String name*)—Returns the byte array value with the specified name.

- getObject(*String name*)—Returns the value of the object with the specified name. This method can be used to return, in objectified format, an object in the Java programming language (Java object) that had been stored in the Map with the equivalent setObject() method call or its equivalent primitive settype() method.

- getMapNames()—Returns an enumeration of all the names in the MapMessage object.

- setBoolean(*String name, boolean value*)—Sets a boolean value with the specified name into the Map.

- setByte(*String name, byte value*)—Sets a byte value with the specified name into the Map.

- setShort(*String name, short value*)—Sets a short value with the specified name into the Map.

- setChar(*String name, char value*)—Sets a Unicode character value with the specified name into the Map.

- setInt(*String name, int value*)—Sets an int value with the specified name into the Map.

- setLong(*String name, long value*)—Sets a long value with the specified name into the Map.

- setFloat(*String name, float value*)—Sets a float value with the specified name into the Map.

- setDouble(*String name, double value*)—Sets a double value with the specified name into the Map.

- setString(*String name, String value*)—Sets a String value with the specified name into the Map.

- setBytes(*String name, byte[] value*)—Sets a byte value with the specified name into the Map.

- setBytes(*String name, byte[] value, int offset, int length*)—Sets a portion of a byte array value with the specified name into the Map. In this method, the parameter offset is the initial offset within the byte array, and the parameter is the number of bytes to use.

- setObject(*String name, Object value*)—Sets an object. In this method, the parameter offset is the initial offset within the byte array, and the parameter is the number of bytes to use.

- itemExists(*String name*)—Indicates whether an item exists in the MapMessage object.

Methods of the MapMessage interface throw the following exceptions:

- JMSException if the JMS provider fails due to some internal error
- MessageFormatException if the type conversion is of invalid type
- MessageNotWriteableException if properties are read-only

The javax.jms.ObjectMessage Interface

An ObjectMessage object is used to send a message that contains a serializable object in the Java programming language (Java object). Only serializable Java objects can be used in this interface.

If a collection of Java objects must be sent, one of the Collection classes provided in the Java Development Kit (JDK) version 1.2 and later can be used.

When a client receives an ObjectMessage, it is in read-only mode. If a client attempts to write to the message at this point, a MessageNotWriteableException is thrown. If the `clearBody()` method is called, the message can then be read from *and* written to.

The ObjectMessage interface has two methods:

- `setObject(java.io.Serializable object)`—Sets the serializable object containing the message's data. It is important that the ObjectMessage contain a snapshot of the object at the time of calling `setObject()`. If you modify the object after calling `setObject()`, it will not affect the ObjectMessage body. It throws a JMSException if the JMS provider fails to set the object due to some internal error, a MessageFormatException if object serialization fails, and a MessageNotWriteableException if the message is in read-only mode.

- `getObject()`—Gets the serializable object containing the message's data. The default value is null. It throws a JMSException if the JMS provider fails to get the object due to some internal error and a MessageFormatException if the object deserialization fails.

javax.jms.StreamMessage Interface

A StreamMessage object is used to send a stream of primitive types in the Java programming language. It is filled and read sequentially. Its methods are based largely on those found in java.io.DataInputStream and java.io.DataOutputStream.

When the message is first created and when `clearBody()` is called, the body of the message is in write-only mode. After the first time `reset()` is called, the message body is in read-only mode. If `clearBody()` is called on a message in read-only mode, the message body is cleared, and the message body is in write-only mode.

StreamMessage objects support the conversion table in Table D.1. A value written as the row type can be read as the column type. The marked cases must be supported. The unmarked cases must throw a JMSException. The StreamMessage interface has 24 methods:

- `readBoolean()`—Reads a boolean from the stream message.
- `readByte()`—Reads a byte value from the stream message.
- `readShort()`—Reads a 16-bit integer from the stream message.
- `readChar()`—Reads a Unicode character value from the stream message.
- `readInt()`—Reads a signed 32-bit integer from the stream message.
- `readLong()`—Reads a signed 64-bit integer from the stream message.
- `readFloat()`—Reads a float from the stream message.
- `readDouble()`—Reads a double from the stream message.
- `readString()`—Reads a string from the stream message.
- `readBytes(`*`byte[] value`*`)`—Reads a byte array field from the stream message into the specified byte[ ] object (the read buffer). In this method, the parameter value is the buffer into which the data is read.
- `readObject()`—Reads an object from the stream message. This method can be used to return, in objectified format, an object in the Java programming language (Java object) that has been written to the stream with the equivalent `writeObject()` method call or its equivalent primitive writetype method. Note that byte values are returned as byte[ ], not Byte[ ].
- `writeBoolean(`*`boolean value`*`)`—Writes a boolean to the stream message. The value true is written as the value (byte)1; the value false is written as the value (byte)0.
- `writeByte(`*`byte value`*`)`—Writes a byte to the stream message as a 1-byte value.
- `writeShort(`*`short value`*`)`—Writes a short value to the stream message.
- `writeChar(`*`char value`*`)`—Writes a char value to the stream message.
- `writeInt(`*`int value`*`)`—Writes an int value to the stream message.
- `writeLong(`*`long value`*`)`—Writes a long value to the stream message.
- `writeFloat(`*`float value`*`)`—Writes a float value to the stream message.
- `writeDouble(`*`double value`*`)`—Writes the double value to the stream message.

- `writeString(String value)`—Writes a string to the stream message.
- `writeBytes(byte[] value)`—Writes a byte array field to the stream message.
- `writeBytes(byte[] value, int offset, int length)`—Writes a portion of a byte array as a byte array field to the stream message. In this method, the parameter offset is the initial offset within the byte array, and the parameter length is the number of bytes to use. A portion of the byte array value is written to the message as a byte array field. Consecutively written byte array fields are treated as two distinct fields when the fields are read.
- `writeObject(Object value)`—Writes an object to the stream message. This method only works for the objectified primitive object types (Integer, Double, Long, and so on), String objects, and byte arrays.
- `reset()`—Puts the message body in read-only mode and repositions the stream of bytes to the beginning.

Methods of the StreamMessage interface throw the following exceptions:

- JMSException if the JMS provider fails due to some internal error
- MessageFormatException if the type conversion is of invalid type
- MessageEOFException if an unexpected end of message stream has been reached
- MessageNotWriteableException if properties are read-only
- MessageNotReadableException if the message is in write-only mode

The javax.jms.TextMessage Interface

A TextMessage object is used to send a message containing a java.lang.String.

TextMessage supports an XML-based text structure because XML will likely become the most popular text representing mechanism in addition to a format for exchanging structured data. Therefore, XML might become a mechanism for representing the content of JMS messages as well as the format used for JMS messages.

When a client receives a TextMessage, it is in read-only mode. If a client attempts to write to the message at this point, a MessageNotWriteableException is thrown. If `clearBody()` is called, the message can then be read from *and* written to.

The TextMessage interface has two methods:

- `setText(`*`String string`*`)`—Sets the string containing the message's data. It throws a JMSException if the JMS provider fails to set the text due to some internal error and a MessageNotWriteableException if the message is in read-only mode.

- `getText()`—Gets the string containing the message's data. The default value is null. It throws a JMSException if the JMS provider fails to set the text due to some internal error.

The javax.jms.QueueBrowser Interface

If you need to check the message on the queue without removing it, you can use the QueueBrowser object and its methods. A client uses a QueueBrowser object to look at messages on a queue without removing them.

The QueueBrowser interface's `getEnumeration()` method scans the queue's messages. The result can be an enumeration of the entire content of a queue, or it can contain only the messages matching a message selector.

New messages might arrive or existing messages expire while the client scans the queue. Therefore, the queue content can change; it is not static. The JMS API does not require the content of an enumeration to be a static snapshot of the queue content. The visibility of these changes while scanning depends on the JMS provider.

The QueueBrowser interface has four methods:

- `getQueue()`—Gets the queue associated with the queue browser.

- `getMessageSelector()`—Gets the queue browser's message selector expression. It returns null if no message selector exists for the message consumer (that is, if the message selector was not set or was set to null or an empty string).

- `getEnumeration()`—Gets an enumeration for browsing the current queue messages in the order they will be received.

- `close()`—Closes the QueueBrowser and releases the resources assigned from the JMS provider.

All methods of the QueueBrowser interface throw a JMSException if the JMS provider fails due to some internal error.

Index

A

Access databases
  PersonInfo table, 73-74
  UserLogin table, 66

accessibility
  entity beans, 54-55, 83-87
  session beans, 47-48, 81-87

acknowledge( ) method (Message interface), 370

advertising, EJB, 40

APIs (Application Programming Interfaces), 11
  J2EE, 11
    EJB, 11
    Java Interface Definition Language.
      See *Java IDL*
    Java Naming Directory Interface.
      See *JNDI*
    Java Server Pages. See *JSP*
    Java servlets, 12
    Java Transaction API. See *JTA*
    JavaMail. See *JavaMail*
    JDBC, 12
    JMS, 11
    JNDI, 15-23, 25-31
    JSP, 13
    LDAP, 14
    RMI, 12
  JAXP, 208, 210-212, 215-218
  JMS. *See* JMS API
  messaging (MOM), 95

applets (Java), 4

Application command (New menu), 310

Application Deployment tool
  applications
    adding, 310-312
    adding web components, 321-330
    beans, 312-318
    deploying, 318-321
    FirstMessage application, 237
    writing, 309-310

  interface, 230, 308
  starting, 307-309

Application Programming Interfaces. *See* **APIs**

applications
  Application Deployment tool
    adding, 310-312
    adding web components, 321-330
    beans, 312-318
    deploying, 318-321
    FirstMessage application, 237
    interface, 230, 308
    starting, 307-309
    writing, 309-310
  business-to-business (B2B)
    applications, 4
  configuration, MOM, 99
  distributed, EJB, 36
  enterprise, 4
  JNDI, 25-31
  message-driven bean, running, 237-239
  servers, EJB, 37
  stand-alone, 4
  Web. *See* JMS Provider

architecture
  EJB, 39-41
  J2EE, 8
    three-tier model, 9-10
    two-tier model, 8-9
  JNDI, 17
  message-driven beans, 223
    bean class, 224-225
    life cycles, 223
  MOM, 94-95, 100
    centralized, 100
    decentralized, 101-102
    hybrid, 101
  ORBs (Object Request Brokers), 96
  Web applications, 115-116
    three-tier architecture, 245-246
    two-tier architecture, 244

Ask Advance Payment application
functionalities, 271
layout design, 258-270
running, 271-275
AskPaymentListener message listener, source code, 266-268
asynchronous message comsumption, 110, 117
MOM, 99, 103-104
p2p messaging model, 129
pub/sub messaging model, 128-130
atomic names, JNDI, 18
attributes, XML documents, 202
aunthentication, JNDI, 21, 25
AUTO_ACKNOWLEDGE option, 123

B

BEA Systems Inc., 333-334
Bean class (EJB), 45, 48-49, 55, 69-72
entity beans, 75-76
message-driven beans, 224-225, 229-237
bean provider (EJB container), 43
bean-managed persistence (entity beans), 54
beans
adding to Application Deployment
applications, 312-318
entity, 11
message, 11
session, 11
bind communications, 335
binding JNDI names, 18
body (message objects), 134
BytesMessage interface, 137
MapMessage interface, 136
Message interface messages, 371
ObjectMessage interface, 135
StreamMessage interface, 138-139
TextMessage interface, 134-135
business methods
entity beans, 75-80
message-driven beans, 222
session beans, 68-72
**business-to-business (B2B)
applications, 4**
bytecode, 6
BytesMessage interface, 137, 371-373

C

case sensitivity, XML, 199
centralized architecture, MOM, 100
CGI (Common Gateway Interface), 12
classes
bean, message-driven beans, 224-225, 229-237
EJB
Bean, 45, 48-49, 55, 69-72, 75-76
primary key, 45, 55
EJBHome, 43
EJBObject, 43
files, 7
javax.jms, 343-344
java.lang.Throwable, 346
QueueRequestor, 344-345
TopicRequestor, 345
JMSException, 346
CLASSPATH variable
configuring for J2EE, 297-299
configuring for J2SE, 290-292
**clearBody( ) method (Message
interface), 370**
**clearProperties( ) method (Message
interface), 369**
clients
access to entity beans, 54-55, 83-87
access to session beans, 47-48, 81-87
applications
p2p messaging model, 152-155
pub/sub messaging model, 162-164, 167-169
communications, 335
Decider, source code, 263, 265
EJB, Web, 60-61
messaging (MOM), 95, 110
PaymentAsker (Ask Advance Payment
application), 258-263
Web. *See* JMS Provider
**CLIENT_ ACKNOWLEDGE
option, 123**
close( ) method
Connection interface, 350
ConnectionConsumer interface, 352
MessageConsumer interface, 365
MessageProducer interface, 361
QueueBrowser interface, 379
Session interface, 355

clustering
  computation, 193
  parallel, 193
  reliability, 192-194
  service, 193

code
  AskPaymentListener message listener,
    266-268
  bytecode, 6
  Decider client, 263, 265
  PaymentAsker client, 260-263
  ReplyPaymentListener message listener,
    269-270

COM (Component Object Model), 10

commands
  New menu, Application, 310
  Tools menu, Deploy, 318

commit( ) method, 182-183, 355

Common Gateway Interface (CGI), 12

**Common Object Broker Architecture
(CORBA), 10, 36**

communications
  bind, 335
  client, 335
  J2EE, 15
  JMS API, 112

compilers, Just-in-time, 6

**Component General Properties dialog
box, 325**

**Component Initialization Parameters
and Aliases dialog box, 325**

Component Object Model. *See* **COM**

Component Security dialog box, 326

component transaction monitors.
  See **CTMs**

components
  adding to Application Deployment
    applications, 321-330
  J2EE, 14
  J2SE, 284

composite names (JNDI names), 19, 21

compound names (JNDI), 18

computation clustering, 193

configurations
  applications, MOM, 99
  J2EE, 295
    CLASSPATH variable, 297-299
    PATH variable, 296-297

J2SE, 287-288
  CLASSPATH variable, 290-292
  PATH variable, 288-290
  resources, MOM, 99

connection factories, 118-119
  p2p messaging model, 119
  pub/sub messaging model, 119-120

**Connection interface (javax.jms
package), 349**
  methods, 349-350
  QueueConnection interface, 350-352

**ConnectionConsumer interface
(javax.jms package), 352**
  JMSException, 352
  methods, 352

**ConnectionFactory interface (javax.jms
package), 348**
  QueueConnectionFactory interface, 348
  TopicConnectionFactory interface,
    348-349

**ConnectionMetaData( ) method
(Connection interface), 350**

Connections, 120
  creating for p2p messaging model, 144
  creating for pub/sub messaging
    model, 144
  myQueueConnection, 177
  myTopicConnection, 177
  p2p messaging model, 121
  pub/sub messaging model, 121-122

**consumption (message), 116-117,
176-177**
  asynchronous, 117
    p2p messaging model, 129
    pub/sub messaging model, 128-130
  JMS Web components, 246
  selectors, 134
  synchronous, 116
    p2p messaging model, 126-127
    pub/sub messaging model, 127

container provider (EJB container), 43

**container-managed persistence (entity
beans), 54**

context
  bridging (MOM networking), 99
  Context Parameters dialog box, 326
  JNDI names, 18

**conversions, StreamMessage interface,
138-139**

CORBA (Common Object Broker Architecture), 10, 36

Coupling (messaging systems), 110

create( ) method
    entity beans, 55, 75
    session beans, 49, 68

createBrowser( ) method (QueueSession interface), 357

createBrowser(Queue queue) method (QueueSession interface), 357

createBrowser(Queue queue, String messageSelector) method (QueueSession interface), 357

createBytesMessage( ) method (Session interface), 355

createConnectionConsumer(Queue parQueue, String messageSelector, ServerSessionPool, parServerSessionPool, int maxMessages) method (QueueConnection interface), 351

createConnectionConsumer(Topic parTopic, String messageSelector, ServerSessionPool parServerSessionPool, int maxMessages) method (QueueConnection interface), 351

createDurableConnectionConsumer (Topic parTopic, String subscriptionName, String messageSelector, ServerSessionPool parServerSessionPool, int maxMessages) method (QueueConnection interface), 351

createDurablePublisher( ) method (TopicSession interface), 360

createDurableSubscriber(Topic topic, String name, String messageSelector, boolean noLocal) method (TopicSession interface), 359

createMapMessage( ) method (Session interface), 355

createMessage( ) method (Session interface), 355

createObjectMessage( ) method (Session interface), 355

createObjectMessage(Serializable myObject) method (Session interface), 355

createPublisher(Topic topic) method (TopicSession interface), 360

createQueue(String queueName) method (QueueSession interface), 356

createQueueConnection( ) class (QueueConnectionFactory interface), 348

createQueueConnection(String userID, String userPassword( ) class (QueueConnectionFactory interface), 348

createQueueSession( ) method, 182

createQueueSession(boolean transacted, int acknowledgeMode) method (QueueConnection interface), 351

createReceiver( ) method (QueueSession interface), 357

createReceiver(Queue queue) method (QueueSession interface), 356

createReceiver(Queue queue, String messageSelector) method (QueueSession interface), 356

createSender(Queue queue) method (QueueSession interface), 357

createStreamMessage( ) method (Session interface), 355

createSubscriber( ) method, 184

createSubscriber(Topic topic) method (TopicSession interface), 358

createSubscriber(Topic topic, String messageSelector, boolean noLocal) method (TopicSession interface), 358

createTemporaryQueue( ) method (QueueSession interface), 357

createTemporaryTopic( ) method (TopicSession interface), 360

createTextMessage( ) method (Session interface), 355

createTextMessage(StringBuffer myString)method (Session interface), 355

createTopic(String topicName) method (TopicSession interface), 357 createTopicConnection( ) method (TopicConnectionFactory interface), 348

createTopicConnection(String userID, String userPassword) method (TopicConnectionFactory interface), 349

createTopicSession( ) method, 182

createTopicSession(boolean transacted, int acknowledgeMode) method (QueueConnection interface), 351

CTMs (component transaction monitors), 37

D

data translation (MOM), 98

data types, MapMessage interface, 374

databases
Access
PersonInfo table, 73-74
UserLogin table, 66
Java Database Connectivity. *See* JDBC
JNDI, 22
mapping, 51-54
ODBC, 67

DCOM, 36

decentralized architecture (MOM), 101-102

Decider client, source code, 263, 265

decoupling (messaging systems), 110

DEFAULT_DELIVERY_MODE value (Message interface), 368

DEFAULT_PRIORITY value (Message interface), 368

DEFAULT_TIME_TO_LIVE value (Message interface), 368

delete( ) method (TemporaryTopic interface), 354

delivery modes
NON_PERSISTEN, 179
PERSISTENT, 178

Demos component (J2SE), 284

Deploy command (Tools menu), 318

deployment
Application Deployment tool applications, 318-321
message-driven bean class, 229-237

Deployment Progress dialog box, 320, 329

Deployment tool. *See* Application Deployment tool

design, JMS API applications, 275
Ask Advance Payment application, 258-271
New Product application, 277-278
Promoting application, 276

Destination interface, 352-353
Queue interface, 353
Topic interface, 353-354

destinations, 117-118
queue, 117-118
topic, 117-118

development (JMS APIs), 143, 257
connections, creating, 144
design layout, 275
Ask Advance Payment application, 258-271
New Product application, 277-278
Promoting application, 276
durable applications, 187-189
lookup lines, 144
Message Consumers, 145
Message producers, 145
p2p messaging example, 146
receiver client applications, 149-152
running client applications, 152-155
sender client applications, 147-149
pub/sub messaging example, 155-156
Message Listener client application, 156-157
message selectors, 164-167
Publisher client application, 157-159
running client applications, 162-164, 167-169
subsrciber client applications, 159-162
receiving messages with receive( ) method, 146
registering message listeners, 146
running Ask Advance Payment application, 271-275
sending messages
with publish( ) method, 146
with send( ) method, 146
sessions, creating, 145

dialog boxes
Component General Properties, 325
Component Initialization Parameters and Aliases, 325

Component Security, 326
Context Parameters, 326
Deployment Progress, 320, 329
Edit Contents, 232
Edit System Variable, 290, 297-298
EJB JAR, 314
Enterprise Bean References, 326
Environment Variables, 287-288
File References, 326
General, 315
Introduction, 319
JNDI Names, 319
New Application, 311
New System Variable, 289, 291, 296
Resource References, 326
Review Settings, 317
Transaction Management, 316
WAR File Environment, 326
directory objects (JNDI) 19-20
directory services, JNDI, 16
distributed programming, 12
EJB, 36
DOCTYPE declarations, 206
Document Object Model. *See* **DOM**
documents, XML
nested elments, 200
processing, 203, 207-208
structure, 200-203
DOM (Document Object Model), 197, 208-209
downloading
Forte for Java Community Edition, 299
J2EE, 293
J2SE, 282-283
DRA (Dynamic Routing Architecture), 337
DTDs (XML), 205-207
DUPS_OK_ ACKNOWLEDGE option, 123
durable subscription transactions, 178, 184
compared to nondurable, 185-186
creating, 186-187
writing applications, 187-189
Dynamic Routing Architecture (DRA), 337

E

ebXML (Electronic Business XML), 197
Edit Contents dialog box, 232
Edit System Variable dialog box, 290, 297-298
EJB (Enterprise Java Beans), 11, 35-37
advertising, 40
architecture, 39-41
compared to JavaBeans, 38-39
entity beans, 39, 43-45, 51-53
Bean class, 45, 55, 75-76
bean-managed persistence, 54
business methods, 75-80
characteristics, 53-54
client access, 54-55, 83-85
container-managed persistence, 54
creating, 72-76
helper methods, 76
Home interface, 44, 55, 74-75
message-drive beans, 225-226
methods, 55-60, 75
primary key, 45, 55
Remote interface, 44, 55, 75
utility methods, 79-80
Web client access, 85, 87
history, 36
application servers, 37
distributed applications, 36
distributed programming, 36
server-side programming, 37
JMS, 61
logical names, 40
message-driven beans, 39, 43, 221-222
architecture, 223
bean class, 224-225, 229-237
business methods, 222
entity beans, 225-226
example, 226-228
methods, 227-228
running applications, 237-239
session beans, 225-226
naming service, 40
physical locations, 40
physical names, 40
portability, 39
remote objects, 42
reusability, 39
servers, 42

session beans, 39, 43-45
  Bean class, 45, 48-49, 69-72
  business methods, 68-72
  client access, 47-48, 81-83
  creating, 65-72
  Home interface, 44, 48, 68
  life-cycle methods, 50
  message-drive beans, 225-226
  methods, 48-51, 68
  primary key, 45
  Remote interface, 44, 48
  stateful, 45-46
  stateless, 45-47
  Web client access, 85-87
three-tier model, 36, 38, 43
Web clients, 60-61

EJB container (J2EE architecture), 10, 41-43
  bean provider, 43
  container provider, 43

EJB Home object, 42

EJB JAR dialog box, 314

EJB JAR page (New Enterprise Bean Wizard), 232

ejbActivate( ) method
  entity beans, 60
  session beans, 51

ejbCreate( ) method
  entity beans, 55, 58
  session beans, 49-50

ejbfindByPrimaryKey( ) method, entity beans, 60

ejbFindByXXX( ) method, entity beans, 60

EJBHome class, 43

ejbLoad( ) method, entity beans, 57-58

EJBObject class, 43

ejbPassivate( ) method
  entity beans, 60
  session beans, 51

ejbPostCreate( ) method, entity beans, 58

ejbRemove( ) method
  entity beans, 59
  session beans, 50

ejbStore( ) method, entity beans, 58

Electronic Business XML. *See* **ebXML**

element tags (XML documents), 203

email, JNDI, 21

encoding information (MOM networking), 98

enterprise applications, 4

Enterprise Bean References dialog box, 326

Enterprise Java Beans. *See* **EJB**

entity beans, EJB, 11, 39, 43-45, 51-53
  Bean class, 45, 55, 75-76
  bean-managed persistence, 54
  business methods, 75-80
  characteristics, 53-54
  client access, 54-55, 83-85
  container-managed persistence, 54
  creating, 72-76
  helper methods, 76
  Home interface, 44, 55, 74-75
  message-drive beans, 225-226
  methods, 55-60, 75
  primary key, 45, 55
  Remote interface, 44, 55, 75
  utility methods, 79-80
  Web client access, 85-87

Environment Variables dialog box, 287-288

equals( ) method, entity beans, 56

exceptions
  IllegalStateException
    Connection interface, 350
    Message interface, 370
    Session interface methods, 356
  InvalidClientIDException (Connection interface), 350
  InvalidDestination
    QueueSender interface, 362
    TopicPublisher interface, 364
  InvalidDestinationException (QueueConnection interface), 352
  InvalidSelectorException (QueueConnection interface), 352
  java.lang.UnsupportedOperation-Exception
    QueueSender interface, 362
    TopicPublisher interface, 364
  JMSException
    BytesMessage interface methods, 373
    Connection interface, 350
    ConnectionConsumer interface, 352

java.lang.Throwable class, 346
MapMessage interface, 375
Message interface, 370
MessageConsumer interface, 365
*MessageEOFException interface
  methods, 373*
*MessageFormatException interface
  methods, 373*
*MessageNotReadableException interface
  methods, 373*
*MessageNotWriteableException interface
  methods, 373*
Queue interface, 353
QueueBrowser interface, 379
QueueConnection interface, 351-352
QueueRequestor class, 344
QueueSender interface, 362
Session interface methods, 356
StreamMessage interface, 378
Topic interface, 354
TopicConnectionFactory interface, 349
TopicPublisher interface, 363
TopicRequestor( ) method, 345
MessageEOFException (StreamMessage
  interface), 378
MessageFormatException
  MapMessage interface, 375
  Message interface, 370
  QueueSender interface, 362
  StreamMessage interface, 378
  TopicPublisher interface, 363
MessageNotReadableException
  (StreamMessage interface), 378
MessageNotWriteableException
  MapMessage interface, 375
  Message interface, 370
  StreamMessage interface, 378
TransactionRolledBackException
  (Session interface), 356
ExoLab, 340
expirations, message, 180
Extensible Markup Language. *See* XML

F

failures
  hardware, 99
  software, 99
FFJ CE. *See* **Forte for Java
  Community Edition**

fields
  headers, 132
  JMSReplyTo, 181
File References dialog box, 326
files
  class, 7
  java, 7
**findByPrimaryKey( ) method, entity
  beans, 56**
**findByXXX( ) method, entity
  beans, 56**
FioranoMQ, 338-339
**FirstMessage application (Application
  Deployment Tool), 237**
flexibility, JavaBeans, 39
flow control (MOM), 98
Forte for Java Community Edition, 299
  downloading, 299
  installation, 299-302
  running message-driven bean
    applications, 237-239
Forte for Java IDE, 26-31

G

General dialog box, 315
**General page (New Enterprise Bean
  Wizard), 233**
**getBoolean(String name) method
  (MapMessage interface), 374**
**getBooleanProperty(String name)
  method (Message interface), 369**
**getByte(String name) method
  (MapMessage interface), 374**
**getByteProperty(String name) method
  (Message interface), 369**
**getChar(String name) method
  (MapMessage interface), 374**
getCity( ) method
  creating entity beans, 76
  entity beans, 75
**getClientID( ) method (Connection
  interface), 349**
**getDeliveryMode( ) method
  (MessageProducer interface), 361**
**getDisableMessageID( ) method
  (MessageProducer interface), 361**

getDisableMessageTimestamp(boolean value) method (MessageProducer interface), 361

getDouble(String name) method (MapMessage interface), 374

getDoubleProperty(String name) method (Message interface), 369

getEnumeration( ) method (QueueBrowser interface), 379

getExceptionListener( ) method (Connection interface), 350

getFloat(String name) method (MapMessage interface), 374

getFloatProperty(String name) method (Message interface), 369

getInt(String name) method (MapMessage interface), 374

getIntProperty(String name) method (Message interface), 369

getJMSCorrelationID( ) method (Message interface), 368

getJMSCorrelationIDAsBytes( ) method (Message interface), 368

getJMSDeliveryMode( ) method (Message interface), 368

getJMSDestination( ) method (Message interface), 368

getJMSExpiration( ) method (Message interface), 369

getJMSMessageID( ) method (Message interface), 368

getJMSPriority( ) method (Message interface), 369

getJMSRedelivered( ) method (Message interface), 368

getJMSReplyTo( ) method (Message interface), 368

getJMSTimestamp( ) method (Message interface), 368

getJMSType( ) method (Message interface), 369

getLong(String name) method (MapMessage interface), 374

getLongProperty(String name) method (Message interface), 369

getMapNames( ) method (MapMessage interface), 375

getMessageListener( ) method
MessageConsumer interface, 364
Session interface, 355

getMessageSelector( ) method
MessageConsumer interface, 364
QueueBrowser interface, 379

getNoLocal( ) method (TopicSubscriber interface), 366

getObject( ) method (ObjectMessage interface), 376

getObject(String name) method (MapMessage interface), 374

getObjectProperty(String name) method (Message interface), 369

getPriority( ) method (MessageProducer interface), 361

getPropertyNames( ) method (Message interface), 369

getQueue( ) method
QueueBrowser interface, 379
QueueSender interface, 362

getQueueName( ) method (Queue interface), 353

getServerSessionPool( ) method (ConnectionConsumer interface), 352

getShort(String name) method (MapMessage interface), 374

getShortProperty(String name) method (Message interface), 369

getString(String name) method (MapMessage interface), 374

getStringProperty(String name) method (Message interface), 369

getText( ) method (TextMessage interface), 379

getTimeToLive( ) method (MessageProducer interface), 361

getTopic( ) method
TopicPublisher interface, 363
TopicSubscriber interface, 366

getTopicName( ) method (Topic interface), 354

getTransacted( ) method (Session interface), 355

H

hardware
  failures, 99
  replacements, 100

hashCode( ) method, entity beans, 56

headers (message objects), 131-132
  fields, 132
  Message interface messages, 370
  methods, 131

helper methods, entity beans, 76

Home interface (EJB), 44, 48, 55, 68, 74-75

HTML, compared to XML, 199

hybrid architecture, MOM, 101

I

IBM, 335

iBus, 339-340

IDEs (Integrated Development Environment), 26-31

IIS (Internet Information Server), 13

IllegalStateException
  Connection interface, 350
  Message interface, 370
  Session interface methods, 356

iMQ, 335-336

in-house developed middleware, 97

initial context, JNDI names, 19

installations
  Forte for Java Community Edition, 299-302
  J2EE, 293-295
  J2SE, 283-287

Integrated Development Environment (IDEs), 26-31

interfaces
  Application Deployment Tool, 230, 308
  EJB
    Home, 44, 48, 55, 68, 74-75
    Remote, 44, 48, 55, 75
  javax.jms, 346-347
    Connection, 349-352
    ConnectionConsumer, 352
    ConnectionFactory, 348-349

    Destination, 352-354
    Message, 134-139, 366-379
    MessageConsumer, 364-366
    MessageListener, 366
    MessageProducer, 360-363
    QueueBrowser, 379
    Session, 354-360

Internet Information Server (IIS), 13

Introduction dialog box, 319

Introduction page (New Enterprise Bean Wizard), 236

InvalidClientIDException (Connection interface), 350

InvalidDestination
  QueueSender interface, 362
  TopicPublisher interface, 364

InvalidDestinationException (QueueConnection interface), 352

InvalidSelectorException (QueueConnection interface), 352

iPlanet, 335-336

itemExists(String name) method (MapMessage interface), 375

J

J2EE (Java 2 Enterprise Edition), 3, 6-7, 14, 198, 281-282, 293
  APIs, 11
    EJB, 11
    Java Interface Definition Language. See Java IDL
    Java Naming Directory Interface. See JNDI
    Java Server Pages. See JSP
    Java servlets, 12
    Java Transaction API. See JTA
    JavaMail. See JavaMail
    JDBC, 12
    JMS, 11
    JNDI, 15-23, 25-31
    JSP, 13
    LDAP, 14
    RMI, 12
  architecture, 8
    three-tier model, 9-10
    two-tier model, 8-9
  components, 14

configuration, 295
  CLASSPATH variable, 297-299
  PATH variable, 296-297
downloading, 293
EJB (Enterprise Java Beans), 35-37
  advertising, 40
  architecture, 39-41
  compared to JavaBeans, 38-39
  entity beans, 39, 43-45, 51-60, 72-80,
    83-87, 225-226
  history, 36-37
  JMS, 61
  logical names, 40
  message-driven beans, 39, 43, 221-239
  naming service, 40
  physical locations, 40
  physical names, 40
  portability, 39
  reusability, 39
  servers, 42
  session beans, 39, 43-51, 65-72, 81-87,
    225-226
  three-tier model, 36, 38, 43
  Web clients, 60-61
EJB container, 41-43
installation, 293-295
JMS API, 114-115
JNDI, 39
services, 15
starting, 307
Web server, 303-305
J2EE 1.3 Reference Server, 336
J2EE Platform Specification, 246
J2SE (Java 2 Standard Edition), 6-7,
281-282
configuration, 287-288
  CLASSPATH variable, 290-292
  PATH variable, 288-290
Demos component, 284
downloading, 282-283
installation, 283-287
Java Sources component, 284
Native Interface Header component, 284
Old Native Interface component, 284
Program Files component, 284
Java, 3
Applets, 4
features, 4-7
servlets. *See* servlets
Java 2 Enterprise Edition. *See* **J2EE**

Java 2 Standard Edition. *See* **J2SE**
Java Database Connectivity. *See* **JDBC**
.java files, 7
Java IDL, 13
Java Micro Edition, 6
Java Naming Directory Interface.
See JNDI
Java Sources component (J2SE), 284
Java Transaction API (JTA), 13, 53
Java Virtual Machine. *See* **JVM**
Java Web Services Developer Pack
(WSDP), 198
Java XML Pack, 197
java.lang.Throwable class, 346
java.lang.UnsupportedOperation-
Exception
  QueueSender interface, 362
  TopicPublisher interface, 364
JavaBeans
  compared to EJB, 38-39
  flexibility, 39
  portability, 39
  reusability, 39
JavaMail, 13
JavaServer Pages (JSP), 3, 13
javax.jms package, 343-344
  classes
    java.lang.Throwable, 346
    QueueRequestor, 344-345
    TopicRequestor, 345
  interfaces, 346-347
    Connection, 349-352
    ConnectionConsumer, 352
    ConnectionFactory, 348-349
    Destination, 352-354
    Message, 134-139, 366-379
    MessageConsumer, 364-366
    MessageListener, 366
    MessageProducer, 360-363
    QueueBrowser, 379
    Session, 354-360
JAXP APIs, 208, 210-212, 215-218
JDBC (Java Database Connectivity), 3,
12, 36
JMQ, 335-336

JMS API, 112
application development, 257
design layout, 258-270, 275-278
functionalities, 271
running applications, 271-275
communication, 112
J2EE, 114-115
Point-to-Point (PTP) messaging, 112-114
vendors, 331-332
BEA Systems Inc., 333-334
criteria for choosing, 332-333
ExoLab, 340
Fiorano, 338-339
IBM, 335
iPlanet, 335-336
Macromedia, 340-341
Progress, 337-338
Softwired, 339-340
Sun Microsystems, 336
TIBCO/Talarian, 337

JMS Provider, Web clients, 243, 246
message consumer example, 250-253
message producer example, 247, 249
three-tier architecture, 245-246
two-tier architecture, 244

JMSException class, 346
BytesMessage interface methods, 373
Connection interface, 350
ConnectionConsumer interface, 352
java.lang.Throwable class, 346
MapMessage interface, 375
Message interface, 370
MessageConsumer interface, 365
MessageEOFException interface methods, 373
MessageFormatException interface methods, 373
MessageNotReadableException interface methods, 373
MessageNotWriteableException interface methods, 373
Queue interface, 353
QueueBrowser interface, 379
QueueConnection interface, 351
QueueConnection interface methods, 352
QueueRequestor class, 344
QueueSender interface, 362
Session interface methods, 356
StreamMessage interface, 378
Topic interface, 354
TopicConnectionFactory interface, 349
TopicPublisher interface, 363
TopicRequestor( ) method, 345

JMSReplyTo field, 181

JNDI (Java Naming Directory Interface), 11, 15-16, 21-25, 39
application development, 25-31
architecture, 17
databases, 22
directory objects, 19-20
directory packages, 19-20
directory services, 16
email, 21
naming packages, 18-19
naming services, 16
network printing, 22
Service Provider Interface (SPI), 17
services
directory, 19-20
naming, 18-19
URLs, 21
user authentication, 21, 25

JNDI Names dialog box, 319

JNDI Names page (New Enterprise Bean Wizard), 236

JRun, 340-341

JSP (JavaServer Pages), 3, 13

JTA (Java Transaction API), 13, 53

Just-in-time compiler, 6

JVM (Java Virtual Machine), 5
bytecode, 6
EJB servers, 42

K-L

layouts, JMS API applications, 275
Ask Advance Payment, 258-270
New Product application, 277-278
Promoting application, 276

LDAP, 14

licensed Sun Microsystems servers, 332
J2EE 1.3 Reference Server, 336
JMQ, 335-336
MQSeries, 335
SmartSockets for JMS, 337
SonicMQ, 337-338
WebLogic Server, 333-334

life cycles
message-driven beans, 223
methods
entity beans, 57
sessions beans, 50

listings
Adding sender application source code transmitting XML documents through the p2p model, 211-212
AskPaymentListener message listener source code, 266-268
Bean class source code named FirstEJB, 309
Business and utility methods of the entity bean, 79-80
Changed lines of Listing 6.4, 227
Client access source code of the sample entity bean, 84
Client access source code of the sample session bean, 81-82
Decider client, 263, 265
DOM parsing of XML files, 209
Hello World example to test the installation (J2SE), 285-287
Home interface of the sample entity bean, 74
Home interface of the sample session bean, 68
Home interface source code named FirstHome, 310
improperly nested elements (XML), 200
inserting DTD file names, 205
JNDI authentication example, 25
JSP component source code named FirstClientWEB, 322
Message listener source code for a pub/sub model, 156-157
namespace syntax for XML files, 207
nested elements (XML), 200
PaymentAsker client, 260-261, 263
Publisher application source code for a pub/sub model, 158-159
Receiver application source code for a p2p model, 150, 152
Receiver application source code reading and processing XML documents through the p2p model, 212, 215
The Receiver Web Client Source Code, 250, 252
Remote interface of the sample entity bean, 75
Remote interface of the sample session bean, 69
Remote interface source code named First, 309
ReplyPaymentListener message listener source code, 269-270
SAX parsing of XML files, 209-210
sayHello( ) method of example application, 30
The screen output after running the client application of the sample entity bean, 85
The screen output after running the client application of the sample session bean, 83
Sender application source code for a p2p model, 148-149
The Sender Web Client Source Code, 247, 249
Simple bean class of the sample entity bean, 76
Simple bean class of the sample session bean, 69
Some lines from the onMessage( ) method of a message-driven bean, 224-225
The source code for the business method of the entity bean, 77-78
Source code of the bean class for a message-driven bean, 228
Subscriber application source code for a pub/sub model, 161-162
The source code for the business method of the sample session bean, 70-71
Web client access to the sample entity bean, 87
Web client access to the sample session bean, 86
XML document of a company's organizational chart, 201

local transactions, 181-182
combinations of processes, 183-184
specifying, 182

logical names, EJB, 40

look-up lines, pub/sub messaging model, 144

M

MapMessage interface, 136, 373
data types, 374
methods, 374-375

markup languages, Extensible Markup Language. *See* **XML**

Message Consumer, 125-126
creating
for p2p messaging model, 145
for pub/sub messaging model, 145
example (JMS Web client application), 250-253
p2p messaging model
asynchronous consuming, 129
synchronous consuming, 126-127
pub/sub messaging model
asynchronous consuming, 128-130
synchronous consuming, 127

Message interface, 366-368
BytesMessage interface, 137, 371-373
exceptions, 370
MapMessage interface, 136, 373
data types, 374
methods, 136, 374-375
message parts, 370-371
methods, 368-370
ObjectMessage interface, 135, 376
StreamMessage interface, 138-139, 376
conversion rules, 138-139
methods, 138-139, 377-378
TextMessage interface, 134-135, 378-379

Message Listener
client applications, 156-157
pub/sub messaging model, 128, 165

Message object
body, 134
BytesMessage, 137
MapMessage, 136
ObjectMessage interface, 135
StreamMessage, 138-139
TextMessage interface, 134-135
headers
fields, 132
methods, 131-132
properties, 132-133

Message Producer, 124
example (JMS Web client application), 247, 249
p2p messaging model, 124-125, 145
pub/sub messaging model, 125, 145

message sending type models (MOM), 105

Message-Drive Bean Settings page, 234

message-driven beans (EJB), 39, 43, 221-222
architecture, 223
bean class, 224-225, 229-237
business methods, 222
entity beans, 225-226
example, 226-228
methods, 227-228
running applications, 237-239
session beans, 225-226

message-oriented middleware. *See* **MOM**

MessageConsumer interface, 364
methods, 364-365
QueueReceiver interface, 365
TopicSubscriber interface, 365-366

MessageEOFException (StreamMessage interface), 378

MessageFormatException
MapMessage interface, 375
Message interface, 370
QueueSender interface, 362
StreamMessage interface, 378
TopicPublisher interface, 363

MessageListener interface, 366

MessageNotReadableException (StreamMessage interface), 378

MessageNotWriteableException
MapMessage interface, 375
Message interface, 370
StreamMessage interface, 378

MessageProducer interface, 360
methods, 360-361
QueueSender interface, 361-362
TopicPublisher interface, 363

messages
acknowledgment, 176-178
beans, 11
expiration, 180
listeners
registering for queue messaging model, 146
registering for topic type messaging model, 146
Message interface, 370-371

MOM, 95, 97, 102
    asynchronous type, 103-104
    message sending type models, 105
    point-to-point type messaging, 105
    publish-and-subscribe type messaging,
       105-106
    synchronization type models, 102
    synchronous type, 102-103
passing, 97
persistence, 175, 178-179
priority level, 179-180
queuing, 97
selectors
    pub/sub messaging model, 164-167
    running pub/sub client applications,
       167-169

messaging systems, 109–110
    advantages, 110-112
    asynchronous messaging, 110
    body, 134
       BytesMessage interface, 137
       MapMessage interface, 136
       ObjectMessage interface, 135
       StreamMessage interface, 138-139
       TextMessage interface, 134-135
    client isolation, 110
    consumption, 116-117
       asynchronous, 117, 128-130
       synchronous, 116, 126-127
    coupling, 110
    decoupling, 110
    destinations, 117-118
    disadvantages, 110-112
    headers, 131-132
       fields, 132
       methods, 131
    Message Consumer. *See* Message
      Consumer
    Message Listener
       client applications, 156-157
       pub/sub messaging model, 128, 165
    Message Producer, 124
       p2p messaging model, 124-125
       pub/sub messaging model, 125
    message transfers, 130
    MOM, 110
    Point-to-Point (PTP), 112-114
    properties, 132
       methods, 133
    receivers, 110, 113-114

reliability, 175-176, 181
    clustering, 192-194
    durable subscription transactions, 184-189
    local transactions, 181-184
    message acknowledgment, 176-178
    message expiration, 180
    message persistence, 175, 178-179
    message priority level, 179-180
    nondurable subscription transactions,
       185-186, 189-192
    temporary destinations, 180-181
selectors, 134
senders, 110, 113-114

methods
    BytesMessage interface, 137, 371-373
    commit( ), 182-183
    Connection interface, 349-350
    ConnectionConsumer interface, 352
    createQueueSession( ), 182
    createSubscriber( ), 184
    createTopicSession( ), 182
    entity beans, 57
       business, 75-80
       create( ), 55, 75
       ejbActivate( ), 60
       ejbCreate( ), 55, 58
       ejbfindByPrimaryKey( ), 60
       ejbFindByXXX( ), 60
       ejbLoad( ), 57-58
       ejbPassivate( ), 60
       ejbPostCreate( ), 58
       ejbRemove( ), 59
       ejbStore( ), 58
       equals( ), 56
       findByPrimaryKey( ), 56
       findByXXX( ), 56
       getCity( ), 75-76
       hashCode( ), 56
       helper, 76
       life-cycle, 57
       remove( ), 56
       setEntityContext( ), 59
       unsetEntityContext( ), 59
       utility, 79-80
    getTheNode( ), 215
    headers, 131
    MapMessage interface, 136, 374-375
    Message interface, 134-135, 368-370
    message object properties, 133
    message-driven beans, 222, 227-228

MessageConsumer interface, 364-365
MessageProducer interface, 360-361
ObjectMessage interface, 135, 376
onMessage( ), 224
publish( ), 146
Queue interface, 353
QueueBrowser interface, 379
QueueConnection interface, 350-352
QueueConnectionFactory interface, 348
QueueSender interface, 362
QueueSession interface, 356-357
receive( ), 146
rollback( ), 182-183
send( ), 146
session beans, 48-51
  business, 68-72
  create( ), 49, 68
  ejbActivate( ), 51
  ejbCreate( ), 49-50
  ejbPassivate( ), 51
  ejbRemove( ), 50
  life-cycle, 50
  remove( ), 50, 68
  setEntityContext( ), 51
Session interface, 355-356
setDeliveryMode( ), 179
setText( ), 147, 157
StreamMessage interface, 138-139,
  377-378
TemporaryTopic interface, 354
TextMessage interface, 379
Topic interface, 354
TopicConnectionFactory interface,
  348-349
TopicPublisher interface, 363
TopicSession interface, 357-360
TopicSubscriber interface, 366
unsubscribe( ), 187
Micro Edition, 6
Microsoft XML. *See* **MSXML**
middleware, 94
  in-house developed, 97
  message-oriented middleware. *See* MOM
**MOM (message-oriented middleware),
11, 37, 93, 97**
  architecture, 94-95, 100
  centralized, 100
  decentralized, 101-102
  hybrid, 101

  history, 93-95
  in-house developed middleware, 97
  ORBs (Object Request Brokers), 96-97
  RPC (Remote Procedure Call), 95-96
  *TPMs (Transaction-Processing
    Monitors), 95*
  messaging, 97, 102, 110
  asynchronous type, 103-104
  message sending type models, 105
  point-to-point type messaging, 105
  *publish-and-subscribe type messaging,
    105-106*
  synchronization type models, 102
  synchronous type, 102-103
  networking features, 98-100
MQSeries, 335
MSXML (Microsoft XML), 203
myQueueConnection connection, 177
myTopicConnection connection, 177

N

names, JNDI
  atomic, 18
  binding, 18
  composite, 19, 21
  compound, 18
  context, 18
  initial context, 19
  namespaces, 18
  naming systems, 18
  subcontext, 18
namespaces
  JNDI names, 18
  XML, 207
naming packages (JNDI), 18-19
naming services
  EJB, 40
  JNDI, 16
  MOM, 99
naming systems, JNDI names, 18
**Native Interface Header component
(J2SE), 284**
nested elements, XML documents, 200
networking, MOM, 98-100
New Application dialog box, 311

New Enterprise Bean Wizard, 231-232
  EJB Jar page, 232-234
  Introduction page, 236
  JNDI Names page, 236
  Message-Drive Bean Settings page, 234
  Review Settings page, 235
New menu commands,
  Application, 310
New Product application, layout
  design, 277-278
New System Variable dialog box,
  289, 291, 296
nondurable subscription
  transactions, 178
  compared to durable, 185-186
  running, 189-192
nonexistent life cycles, message-driven
  beans, 223
nonlicensed Sun Microsystems
  servers, 332
  FioranoMQ, 338-339
  iBus, 339-340
nontransacted sessions, 176
NON_PERSISTENT delivery
  mode, 179

O

Object Management Group. *See* OMG
Object Request Brokers. *See* ORBs
object-oriented languages. *See* OOLs
Object-Oriented Programming.
  See OOP
ObjectMessage interface, 135, 376
objects
  connection factories, 118-119
    p2p messaging model, 119
    pub/sub messaging model, 119-120
  destinations. *See* destinations
  EJB Home, 42
  EJB remote, 42
  JNDI directory, 19-20
ODBC connections, creating, 67
off state transaction sessions, 123
Old Native Interface component
  (J2SE), 284
OMG (Object Management Group), 97

onMessage method( ), 222, 224
OOLs (object-oriented languages), 37
OOP (Object-Oriented
  Programming), 4-5
open source Sun Microsystems
  servers, 332
  ExoLab, 340
  JRun, 340-341
ORBs (Object Request Brokers), 37,
  96-97

P

p2p messaging model, 112-114, 146
  asynchronous consuming, 129
  connections, 119, 121, 144
  creating Message Consumers, 145
  creating Message Producers, 145
  creating sessions, 145
  Message Producer, 124-125
  receiver client applications, 149-150, 152
  receiving messages, 146
  running client applications, 152-155
  sender client applications, 147-149
  sending messages, 146
  sessions, 123
  synchronous consuming, 126-127
packages (class), javax.jms, 343-347
  Connection interface, 349-352
  ConnectionConsumer interface, 352
  ConnectionFactory interface, 348-349
  Destination interface, 352-354
  java.lang.Throwable class, 346
  Message interface, 134-139, 366-379
  MessageConsumer interface, 364-366
  MessageListener interface, 366
  MessageProducer interface, 360-363
  QueueBrowser interface, 379
  QueueRequestor class, 344-345
  Session interface, 354-360
  TopicRequestor class, 345
parallel clustering, 193
param2 values, 177-178
parsers (XML), 203, 207-208
PATH variable
  configuring for J2EE, 296-297
  configuring for J2SE, 288-290
PaymentAsker client (Ask Advance
  Payment application), 258-263

persistence
entity beans, 54
messages, 175, 178-179
PERSISTENT delivery mode, 178
PersonInfo table, creating entity beans, 73-74
physical locations, EJB, 40
physical names, EJB, 40
Point-to-Point (PTP) messaging, 105, 112-114
portability
EJB, 39
JavaBeans, 39
MOM, 99
primary key (EJB), 45, 55
printing, JNDI, 22
priority levels (message), 179-180
processors (XML), 203, 207-208
Program Files component (J2SE), 284
Promoting application, layout design, 276
properties (message objects), 132
Message interface messages, 370
methods, 133
propertyExists(String name) method (Message interface), 369
protocols
LDAP, 14
MOM networking, 99
PTP (Point-to-Point) messaging, 112-114, 146
asynchronous consuming, 129
connections, 119, 121, 144
creating Message Consumers, 145
creating Message Producers, 145
creating sessions, 145
Message Producer, 124-125
receiver client applications, 149-152
receiving messages, 146
running client applications, 152-155
sender client applications, 147-149
sending messages, 146
sessions, 123
synchronous consuming, 126-127
pub/sub messaging model, 110, 114, 155-156
asynchronous consuming, 128-130
connections, 119-122, 144

creating Message Consumers, 145
creating Message Producers, 145
creating sessions, 145
look-up lines, 144
Message Listener client application, 156-157
Message Producer, 125
message selectors, 164-167
Publisher client application, 157-159
receiving messages, 146
running client applications, 162-164, 167-169
sending messages, 146
sessions, 123-124
subscriber client applications, 159-162
synchronous consuming, 127
Publish Client applications, 165-166
publish( ) method, sending messages, 146
publish(Message message) method (TopicPublisher interface), 363
publish(Message message, int deliveryMode, int priority, long timeToLive) method (TopicPublisher interface), 363
publish(Topic topic, Message message) method (TopicPublisher interface), 363
publish(Topic topic, Message message, int deliveryMode, int priority, long timeToLive) method (TopicPublisher interface), 363
publish-and-subscribe type messaging (MOM), 105-106
PublisherClient (Forte for Java Community Edition)
client applications, 157-159
running message-drive bean applications, 238-239
publishers (messaging systems), 110, 113-114

Q

queue destinations, 117-118
Queue interface, 353
methods, 353
TemporaryQueue interface, 353

queue messaging model, 146

QueueBrowser interface, 379

QueueConnection interface
   exceptions, 351
   JMSException, 351
   methods, 350-352

QueueConnectionFactory
interface, 348

QueueReceiver interface, 365

QueueRequester class (javax.jms
package), 344-345

QueueSender interface, 361
   exceptions, 362
   methods, 362

QueueSession interface, 356-357

R

readBoolean( ) method
   BytesMessage interface, 371
   StreamMessage interface, 377

readByte( ) method
   BytesMessage interface, 371
   StreamMessage interface, 377

readBytes(byte[ ] value) method
   BytesMessage interface, 372
   StreamMessage interface, 377

readBytes(byte[ ] value, int length)
method (BytesMessage interface), 372

readChar( ) method
   BytesMessage interface, 371
   StreamMessage interface, 377

readDouble( ) method
   BytesMessage interface, 372
   StreamMessage interface, 377

readFloat( ) method
   BytesMessage interface, 372
   StreamMessage interface, 377

readInt( ) method
   BytesMessage interface, 371
   StreamMessage interface, 377

readLong( ) method
   BytesMessage interface, 371
   StreamMessage interface, 377

readObject( ) method (StreamMessage
interface), 377

readShort( ) method
   BytesMessage interface, 371
   StreamMessage interface, 377

readString( ) method (StreamMessage
interface), 377

readUnsignedByte( ) method
(BytesMessage interface), 371

readUnsignedShort( ) method
(BytesMessage interface), 371

ready life cycles, message-driven
beans, 223

receive( ) method
   MessageConsumer interface, 364
   sending messages, 146

receive(long timeout) method
(MessageConsumer interface), 365

receiveNoWait( ) method
(MessageConsumer interface), 365

receiver client applications, p2p
messaging model, 149-150, 152

receivers (messaging systems), 110,
113-114, 215-218

receiving messages with publish( )
method, 146

recover( ) method (Session
interface), 355

reliability, 175-176, 181
   clustering, 192-194
   durable subscription transactions, 184
      compared to nondurable, 185-186
      creating, 186-187
      writing applications, 187-189
   local transactions, 181-182
      combinations of processes, 183-184
      specifying, 182
   messages
      acknowledgment, 176-178
      expiration, 180
      persistence, 175, 178-179
      priority level, 179-180
   nondurable subscription transactions
      compared to durable, 185-186
      running, 189-192
   temporary destinations, 180-181

Remote interface (EJB), 44, 48, 55, 75

remote objects (EJB), 42

Remote Procedure Call. *See* RPC

remove( ) method
 entity beans, 56
 session beans, 50, 68
**ReplyPaymentListener message
 listener, 269-270**
**reset( ) method (BytesMessage
 interface), 373**
Resource References dialog box, 326
resources, MOM, 99
reusability
 EJB, 39
 JavaBeans, 39
Review Settings dialog box, 317
Review Settings page, 235
RMI, 12, 36
**rollback( ) method (Session interface),
 182-183, 355**
rolling back, 181
root elements (XML documents), 202
RPC (Remote Procedure Call), 95-96
run( ) method (Session interface), 356
running
 Ask Advance Payment application,
  271-275
 client applications
  p2p messaging model, 152-155
  pub/sub messaging model, 162-164,
  167-169
 nondurable subscription transactions,
  189-192
 receiver applications, 215-218
 sender applications, 215-218

S

**SAX (Simple API for XML Parsing),
 197, 209-210**
schemas (XML), 205-207
security, JNDI authentication, 21, 25
selectors (message), 134
send( ) method, sending messages, 146
**send(Message message) method
 (QueueSender interface), 362**
**send(Message message, int
 deliveryMode, int priority, long
 timeToLive) method (QueueSender
 interface), 362**

**send(Queue queue, Message message)
 method (QueueSender interface), 362**
**send(Queue queue, Message message,
 int deliveryMode, int priority, long
 timeToLive) method (QueueSender
 interface), 362**
sender applications
 p2p messaging model, 147-149
 running, 215-218
**senders (messaging systems), 110,
 113-114**
sending
 messages with publish( ) method, 146
 messages with send( ) method, 146
server-side programming (EJB), 37
servers
 EJB, 37, 42
 ExoLab, 340
 FioranoMQ, 338-339
 iBus, 339-340
 iMQ, 335-336
 J2EE 1.3 Reference Server, 336
 JMQ, 335-336
 JRun, 340-341
 MQSeries, 335
 SmartSockets for JMS, 337
 SonicMQ, 337-338
 Web, 303-305
 WebLogic, 333-334
Service Provider Interface. *See* **SPI**
services
 clustering, 193
 J2EE, 15
 JNDI
  directory, 16, 19-20
  naming, 16, 18-19
servlets, 3, 12-13
session beans, EJB, 11, 39, 43-45
 Bean class, 45, 48-49, 69-72
 business methods, 68-72
 client access, 47-48, 81-83
 creating, 65-72
 Home interface, 44, 48, 68
 life-cycle methods, 50
 message-driven beans, 225-226
 methods, 48-51, 68
 primary key, 45
 Remote interface, 44, 48
 stateful, 45-46

stateless, 45–47
Web client access, 85–87

Session interface, 354
  methods, 355–356
  QueueSession interface, 356–357
  TopicSession interface, 357–360
  XASession interface, 360

Session.AUTO_ACKNOWLEDGE value (param2), 177

Session.CLIENT_ACKNOWLEDGE value (param2), 177

Session.DUPS_OK_ACKNOWLEDGE value (param2), 177

sessions, 122–123
  acknowledgement options, 123
  creating for p2p messaging model, 145
  creating for pub/sub messaging
    model, 145
  Message Producer, 124
    p2p messaging model, 124-125
    pub/sub messaging model, 125
  nontransacted, 176
  off state transactions, 123
  p2p messaging model, 123
  pub/sub messaging model, 123–124
  termination, 178
  transacted, 176
  transactional contexts, 122

setBoolean(String name, boolean value) method (MapMessage interface), 375

setBooleanProperty(String name, boolean value) method (Message interface), 369

setByte(String name, byte value) method (MapMessage interface), 375

setByteProperty(String name, byte value) method (Message interface), 369

setBytes(String name, byte[ ] value) method (MapMessage interface), 375

setBytes(String name, byte[ ] value, int offset, int length) method (MapMessage interface), 375

setChar(String name, char value) method (MapMessage interface), 375

setClientID(String ID) method (Connection interface), 350

setDeliveryMode( ) method, 179

setDeliveryMode(int deliveryMode) method (MessageProducer interface), 361

setDisableMessageID(boolean value) method (MessageProducer interface), 360

setDisableMessageTimestamp(boolean value) method (MessageProducer interface), 361

setDouble(String name, double value) method (MapMessage interface), 375

setDoubleProperty(String name, double value) method (Message interface), 370

setEntityContext( ) method
  entity beans, 59
  session beans, 51

setExceptionListener( ) method (Connection interface), 350

setFloat(String name, float value) method (MapMessage interface), 375

setFloatProperty(String name, float value) method (Message interface), 370

setInt(String name, int value) method (MapMessage interface), 375

setJMSCorrelationID(String correlationID) method (Message interface), 368

setJMSCorrelationIDAsBytes(byte[ ] correlationID) method (Message interface), 368

setJMSDeliveryMode(int deliveryMode) method (Message interface), 368

setJMSDestination(Destination destination) method (Message interface), 368

setJMSExpiration(long expiration) method (Message interface), 369

setJMSMessageID(String ID) method (Message interface), 368

setJMSPriority(int priority) method (Message interface), 369

setJMSRedelivered(boolean redelivered) method (Message interface), 368

setJMSReplyTo(Destination replyTo) method (Message interface), 368

setJMSTimestamp(long timestamp) method (Message interface), 368

setJMSType(String type) method (Message interface), 369

setLong(String name, long value) method (MapMessage interface), 375

setLongProperty(String name, long value) method (Message interface), 370

setMessageListener( ) method (Session interface), 356

setMessageListener(MessageListener listener) method (MessageConsumer interface), 364

setObject(java.io.Serializable object) method (ObjectMessage interface), 376

setObject(String name, Object value) method (MapMessage interface), 375

setObjectProperty(String name, Object value) method (Message interface), 370

setPriority(int defaultPriority) method (MessageProducer interface), 361

setShort(String name, short value) method (MapMessage interface), 375

setShortProperty(String name, short value) method (Message interface), 370

setString(String name, String value) method (MapMessage interface), 375

setStringProperty(String name, String value) method (Message interface), 370

setText( ) method, 147, 157

setText(String string) method (TextMessage interface), 379

setTimeToLive(long timeToLive) method (MessageProducer interface), 361

SGML (Standard Generalized Markup Language), 198

Simple API for XML Parsing. *See* SAX

Simple Object Access Protocol. *See* SOAP

skeletons, EJB architecture, 40–41

SmartSockets for JMS, 337

SOAP (Simple Object Access Protocol), 197

software failures, MOM, 99

SonicMQ, 337–338

specifying local transactions, 182

SPI (Service Provider Interface), 17

stand-alone applications, 4

Standard Generalized Markup Language. *See* SGML

start( ) method (Connection interface), 350

starting
    Application Deployment tool, 307–309
    J2EE, 307

stateful session beans, 45–46

stateless session beans, 45–47

stop( ) method (Connection interface), 350

StreamMessage interface, 138–139, 376–378

stubs (EJB architecture), 40–41

subcontext, JNDI names, 18

subscribers (messaging systems), 110, 113–114
    client applications (pub/sub messaging model, 159–162, 166–167
    nondurable, 178

Sun Microsystems, 336
    Java. *See* Java
    licensed servers, 332
        J2EE 1.3 Reference Server, 336
        JMQ, 335–336
        MQSeries, 335
        SmartSockets for JMS, 337
        SonicMQ, 337–338
        WebLogic Server, 333–334
    nonlicensed servers, 332
        FioranoMQ, 338–339
        iBus, 339–340
    open source servers, 332
        ExoLab, 340
        JRun, 340–341

synchronous message comsumption, 102–103, 116, 246
    p2p messaging model, 126–127
    pub/sub messaging model, 127

syntax, XML, 199

T

tables
PersonInfo, 73-74
UserLogin, 66

tags, XML, 203

temporary destinations, 180-181

TemporaryQueue interface, 353

TemporaryTopic interface, 354

termination sessions, 178

testing
Forte for Java Community Edition
installation, 301-302
J2EE installation, 295
J2SE installation, 285-287

TextMessage interface, 134-135, 378-379

three-tier architecture (JMS Web applications), 245-246
EJB, 36, 38, 43
J2EE, 9-10

Throwable class (javax.jms package), 346

TIBCO/Talarian, 337

Tools menu commands, Deploy, 318

topic destinations, 117-118

Topic interface, 353-354

topic type messaging model, 146

TopicConnectionFactory interface, 348-349

TopicPublisher interface, 363

TopicRequestor class (javax.jms package), 345

TopicSession interface methods, 357-360

TopicSubscriber interface, 365-366

toString( ) method
Queue interface, 353
Topic interface, 354

TPMs (Transaction-Processing Monitors), 95

transacted sessions, 176

Transaction Management dialog box, 316

Transaction Management page (New Enterprise Bean Wizard), 234

Transaction-Processing Monitors. *See* TPMs

transactional contexts, sessions, 122

TransactionRolledBackException (Session interface methods), 356

transactions
committing, 181
durable subscription, 184
compared to nondurable, 185-186
creating, 186-187
writing applications, 187-189
local, 181-182
combinations of processes, 183-184
specifying, 182
nondurable subscription
compared to durable, 185-186
running, 189-192
off state, 123
rolling back, 181

transformation technologies, XML, 210

two-tier architecture
J2EE, 8-9
JMS Web applications, 244

U

UDDI (Universal Description Discovery, and Integration), 197

Uniform Resource Locators (URLs), 21

unsetEntityContext( ) method, entity beans, 59

unsubscribe( ) method, 187

unsubscribe(String name) method (TopicSession interface), 360

URLs (Uniform Resource Locators), 21

user interfaces. *See* interfaces

UserLogin table, creating session beans, 66

utility methods, entity beans, 79-80

V

validation (XML), 203-205
DTDs, 205-207
schemas, 205-207

variables
   CLASSPATH
      configuring for J2EE, 297-299
      configuring for J2SE, 290-292
   PATH
      configuring for J2EE, 296-297
      configuring for J2SE, 288-290
vendors, JMS API, 331-332
   BEA Systems Inc., 333-334
   criteria for choosing, 332-333
   ExoLab, 340
   Fiorano, 338-339
   IBM, 335
   iPlanet, 335-336
   Macromedia, 340-341
   Progress, 337-338
   Softwired, 339-340
   Sun Microsystems, 336
   TIBCO/Talarian, 337

W

W3C web site, 198
WAR File Environment dialog
   box, 326
web applications, JMS, 243, 246
   message consumer example, 250-253
   message producer example, 247, 249
   three-tier architecture, 245-246
   two-tier architecture, 244
web clients
   accessibility
      to entity beans, 85, 87
      to session beans, 85-87
   EJB, 60-61
   JMS Provider, 243, 246
      message consumer example, 250-253
      message producer example, 247-249
      three-tier architecture, 245-246
      two-tier architecture, 244
web components, adding to
   Application Deployment tool
   applications, 321-330
web container (J2EE architecture), 10
Web Services Description Language.
   See WSDL
web sites
   BEA Systems, Inc., 334
   W3C, 198
   XML, 198

WebLogic Server, 333-334
wizards, New Enterprise Bean Wizard,
   231-232
   EJB Jar page, 232-234
   Introduction page, 236
   JNDI Names page, 236
   Message-Drive Bean Settings page, 234
   Review Settings page, 235
writeBoolean(boolean value) method
   BytesMessage interface, 372
   StreamMessage interface, 377
writeByte(byte value) method
   BytesMessage interface, 372
   StreamMessage interface, 377
writeBytes(byte[ ] value) method
   (BytesMessage interface), 372
writeBytes(byte[ ] value, int offset,
   int length) method (BytesMessage
   interface), 373
writeChar(char value) method
   BytesMessage interface, 372
   StreamMessage interface, 377
writeDouble(double value) method
   (BytesMessage interface), 372
writeFloat(float value) method
   (BytesMessage interface), 372
writeInt(int value) method
   BytesMessage interface, 372
   StreamMessage interface, 377
writeLong(long value) method
   (BytesMessage interface), 372
writeObject(Object value) method
   (BytesMessage interface), 373
writeShort(short value) method
   BytesMessage interface, 372
   StreamMessage interface, 377
writeUTF(String value) method
   (BytesMessage interface), 372
writing applications, 143
   creating connections, 144
   creating Message Consumers, 145
   creating Message Producers, 145
   creating sessions, 145
   look-up lines, 144
   p2p messaging example, 146-155
   pub/sub messaging example, 155-169
   receiving messages with receive( )
      method, 146

registering message listeners, 146
sending messages with publish( )
   method, 146
sending messages with send( )
   method, 146
**WSDL (Web Services Description
Language), 197**
**WSDP (Java Web Services Developer
Pack), 198**

X-Z

XASession interface, 360
**XML (Extensible Markup Language),
197–198**
 compared to HTML, 199
 document structure, 200–202
   attributes, 202
   element tags, 203
   root elements, 202
 DOM, 197, 208–209
 ebXML (Electronic Business XML), 197
 JAXP API, 210–212, 215
   running receiver applications, 215-218
   running sender applications, 215-218
 namespaces, 207
 nested elements, 200
 processing documents, 203, 207–208
 SAX, 197, 209–210
 syntax, 199
 transformation technologies, 210
 UDDI (Universal Description Discovery,
   and Integration), 197
 validation, 203–205
   DTDs, 205-207
   schemas, 205-207
 web sites, 198
 WSDL (Web Services Description
   Language), 197
 XSL, 210
XPath, 210
XSL (XML Stylesheet Language), 210
**XSLT (XML Stylesheet Language
Transformation), 197**

VOICES THAT MATTER

HOW TO CONTACT US

VISIT OUR WEB SITE

WWW.NEWRIDERS.COM

On our web site, you'll find information about our other books, authors, tables of contents, and book errata. You will also find information about book registration and how to purchase our books, both domestically and internationally.

EMAIL US

Contact us at: **nrfeedback@newriders.com**

- If you have comments or questions about this book
- To report errors that you have found in this book
- If you have a book proposal to submit or are interested in writing for New Riders
- If you are an expert in a computer topic or technology and are interested in being a technical editor who reviews manuscripts for technical accuracy

Contact us at: **nreducation@newriders.com**

- If you are an instructor from an educational institution who wants to preview New Riders books for classroom use. Email should include your name, title, school, department, address, phone number, office days/hours, text in use, and enrollment, along with your request for desk/examination copies and/or additional information.

Contact us at: **nrmedia@newriders.com**

- If you are a member of the media who is interested in reviewing copies of New Riders books. Send your name, mailing address, and email address, along with the name of the publication or web site you work for.

BULK PURCHASES/CORPORATE SALES

The publisher offers discounts on this book when ordered in quantity for bulk purchases and special sales. For sales within the U.S., please contact: Corporate and Government Sales (800) 382-3419 or **corpsales@pearsontechgroup.com**. Outside of the U.S., please contact: International Sales (317) 581-3793 or **international@pearsontechgroup.com**.

WRITE TO US

New Riders Publishing
201 W. 103rd St.
Indianapolis, IN 46290-1097

CALL/FAX US

Toll-free (800) 571-5840
If outside U.S. (317) 581-3500
Ask for New Riders
FAX: (317) 581-4663

New Riders

WWW.NEWRIDERS.COM

Solutions from experts you know and trust.

www.informit.com

VIEW CART 🛒   search ⊙

▸ Registration already a member? Log in. ▸ Book Registration

Publishing the Voices that Matter

OUR AUTHORS

PRESS ROOM

| ▦ web development | ▦ design | ▦ photoshop | ▦ new media | ▦ 3-D | ▦ server technologies |

EDUCATORS

ABOUT US

CONTACT US

You already know that New Riders brings you the **Voices that Matter**. But what does that mean? It means that New Riders brings you the Voices that challenge your assumptions, take your talents to the next level, or simply help you better understand the complex technical world we're all navigating.

Visit **www.newriders.com** to find:

- ▸ **10% discount** and **free shipping** on all purchases
- ▸ Never before published chapters
- ▸ Sample chapters and excerpts
- ▸ Author bios and interviews
- ▸ Contests and enter-to-wins
- ▸ Up-to-date industry event information
- ▸ Book reviews
- ▸ Special offers from our friends and partners
- ▸ Info on how to join our User Group program
- ▸ Ways to have your Voice heard

New Riders

WWW.NEWRIDERS.COM

RELATED NEW RIDERS TITLES

Jython for Java Programmers

Robert Bill

Delve into the new and exciting world of Jython, a speedy and efficient scripting language written in Java. After a brief introduction, the book utilizes examples to ensure that you increase your programming productivity and get the most from Jython.

ISBN: 0735711119
460 pages
US$49.99

JSP and Tag Libraries for Web Development

Wellington L.S. da Silva

This book, with its explanation of tag library technology and examples of implementation, helps to bring the capabilities of tag libraries to the arsenals of current JSP programmers.

ISBN: 0735710953
464 pages
US$39.99

JXTA

Brendon J. Wilson

JXTA technology is a set of open source, peer-to-peer protocols that allow any connected device on the network from cell phone to PDA from PC to server to communicate and collaborate in a peer-to-peer manner. JXTA technology enables new and innovative network applications to be created, giving complete access to content on the expanded web. This is an implementation book that covers the protocols and how to use them.

ISBN: 0735712344
512 pages
US$45.00

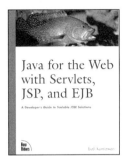

Java for the Web with Servlets, JSP, and EJB

Budi Kurniawan

This book teaches three of the most important technologies for Java web programming: Servlet, JSP, and EJB. Each topic offers real world examples. The CD-ROM includes all the code samples from the book, a copy of the latest version of JSP, Servlet, and EJB, and a copy of Budi's File Upload software are on the CD-ROM.

ISBN: 073571195X
992 pages with CD-ROM
US$49.99

Inside XML

Steve Holzner

Inside XML is a foundation book that covers both the Microsoft and non-Microsoft approach to XML programming. It covers in detail the hot aspects of XML, such as DTD's vs. XML Schemas, CSS, XSL, XSLT, Xlinks, Xpointers, XHTML, RDF, CDF, parsing XML in Perl and Java, and much more.

ISBN: 0735710201
1152 pages
US$49.99

XML, XSLT, Java, and JSP

Westy Rockwell

A practical, hands-on experience in building web applications based on XML and Java technologies, this book is unique because it teaches the technologies by using them to build a web chat project throughout the book. The project is explained in great detail, after the reader is shown how to get and install the necessary tools to be able to customize this project and build other web applications.

ISBN: 0735710899
768 pages with CD-ROM
US$49.99

Colophon

The image on this book's cover depicts the ancient ruins of sculptures and columns on a stone path in Ephesus, Turkey. Levent Erdogan, the author of this book, is from this part of Turkey and enjoys the natural beauty and history of his homeland. The photograph was captured by Andrew Ward/ Life File/Photodisc.

This book was written and edited in Microsoft Word, and laid out in QuarkXPress. The fonts used for the body text are Bembo and MCPdigital. It was printed on 50# Husky Offset Smooth paper at R.R. Donnelley & Sons in Crawfordsville, Indiana. Prepress consisted of PostScript computer-to-plate technology (filmless process). The cover was printed at Moore Langen Printing in Terre Haute, Indiana, on Carolina, coated on one side.